How to
SURVIVE
Anything, Anywhere

A HANDBOOK OF SURVIVAL SKILLS FOR
EVERY SCENARIO AND ENVIRONMENT

How to SURVIVE Anything, Anywhere

A HANDBOOK OF SURVIVAL SKILLS FOR EVERY SCENARIO AND ENVIRONMENT

CHRIS McNAB

Camden, Maine • New York • Chicago • San Francisco • Lisbon • Madrid • Mexico City • Milan • New Delhi • San Juan • Seoul • Singapore • Sydney • Toronto

The McGraw·Hill Companies

First published in North America in 2004 by
The McGraw-Hill Companies
Camden ME 04843
www.books.mcgraw-hill.com

© 2004 Amber Books Ltd

Reprinted in 2007 (twice)

ISBN-13: 978-0-07-144053-0
ISBN-10: 0-07-144053-4

Editorial and design by:
Amber Books Ltd
Bradley's Close
74–77 White Lion Street
London N1 9PF
United Kingdom
www.amberbooks.co.uk

Project Editor: Michael Spilling
Designer: Zoe Mellors
Illustrations courtesy of Art-Tech

Printed and bound in Singapore

Contents

CHAPTER ONE

SURVIVAL PSYCHOLOGY

Willpower can be a defining factor in survival. A determination to survive whatever the cost will often compensate for a limited knowledge of survival skills.

THE GREATEST THREAT to survival comes from our normal standard of living. The generally high comfort levels of a modern lifestyle cushion us from threats from nature and the environment. In an emergency scenario all the things we take for granted – warm, secure buildings, professional health care, ample supplies of food and water – instantly vanish. You may be left with only the clothes you stand in and no food, water or shelter. On your decisions hangs your survival or your death. The psychological effects of this dislocation can be profound ones. At the very moment when you need clear mental faculties and physical toughness, you may instead fall into a fatal condition of shock and demoralization. So how do you make sure that you remain mentally strong in a dire emergency?

PSYCHOLOGICAL THREATS

Recognize that negative mental conditions might be the result of the environment itself. Cold, for example, retards blood flow and induces sleepiness. This is not only mentally disabling, but it can also be a prelude to hypothermia. Equally, high temperatures can lead to dehydration, which has a chronic impact on the brain's efficiency (brain tissue is 85 per cent water). Food deprivation leads to dizziness and blackouts, with an increased vulnerability to cold and thirst.

If you suspect your mental state is caused by environmental factors, tackle those issues first. If cold, seek or make shelter, and build a fire. Keep up your intake of water; if water is scarce, cut down on food, as the body uses large amounts of fluids in the process of digestion, particularly of fatty foods. If hungry, make increasing your food intake your priority. If fatigue – the primary cause of much depression and anxiety – is at the root of your feelings, schedule 20-minute naps.

Keep busy – accepting total self-sufficiency is the best remedy for many negative mental conditions. Do not aim for unrealistic goals, but set clear objectives one at a time, and feel a sense of satisfaction and optimism as each one is accomplished. Staying busy will distract your attention from fear and pain, and instil you with a greater sense of optimism.

STRESS AND MENTAL BREAKDOWN

The stress response in human beings was designed for prehistoric humans, who regularly required a sudden rush of energy to face mortal dangers from wild animals or rival groups of hunters. Today we rarely face life-or-death situations and are unfamiliar with the sensations of the response to stress. Often people thrust into sudden danger are literally paralyzed, their bodies flooded with unfamiliar hormones that trigger physical and mental deadlock.

If such experiences are repeated over time, as may happen in a survival situation, they can precipitate complete mental breakdown. Mental instability can result after about five or 10 days of extreme danger depending on how effectively the survivor's basic needs (food, sleep and so on) have been catered for.

Signs that a person is succumbing to the stress reaction are many. Indicators to watch for in yourself and others include aggression, dramatic mood swings, an increase in alcohol and drug use (which ironically aggravates the condition), severe anxiety that disrupts sleep and intelligence, extreme and inexplicable body temperature variations, and chronic depression. Memory loss (even instructions given only seconds earlier might vanish from recollection), reckless actions, chronic fatigue even after rest, poor communications skills and pronunciation, and obsessive activities (such as constantly cleaning tools beyond normal maintenance requirements or dwelling obsessively on one subject) are also signs to be watched for.

All these conditions are dangerous in a survival situation because the sufferer starts to withdraw into himself and ignore external hazards rather than deal with them. At the extreme end of symptoms, the stress sufferer may become catatonic, unable to move his limbs even under extreme coercion, may stop eating and drinking, and vomit when he attempts to do so, and may exhibit loss of bowel and bladder control. The sufferer might suddenly inhabit an imaginary or even hallucinatory world, and not respond to external stimuli.

Team survival
One of the best ways of staying mentally focused in a survival situation is to concentrate on the welfare of the other team members, such as this man applying a treatment for hypothermia. Do not, however, jeopardize your own safety through attending to others.

Arctic clothing from animal skins
Survival requires a resourceful attitude which utilizes all available materials and opportunities. Here a woman has fashioned improvised arctic clothing out of sections of animal skins.

Rope rescue

Your first priority in a survival situation is the immediate safety of yourself and others. Remove yourself and others from life-threatening dangers before addressing the long-term survival issues.

Such severe symptoms disable an individual's capacity to survive and increase the burden on other survivors. However, entire groups can suffer from stress symptoms, too. Group cohesion may disintegrate, discipline may become poor and important tasks may be left undone or completed slowly. Physical fights may even break out.

Such problems become more acute if the survivors are suffering from sleep deprivation. Sleep deprivation is one of the central catalysts for mental breakdown. Disrupted sleep patterns, particularly between 02:00 and 06:00 (the times of deepest sleep), aggressively attack intelligence and emotions. Sleep deprivation for more than 48 hours results in individuals and groups suffering extreme psychological disorders, including auditory and visual hallucinations. When sleep is withheld, rates of illness increase dramatically, and the body's immune system begins to grow progressively weaker. Further, sleep deprivation is compounded if it comes at the end of long-distance travel, especially if the person has crossed time zones and is suffering from jet lag.

TAKING CONTROL

What separates those who can cope with the stress of life-or-death survival situations from those who just give up and pay the price? The answer: possessing sound survival skills, probably the best tools for handling stress. Having the correct skills means a survivor is far less likely to suffer from helplessness and more likely to develop a systematic plan for survival. Such individuals also increase group survival rates by offering a focus of well-judged decision-making skills. Confidence also comes from group support. Before embarking on any wilderness adventure, take time for hard training with the group of people with which you actually intend to travel. The training will reveal individual strengths and weaknesses, and you will, hopefully, come to have an implicit trust in one another and learn each person's strong points. In a survival situation, this trust translates into motivation because nobody will want to let the others down. As a result, adverse stress responses are far less likely to set in because the

RELAXATION

Relaxation techniques are excellent tools for helping you cope with the stress of survival. The easiest to master is simple breathing meditation, such as the kind used in Buddhism and other contemplative religions. Breathing-based meditation has clear benefits. During a meditative state, the rate the heart beats slows down and the blood pressure drops, both inducing a sense of peace and improving composure and concentration.

To perform breathing relaxation, find a safe, quiet place, sit down, and close your eyes. Direct all your concentration on to the sound and sensation of your breathing. Breathe slowly and deeply, drawing the air in through your nose, then expelling it slowly through your mouth. If your attention wanders – which it will – simply bring it back to your breathing. Do this exercise for only five minutes, and when you stop you should have a renewed sense of peace as well as the ability to think more clearly about your situation.

survivors will maintain an outward-looking perspective and remain conscious of the needs of others.

Fear is perhaps the root of any psychological breakdown in survival situations. To control fear, first realize it is your friend, not your enemy. Fear produces adrenaline and other body responses that make you more resilient to pain, give you faster reactions, focus all your attention on survival and make you physically stronger. The key is to control your fear and channel it into

Hypnosis positions

Self-hypnosis is the practice of making positive visualizations while in a state of deep relaxation. It can be performed in a sitting or prone position, and has practical usage in a survival situation.

Taking 10 minutes out from danger to perform relaxation exercises will give you greater clarity of thought and so help you to avoid bad decisions.

AVOIDING PANIC

In the immediate aftermath of a car or aircraft crash, your mind will be in a state of disorientation and panic. To restore your focus, do the following:

- Get away from the immediate vicinity of the wreckage in case of explosions of fire; however, don't go so far away that you lose the accident location, something possible in bad weather or heavily wooded terrain. Don't blindly stumble into unknown territory, especially if it is dark. This response will only result in you getting lost and risking serious injury.
- Remove yourself from the presence of corpses (after checking for any survivors). They will distract the focus of your thinking and produce a very negative mind set.
- Once out of danger, find yourself a sheltered and safe spot. Spend a few minutes slowing down your breathing and calming yourself.
- Once you are more composed, design a survival plan. Do not make the plan too complex; it should consist of no more than two or three easily memorable points at first. Anything too detailed is unlikely to be remembered.
- Having made the long-term plan, deal with your immediate survival priorities one step at a time. Don't look too far into the future – you'll simply feel overwhelmed. Instead, concentrate on getting through each day alive and healthy, while slowly achieving the goals of the survival plan.

Controlling fear

Handling fear is paramount in any survival scenario, from an air crash to a hostage-taking situation. Counter negative thoughts immediately with positive strategies for survival.

action. There are two main ways you can do this.

First, counter every negative thought with a positive one. Fear encourages a disaster-oriented inner voice. It says things such as 'I'm going to die', 'I don't know what to do' and 'I can't cope with this'. The instant these thoughts appear, immediately contradict them with positive opposites – 'I can handle this', 'I'm going to survive' and 'I'm in control'. Don't worry if this feels artificial at first. It will keep your mind occupied and prevent you from succumbing to panic. The key point is to counter any negative with a positive immediately, and never allow any negative to go unchallenged, no matter how desperate the situation.

Another way of handling fear is to control body posture. Our bodies are capable of creating fear, as well as expressing it. When afraid, we tend to stoop and wrap our arms around ourselves as we revert to an infant state. Our eyesight becomes unfocused – we don't want to see the thing that scares us. Voice tone become higher pitched and trembles as the throat tightens and our breathing becomes shallow and rapid. Movements are erratic and uncertain. Such responses actually increase fear.

Research has shown that the emotions often

Milling

'Milling' is a form of aggression training used by the British Parachute Regiment. Supervised combat training is an excellent way to build up stress-handling capabilities and to control fear.

take their lead from what the body is doing, rather than the other way around. Force yourself to express confidence with your body, not fear. Keep your chin up (literally), as this raises your head and makes you focus your eyes outward. Stand up straight and pull your shoulders back. Breathe deeply from the abdomen. Speak slowly and deliberately, pushing your voice up from the abdomen to give it a deeper tone. Move decisively and with confidence. You need to play the role of a confident individual, as an actor would do in a film. Visualize a tough, independent character, such as John Wayne or James Bond, if it helps, and respond as you imagine they would. Even if your mind still shakes with fear, keep with it. You will soon find that the mind adopts the confidence of the body. After all, it is easier to control your physique than your thoughts.

EMERGENCY CONDITIONING
One way to produce psychological strength in times of emergency is to condition the mind for emergencies in advance. Such is what soldiers call 'battleproofing' or 'battle inoculation', but what we might call 'emergency conditioning' (EC). EC is based on making the mind 'familiar' with the shock of survival through realistic

Equipped for the job
Having the right equipment will go a long way to alleviating fears and concerns when faced with an emergency. Ensure that clothing is precisely adapted to the specific environment.

RULE-OF-THREE THINKING

If you find yourself wracked by indecision about your best course of action in a survival situation, use the 'rule-of-three' decision-making process as taught to the US Marines. When faced with a problem, think of three different solutions. Any fewer than three and you do not have enough options, and any more than three and you have too many alternatives. Honestly assess the positive and negatives of each option, then, without dwelling obsessively on detail, choose what seems the best. Importantly, stick with your choice once it is made. US Marine officers are taught that the biggest danger in extreme circumstances is not making the wrong decision, but rather not making any decision at all. Do not worry too much if there are still problems in your plan; you can negotiate these as you go along. Rule-of-three thinking has the advantage of giving a structure to your thinking processes in extreme circumstances.

training. Possessing a basic understanding of how the human brain processes memory is helpful when it comes to utilizing EC.

The human brain is essentially like a large filing system. All experiences are compared against the 'files' of memory to see if there is a similar experience in the past to guide future actions. If there is a match, the individual is able to respond appropriately to the situation. Sometimes the match is so strong, such as the oft-repeated file for making a cup of coffee, that the action is performed almost unconsciously. If, however, there is no previous experience to guide the response, the brain finds the nearest equivalent and uses it to create a new file based on the results of the action.

The problem with survival is that, unless you have been in life or death situations before, you are unlikely to have any relevant files at all. The result is psychological distress and paralysis. This is where EC comes in.

The first and most vital part of EC is hard training because it enables the brain to establish those important emergency files. Replicate as many different disasters as realistically as possible without putting yourself in actual danger. If you are a diver, for instance, practise losing your mask or supply of oxygen underwater. If you are an explorer, make a shelter or safely build a fire from scratch in freezing conditions. If you frequent rough areas of a city, learn to defend yourself by undergoing hard training, with real pain involved. By generating as much realism in

Avoiding fatigue

As soon as you face a survival situation, you should eliminate all unnecessary physical activities to conserve your energy and bodily resources. When running or walking, avoid the high-leg step shown here in preference for a low, loping movement which is far more energy efficient.

Demotivation

Willpower is a central ingredient in survival. Avoid spending too much time contemplating the danger you are in, as you are likely to sink into depression and demotivation.

training as possible, you eliminate the shock factor from actual survival situations.

The training exercises must be undertaken with a real sense of emergency and repeated constantly until the correct responses become almost second nature. Through repetition the sensations and mental processes of survival enter the 'files' of the familiar. In a real survival situation, the brain will be less traumatized by the experience than the brain of someone who has not undergone training.

In addition to the physical aspect of training, there is a method of EC called 'visualization'. Scientific research has shown that, if the brain imagines something in deep and vivid detail, then that imagination actually becomes part of the person's experience files, and these files will guide future actions.

Visualization involves sitting in a quiet place with the eyes closed, imagining an emergency situation as vividly as possible, re-creating every sight, sound and sensation in the mind. Visualization is useful for EC because it allows individuals to perform their own internal 'battleproofing' by imagining themselves coping with situations about which they are fearful. If you are particularly afraid of being buried in an avalanche, for example, imagine yourself deep under the snow in the darkness. But instead of

succumbing to terror, picture yourself getting
your orientation, suppressing panic, then boldly
striking for the surface. Thus if the worst actually
happens, the brain will use that positive file to
tackle the situation. While the technique is not a
substitute for physical training itself, it can help
to control the stress response in an emergency.

BEING A SURVIVOR
Positive thinking alone will not save you in a
survival situation. You need a definite survival
plan as well. A survival plan has two
interconnected objectives: 1) stay safe and well,
and 2) reach a position of safety. A survival plan
starts with an appraisal of the situation.

First, remove yourself from the immediate
danger and find a place that is sheltered so that
you can sit down and think. Evaluate your
surroundings. Every environment in the world has
its own advantages and disadvantages. If surviving
in arctic conditions, for example, the extreme cold
is a central danger, but on the positive side you
should have an abundance of water from melted

Effects of dehydration
**Dehydration has a major detrimental impact upon
the psychological state, as the brain relies heavily
upon fluid for its function. Always make adequate
hydration a no. 1 survival priority.**

Depression
**Depression results in poor judgement skills and
a lack of motivation. Survival situations court
depression, but the best countermeasure is to stay
occupied and direct all energies towards rescue.**

THE STRESS RESPONSE

The human body has an advanced stress-response system to maximize the chances of survival. When we encounter a life-threatening situation, the part of the brain known as the hypothalamus triggers the release of stress-response hormones such as adrenaline into the bloodstream. Here they prepare the body for life-saving action through the 'fight or flight' reaction. Blood is diverted away from the brain and the skin (which is why frightened people go pale) to the muscles, to give them more physical energy. Simultaneously, heartbeat and breathing are increased to provide the muscles with the increased blood-borne oxygen necessary for strenuous action. In a further response to bolster energy levels, the liver releases glucose into the bloodstream. Psychologically, the brain adopts a tunnel vision, shutting out almost every sensation that does not contribute to the survival of the individual. All these responses give the person tremendous energy and an increased ability to withstand pain.

Signs of stress

Aggression is an indicator of several possible physical or mental states. It might suggest fatigue, hypo- or hyperthermia, depression, altitude sickness or simple frustration. Calm an aggressive individual down with reasoned, soft words.

snow and ice. In the tropics, you should find plentiful food, but heat and humidity will be hazards. Be completely objective and weigh up all the positive and negative aspects of the situation you are in. Try to make the assessment in daylight rather than at night, when it is less easy to make an accurate and more objective assessment of a situation. And take your time. Acting in haste can result in general disorientation, bad decisions and the danger of losing equipment.

Next, assess your physical condition. Do you have any wounds that need treatment? Do you require extra clothing, or food and water? Base any survival plans on your realistically available energy and condition. Assess the conditions, usage and value of any equipment you may have. Your main survival priorities are shelter, fire, water and food. If you have plentiful wood fuel for a fire, you will also have shelter-building materials and, most likely, plant foods. Combine this with a nearby stream for water plus evidence of animal life, and it means your current location satisfies all main survival priorities and you can stay where you are in the short term.

Don't be in a hurry to move unless there is an immediate danger. For example, if you survive

an aircraft crash, there may be useful survival materials to be had from the wreckage. For instance, the foam-rubber seats can make excellent fire-starter material (unless they are specifically fire-retardant) or can be shaped into warm foot protection. Batteries from the aircraft can be used to start fires, and if set alight the aircraft's tyres will produce excellent signal smoke visible over long distances. The moral is, think before walking away from an immediate accident in case you deprive yourself of useful items of equipment. Also remember, in the case of an aircraft crash or shipping accident your position will probably have been relayed to emergency authorities just prior to the accident. The rescue services will therefore know your approximate position, and search teams will probably be on their way. Don't let this stop you from thinking for yourself. You must not just sit and wait for rescue. Think constantly about the dangers of the future, and try to obviate them in advance. Rely on yourself to stay alive, not on other people.

CHAPTER TWO

SURVIVAL CLOTHING

Your clothing is the front line of your protection against the elements. Survival experts often use the saying, 'There is no such thing as the wrong weather, just the wrong clothing.'

THE CORRECT SELECTION of clothing is vital for any outdoor adventure. Your clothing will, if appropriate, not only keep you warm, but also protect you from wind, rain, extreme heat, and sunlight. Bear in mind, though, that much outdoor clothing designed for everyday wear in a temperate climate will not stand up to the climatic conditions of the arctic, tropics or desert.

When purchasing survival clothing, get the best you can possibly afford. This is easier said than done. There is an excessive variety of clothing for the outdoors available, with huge variations in price and quality. If you do not have the prior knowledge, ask trained staff in a specialist retailer, outlining the specifics of your intended pursuit and the likely climatic conditions you will face. They should be able to provide you with straightforward advice on what you need.

The worst case scenario for clothing occurs when you have a survival situation unexpectedly thrust upon you. For example, you might find yourself dressed in light, urban clothing that provides little or no protection in the event of an unexpected but extreme change of weather or in the wild. Make sure you get into the habit of throwing a substantial coat, good boots, a hat and some waterproof clothing into the car before a long journey. It may seem overzealous, but these items could well save your life.

LAYER PRINCIPLE
The fundamental principle of survival clothing is layering. The essence of layering is to trap still air between numerous layers of clothing, to reduce the temperature gradient between the body and its surrounding environment. Each band of air is warmed by the body and produces multiple layers of insulation. The more layers you wear, the warmer you become. You can readily add or take away layers as a method of temperature control, and several light layers are more effective than a single heavy layer.

For an extreme cold-weather climate, here are the layers you should wear.
- Next to the skin wear long-sleeved and long-legged underwear made from tight-weave thermal materials.
- The second layer should be a woollen or wool-mixture shirt. Avoid cotton T-shirts as these are easily soaked by sweat.
- Next put on a woollen or wool-mixture sweater (wool-mixture sweaters offers better warmth and windproofing). Polo neck or turtleneck sweaters are recommended, as they enclose the carotid arteries and jugular veins in the neck, through which much heat is lost.

MAINTAINING FOOTWEAR

Obey the following procedures to keep boots in optimum condition:
- Apply boot wax or polishes to keep the uppers supple and waterproof.
- Before putting your boots on, check them for signs of damage such as severely worn treads, cracked soles, broken seals or stitching, cracked leather and broken fastening hooks.
- To dry wet boots, stuff them with newspaper if available, and dry them in a warm, airy place. You can place them near a fire to assist drying, but not too close. Too much direct heat will bake and crack the leather.
- Always carry at least two spare pairs of laces. To preserve laces in cold weather, rub silicone or wax into them. It will prevent them from freezing if they become wet.

- The penultimate layer should be a jacket of modern synthetic fleece material, or a Hollofil (man-made fibrefill) jacket. It should have long sleeves and full-length legs. Do not use down materials as they lose much of their insulating properties when wet. The jacket should have a large hood with a drawstring cord around the face to prevent loss of heat through the head.
- Finally, light windproof and waterproof trousers and jackets will protect from wind chill, and wet. The waterproof layer must pull easily over other clothing (including boots) without being tight-fitting. Remember, once soaked, clothing loses its heat-retaining properties, so never shed waterproofs if the conditions are very wet.

THE 'COLDER' PRINCIPLE

In US military survival training, the correct procedures for the wearing and repair of survival clothing are remembered by the acronym 'COLDER'. This stands for:

C   Clean – keep clothing free of mud and dirt
O   Overheating – avoid becoming too hot and excessive sweating
L   Loose layers – wear clothing loose and in layers
D   Dry – dry out clothing when wet
E   Examine – monitor your clothing for any defects and wear
R   Repair – repair clothing as soon as it is damaged (make sure you pack a sewing kit)

Personal flotation device (PFD)

A good personal flotation device (PFD) should always include automatic CO_2 self-inflation, a manual top-up tube, a whistle and a strobe light to increase your visibility in the dark.

Carry duplicate items of all clothing up to the final jacket and waterproof layer. This enables you to change out of sweat-soaked inner clothing when you break from exercise.

FABRICS

When selecting survival clothing, particularly outer jackets and waterproof clothing, pay close attention to fabrics. Your fabrics must release the sweat from the body, which inevitably builds up when exercising in substantial clothing. If you sweat in a freezing climate, the sweat-soaked clothing acts a conductor to draw away body heat into the air. To prevent this, choose 'breathable' materials that will not absorb sweat and become wet, cold, and uncomfortable. Gore-Tex is the best known of these materials, but other names include Ultrex and Extreme. The micro-porous Gore-Tex

Cold-weather clothing

This man is fully equipped in arctic survival clothing. His extremities are well protected by thermal balaclava and mittens. Note the mittens are on a cord to prevent them being lost in snow.

Warm-weather clothing

Warm-weather clothing should provide maximum body coverage to prevent sunburn and heat exhaustion. A wide-brimmed hat is essential for heat protection.

Jacket fastenings are important, as much body heat is lost from loose openings around the wrists, neck and hood. All zippers, particularly the main zip, should feature storm flaps sealed by both stud fastenings and Velcro to prevent the wind and wet from entering. The wrists should have adjustable fastenings that can be tightened. The jacket's hood must have enough space for a hat to be worn underneath, and it should also fasten up to cover the lower part of the face. A wire stiffener and drawstrings will allow you to pull the hood close around the face, preventing both heat loss and the wind blowing the hood off the head.

On the issue of colour, choose something that makes you easier to see in an emergency. Bright colours stand out and increase the chances of a rescue patrol seeing you in an emergency. The only exception to this rule might be if you are doing any hunting, in which case camouflage is the best choice. The ideal in this situation would be a light camouflage waterproof layer over a bright jacket – the waterproof layer can be removed if conditions are dry.

membrane allows perspiration to evaporate while remaining fully waterproof to external water. It achieves this by having nine billion pores per square inch, each pore being 20,000 times smaller than a water droplet, but 700 times bigger than a molecule of water evaporation. An important point about such fabrics is to keep them clean. If they become plastered in mud, the pores are blocked and the water-release properties of the garment are compromised.

SPECIAL ITEMS AND REQUIREMENTS
Jackets

The principal quality of an outer jacket is that it should be windproof and waterproof, and feature a breathable fabric such as Gore-Tex. The jacket should have the capacity to accommodate several layers of clothing without being tight and should be knee-length with drawstrings at the waist and hem. It should have at least two large outside pockets with waterproof flaps, and it is best to have a large inside pocket that can hold a map.

IMPROVISED CLOTHING

If caught in the wilderness without adequate clothing, there are several measures you can follow to increase your chances of survival.

- If involved in a vehicle accident or plane crash, salvage as much material and fabric as you can from the crash site, including towels, cushions, and seat covers. Convert as much of this as possible into clothing.
- Place dry grass or moss and leaves from deciduous trees between two layers of clothing, and stuff the material into cuffs and waistbands to increase insulation. Other types of insulation include paper, feathers and animal hair.
- Make waterproof clothing from plastic bags or sheets. The inner bark of birch trees can be inserted under clothing as a waterproof barrier as well. Rubbing animal fat into clothing can make it waterproof, but it also reduces the clothing's insulating properties, so this should not be done in cold climates.
- Basic footwear can be made from rubber tyres or a piece of leather. Punch holes around the edges for thongs to tie them into place.

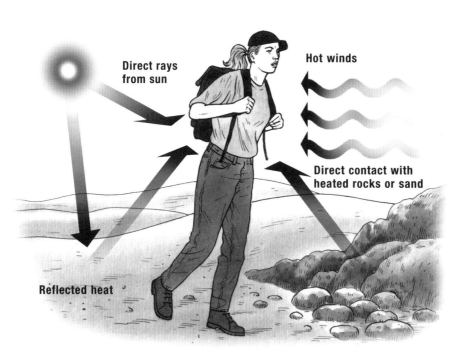

Direct rays from sun

Hot winds

Direct contact with heated rocks or sand

Reflected heat

Sources of heat gain

The sun is not the only source of heat to contend with in an arid area. Rocks, heated wind and ground-reflected heat all contribute to the burden. This woman should be wearing a hat or head scarf which covers the back of the neck, as well as the skull. The neck contains many major blood vessels; heating of these by the sun can lead to heat exhaustion.

Trousers

Light trousers will suffice in cold, though not extreme, climates as long as your upper body is warm. All trousers should be quick-drying and made of a strong material – synthetic/cotton gabardine-type twill weaves are best. Make sure that they allow free leg movements and are not too tight, otherwise your legs will sweat more. All pockets should be large and fastened with zippers covered by storm flaps. Reinforced knee-covers are useful, particularly if you are heading for mountainous terrain. In addition to your standard trousers, you should have a pair of windproof and waterproof trousers. These are worn over your regular trousers and feature a zipper at the side around the ankle to allow you to put them on while wearing boots. Make sure these outer trousers are made of breathable fabric.

Footwear

It is hard to overstate the importance of good footwear for survival situations. Do not wear athletics shoes for wilderness activities, as the soft construction will not provide adequate protection against twisting and impact, or cope with cold and sweat. For general backpacking,

invest in a pair of high-quality walking boots with a flexible sole and deep tread. Ideally, choose boots with waterproof leather and breathable fabric linings such as Gore-Tex, Cordura and Cambrelle to offer greater comfort. Additional waterproofing is offered by wearing nylon gaiters over the boots to help keep water from entering through the lace eyelets and the ankle opening.

Above all, choose boots that are suitable for your activity. A mountain boot, for example, is more rigid than a standard walking boot, and will make for tough going over flat land. Before buying anything, seek advice or read the reviews in specialist magazines. Purchase the boots long before you plan to put them to heavy use, and wear them around the house to increase their flexibility and so avoid blisters. When buying boots, it is a good idea to put on the layers of socks you will need to wear, and always try them on in the afternoon when your feet are warm and expanded.

Headgear

With up to half of our body heat lost through the head, it is vital to invest in several good hats. Hats are equally vital in hot climates to guard against heat stroke. For cold environments, pack

CLOTHING FOR HOT CLIMATES

The vital principle of hot-weather clothing is that the skin and the head should be protected from direct sunlight and heat. Wear light ankle-length trousers and a long-sleeved shirt with a collar to filter out the sun's UV radiation. Not all materials block out UV radiation, so it is worth obtaining special clothing from an outdoor supplier. The head and eyes require a sun hat and sunglasses, respectively. The neck is vulnerable to burning and high temperatures so the hat should feature a covering for the neck, such as is seen on the hats worn by members of the French Foreign Legion. To prevent temporary sun blindness, the sunglasses must offer a strong filter against UVA and UVB rays. If, in an emergency, sunglasses are not available, then wrap a cloth over the eyes with slits for vision. Rubbing streaks of charcoal (from burnt wood) under the eyes also helps to reduce the glare. Remember to protect the extremities, and use a sun block with a sun protection factor of 25 or higher. Apply it generously to all exposed skin, including the feet, neck, ears, hands and nose. Don't forget to bring some warm clothing with you as well. In tropical or desert climates, temperatures can drop precipitously at night, even to below freezing.

conditions such as frostbite. Good socks, readily available from outdoor clothing suppliers, will help to protect your feet from the agony of blisters.

For socks, a woollen sock or cotton-blend sock is good, with Lycra grip sections around the ankle and instep to prevent the sock slipping. Socks are classified under different categories, such as for walking and climbing. Wearing two pairs of socks helps prevent blisters and increases comfort. Try various combinations of thickness before embarking on your activity to make sure they are suitable. Avoid socks that are too tight as these restrict the circulation and can promote frozen feet. Take plenty of spare socks so you can put on a dry pair when necessary. Wearing wet socks for any length of time puts you at risk of developing trench foot. Some socks are impregnated with antibacterial agents to maintain the health of the garment; if not, wash out old socks on a regular basis.

Choosing the right gloves is just as important as choosing the right socks. There are many woollen and ski gloves available, but in severely cold climates mittens provide better insulation. Wearing a pair of thin thermal gloves under your mittens allows you to use your fingers when you need to, but make sure the mittens are attached to the jacket by a cord or they can be easily lost.

at least a couple of balaclavas or woollen hats that cover the ears and the back of the neck. Remember, if conditions are wet, wear a waterproof hood over the hat – a soaking wet woollen hat will actually accelerate heat loss.

In hot climates, wear an Arab headdress, known as a 'keffiyeh' or 'shemagh'. These can be purchased from many markets in the Middle East and North Africa, but are also relatively easy to make. Take a piece of light, sun-reflective cloth (obtainable from survival stores), ideally white in colour, about 100cm (3ft 3in) square, and fold it over the head, neck and shoulders. Secure in place with a cord around the top of the head. When completed, there should be enough excess material to be wrapped around the face when necessary (such as in a sandstorm).

Socks and gloves

Both sock and gloves protect the vulnerable extremities from heat loss and more severe

Keeping active

Even in the most restricted survival environments, such as this inflatable dinghy, try to keep as active as possible, washing clothes, repairing kit and trying to collect food and drinking water.

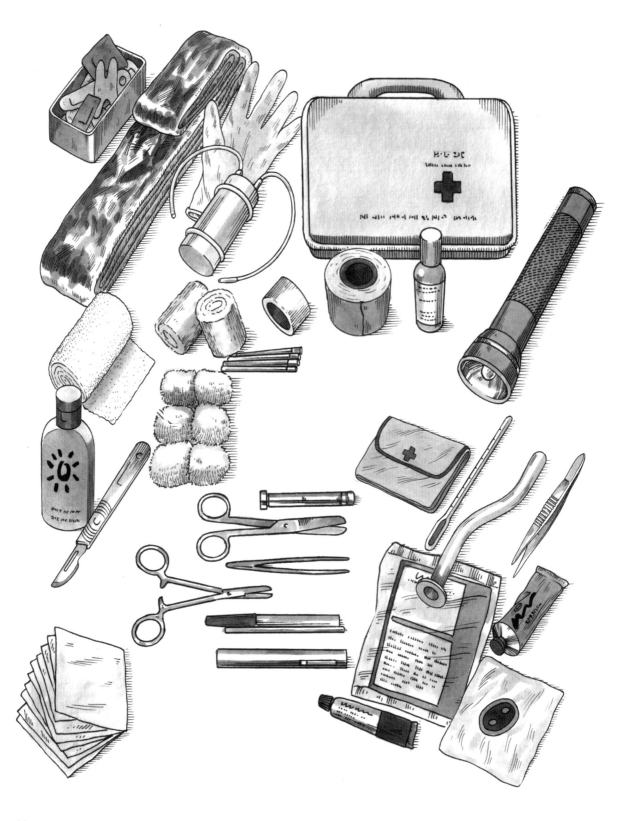

CHAPTER THREE

SURVIVAL KIT

The fundamental principle when packing a survival kit is to pack nothing extraneous. Take with you only those items essential for survival in the wilderness.

WHEN CHOOSING THE items in your survival kit, you should consider two factors: the type of emergencies likely to occur and the climate and territory you will face. Judge everything in terms of function, and ask yourself one question: does this item directly contribute to my physical welfare? If not, leave it behind.

Be wary of packing those 'little luxuries' you feel you just cannot do without. Limit in particular the number of books you carry because these quickly pile up the weight. That said, one or two light paperbacks may help stem the boredom that so often accompanies survival situations.

Here we will look at the most important items of survival kit in turn.

TIPS ON TENT CARE

- Never pack a tent away wet, as this will result in a build-up of mildew and bacteria that will damage the material. Clean any mildew off immediately with warm water, and hang the tent up to dry before packing.
- Always peg the tent out with the correct tension. Too tight, and the tent will be rigid, lacking the flexibility to withstand strong winds. Too slack, and the tent will whip against itself and could easily tear.
- Put a ground cloth under the tent to protect it from damage by rocks or sticks.
- Ventilate the tent well in the morning to clear out condensation from inside.
- Do not wash a tent using common detergents, which can damage the waterproofing.
- Waterproof all seams with a recommended seam-sealer product, even if the tent claims to be 100 per cent waterproof.

TENTS

A variety of tents are available, from large summer shelters designed for family use (and usually carried in a car) to ultra-lightweight mountain and arctic models. As always, take expert advice when purchasing a tent, and be very specific about your planned needs.

The two types of tent relevant to our discussion here are backpacking tents, designed for mild weather use, and winter tents. When purchasing either type, look for the following:
- Full waterproofing, with seams that are taped and lap-felled (meaning that the layers of fabric interlock)
- A breathable nylon inner wall
- Feature poles linked together with shock-cords for easy construction
- Poles made out of aircraft aluminium – these are stronger and more durable than poles made from fibreglass
- A vestibule section, for storing wet equipment and for cooking
- Mosquito nets, for zipping over the entrances – especially important if you are travelling to a tropical or summertime location

In addition to this, each type of tent has its own specific requirements:

Backpacking tent
- Light weight – no more than 2.72kg (6lb) for a two-person tent

Winter tent
- A weight of 3.63–4.54kg (8–10lb) – the extra weight provides the tent with greater sturdiness in winter conditions
- Extra capacity to handle the larger amounts of equipment carried in winter explorations.

- Sometimes there is enough space between the fly sheet and the inner tent for extra storage

Regarding tent shape, geodesic (dome-shaped) tents are a good choice. These not only provide plenty of internal space, but also their shape is ideal for resisting high winds.

For solo camping, 'bivi-bags' are another, limited alternative to tents. These are portable shelters constructed using hoops, which erect into low-profile, one-man tunnel tents. Their use is not ideal for extended pursuits, as you cannot cook or even store any significant equipment in a bivi-bag. They are, however, windproof and waterproof, and weigh only 540g (1.19lb), so they are easily packed as a backup to the main tent or for use during one- or two-day activities in temperate conditions.

SLEEPING BAGS
A good sleeping bag is vital for ensuring rest and warmth during an expedition into the wilds. In terms of shape, close-fitting sarcophagus-shaped or semi-rectangular bags are best, as they minimize the air space surrounding you, which will require body heat to warm up.

For insulation, select a sleeping bag filled with down filling, one of the best insulating materials, or an equivalent synthetic material such as Thinsulate, Qualofill, Hollowfil or Polarguard. In wet conditions, a waterproof cover for a down-filled bag is essential, as down will lose its insulating properties when wet.

Most sleeping bags are graded according to the lowest temperature for which they are suitable (e.g. '0°–25°C'), so choose the right bag for your intended destination. Alternatively, you could opt for an all-weather sleeping system consisting of a sleeping bag, a fleece liner and a bivi-bag.

Sleeping mats are an important addition if you are planning to sleep out for any length of time, and some modern ones come with self-inflating and deflating functions. Do not sleep directly on cold ground – more heat will be lost through contact with cold ground than with cold air.

In tropical climates where staying warm is not an issue, a hammock may be a better form of bed than a sleeping bag because it is cooler and packs up much smaller. If tying the hammock between trees, put insect repellent on the ropes to prevent visits from unwelcome insects.

BACKPACKS
The first issue in selecting a backpack is capacity. Backpacks range from small 20l (1220ci) capacity packs to large 100l (6100ci) capacity bergens. Select a pack large enough only for your purpose; anything too large will encourage excess weight carriage. A filled backpack should be no more than one-third of the carrier's body weight. In terms of design, select one that offers maximum comfort and strength. Modern packs often come with anatomically shaped shoulder straps, hip belts and lumbar pads, and have aluminium frames to reduce pack weight. Traditional H-frame packs, however, can be better if carrying heavy loads for long periods.

There are several features which you should look for in a good backpack:
- Side pockets – essential for carrying items requiring quick access
- A separate base compartment for storing wet or infrequently accessed items
- Extendible flaps over the pockets and main openings, which allow you to vary the backpack capacity
- Double stitching, taped seals, storm flaps over zippers and bar tacks to increase the backpack's strength and waterproofing.

Packing a backpack is a structured process. Pack all the items you will need regularly or suddenly – such as food or a dry pullover or sweater) – in the side pockets or top section, where they can be accessed easily. Items which are needed infrequently – such as sleeping bags – will go towards the bottom of the pack (unless their bulk requires separate storage in a roll outside the backpack). The top flap of the backpack is ideal for storing wet-weather clothing, so it is quickly accessible. Increase waterproof protection for the bag contents (particularly sleeping bags) by packing them in several separate, strong plastic bags for protection in case of a sudden ingress of water, as might occur if you fall into a river.

During the early days of wearing a new backpack, watch out for points that are rubbing or numbness in your limbs. These indicate that straps are too tight or badly adjusted; lengthen or shorten the straps accordingly, or pad with foam pieces until the backpack is a perfect fit. Wear your backpack high up the back, with the weight centralized. The high position allows your legs to

Backpack

A backpack should be made of tough, waterproof materials and should feature multiple isolated storage compartments. Tie up any loose straps to prevent them snagging on plants, walls, etc.

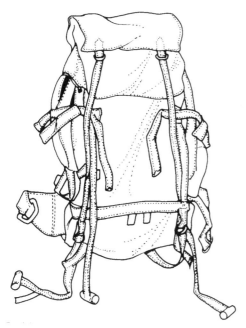

Horseshoe pack

A particularly useful form of improvised backpack is the horseshoe pack. Lay a rectangular piece of material 1.5 x 1.5m (5 x 5ft) on the ground. Place all the items you need to carry on one side of the material, then roll the items up in the material, going right to the opposite edge. Tie knots in each end of the now sausage-shaped roll, then add another two ties to divide the roll into thirds. Finally, tie both ends together to form a pack which can be worn over the shoulder and diagonally across the chest.

take more of the weight and also reduces the possibility of back strain. Edges or corners of cans, footwear and hard objects must be kept towards the centre of the bag so that they do not rub against your back.

As with clothing, keep backpacks in a good state of repair. Take with you repair materials, particularly strong tape, a tube of superglue, some nylon patches and strong sewing thread. With these materials, you can mend most torn seams or punctured fabric.

COOKING EQUIPMENT

The most important item of cooking equipment is a portable stove. This should be lightweight – 500–700g (1.1–1.54lb) – and also compact, without too many loose attachments. Your choice of fuel – butane/propane, methylated spirits (denatured alcohol), paraffin (kerosene) or petrol (gasoline) – depends on how the stove will be used. For instance, when used in a tent, paraffin stoves require a lot of ventilation to disperse toxic gases. Never use hexamine blocks (small blocks of inflammable material that burn with a hot flame for around 10 minutes) or leaded petrol within a tent; unleaded petrol is safe if there is plentiful ventilation. Consider also environmental conditions. Cooking gas, for instance, can freeze in subzero temperatures.

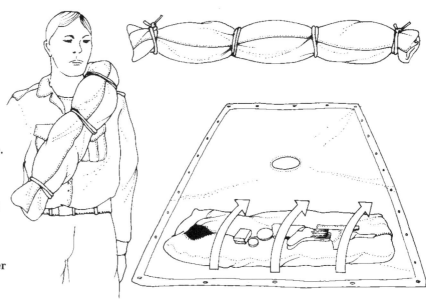

When it comes to cookware, you can buy compact cooking sets made of stainless steel, and with four or five items, each storing inside another. For short trips, however, two vessels may suffice. For crockery, use lightweight plastic plates and bowls.

FOOD

We discuss this in more detail in later chapters, but it is worth pointing out here that modern dehydrated food packages are ideal for survival use. Avoid cans, which may rust and are also heavy and bulky. Dehydrated food packages are light in weight, and good brands provide recommended levels of carbohydrates, calories, protein and vitamins. Two or three such packs should provide at least 4500 calories a day to maintain high levels of physical activity – look on the back of the package for calorie details. The only preparation required is to add hot water and stir, then wait for 2–3 minutes. Some survival packages even come ready hydrated and are self-heating. Pulling a cord on the package activates a chemical heating process, and the hot meal is ready in minutes.

A typical survival menu for a day's outdoor activity might look as follows:

Breakfast – oat porridge, hot tea/coffee

Snacks – beef spread, biscuits and chocolate, nuts, raisins, dextrose energy sweets (candies)

Main meal – chicken soup, beef granules and mashed potatoes (made with potato powder), peas, apple flakes (chips)

Such a menu will provide all the day's nutritional needs. Store the main meal foodstuffs in a separate backpack compartment, but also carry an easily accessible 'mess pack' containing snack items. A typical mess pack might contain: chocolate, rice cakes, soup sachets (pouches), tea/coffee sachets, milk and sugar sachets.

Selection of travel foods

Pre-purchased foods, which are a good idea to have in your supplies in all survival situations, should be light in weight, compact, have a high nutritional or calorific content, and a long shelf life. The following are good examples:

A. boiled sweets (hard candies)
B. trail mix
C. muesli or granola
D. dried fruit
E. oats
F. rice
G. lentils
H. kidney beans
I. chocolate bar

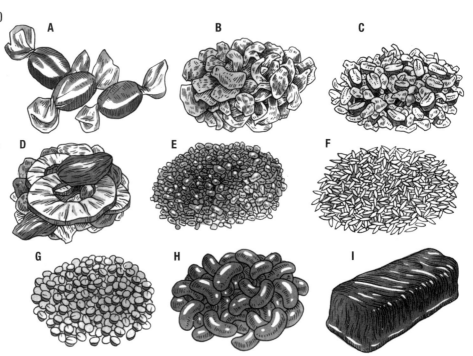

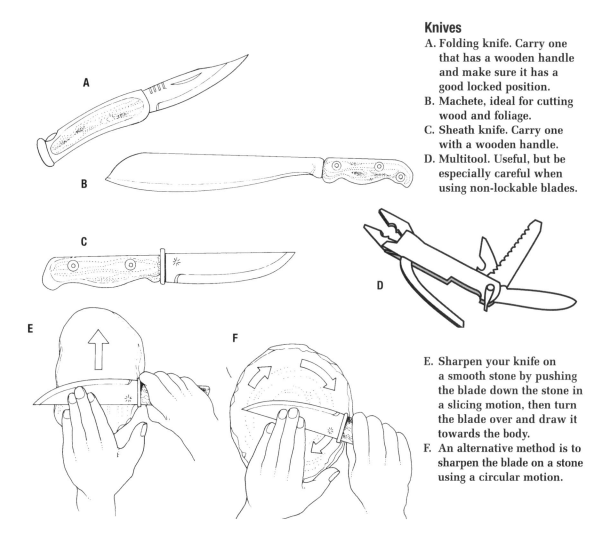

Knives
A. Folding knife. Carry one that has a wooden handle and make sure it has a good locked position.
B. Machete, ideal for cutting wood and foliage.
C. Sheath knife. Carry one with a wooden handle.
D. Multitool. Useful, but be especially careful when using non-lockable blades.

E. Sharpen your knife on a smooth stone by pushing the blade down the stone in a slicing motion, then turn the blade over and draw it towards the body.
F. An alternative method is to sharpen the blade on a stone using a circular motion.

KNIVES
A good knife is probably the most useful single tool to have on hand in a survival situation. It can be used for everything from skinning animals to making shelters. The best type of knife is one that has a single, strong blade sharpened on one side only, with a broad opposite edge and a wooden handle securely fitted with rivets which pass right through the tang. As a backup, carry a small but sturdy lock knife. A multi-blade knife such as a Swiss Army Knife is useful, but the absence of a locking system can make it dangerous to the fingers during heavy use – you don't want to be adding to any injuries you may have.

Look after your knife well. Keep it clean and sharp, and always carry it within a protective scabbard (to protect both you and the blade), especially when travelling. To sharpen it, use a sharpening whetstone and a leather strop. Keeping the blade about 30° from the flat of the stone (which should be dampened with water or a thin oil), stroke the blade across the whetstone about six times in an outward direction before sharpening the other side of the blade with another six strokes, this time running towards you across the stone. Once sharpened, strop the blade backwards and forwards on the leather strop to strengthen the edge.

Mess pack and contents

A Mess tin, B Tea and coffee pouches, C Milk and sugar pouches, D Rice cakes, E Chocolate, F Chocolate candy, G Half-toothbrush, H Half-razor, I Mini toothpaste tube, J Mini shaving foam, K Soap and flannel (washcloth), L Fluorescent survival bag, M Small flashlight

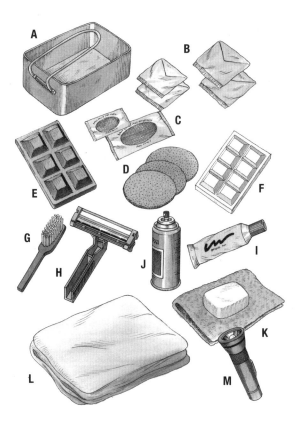

One final rule about knives: never stick or throw them into tree trunks or branches, or even soft ground; the hard wood and grit in the soil will damage and blunt the blade.

SURVIVAL TIN AND SURVIVAL PACK

The survival tin is a portable container for carrying the basic tools of survival. Carry the tin around with you at all times when heading into or through the wilderness, preferably in a jacket pocket. Do not put it in your backpack, in case that is lost or stolen. The basic contents of a good working survival tin are as follows:

BINOCULARS

Binoculars are an excellent survival tool, with uses ranging from surveying terrain to spotting distant rescue parties. Here are some tips on the purchase of binoculars:

- Select an appropriate power. Binocular power is expressed by the equation 'magnification x the diameter of lenses'. A useful and compact pair of binoculars is 8 x 30, although binoculars with larger diameter lenses have greater image intensification in low-light conditions. A pair of 8 x 42s or 10 x 50s is a good choice, but only as long as the binoculars are compact and lightweight.
- Ensure that the binoculars are suitable for heavy outdoor use, being waterproof and rugged. Good lenses will feature anti-fogging treatments ideal for use in damp conditions.
- Choose binoculars with 'fully multicoated' lenses. These will provide optimum light transmission and intensification.
- If you wear glasses, buy binoculars fitted with rubberized, adjustable eyepieces. These allow you to push your eyes close up to the lenses, and so give you the full field of view.

- Matches – dip the heads in melted candle wax and let them dry to give a waterproof coating
- Candle – not only for light and fire, but also because tallow wax is edible in an emergency
- Flint and striker – the most essential piece of fire-starting kit
- Water purification tablets – pack enough to provide a week's supply of clean drinking water
- Small hand mirror – used for signalling by flashing sunlight
- Safety pins – can repair clothing and be used as improvised fishing hooks
- Sewing kit – for stitching damaged clothing or making clothing out of animal skins
- Fish hooks, line and split lead weights – the fishing line can also be used to catch birds (see also Hunting chapter)
- Clear plastic bag – ideal for storage solutions or for use as a solar still
- Brass snare wire – use for animal traps
- Wire saw – use for cutting thick branches
- Button compass – carried as a backup to your main compass

Safety and first-aid equipment

Even for the simplest hiking trip, make sure you pack essential kit such as a map and compass, head torch (flashlight), including a spare battery and bulb, a whistle, knife, rations and survival bag/tin.

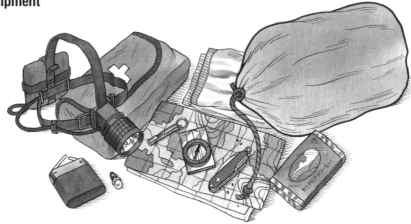

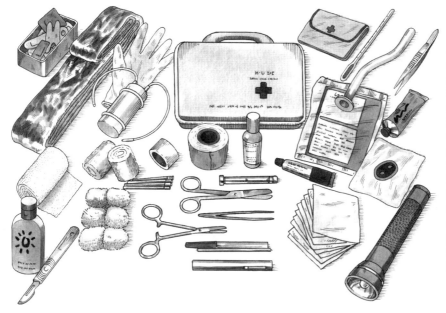

A good first-aid kit should include sticking plasters (adhesive bandages), elastic or crepe bandages, cotton wool, padded dressings, medical tape, scissors, tweezers, antiseptic, iodine, hermometer, torch (flashlight), sunblock and any prescription medicines needed by team members.

That last item, the button compass, is a vital element of your survival tin/survival pack. Check both it and your main compass regularly for leaks (the needle is usually floated on oil), and learn basic methods of compass navigation before venturing into the wilderness. Also pack a magnet and a pin, from which you can make an improvised compass as follows. Stroke the magnet down the pin in one direction only, then push it through something which floats – such as a cork or a few matchsticks. Next float it in water in a non-metallic container; the magnetized pin will be attracted to north. Remember that the pin will need frequent re-magnetizing.

Regularly check the contents of your survival tin for signs of deterioration. Make sure any medications or tablets do not go beyond their expiration date. Prevent damage from shaking by packing the contents with cotton balls or cotton wool (absorbent cotton), which can also be used for making fire. Coat any metal objects in a thin film of grease to protect them against rust.

If space allows – usually when travelling in a vehicle – it is a good idea to put together a larger

Ration kit

A. Jar of powdered yeast – a good source of vitamin B complex
B. Boiled sweets (candies) – fruit flavour in a resealable tin, with glucose powder
C. Ginger biscuits – ginger in any form helps to ward off seasickness
D. Canned fruit
E. Chocolate bars – these are degradable, so replace regularly
F. Muesli or granola bars – these are degradable, so replace regularly
G. Onions – the most vitamin-rich vegetable, but degradable, so replace regularly

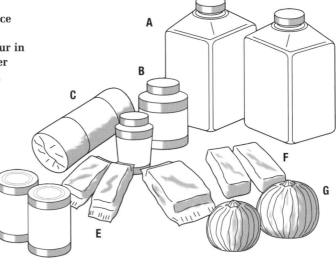

survival kit contained in a large bag. The purpose of a survival bag is to provide more extensive survival resources, especially when travelling with family or friends.

Additional items for the survival bag might include: pliers with wire cutter; folding snow shovel; a large bright signal cloth about 1 x 1m (3 x 3ft); two orange smoke signals; space blankets – metallic blankets designed for optimum heat retention, so pack enough for everyone present; magnifying glass – good for starting fires in sunny conditions; 67m (225ft) of nylon cord; insect repellent; whistle; one pair of work gloves; flashlight with extra batteries and extra bulbs; additional candles; butane lighter; slingshot and ammunition (small ball-bearings are ideal); knife sharpener; water-purification pump; multivitamins; protein tablets; large chocolate bar; dried eggs; dried milk; can opener; plastic cup(s); cutlery set; and soap.

As well as these items, you can duplicate items already contained in the survival tin, but pack them in greater number. As with the survival tin, check the contents of the survival bag for any signs of deterioration.

ADDITIONAL USEFUL ITEMS

Always bear in mind the earlier caution about excess packing, but remember, too, that for major expeditions there are several other items which may increase your comfort and, more importantly,

your chances of survival. A simple whistle will provide an auditory signal, and you should also consider modern communication or signalling tools. Strobe lights and flares can be seen for miles at night, while a VHF radio or satellite telephone provides excellent mayday facilities, as does a tri-band mobile phone. Make sure that the phone's account and technology are configured for your destination before you arrive there. Also remember to take spare battery packs, as you are unlikely to find a recharging point in the wilderness.

A luminous light is a useful pack addition, especially for consulting maps or compasses in the dark. Available from climbing and outdoor pursuits suppliers, they produce light through chemical process rather than battery power, and so provide a permanent light source. On the subject of maps, take with you a good map case with waterproof fittings and a cord so that it can be worn around the neck.

The ultimate navigation aid is a Global Positioning Satellite (GPS) receiver. These triangulate your position using signals sent from military satellites, and will provide you with your coordinates to within a 10m (33ft) accuracy or better. In itself, this will not save your life, but it is an excellent tool if lost. Modern GPS systems allow you to plot hundreds of waypoints as you go through your journey. If you get lost, the receiver can then direct you back through the waypoints to your start position.

Survival tin contents

Typical survival
tin (A) contents
include:
B. matches,
C. candle,
D. flint and
    striker,
E. sewing kit,
F. water purification
    tablets,
G. compass,
H. signalling mirror,
I. safety pins,
J. fishing line,
K. wire saw,
L. plastic bags,
M. snare wire,
N. potassium
    permanganate.

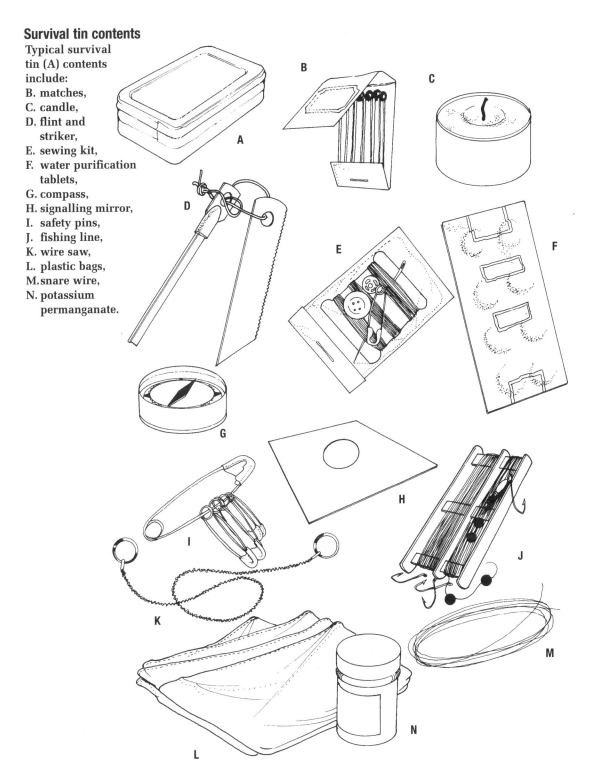

• CHAPTER FOUR

PLANNING AND PREPARATION

Good planning and preparation provide the groundwork for survival. By preparing for every foreseeable emergency, your chances of surviving a real disaster are maximized.

PREPARATION FOR OUTDOOR pursuits is not simply a matter of packing equipment and knowing where you are going. It extends to everything from researching the culture you are visiting to delegating group responsibilities in advance. You must invest the preparation stages of an outdoor adventure with a serious and meticulous attitude. Continually ask yourself the question: 'What if?' What if the vehicle breaks down on an isolated road? What if I injure myself miles from base camp? What if the temperatures at night drop below zero? Think realistically and logically about possible disasters, and try to ensure that your equipment and planning have prepared you to deal with them.

GATHERING INFORMATION
The first stage in preparation is information gathering. Investigate the area you are travelling to as thoroughly as possible. Travel guides, widely available in bookstores, provide convenient literary sources. Inside you will find information about places to go to, what inoculations to have and what cultural customs to observe. You will also find advice about environmental and legal dangers, places to avoid and documentation requirements. Make sure the publication is an up-to-date edition.

As well as guide books, purchase high-quality maps on the region you in which will be travelling. Detailed maps at 1:50,000 are good for revealing significant natural features, small tracks and distinctive landmarks. Be sure the map is recent – you don't want to go through an area of natural beauty to discover it became a military firing range sometime in the past few years.

The Internet is another useful resource for research. The official websites of government foreign departments often contain cultural and political information about world countries, including listings of countries to avoid (the CIA has a very comprehensive website). The Web also features numerous message boards and news groups where individuals post accounts of their travels. You can use their experience to help your own preparation, though try to use only reputable websites, as the information is usually not verified by external authorities.

ENVIRONMENTAL RESEARCH
The first major stage of preparation and planning is environmental research. This means researching the climate, geography, flora and fauna of the country or region you intend to visit. First, the time of year you intend to travel is vitally important, determining weather conditions. For example, the Caribbean and eastern seaboard of the United States are prone to hurricanes and other extreme phenomena between June and November. Regions of Australia suffer from forest fires and the Sahara from sandstorms during their summer months. Tropical areas of Australia are prone to cyclones during the wet season. Insect life can intensify with the seasons, such as malarial mosquitoes in many tropical and subtropical regions during the monsoons, and biting insects in the Scottish Highlands between May and August. Desert travel is best attempted in cooler months, and an Antarctica expedition at any time in the short southern summer. Tropical expeditions should be planned either side of the summertime monsoon.

Seasonal changes don't just affect the weather. In extreme northern or southern latitudes, seasonal daylight variations are dramatic, with long hours of daylight in summer and almost permanent night in winter.

Nearer to the time of your expedition, monitor the weather conditions of your chosen destination carefully. International weather forecasts are readily available over the Internet, and forecasts can even be texted to you directly on some services. If you have a radio, tune into local radio stations for forecasts when you reach your destination (assuming you understand the language). In addition, forecasts for national parks and other popular outdoor recreation areas are often posted each day at information offices.

Special environmental research should be applied to journeys by boat. Be rigorous in fact gathering. Find out about the patterns of the tides, where the nearest safe port is, what the prevailing currents are and what the sea conditions are like. If you are inexperienced in sailing, only go out in sheltered bays or lakes, and only during good weather and no more than a light breeze (a Force 2 to 3 wind). If kayaking, don't go out in winds of more than Force 3 unless you are very strong and competent. Once wind conditions reach Force 6, only an experienced helmsman will be able to handle a small sailing boat, so only pitch yourself against conditions you can really handle.

As well as wind strength, consider wind direction. A strong offshore wind can blow you far out to sea in a light vessel, whereas a strong lee shore wind can drive you into breaking shore waves and rocks. Make sure that you and your vessel can safely negotiate windy conditions.

ACCLIMATIZATION

Acclimatization is important if journeying to extreme climates with which your body is not familiar. In tropical conditions or at high altitude, you should allow around two to four days with only light exercise to let your body adjust to the new demands. This is extremely important if you are attempting a high-altitude adventure; acute mountain sickness (AMS) is a potentially life-threatening condition.

AMS is caused by the way atmospheric pressure decreases with height. The effects of altitude begin to be felt above 2400m (8000ft) and at around 5500m (18,000ft) altitude. Here, air

pressure is about half of what it is at sea level, and this means a dramatically reduced oxygen intake on inhalation. The following AMS symptoms can occur with sudden exposure to high altitudes:

Stage 1 (mild) – shortness of breath, mild headache, nausea, fatigue, slight dizziness

Stage 2 (moderate) – fatigue, severe headache, persistent nausea, vomiting

Stage 3 (severe) – chronic fatigue, severe breathing difficulties, fluid in the lungs, cyanosis, cerebral and pulmonary oedema, staggering, confusion, unconsciousness, even death

The way to avoid AMS is through acclimatization, allowing the body to adjust to the reduced oxygen levels before putting it under the strain of exercise. If taken by helicopter or light aircraft to a high-altitude position (not advisable for the inexperienced, as the transition from low to high altitudes is abrupt), spend two or three days becoming acclimatized and allowing the body to adjust its operation to the reduced air pressure. The best method is to hike to a high mountain

Pre-trip planning
Always read about and research a travel destination thoroughly before setting out. Look into culture, customs and politics as much as flora, fauna and geography, and only use up-to-date sources for information.

DOCUMENTS AND MOVEMENT

Having incorrect documentation can have some very unpleasant legal ramifications in certain countries, particularly those with heightened states of security. The following tips will help you to ensure you have all the documentation you need:

- Always carry a valid passport. Write down the number and issue date (better still, make photocopies) in case it is lost. Also check its expiry date – some countries insist on your passport being valid for at least six months from the date of entry into their land, regardless of your actual length of stay.
- Be aware that certain stamps on your passport might ring alarm bells with passport control in other countries. Arab countries in the Middle East and Africa can refuse entry to Israeli nationals, as well as anyone with an Israeli stamp in their passport. Check with government sources about any possibly travel restrictions before setting off.
- Visa requirements must be clarified before travel – do not assume that you can get a visa at border control. And take with you a large collection of passport photographs for any unexpected documentation you might have to fill in.

area over a period of several days to provide a slow transition. An acclimatization period of two to three days should cure someone with mild AMS, but if moderate AMS develops the casualty should descend by 300–600m (1000–2000ft) and rest until the symptoms disappear. Severe AMS requires an immediate, emergency descent of at least 600–1200m (2000–4000ft), preferably by helicopter or some other high-speed vehicle.

ROUTE PLANNING

Route planning is an essential element of your preparation. Never head off into the wilderness without a clear idea of where you are going, how you are going to get there and how long it will take. Route planning dictates the type of safety equipment, and the correct quantities of food and water to take. Don't overestimate how fit you or your companions are when planning a route – honesty about your capabilities will make for a much more enjoyable and safe activity. Two or

Researching land patterns

Research the direction of major land masses in your destination. Knowing that a mountain range runs, say, from north–south will give you a constant navigational reference in easy view.

three days of consecutive hiking up steep gradients with a full backpack will be far harder than a single day of hiking with light gear. If there are people in your party with questionable fitness, plan a route with easy and regular escape options by crossing close to areas of habitation and public transportation routes.

Base your route planning on a realistic expectation of how fast you can cover ground. For a generally fit person carrying a heavy backpack over rough trails for more than one day, 3km/h (2mph) is a realistic speed. Introduce an upward gradient, and that speed will fall to 2km/h (1.3mph). Bear in mind that the slowest member of the group will dictate your speed.

Based on this estimate, you can then plan your journey from point to point, plotting the route taken on a route card. A route card is simply a written record of your planned route, and should include compass bearings, map coordinates and the times you expect to arrive at each point. Make out a separate card for each day of travel, and leave copies behind with a responsible person and ideally with park rangers or mountain rescue

Route planning
Make sure your route planning phase takes into account all the features which will slow your progress, such as dense woodland, river crossings and hilly/mountainous areas.

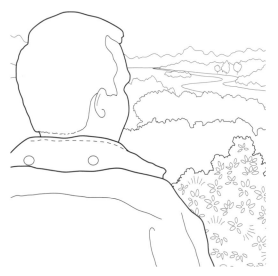

officers. Arrange to phone your main contact as you reach each travel point, and agree in advance when he or she should contact the rescue services if you fail to make contact. Also, compare your progress with the estimated times on your card. Shorten the trip or inform your contact of new times if you fall behind schedule.

As well as planning your main route of travel, plot out one or two alternative routes. Bad weather can force a sudden change of direction, particularly if crossing rivers or mountains. Plot possible routes for escape as well. These should be safe routes of easy going and clear navigation, which take you directly to habitation, public transportation or at least a point from which you can contact the emergency services. Planning escape routes in advance means that you have all the necessary bearings and distances written down ready for use, which helps your decision-making process greatly if you find yourself in the confusion of a survival situation. Make sure that any alternative or escape routes are also conveyed to your contact person.

Whatever country you move in, find out about any restricted-access laws relating to specific zones and territories. Take great care around military installations (especially firing ranges) and border zones between antagonistic countries (such as India and Pakistan). Be wary of using cameras and binoculars around such areas in case you are accused of spying, and never display such instruments around armed personnel.

CULTURAL RESEARCH
Cultural research is as important as environmental research. During foreign travel, showing disrespect towards or ignorance of the customs of the indigenous population can land you in serious trouble, if not outright danger in more lawless regions. Watch that you respect any religious sites or artifacts, and dress appropriately for the culture. This latter point is particularly relevant for women as Western styles of dress can attract severe legal penalties in certain parts of the world, especially in Arab and Muslim cultures. (Very aggressive sexual conduct is also prosecuted in this part of the world.) In the Algerian south, for example, women over the age of 12 who aren't veiled or covered are regarded as little more than prostitutes, and may find themselves in jail or raped. Dress codes also affect men, however. In Malawi, not

Route card

Fill out a route card before every journey into the wilderness and leave it with a responsible person. If the area you will be travelling through is particularly remote, consult with local ranger/mountain rescue officers while planning out your route so that they can highlight pitfalls or overlooked dangers before you set off.

ROUTE PLAN										
Date:		Time:						Starting point reference:		
Weather forecast:										
Members of party:										
Description:										
To (grid reference)	Description (of target)	Direction	Distance	Time (for distance)	Height gain	Time (for height)	Total time	Description (of route and terrain)	Possible alternative route	Escape route
Finishing point reference:					Estimated pick-up time:					
Description:					Estimated phone in time:					

only is it illegal for women to wear trousers or skirts that don't cover their knees, but also men with long hair or wearing shorts without long socks can be barred from entering the country.

Find out as much as you can about social customs and etiquette, and also about criminal or political activity that may affect your travel. Learn a few key phrases in the language, including how to make an apology if you cause offence. Do not, however exciting it may seem, go to countries in the throes of conflict. If you get yourself into trouble in such places, someone may ultimately have to risk his or her life to get you out.

The following are some general guidelines about travel within specific continents and regions. Some of the points apply across the world, but, as always, do your own research before setting off, as political and social circumstances are apt to change.

AFRICA

Africa is a popular destination for adventure tourists. Unfortunately, many African countries are blighted with poverty, crime, civil war and even outright anarchy, which make them unsuitable for travellers. As a general and current rule, avoid the following countries: Algeria, Angola, Burundi, Chad, Liberia, Mozambique, Sierra Leone, Somalia, Sudan, Uganda and Zimbabwe. South Africa is a popular travel destination, but it is best to stay within clear tourist areas. The impoverished townships have one of the highest murder rates in the world (military doctors are often sent for training in Johannesburg hospitals as they will see numbers of violent casualties close to wartime levels). Almost all African cities and towns have high rates of theft and theft-related violence, so be extremely careful where you go in these areas.

There are several other general considerations

for African travel. Hitchhiking is acceptable, though remember that sticking out your thumb is an obscene gesture in many African countries. Carry your money split between many pockets. Not only will this protect you from the pickpockets prevalent in many African towns and cities, but it also enables you to pay 'fees' to government and military officials (objecting to this de facto extortion can make life unpleasant) without producing a bulging wallet or large roll of notes. Note that openly carrying expensive items such as cameras is inadvisable in many African countries owing to endemic problems of violent theft or straightforward confiscation by police and border officials. In Sudan, alcohol is illegal under Islamic law, with penalties for possession ranging from a fine to flogging.

Do not mess with African military forces, particularly in countries such as Botswana, Burkino Faso, Congo and Namibia. The latter, for example, has some very trigger-happy troops around the presidential summer palace in Swakopmund and the Sperrgebeit prohibited diamond area. Any

Banana Plants

Banana plants contain drinkable water. Make a banana well out of the plant stump by cutting out and removing the inner section of the stump. While it is filling, place a leaf from the plant over the bowl to prevent contamination by insects.

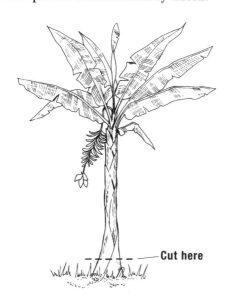

----- **Cut here**

diamond-rich area in Africa is likely to be fiercely guarded and politically sensitive. Any travellers wandering through the Zairian diamond mining towns of Mbujimayi and Tshikapa are likely to be classified and treated as diamond smugglers.

Be compliant at roadblocks and checkpoints, and never go to help locals who are being beaten up by police officers – the officers are likely to shoot or imprison you.

Be friendly with people, but watch who you talk to. In the Congo, the government employs plainclothes police in the towns and cities to monitor political subversion, so be cautious about talking politics. Cameras are a perennial cause of trouble for foreigners. Do not take anyone's picture without asking permission, and if you do don't be surprised if they ask for a small fee. Many African governments place restrictions on what can be photographed, and as a general rule avoid taking pictures of military installations, personnel or vehicles, bridges, radio and television stations, railway stations, post offices, prisons and port facilities. Certain countries require a photography permit, including Angola, Benin, Burkino Faso, Cameroon, Chad, Equatorial Guinea and Somalia, before you can take pictures around the country.

The general cautions concerning photography given here apply throughout much of the world, particularly the Middle East, Central Asia, the Far East and South America.

THE MIDDLE EAST

Visitors to the Middle East should obey the same rules for photography as for Africa, but be even more cautious about taking pictures around military installations because of the Middle East's acute political and military tension. You should also refrain from taking pictures of women. Women travellers have extra considerations to take into account when moving among the predominantly Muslim peoples. Some Islamic laws restrict the movement and opportunities of women, and just because you are a foreigner does not mean you are exempt – check up on any relevant laws before travelling. In Saudi Arabia, for example, women are prohibited from driving and riding public transportation without a husband or male relative. A woman should avoid travelling alone and dress conservatively, with the arms, legs and head covered and no tight garments. (Men should wear full-length trousers

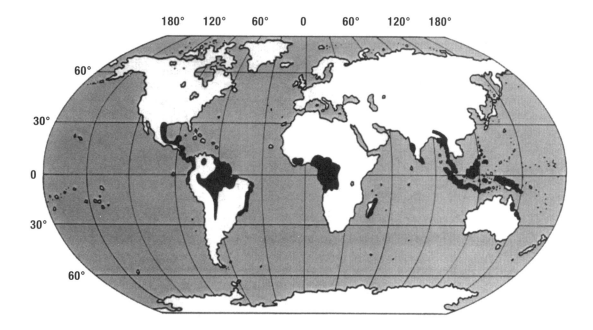

and shirts when visiting mosques, and both sexes should remove their shoes.) However, whether you are male or female, do not imitate Arab dress; it may be interpreted as mockery. Avoid flirtation or even eye contact with unknown men. Do not ride in the front seat of taxis. During the holy month of Ramadan, many Muslims fast from dawn until dusk. Within certain fundamentalist regions, everyone is required to observe the fast when in public, and penalties for breaking it can be severe. Check the dates of Ramadan before travelling and also look up any other local holy days that may affect conduct.

In the Middle East, and in certain parts of Africa, terrorism and conflict can be your biggest dangers. Certain countries such as the Lebanon, the Palestinian territories of Israel, and Iraq suffer from major internal conflicts. A foreign tourist could end up as a target for the armed forces or from any of a number of terrorist groups looking for a hostage or a killing that could generate lots of publicity. Try to avoid countries with a marked cultural hostility to your home country.

Also avoid former battlefields. While fascinating, they are often littered with antipersonnel mines and other unexploded munitions, which rob thousands of people each year of life or limb. If such areas are unavoidable, stick to well-used

Tropical rainforest regions

Many tropical rainforest regions cover areas noted for political unrest, terrorist concentrations and criminal activities. Always take advice from government organizations before travelling to remote parts of South America, Africa, Indonesia and the Pacific Islands.

tracks, and don't wander off into grassy areas either side of the road. Beware of objects you cannot identify. What appears to be a large tin can might be an unexploded bomblet from a cluster mine. Do NOT touch it.

CENTRAL ASIA

Travel in Central Asia involves many of the considerations already discussed, particularly those regarding safety for women in terms of dress and conduct, and also concerning photography (do not, for example, take pictures of tribal women – the men will react badly). As long as conservative conduct and dress are observed, many supposedly hostile countries, such as Iran, will actually be fairly welcoming. The biggest dangers will come from theft and, if in isolated countryside, violent banditry. Try to get a trusted local to define safe routes of travel through the

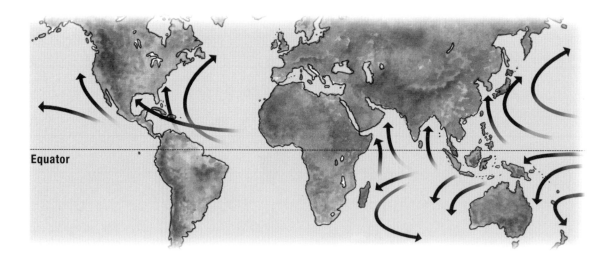

Equator

wilderness, as many bandit gangs operate within defined geographical areas.

Certain Central Asian countries remain no-go areas. Afghanistan may have been freed from the Taliban in 2002, but avoid this war-ravaged country with its numerous violent gangs and general lawlessness. In addition, the countryside is littered with mines left over from past wars.

Terrorist violence and crime pose a real threat to Western visitors in Kyrgyzstan (particularly in the rural areas south and west of Osh), the Afghanistan–Pakistan border, Kashmir and the border areas of Uzbekistan and Tajikistan. Travellers in Kazakhstan are vulnerable to banditry on the country's isolated roads and on its trains – make sure you always travel in groups. Currently, all non-essential travel to Nepal should be avoided – in a country of spiralling civil conflict, hikers are often forced (sometimes at gunpoint) to pay exorbitant 'taxes' to local guerrilla forces.

THE FAR EAST
In the Far East, dress codes can be Western in style, although police and other government officials may take a dislike towards untidy or revealing clothing. Dressing smartly should ease your passage through customs and other official offices. The Far East is well visited by foreign tourists, but the region actually contains some of the world's more dangerous places. There are many no-go areas, especially in Cambodia,

Paths of tropical cyclones
Plan a journey abroad taking into account the times and routes of tropical storms, which usually move in from warm seas. In the northern hemisphere, the hurricane season is from July to October, while in the southern hemisphere they run from November to April.

Myanmar (formerly Burma), North Korea and across China (the Chinese border areas are very sensitive). Cambodia, Laos and Vietnam are also riddled with unexploded military ordnance from five decades of warfare, so do not stray from well-travelled roads. Northwest Laos is also an area for heroin production, and foreign tourists will definitely be unwelcome. Poverty stretches across the Far East, with robbery and violence common in both country and city, so watch valuables and do not make ostentatious displays of wealth.

Be very careful about your luggage being used for drug trafficking. Make sure your backpack has secured zip fastenings and, if you sense there is something in your luggage you didn't pack, notify the authorities without touching the suspect object (you don't want to put your fingerprints on a drug package or disrupt a possible terrorist bomb).

SOUTH AMERICA
South America has some acutely troubled regions, with terrorism, war, extreme poverty, lawlessness

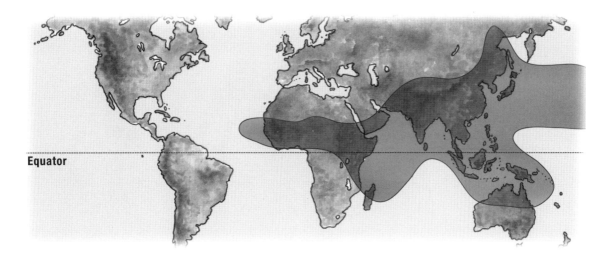

Monsoon areas of the world

Monsoon conditions can turn a trip to paradise into a journey through hell if a traveller is caught unexpectedly. If travelling into wilderness areas, do so outside of the monsoon seasons – check with a travel agent or tourist office for the months and duration of monsoon weather.

and massive narcotics production blighting many spectacular and beautiful places. Do not draw attention to yourself through clothing, jewellery or other valuable items. Do not travel at night, or alone, and always carry your passport and relevant identification papers in case the military or police stops you. Your checkpoint conduct should match that used in Africa – deferential and responsive. Dress codes in South America are generally liberal, but avoid military-style clothing as many people loathe the military because of its role in repressive regimes and coups.

Terrorism remains endemic through Central and Latin America, with terrorist factions concentrating themselves in certain geographical strongholds. Travellers to Peru, for example, should avoid the area from the upper Huallag valley and just south of Cajamarca down to the Abancay area in the south. Marxist guerrilla forces dominate this area. An additional problem is territory controlled by drug warlords. In Bolivia and Colombia, entire regions are ruled by narcotics magnates and any intruders, however innocent, are likely to be

Travelling alone

Unless you know the territory and local people extremely well, never travel alone. Western travellers are clear targets for criminals, the backpack usually advertising valuable contents.

killed or taken hostage. In Bolivia, production is concentrated in the Chapare region: do not wander off the Cochabamba-Santa Cruz highway. Likewise in Colombia, avoid the highway between the Venezuelan border and Riohacha. Learn to recognize what an opium-poppy field looks like, and avoid them. Also stay well away from any factory units posting armed guards around them.

EUROPE

Western Europe is a generally safe place for travellers, with some exceptions. The former Yugoslavia is redeveloping its tourist industry following the bitter civil war, and many locations in Croatia are fine for visiting. However, be careful about venturing into some of the isolated territories in Serbia and Bosnia. These countries are still awash with guns, and resentment against certain foreign nationals can still run high. When in an

Travelling as a group
If travelling with children, modify your route planning accordingly. Small children may have prodigious short-term energy, but can easily succumb to fatigue over several hours of exertion. Set a realistic objective which is based on the capabilities of the weakest, not the strongest, member of the group.

unfamiliar city, ask a police officer if there are any districts you should avoid (get him or her to mark the districts on your map so you don't forget).

Many of the former southern Soviet republics are places to avoid, particularly Chechnya, which is almost destroyed by bloody conflict with Russia. Here travellers, foreign workers and reporters have been kidnapped, tortured and murdered, so stay away. Other countries in this region with deep ethnic troubles and terrorism include Armenia, Azerbaijan and Georgia.

GROUP PREPARATION

Having done all your individual preparation, check that the entire group is equally prepared. Elect a recognized leader, ideally the person with the most wilderness experience and a decisive leadership manner. The leader should not be autocratic, but consult the group and gather opinions when a decision needs to be made. However, his or her decision should be accepted as the final word.

While moving, the leader should take position towards the front of the group, with another experienced member at the rear. Every other person in the group should have an allotted responsibility. Use the fitter and more confident members of the group as scouts if needed. Their job will be to search out viable routes through difficult terrain. Decide in advance who will take charge of the main medical kit and the most important

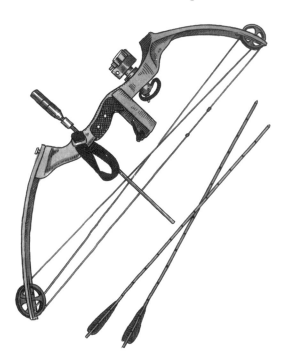

Bow and arrow – commercial model
A bow and arrow can be a suitable hunting weapon to take to a foreign country if transporting firearms is too difficult, although always check with customs officials before packing any weapon.

USING AN EMBASSY

If you find yourself in trouble in a foreign country, make contact with your nearest embassy or consulate. Although the embassies of different nations have different procedures and powers, it is good to have a prior understanding of their capabilities and limits. Embassy staff can:
- Issue passports and other documents, and tell you how to transfer money
- Facilitate medical treatment by liaising with your insurance provider
- Provide advice on local doctors, lawyers and interpreters
- Advise you on local cultural and safety issues
- Inform next of kin if you are in trouble and advise them on procedures
- Visit you if you have been arrested or put in prison
- Arrange rescue attempts if you are in life-threatening danger

However, embassies are usually unable to:
- Get you out of prison, interfere in local court proceedings or give legal advice
- Investigate crimes
- Pay any sort of bill for you, including legal, medical or transportation bills
- Provide you with travel details
- Issue you with in-country work permits or visas
- Find you work

Most crucially, remember you are subject to the laws of the country you are visiting. Employees at your embassy are unable to influence the legal process.

communications equipment, and also define what each person's role will be in an emergency.

If you are travelling in a large group, the military 'buddy system' provides a good social safety net. Each member of the group takes responsibility for one other person, his or her 'buddy'. He or she will then monitor the welfare of their buddy, checking on everything from morale to injuries, and receiving the same in return. Taking responsibility for each other is an essential ingredient of survival in an emergency, so any enmities or hostilities in a group must be eradicated (even if it means leaving people behind) before setting off into the wilderness.

•CHAPTER FIVE

FIT TO SURVIVE

Survival in the wild is one of the most punishing ordeals for the human body. Strengthening and conditioning the body in advance is the best measure to take against injury and fatigue.

BEING FIT AND healthy has several key advantages for someone engaged in a survival situation. First, having flexible and toned muscles decreases the likelihood of muscle, joint and bone injuries, and provides the muscles with greater endurance capabilities. Secondly, a high level of aerobic fitness will ward off fatigue and protect the heart and lungs from potentially fatal over-stressing during exercise. Finally, a fit body is better able to regulate and adapt its temperature control and digestive processes in harsh conditions.

FITNESS AND LIFESTYLE

Developing a programme of fitness training begins with an honest evaluation of your current standard of fitness. Your lifestyle is a good initial guide to how fit you are. If you have a diet high in fatty foods, combined with a sedentary job and you smoke, the chances are that you are unfit for any arduous outdoor activity.

Obesity is a particular problem, not only because it can cause a heart attack, cancer, diabetes and strokes in later life, but also because excess fat around the waist and hips limits mobility and endurance. The heart and lungs of an obese person have to cope with the extra strain of carrying their excess body weight. This, combined with the sudden physical demands of a survival situation, can lead to a sudden coronary attack. An equal but rarer problem is being underweight. Hard endurance activities draw heavily on the body's fat reserves, particularly when they are not being replenished by adequate nutrition. Someone chronically underweight might not have the basic body reserves to cope with a sudden collapse in food intake.

Lifestyle reform is an essential factor in any survival fitness programme. Stop smoking. Smoking dramatically reduces lung efficiency (which you

will really need in a survival situation), as well as carrying some fairly appalling long-term health risks. If necessary, join a local support group to help you quit. Watch your alcohol consumption. Alcohol has a very high calorific content and is an easy route to weight gain. Most importantly, alcohol impairs thought processes – do not attempt to train or embark into the wilderness while still under the influence. After a heavy night's drinking allow at least 24 hours for the alcohol to work its way out of your system.

In terms of general lifestyle changes to improve fitness, try the following:

- Always use the stairs.
- Walk more. Try not to use the car for any journey under a mile. When you do drive, park the car farther away from the entrance so that you have to walk farther.
- Go shopping. A trip around the supermarket can burn many calories. Avoid ordering too many products over the Internet.
- Be more active at home. Do your own gardening chores. Play energetic games with the children. Take them and the dog for long walks.
- Limit the amount of television you watch each day, and if you are watching TV get up and walk around during the commercials.

For survival endurance, however, general changes in fitness are not enough. You must invest in a dedicated training regime to raise your fitness to high-performance levels. This regime has two key goals: 1) to increase the strength and flexibility of all major muscle groups; and 2) to develop aerobic fitness and endurance levels.

MUSCLE DEVELOPMENT

Muscle development is not merely about strengthening, but also about increasing muscle

Lunges

A good work-out of the thighs and upper leg muscles.

- Place the hands behind the neck and move one leg forward, taking a longer stride than usual.
- Bend the leading leg until the thigh is parallel with the ground.
- Repeat the exercise using the other leg.

Push-ups

- Place the palms of your hands flat on the floor, one shoulder-width apart. Keep the legs straight, and pivot on your toes.
- Bend the arms, and lower the body until it just brushes the floor. Now push down, straightening the arms, and raise the body back to the start position. Do not bend the torso.
- Variations: Repeat the exercise with the arms wide apart, and rest the body on the fingertips. Also try lowering the body until it almost touches the ground, and hold for five seconds.

flexibility. While improving strength increases stamina and load-carrying capabilities, both important for outdoor activities, the flexibility training gives muscles an enhanced range of movement and, further, protects them from sprain and strain injuries.

Weight and resistance training are the primary vehicles of muscle strengthening. Gyms and specific equipment are not required, as there is a whole range of well-known exercises ideal for building up the muscle groups. These include push-ups (also called press-ups), chin-ups, parallel dips, crunches and lunges (see illustrations). However, weight training using free weights or weight machines remains probably the best route to scientific muscle conditioning, as each exercise or weight machine is specifically designed to enhance an isolated muscle group.

SAFE TRAINING

There are some general rules to follow for safe and productive weight training. Develop muscle strength slowly, and never attempt to compete with others for lifting the heaviest weight. Instead, train at a particular weight until you can lift, pull or push it with proper technique for 15 consecutive repetitions. Once you can do this, increase the resistance by a small increment and repeat the process. Make sure that you work on every major muscle group. Muscle groups are often set in opposing relationships, and developing one of these 'antagonistic muscles' but not its companion can result in physical damage or an unbalanced musculature. For example, if you do an exercise for your biceps, follow it with one for your triceps; if toning the abdominal muscles, switch to the erectors (lower back) and latissimus dorsi (middle back). All weight training should be done slowly and methodically. Never snatch or jerk the weight – movements likely to tear or strain ligaments and muscles – but instead move it steadily through the full range of the technique. Do your weight training in a reputable gym with expert instructors who can demonstrate safe and productive equipment use.

Weight training, like any sport, can be addictive, so make sure you don't train to excess. Two or three two-hour sessions per week is fine, and gives your body time to recuperate in between (rest periods are actually integral to the muscle strengthening process). Training too much

can result in injured muscles and an unwelcome accumulation of muscle-weakening scar tissue. Mix the weight training with various aerobic sports to provide an all-round level of fitness.

Good posture is a vital for training with weights safely. Always sit or stand with the back straight when performing any weight exercise, as this allows the vertebrae to distribute the strain along the full length of the spine, rather than concentrate it in one spot. If seated at a weight machine, avoid slouching by pushing the buttocks to the back of the seat, looking directly forward and pulling your shoulders back. Keep the feet flat on the floor and drawn slightly back with your toes beneath your kneecaps. If standing, tuck the buttocks slightly forward, but adopt the same back, chin and shoulder posture.

Proper breathing technique should be used throughout weight training to ensure a good supply of oxygen essential to working muscles. Deprive the muscles of oxygen through poor breathing, and the risk of injury increases. There is a specific technique for breathing: draw in the breath through your nose, pulling it deep down into your abdomen, then exhale from the mouth making sure you expel all the air in the lungs. In weight training, breathe out during the 'power phase' – when you apply power to the weight – and breathe in during the 'return phase'. Both phases should take around three seconds. Never hold your breath, as in extreme cases the oxygen deprivation combined with the effort of lifting can result in a stroke or aneurysm. The power phase and return phase should each take about three full seconds to complete.

Be systematic in your programme of weight training. Discover a productive range of exercises for each muscle group, and use them diligently. Divide your training session equally between four zones: upper body (shoulders and chest); arms

MEDICAL CONDITIONS

Before beginning any programme of exercise, consult your doctor if you suffer from any of the following complaints:
- High blood pressure
- Heart disorders
- Respiratory problems
- Blood disorders
- Muscle and bone problems
- Obesity

Crunches

- Lie on your back with your hands behind your head.
- Bring both knees up together, at the same time raising your head to meet them over the torso. Keep your knees raised and stationary for as long as possible.
- Finally, lower head and knees back to the floor.

Twisting crunches

- Lie on the floor with your hands behind your head.
- This time, as you raise your legs and upper body, twist your torso so that your left elbow touches your right knee.
- Repeat, alternating left and right elbows to touch right and left knees. Feel that stretch at your waist.

and back; abdominal muscles; legs. By giving the correct attention to each zone, you won't end up with a structural imbalance in your musculature. Mix heavy weights/low repetitions with light weights/high repetitions to give the muscles strength without making them slow and inflexible.

FLEXIBILITY

Flexibility training is surprisingly important for outdoor pursuits. It maximizes the body's range of movement by progressively lengthening the muscles and ligaments, and reducing the muscles' tendency to tighten and contract when stretched, thus ensuring that muscular movement is more efficient and less prone to fatigue. In addition, a flexible muscle and ligament are more likely to escape injury if a body part is suddenly put through an extreme range of movement, such as when an ankle is twisted. It also benefits the gymnast by reducing the possibilities of sprains and helping sore and stiff muscles to recover from heavy workouts.

Although there are several different types of stretching technique, only two are recommended: resistance stretching and static stretching.

Resistance stretching works by systematically tensing, relaxing and stretching the muscle, and often uses the 'Contract-Relax' (CR) technique. A hamstring stretch using this technique, for example, begins by sitting on the floor with the legs straight out in front of you. Bend from the waist, and slide your hands as far down the legs as they will go, keeping the back straight all the time. Now tense the muscles of the legs, and hold the tension for about five seconds. Release the contraction, relax the muscles and try gently to push the stretch down further. Repeat three or four times until at maximum stretch, breathing deeply throughout the stretch. Improved results from the CR technique can be obtained by working with a partner, who gently pushes or lifts you further into a stretch during the moments of relaxation.

Static stretching is a typical form of solo stretching and follows a set pattern. The limb or muscle group is stretched to the point at which tension is felt. Next, the position is held for up to 10 seconds, and the muscles are relaxed. Then the stretch is extended a little more, using the relaxation of the muscles to go further. Finally,

Seated hamstring stretch
- Sit on the floor, legs straight out in front.
- Bend forward and grasp your ankles, gently pulling forward to stretch the hamstrings.
- Do this exercise to a count of four and perform 10 repetitions.

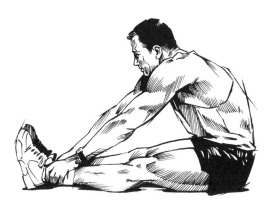

Quadriceps stretch
- Stand with your right hand against a wall for support (or grasp the back of a chair).
- Reach down and grasp your left foot at the instep, and draw the heel towards the buttocks.
- Hold for 30 seconds.
- Slowly let go of your foot, and repeat the exercise with your right leg.

the process is repeated to the limit of the stretch, before the stretch is gently pulled in.

Some specific examples of static stretches and the other stretching types are explained through the captions and illustrations in this chapter. The secret to stretching successfully is patience – it can take a long time to build up decent flexibility, but the effort is worth it. For safe stretching, take advice from your doctor if you have any muscle, joint or bone injuries, and always stop stretching immediately if you feel nauseous, faint or otherwise unwell, or experience pain or burning sensations in the muscles, tendons or ligaments. Always warm up before stretching (see below), and keep breathing deeply through a stretch to supply the muscles with oxygen.

For survival purposes, it is useful to develop flexibility throughout the body. Pay particular attention to the hips, legs and abdomen because the muscles here will be used hard in endurance walking. If climbing is involved in your activity, add many shoulder and neck-stretching exercises.

ENDURANCE TRAINING
Endurance training develops sustained cardiovascular stamina. Physical endurance is absolutely essential for survival situations, not least because you will have to transport a

Inner thigh stretch
- Remain seated and draw your legs towards you so that the soles of your feet touch.
- Place your hands on your knees and gently force your knees down.
- Do this to a count of four, and do 10 repetitions of the exercise.

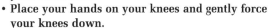

backpack – which could weigh around half your body weight – long distances. Inadequate endurance levels could mean you get left behind by your group, or that you hold them back, both undesirable situations.

Probably the best endurance exercise of all is running. Running conditions both the heart and the lungs for speed and sustained effort. Like stretching, a programme of running training should be developed slowly, increasing distances and speeds week by week. Training for survival,

Seated dumb-bell presses

- Sit at one end of a bench with a dumb-bell in each hand.
- Hold the dumb-bells at shoulder height, with palms facing forward.
- Pushing elbows out at the sides, extend both arms upwards until at full stretch.
- Hold briefly before lowering to the start position.
- Do 10 repetitions with weights of 5–7kg (10–15lb).

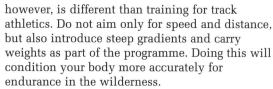

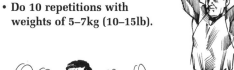

however, is different than training for track athletics. Do not aim only for speed and distance, but also introduce steep gradients and carry weights as part of the programme. Doing this will condition your body more accurately for endurance in the wilderness.

For survival endurance training, combine different forms of running in a systematic programme, aiming to run every other day. You should combine three basic types of run: speed runs, distance runs and endurance runs.

Speed runs are designed to improve short-distance speeds. Start with a short, flat route of about 5km (3 miles) and run it as fast as possible, noting the finish time. Progressively attempt to beat this time or, alternatively, try to run a greater distance within the original time (this has the virtue of not shortening your training period as you become fitter). If you are unaccustomed to running, do speed runs gently at first, but slowly increase the pace. As your body becomes stronger, you can increase the distances, introduce some light belt and then pack weights, and include some gradients.

Distance runs, as the name suggests, are used for building endurance over considerable distances. A distance of 16km (10 miles) is a good target to work towards, but build up to this slowly from around 5km (3 miles) and add 0.6km (1-mile) increments each week. A practical way of planning distance runs is to run for fixed time

Upright rows

- Stand with feet one shoulder-width apart, holding the barbell at arm's length down in front of the body.
- Keeping the bar as close to the body as possible, lift it smoothly upwards to just below the chin, with the elbows out to the sides.
- Do 10 repetitions with weights of 7–9kg (15–20lb).

periods. Start with about 60-minute runs during the first few weeks, and increase the time (and therefore the distance covered) as your fitness improves. If you feel yourself losing energy during the run, revert to a fast walk to allow your body to recover, then move back into a jogging pace when you feel ready. Introduce light weights after time, and vary the route constantly to take in new gradients and challenges. Alter the pace in certain sections, occasionally sprinting for 100m (100yd) stretches.

Endurance runs are designed to mimic emergency survival conditions, and should only be attempted when you are comfortably handling speed runs and distance runs. They key to a good endurance run is terrain. Pick an unpaved route featuring plenty of hills and different surfaces (such as grass, sand or gravel). Do the run wearing a light backpack at first, but increase the weight over time until it approaches the load you will actually carry in the field. Take your time over endurance runs, and switch between running and speedwalking to avoid exhaustion and negotiate

Bench presses

- Lie flat on a bench and grasp the bar with hands slightly wider apart than the width of the shoulders.
- Lift the bar off the rack, and hold it straight overhead with the arms fully locked.
- Now, lower the bar slowly until it just touches the chest.
- Press it back up to the start position.
- Do not arch the back during this exercise. Keep shoulders firmly on the bench.
- It is always wise to train with a partner, then if you do run out of steam, he or she can help replace the bar on the rack.
- Do three sets each of 10 repetitions with weights of 36–54kg (80–120lb).

Deadlifts

- Stand with your feet one shoulder-width apart, then squat down to grasp the bar in front of you. Hold the bar in an overhand grip with one hand and an underhand grip with the other. These two grips will help to maintain balance.
- Keeping your back straight, lift the weight by straightening the legs.
- Shrug your shoulders back, keep your chin up and back arched.
- When lowering, use the legs as much as possible to control the weight.
- Do three sets each of 10 repetitions with 36–45kg (80–100lb) weights.

difficult terrain types. The actual running technique varies according to the type of run, but there are general rules to ensure safety and efficiency. Adopt a natural style when running, swinging the arms and legs smoothly and in a coordinated fashion. Keep the arms and shoulders loose; do not clench your fists as this stops the arms from swinging normally. Make your breathing regular – there should be no erratic gasping – and swing your feet fairly low to the ground to reduce the impact on your ankles, knees and hips.

Here we have focused on running for improving stamina and endurance, but there are many other aerobic activities you can, and should, blend into you training. Circuit training

Leg extensions

For this exercise you will need a bench equipped with a leg extension machine.
- **Sit comfortably on the bench with your feet under the padded bar.**
- **Grip the sides of the bench firmly, and straighten your legs slowly until they are locked.**
- **Lower slowly back to the starting position.**
- **Do three sets of 10 repetitions utilizing 36–45kg (80–100lb) weights.**

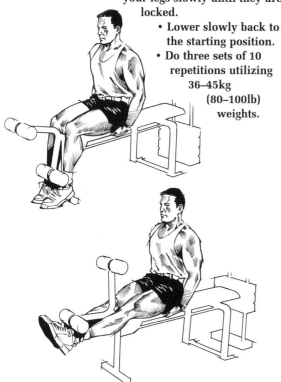

is excellent for developing all-round body fitness as it builds up not only stamina, but also strength and flexibility. Swimming works every major muscle group simultaneously, and is a terrific way to develop endurance. During a swimming session, vary the type of stroke you use. A good combination is the breaststroke, crawl and backstroke. Switch between speed swims of around 100m (100yd) and long-distance swims. If possible, try swimming fully clothed and wearing shoes (but only in a safe, monitored environment). Such practice is invaluable if you ever have to swim for your life.

NUTRITION AND EXERCISE
What we eat has a tremendous impact on our general levels of health and fitness, so any fitness programme should be backed up with appropriate nutritional changes.

Sport nutrition is an extensive subject, but in essence it involves a balanced diet that provides the body with all the essential proteins, carbohydrates, vitamins and minerals.

Seated pull-downs
- **Sit down, and reach up to grip the bar.**
- **Pull the bar down behind the neck, then allow it to rise under control. Keep the back straight.**

Leg stretch

The person stretching places his ankle on his partner's shoulders and relaxes the leg muscles. The partner then slowly raises the leg upwards, increasing the stretch very slowly until the stretcher signals his limits, when the leg is gradually lowered to the ground. Keep the torso upright throughout this stretch.

Cut out or limit the amount of high-fat and sugary foods you consume. This especially applies to deep-fried foods such as fries, fast foods such as hamburgers and donuts (both have very high fat contents), foods heavy in artificial additives, sugary carbonated drinks, and processed foods, which use large amounts of artificial colourings and preservatives. Sugary foods are often eaten for an energy boost, but actually do a poor job as the sugar is quickly burnt off, leaving the eater feeling fatigued. The same is true of drinks containing caffeine, such as tea and coffee.

Replace high-fat, high-sugar foods with fresh produce, cooked in a healthy manner. For maximum energy eat foods high in carbohydrates, including pasta, rice, bread and porridge, and fresh fruit and vegetables. If cooking meat, select lean cuts and use healthy cooking processes. Good options are grilling and stir-frying. (When sir-frying, use a minimum quantity of oil and make sure it is very hot before putting the meat in.) For immediate energy fixes, rely on drinks

WARMING UP

Warming up is the process of preparing your body for exercise and should precede every physical training activity. The warmup routine consists of light exercise and stretching designed to increase the heart rate in preparation for harder physical exertion and warm and loosen the muscles – cold muscles are inflexible and are easily damaged if subjected to sudden high-impact exercise. A typical warmup routine might take the following sequence:

1 Walk briskly for five minutes to raise the heart rate and body temperature.
2 Stand upright with feet shoulder-width apart. Gently twist the head from side to side 10 times (five each side), then rotate it in a full circle without letting the head go too far backward at the top of the circle – stretch up, rather than back.
3 To warm up the shoulder muscles, swing both arms forward in large circles 10 times, then reverse the direction for another 10 revolutions.
4 Still standing with both feet shoulder-width apart, place your hands on your hips, and rotate them as if spinning an imaginary hula-hoop. Do this about five or six times in one direction, then reverse. This exercise will warm up the hips.
5 Stretch out the leg muscles. Stand on one leg, and grip the other leg just below the knee. Stay standing upright, and pull the knee up to the chest as far as it will comfortably go. Repeat for the other leg. Now reach your hand down behind your body and take hold of the ankle of the first leg. Pull the leg backward so that the back of the heel touches the back of your thigh (or as far as you can go). Repeat on the other side.
6 Shake the body loose. You are now ready to exercise. Follow a similar routine when you finish exercising as well, so that the muscles don't tighten as you cool down.

containing natural sugars, such as fruit juices, rather than drinks with sugar or caffeine.

Supplement a good diet with a high intake of water. Water is involved in almost all bodily process and constitutes around 75 per cent of our cellular content. Everything from brain function to skin tone is dramatically affected if we are not properly hydrated. Drink about 2–3 litres (3.5–5.3 pints) of water each day to hydrate the body.

• CHAPTER SIX

FINDING WATER

Finding water is among the highest survival priorities. Without clean, fresh drinking water, survival for more than a few days is unlikely.

ABOUT THREE-QUARTERS of our bodies consists of water, but we are in a constant process of using up this precious fluid. Urine output alone counts for approximately 1.5 litres (0.33 gallons) of water lost per day. Defecation uses 0.2 litres (7 ounces) and sweat/skin diffusion releases 0.5 litres (17 ounces). As a general rule, each person of average build, living in a temperate climate and going about their normal activity, will lose about 2–3 litres (3.5–5.3 pints) of body fluids each day. Even if he lay still on a bed for 24 hours, he would still lose about 1 litre (34 ounces). These figures climb dramatically under conditions of high temperature, illness (particularly vomiting or diarrhoea), injury (especially burns, which use large amounts of fluid in body repair) or physical exertion. In tropical heat, for example, an individual can lose up to 4 litres (1 gallon) of water per day through perspiration alone, and someone working hard in desert conditions during the daytime could require up to 25 litres (6.6 gallons) of drinking water each day.

We offset fluid loss against fluid intake through drinking. The intake should match or exceed output. In survival situations, however, sources of drinkable water may be scarce, and the equation will often mean water loss. Dehydration is the primary threat. Dehydration begins if only 1–5 per cent of body fluid is lost and not replaced, producing symptoms such as thirst, confusion, nausea, fatigue and other troubling conditions.

Serious medical problems accrue as the dehydration increases and affects blood pressure, kidney function, digestion, brain processes and body waste disposal. Losing one-tenth of the total body water content results in severe illness, including headaches, dizziness, shaky limbs, blurred vision and difficulty in breathing. If the proportion of body fluids lost goes beyond

one-tenth, the individual goes into circulatory shock (see Chapter 13) and is likely to die if the fluid equation is not quickly balanced.

WATER SOURCES

The best way to prevent dehydration is to have adequate supplies of drinking water with you. If you have a vehicle, pack at least 3 litres (5.3 pints) for every day of travel; double this amount if travelling in tropical conditions. Store the water in secure containers, with tightly fitted lids to ensure no water is lost through evaporation or spillage. Follow the 'little but often' rule for drinking, but should an emergency survival situation strike immediately ration the remaining water to last as many days as possible with a reasonable drinking supply. Do not break the ration unless there is a significant increase in air temperature or levels of exertion.

If you cannot transport large amounts of water, take with you water-storage containers such as flasks and water bottles for holding the water you collect. Large collapsible water bags are available from good outdoor adventure stores. These hold up to 15–20 litres (4–5 gallons), but when empty they can be folded down small enough to fit into a pack. If supplies of drinking water run out or are not available, then you must find drinkable water in the natural environment. The primary natural water sources are open water (lakes, rivers, streams, snow and ice), falling water (rain, snow and hail), underground water, condensation and water from plants.

READING THE LANDSCAPE

The landscape around you is one of the best guides for hunting for water. Obviously, open water is the ideal source, as long as you obey all the requirements for filtering and purification. In flat, agricultural land, water sources may not be obvious, but look for irrigation ditches between fields, and in gullies or culverts. Don't disregard dew as a source of open water. A field of grass or plants – unless in the most arid regions – is covered with literally gallons of dew in the early morning (remember that many large grazing animals thrive almost exclusively on dew water). Collect dew by simply running a cloth over the grass or plants to soak it, then wringing out the water into a container. You will need to do this at first light, before the daytime sun has time to dry up the landscape.

Following the basic principle that water flows from high ground to low ground, with valley floors among the richest places for finding water. The sea-facing slopes of large hills or mountain ranges are also usually rich in water. Moisture-laden air from the sea rises up the sea-facing slopes, and produces clouds with accompanying precipitation (note that the opposite side of the range can receive surprisingly little rain). The

Professional water storage

Take with you as much stored water as you can viably carry, and back up your water supplies with empty containers to store rain and river water in an emergency. Check all containers regularly for leaks.

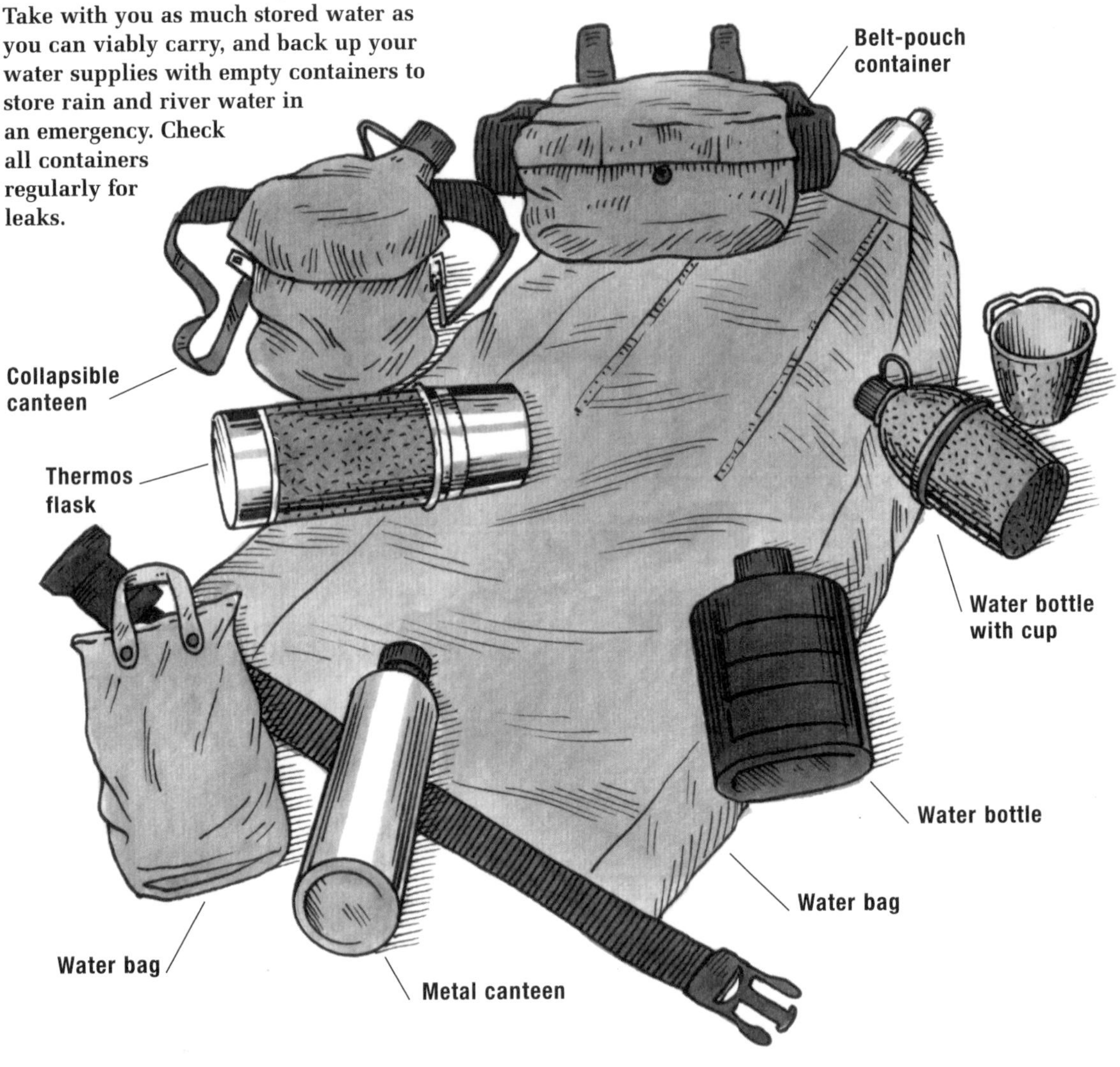

Belt-pouch container

Collapsible canteen

Thermos flask

Water bottle with cup

Water bottle

Water bag

Water bag

Metal canteen

Finding water

A dried-up riverbed will usually still contain deposits of water under the ground. Dig down at the places where water would have last evaporated, usually the river's outer bends, any deep recesses in the riverbed, and in shaded and rocky sections.

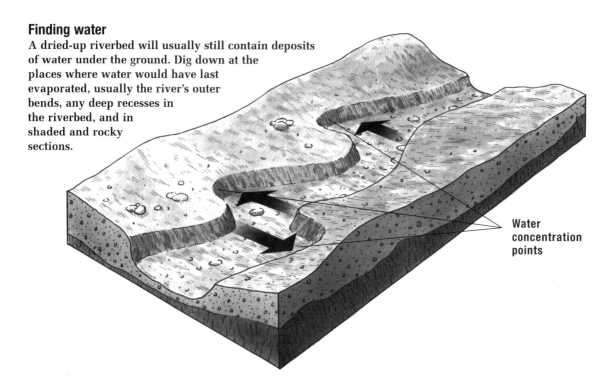

Water concentration points

rain (or meltwater from snow) then begins to flow down the mountain, following any natural channels. Snow-capped mountains are especially good water providers on the warmer south-facing (in the northern hemisphere) side, which produces more meltwater.

Look for cracks in rock faces down which water flows. In particular, watch for cracks that widen from top to bottom (the widening is usually caused by water erosion) and have shingle or mud deposits around their edges. Cracks with bird dung outside may indicate an internal water source that can be reached by a straw. Look also for concave sections of rock where water may collect, often found along ridges. In any rocky terrain, even flat ground at sea level, look for springs and seepage bubbling up through the rock. Limestone and lava rocks often have underground water sources beneath, and can feature substantial springs.

It is true that it takes a lot of effort to gain access to underground water, but it is a vital source in desert, coastal or arid environments. Look for underground water in places where water has been present, but dried up on the

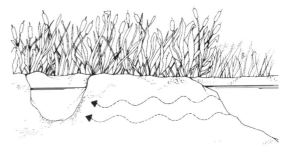

Sediment hole

Digging a hole into damp earth will allow water moisture in the soil to seep into the hole and gradually fill it with water. The water will require filtration to remove soil sediments.

surface – dried-up riverbeds, the bottom of valleys, dry ditches or culverts. In other words, look for any low point between two high points where water has flowed or gathered. Muddy textures to the earth or fresh patches of green vegetation are good indicators of the presence of water beneath the surface. For dried riverbeds, dig beneath the outside edge of a bend – usually the last place from which surface water evaporated or beneath a section heavily shaded by trees. In sandy environments, target the trough between two sand dunes. On a beach, dig above the high-tide mark. The sand filters out the brine, and the hole will steadily fill with fresh water. Regardless of the terrain, dig for water by digging straight down until the earth becomes wet and water seeps into the hole. At first the water will be dirty and full of silt, but will become clearer with time. Collect it, then filter and purify it for drinking.

NATURAL WATER INDICATORS
Plants and animals are useful indicators of water sources. Certain plants predict future rain, and such advance warning is useful for preparing rain-collecting vessels. Because they open their spores in preparation when rain is coming, all plants release stronger scents, usually an earthy, musty or perfumed smell. Pine cones expand with the increased air moisture indicative of approaching rain, and close in dry weather.

As explained above, fresh, green vegetation always denotes water being present, either as an open water source or underground. If no open water is nearby, and plants only extend to around 1.5–1.8m (5–6ft) in height (any higher, and the water table is likely to be too deep), you may be able to tap into underground water directly

Open water
Never drink water straight from an untreated source. Always filter and purify the water; simply putting water through a rolling boil for 10 minutes will make it safe to drink.

Signs of a poisonous water supply
Signs such as the profusion of cattails and rushes and the lack of water flow indicate that stagnant water such as this may be unsuitable to drink.

around the root system. Dig straight down to the roots, following the root system where it goes (as long as this does not expend too much valuable energy) and collecting water where you find it.

Most animals, like humans, are utterly dependent on water for their survival. Their senses are better attuned to finding natural water than ours, so observing them can lead you to water. Grazing animals usually head for watering holes around dawn and dusk; if you can't see the animals themselves, look for large numbers of tracks gathering at a single point. (Don't follow carnivorous animals, as they derive much of their essential fluid from prey, rather than open water.)

Wild animals may also indicate the approach of rain through their sensitivity to changes in barometric pressure. When poor weather is on its way, herding animals usually move to lower ground and gather there, but bear in mind that they can start this procedure up to two days before the rain arrives.

Insects are fairly secure water indicators. Flies and mosquitoes, for example, tend to keep water sources within 100m (328ft) distance – the density of such creatures often increases the closer you get to water. Ants march to water sources in column, often ascending a tree to visit a water reservoir in the trunk.

WATER FROM THE AIR

The air offers two water sources – rain (snow precipitation is covered in Chapter 18) and condensation. As soon as rain begins, put out as many open receptacles as possible. You can direct water into these by making gutters out of waterproof fabric, large leaves or pieces of bark. If weather, plant or animal indicators give good advance warning of rain, dig a deep hollow into the ground, and line the hollow with a single piece of waterproof material, such as a camping groundsheet, securely weighted with stones around the edges. You can also make a natural waterproof lining by smearing wet clay over the surface of the hole and allowing it to dry. Dig the hole right down to clay or bedrock, to add further resistance to water drainage.

Large amounts of water gathered during a rainstorm can be wasted if not subsequently stored

properly. We have already mentioned professional storage containers, and the water-collecting pit just described can be used to store water if properly handled. Keep stored water covered over at all times and in the dark if possible, as direct sunlight encourages the growth of green algae. (You can test this by leaving a glass of drinking water on an exposed windowsill for a few days.) Although rainwater is pure when first caught, and can be drunk immediately, filter and purify rainwater which has been stored for more than two days (less if the water has obviously been contaminated) to remove foreign bodies, parasites and germs.

In extreme emergencies, small but valuable amounts of water can be obtained by extracting condensation from the air, plants or soil through a process called 'transpiration'. The two pieces of survival apparatus you should learn to construct are a solar still and a transpiration bag.

To make a solar still, first take a sheet of (preferably clear) plastic, ideally 1m (3ft) long on each side, but use whatever is available. Dig a hole in the ground of a diameter several inches less than the diameter of your sheet, and place a container in the bottom as a water catcher. Spread the plastic over the hole, and weight down the perimeter

Solar still

The secret to making a good solar still is to seal the perimeter of the plastic sheet tightly to the ground so that no captured water vapour is allowed to evaporate to the outside world.

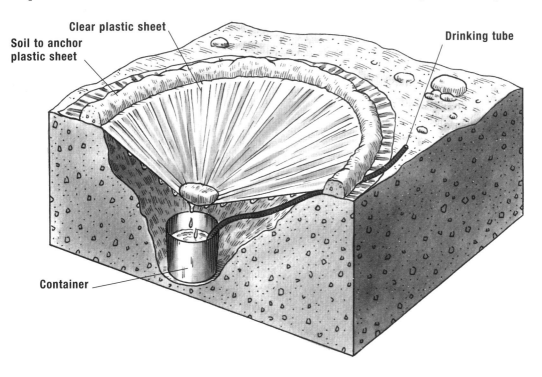

Clear plastic sheet

Soil to anchor plastic sheet

Drinking tube

Container

with plenty of heavy rocks and stones, leaving no gaps. Weight the middle of the sheet with a stone, so the sheet dips down directly over the container.

Now leave the solar still for 24 hours. The soil is heated by sunlight and releases its water vapour. During the day sunlight will heat up the soil, and the soil will release water vapour into the hole. The vapour condenses on the cooler underside of the plastic, and the condensation runs down the plastic into the container. It also works at night when the sheet is cooled, but the trapped air in the hole remains warm. Insert a tube, if available, underneath the plastic into the container so that you can drink without having to

Water soak

Wrap a cloth around a tree, one end hanging above a container. Rainwater running down the tree will soak into the cloth, then flow through the material before dripping into the container. Rainwater is usually drinkable without purifying when caught by this method.

Rain collection

As soon as rain approaches, make rain collection systems. These should be as large as possible to maximize the amount of water collected. A waterproof tent groundsheet is ideal, with rocks improvising a gutter effect in the surface of the sheet.

Rain trap

Large leaves make excellent gutters for diverting rain flow into containers, although use only edible plant types to ensure that no plant poisons enter the water and contaminate it.

Water reservoir

A pit lined with a groundsheet or clay will make a large water reservoir. Don't allow any of the water collected in the reservoir to go stagnant; it may be necessary to empty the reservoir periodically, by digging a draining channel.

dismantle the still. However, make sure the plastic is sealed tight around the tube, or the water inside the still will evaporate into the outside air.

A variation on the solar still principle is the transpiration bag. Tie a plastic bag (avoid bags with moulding holes in their surfaces) over a green patch of foliage – dead foliage will not water. The condensation produced by the plant during photosynthesis condenses against the inside of the bag, then runs down to the lowest corner.

MAKING WATER SAFE

All water collected from nature must be filtered and purified before drinking. Even the purest-looking waters will usually contain organic materials, aquatic parasites or, at worst, waterborne diseases (the exception is rainwater if it falls directly into a container without running across surfaces first). Drinking contaminated water will

result in illness, often accompanied by vomiting or diarrhoea, which accelerate dehydration.

There are some types of water you should avoid drinking altogether. Steer clear of pools of water with strong smells, powder or foam deposits on the surface or edges (both of which can indicate chemical pollutants), and gaseous bubbles or green slime on the surface. If you suspect pollutants, boil a small amount of water until it entirely evaporates, and see if any suspicious residues remain. Observe the surrounding plant and animal life; dead plants or animals are obviously a bad sign. Be careful of taking water from isolated pools which have no water inlets or outlets; these usually stagnate and breed germs and bacteria (in deserts they are probably salt lakes). Stagnant water tends to attract certain foliage, particularly cattails and rushes. If a river or stream is crowded with algae and choking amounts of weeds, agricultural chemicals are the probable pollutants.

If you have collected water from a safe location, filter it first to remove particles of organic or mineral matter. Pour the water several times through a close-woven piece of fabric – such as cotton – into a container. This removes most of the larger particles of dirt and vegetation, and renders the water clear enough for purification. Even better, large filtering bags are commercially available, and these strain out even fine particles and some bacterial elements.

The most rudimentary but still effective method of purification is boiling. Boiling water

WATER FROM PLANTS

Some plants not only indicate water nearby or underground, but also they can store water within themselves. Check the following for water, but ensure that the plant type is not poisonous before treating and ingesting the fluids:

- Upturned, cup-shaped flowers (which are particularly common in the tropics) can act as water reservoirs.
- Examine holes in a tree for water, and also look in the tree's fork for gathered rainwater.
- As long as a plant isn't poisonous, rainwater can be licked directly off leaves, or at least directed down the leaf into a container.

Transpiration bags

When using transpiration bags, try to keep the vegetation from pressing against the sides of the plastic so that the wood and leaves do not reabsorb the water as it runs down the plastic.

for a minimum of 10 minutes will kill off bacteria and all germs, although it will not negate chemical risks. Beyond boiling, however, there are several professional options for purification, if you have the kit with you. There are three main chemical additives for water purification: iodine, potassium permanganate and chlorine. Iodine and potassium permanganate come as liquid and granules, respectively. When added to water (follow instructions closely), these chemicals turn the water slightly pink and give it a chemical taste, but render it safe to drink. Chlorine tends to come in tablet form, and usually one tablet is added to 0.5 litres (17 ounces) of water to make it safe to drink. Again there is a distinct chemical aftertaste. Adding charcoal to the purified water removes some of the chemical taste. However, you must do this only once the purifying chemical has stopped working.

Purification pumps are a convenient method of providing instant pure water. These are machines containing a cylinder full of purifying chemicals (usually iodine). Water is pumped through the cylinder, purified in its passage, then pumped out of an outlet tube into a waiting container. Purification pumps are available from good outdoor activity suppliers.

REDUCING WATER LOSS
As well as finding sources of water, the survivor should also be aware of techniques to conserve as

Saltwater still

Saltwater can be converted to drinking water by boiling it with a cloth over the top. The freshwater steam will soak the cloth, which can then be wrung out into a container. The cloth will be red hot, so care is needed to avoid burns.

Water filter

Ideally water filters should consist of multiple layers of filtering material to remove the full range of particles suspended in the water. The coarsest filters are rocks, the finest sand and man-made fabrics, with grass an intermediary.

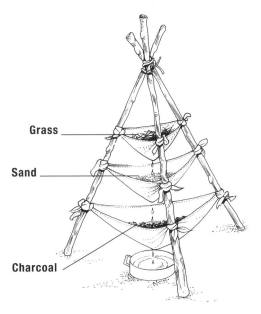

Grass

Sand

Charcoal

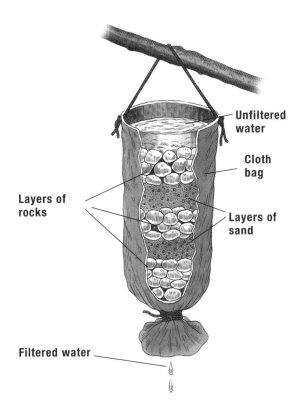

Unfiltered water

Cloth bag

Layers of rocks

Layers of sand

Filtered water

much water as possible within the body. The loss of water cannot be stopped, but modifying patterns of movement, food intake and routine can reduce the rate of water depletion.

A large amount of water output occurs simply through breathing, as the lungs saturate air with water vapour before expelling it into the outside air (it is this vapour we see when our breath billows out on a cold day). Breathe through your nose, not your mouth, as much as possible to prevent the evaporation of saliva from the mouth. For this reason, do not talk much, restricting conversation only to essential survival issues.

Increased breathing rate through exercise, cold temperatures and high altitudes also raises the levels of fluid loss through breathing. To conserve

fluids, don't overexert yourself or perform any unessential tasks, and rest frequently. Make all movements slow and energy-efficient. Walk or run with the feet moving in a low, sliding action and the arms loose by your sides. Restrict most of your heavy duties to the cooler early mornings or late afternoons, or at night if you have the visibility.

In hot climates, water conservation measures are even more crucial to your survival. Keep out of direct sunlight, stay in the shade and avoid lying on hot ground or other surfaces (put some insulating material, such as foliage, between you and the ground). Wear pale clothing to reflect the sun's rays, and try to keep as cool as possible. But don't remove sweaty clothing, as the sweat in the fabric will act to cool the air trapped between the clothing and the skin, reducing the activity of your body's sweat glands.

In all climates, you need to watch patterns of food consumption, as the digestion process is heavy on water consumption. If you have a daily ration of water of only about 0.5 litres (17 ounces) of water, then avoid food altogether. If water is scarce, you should avoid eating fatty foods. Fat is indissoluble in water, so a lot of body fluid is used to break fats down. Also avoid high-protein foods. Tea, coffee and alcohol also need to be avoided as they increase urination. Smoking also increases water loss during respiration.

• CHAPTER SEVEN

PLANT FOOD AND SURVIVAL NUTRITION

Plants are the first choice for survival foods. While hunting animals takes energy and skill, gathering plants requires only the ability to identify edible varieties.

SURVIVAL NUTRITION IS a matter of supplying the body with all the food elements essential for health, and maintaining a calorie intake equal to activity levels. The essential elements of any diet are proteins, carbohydrates, fats, vitamins and minerals. Proteins are essential for the growth and repair of body tissue and muscular strength; high concentrations of protein are found in meat (including fish), milk, cheese and cereal grains. Carbohydrates, found in fruit, vegetables, chocolate, milk, rice, pasta and cereals, are the human body's main energy source and should form around half of daily food intake in a survival situation. Fats are a further energy source. The body draws more heavily on fats as an energy source once the body has depleted its reserves of carbohydrates. Fats are found in cheese, butter, and margarine, oils and animal fats, nuts and eggs.

Vitamins and minerals regulate a long list of body functions from skin condition to oral health. The list of vitamins and minerals, and their functions, is extensive, but if a diet is balanced – i.e. a mixed selection of meats (if you are a meat eater), vegetables, fruits, nuts, rice and pasta – then all the essentials should be supplied. In a survival situation, however, food becomes scarce and the diet often unbalanced as one more accessible food source is eaten at the expense of finding others. The result is illness and fatigue, adding to the already severe burdens of body and mind. You therefore need to construct a survival diet from as many different food sources as possible. For example, a couple of small fish, a boiled rootstock and some boiled leaves, plus

a handful of nuts and berries, should give you all the daily nutritional needs.

A final important consideration for a survivor is calorie intake. Calories are a measurement of the energy value of food, and in normal domestic routine a man tends to need around 3000 calories a day and a woman up to 2000 calories. In a survival situation, particularly one which demands high levels of energy, the intake for both sexes should be around 4000–6000 calories, the required calorie intake increasing with cold temperature. As a guide, 100g (3¾ oz) of butter provides 770 calories, and the same weights of beef, salmon, bananas and brazil nuts provide 300, 200, 77 and 644 calories, respectively. In a true survival emergency, the need for a high calorie intake and a balanced diet means that a large percentage of each day will be spent gathering and preparing food.

PLANT FOOD – EDIBILITY AND SAFETY
Not all plants are safe to eat. Some will induce illness, while a select group of other plants will kill within hours if ingested. Plant identification, therefore, is crucial. Before travelling to a particular location, do thorough research on edible and poisonous plant types in the region. Study high-quality botanical books with clear photographs or illustrations, and visit botanical gardens for a real-life view of the plants. Don't learn about too many plants at first, just a basic selection of around 10 edible plants common to your destination, but learn everything about them (such as habitat, scent, seasonal changes and so on) so you can identify them with confidence.

Soon we will look at some specific edible plant types commonly found in temperate regions (edible plants in other climates are dealt with in Chapters 18–22), but there are some general edibility rules that are useful when plants cannot be identified. Note that these are guidelines only; the Universal Edibility Test (see feature box) should be used as a final arbiter of a plant's edibility.

UNIVERSAL EDIBILITY TEST

Use this test for establishing whether a plant is safe to eat if you cannot positively identify it. Reject the plant if an adverse body reaction is experienced at any point during the test. Note that the test cannot be applied to fungi.

• Avoid eating, if possible, for eight hours before the test to guarantee the accuracy of the results, and during the test drink only water and eat only the plant sample. (However, if immediate starvation is a threat to health, then you may have to ignore these guidelines.)

• Divide the plant into its basic constituents – leaves, stems, roots and so on – and test only one part of the plant at a time.

• Smell the plant for strong, acid or almond-like scent, and crush some of the plant to release potentially hidden smells. If you detect unpleasant smells, reject the plant.

• Place a sample of the plant on the inside of your elbow or wrist. Wait 15 minutes to see whether there is any adverse reaction such as blistering or irritation.

• If there is no skin reaction, place a small piece of the plant on the outer surface of the lip to test for burning or itching. Leave for three minutes.

• Put the piece of plant onto your tongue; hold it there for 15 minutes without chewing.

• Now chew the piece of plant, but do not swallow. Hold the chewed plant in your mouth for another 15 minutes.

• Swallow the food and wait for eight hours. Should you start to feel ill, induce vomiting, and drink plenty of water. If there is no adverse reaction, eat a handful of the plant and wait another eight hours. If there is no sign of illness, the plant is safe to eat when prepared in the same manner as used during the test.

Plants to avoid eating
• Any type of bulb
• White and yellow berries. About half of red berries are safe, so eat only if you can make a positive identification
• Red plants
• Overripe fruit
• Fruit marred by mildew or fungus
• Any plant with an almond-like scent, indicating a cyanide compound (crush up some of the leaves to release the smell)
• Plants with a white, milky sap, unless you know the plant is safe (such as dandelion)
• Five-segmented fruits
• Plants with three-leaved structures
• Uncooked legumes (beans and peas) – these absorb minerals from the soil and cause digestive problems
• Plants with tiny barbed hairs on the stem and leaves; these can be laced with irritant chemicals
• Any plant which irritates the skin on contact
• Any dead or diseased plant
• Plants with umbrella-shaped flowers, although carrots, celery, and parsley (all edible) are members of this family.
• Grain heads with pink, purplish or black spurs

Also note: do not think that a plant is safe to eat because an animal is seen eating it. Many animals have digestive systems resistant to toxins that would make humans severely ill.

Positive signs of edibility
• Blue and black berries are usually safe to eat (there are exemptions, such as the highly poisonous black berries of deadly nightshade)
• Single pieces of fruit hanging on a stem, or aggregated fruits

Note that the number of negatives far outweighs the number of positives in these lists. The identities of edible plants really need to be memorized individually. Also, pay attention to the environment of a plant, which in certain cases can turn a normally edible plant into a poisonous plant. Proximate inedible plants may contaminate edible plants, and plants in or surrounding agricultural fields may be covered in harmful pesticides. Never eat plants growing around obviously polluted water, and be sure to clean plants thoroughly of any dirt before consumption.

EDIBLE PLANT TYPES

The following are common edible plants, many of which are found throughout the world, but there are literally hundreds more. The emphasis here is on plants found mainly in temperate zones, while subsequent chapters in the book will deal with plant foods found in tropical, arctic and desert environments.

Almond

Common to warmer temperate and arid areas, the almond tree provides a good source of nutritious edible nuts, each nut being covered by a thick, brown, dry skin.

Beech

Beech trees are found in most temperate zones, and feature a light grey bark and dark-green oval leaves. The husks contain a group of 2–4 edible nuts that can be eaten or crushed down for oil.

Bistorts

Found in grassy areas and woodland, bistorts grow up to 60cm (24in) tall and feature pink or white flowers. The roots are edible after soaking and cooking.

Blackberry and raspberry

Well-known accessible fruits found throughout temperate regions in woody areas or waste ground. Fruit can be eaten raw, and leaves boiled to make tea.

Bracken

Only the young shoots (never mature bracken) and the roots of this almost universal plant are edible. Boil the shoots for 30 minutes, but eat only small amounts, and boil or roast the roots before eating.

Cat's tail

Cat's tail grows around fresh water and can reach 5m (15ft) high. Its defining feature is a sausage-shaped flower head. The rootstock and stem are edible raw, while the leaves and young shoots are edible after boiling.

Chicory

Chicory has edible leaves and roots (the roots must be boiled first). It is found throughout much of the world, and it has leaves similar to a dandelion's and light blue flowers.

Crab apple

Crab apple trees grow 1–12m (3–40ft) high, with white and pink blossoms. Their small apples can be eaten raw or boiled, and can be sliced and dried. Eating too many crab apples may result in diarrhoea.

Dandelion

Dandelions are completely edible, nutritious and extremely common. Jagged leaves and distinctive yellow flowers identify it. Boil or roast the roots, or eat the young leaves raw (older leaves require boiling).

Good King Henry

Common to grassy and waste areas and growing up to 60 cm (24 in) tall, Good King Henry features triangular leaves and slim clusters of green flowers. Both the leaves and shoots are edible, raw or boiled.

Hawthorn

The red fruit of the autumnal (fall) hawthorn is edible raw, providing a useful source of nutrition at a time of year when the variety of plant food types is often in decline.

Juniper

Juniper is found in many places outside of South America. It has evergreen leaves resembling needles and small berries, which can be eaten raw when ripe, although cooking improves taste. The seeds can be roasted as substitute coffee grains.

Nettle

Nettles are nutritious plants found almost everywhere in the world. Boil the plant for around 15 minutes to cook and kill the plant's stinging parts. Nettle tea makes a healthy drink.

Oak

The oak tree's acorns are edible, but should be shelled first and boiled in several changes of water, then roasted before being eaten. Alternatively, soak the acorns for several days in water before cooking.

Pine

Throughout much of Europe, North and South America, North Africa, the Middle East and in parts of Asia, pine trees are a familiar sight. The cones produce pine nuts (release them by heating the cone), to be eaten raw or roasted. Boil pine needles to make a tea.

Reed

Reeds grow around fresh water throughout the temperate world. The roots are edible when boiled; the grass itself is edible raw or cooked.

Sweet chestnut

(Important: this plant must be distinguished from horse chestnut, which has poisonous nuts.) Sweet chestnuts grow up to 30m (90ft) and produce nuts contained in thick, green, spiky husks. Crack the husks open to obtain the nuts, then peel and boil them.

Walnut

A good handful of walnuts provides over 600 calories. The walnut tree grows up to 30m (90ft) and encloses its brown nuts in a green husk. Break the husks open and eat the walnuts raw or roasted.

White mustard

The white mustard plant grows to 60cm (24in) with crinkled leaves and yellow flowers, and is found throughout Europe and Asia. You can eat the young leaves and flowers raw, but boil all other parts of the plant.

Curled dock and wild sorrel

These are common plants with narrow leaves and small green or reddish clusters of flowers. Boil the young leaves.

Wild parsnip

Wild parsnip grows around 1m (3ft) tall in grassy areas, with a strong scent and clusters of small, yellow flowers set at the end of stalks. Eat the roots either raw or boiled.

Wild rose

Found throughout the northern hemisphere, the wild rose is an excellent source of vitamin C. It is a prickly shrub with red, pink or yellow flowers. Avoid eating the seeds, but eat the rose hips raw or boiled.

POISONOUS PLANT TYPES

Poisonous plants are found in abundance in nature, and some are very powerful indeed. A single mouthful of water hemlock, for example, is capable of killing a grown adult within hours. Unfortunately, several poisonous plants are easily confused with common edible types – death camas resembles wild onions, and comfrey can be confused with the poisonous foxglove. The following is a list of some of the most common types of poisonous plant. Rather than work with a brief description here, spend time with a reputable botanical reference work, and learn to identify these plants with total confidence – your life could depend on it.

FUNGI

The overriding rule for eating fungi is not to eat anything you can't identify positively. Fungi are high in vitamins, minerals and proteins, and even contain fats, and so are a first-rate survival food. However, there are numerous inedible varieties, some with positively lethal poisonous content (death cap is fatal in 9 out of 10 cases of ingestion, killing through inducing liver failure).

Common poisonous plants

Water hemlock (A), hemlock, poison ivy, baneberry (B), poison sumacs, death camas (C), foxgloves (D), monkshood (E), deadly nightshade (F), buttercups (G), lupins (H), vetches or locoweeds, larkspur (I), oleander

The poisons in fungi are not killed by cooking, nor can the Universal Edibility Test be used with fungi (the dangers are too great, and some fungi poisons operate over long time periods).

As a backup only to a detailed knowledge of fungi species, there are some general principles to guide you as to which fungi are safe to eat. Don't eat fungi that have white gills. Avoid fungi with a volva (a cuplike structure around the base of the stem) or rings around the stem, and don't eat old or decomposing fungi.

Edible fungi are prepared in a variety of ways. They can be simply eaten raw, or boiled in soups or stews (soak tough fungi in water to soften for cooking). Fungi are a long-term storage food when air-dried. Place the separated caps and stems on a rock in the sun until they are dehydrated, then store them in an airtight container. Soak them in water to rehydrate them before eating.

EDIBLE FUNGI

The following are common types of edible fungi. Note that there are two basic categories: ground fungi, which grow from the earth, and bracket fungi, which grow out of trees.

Beefsteak fungus

A bracket fungus with a red and pink coloration and rough texture, these are not pleasant-tasting, but are edible.

Brain fungus

A bracket fungus resembling a brain or coral.

Chanterelle

A summertime ground fungus which is found in forests. Features an irregularly shaped orange or yellow cap.

Field mushroom

The common field mushroom is a summer fungus and, as its name suggests, it can be found growing in open, grassy fields. All parts of a field mushroom can be eaten after cleaning.

Giant puffball

Appears like a white football 30cm (1ft) wide in grassland and woodland from late summer through to autumn (fall). An edible puffball is white throughout; reject if there is any discoloration.

Oyster mushroom

Grows on rotting tree trunks from midsummer to late autumn (fall). Olive-coloured cap when young, fading with age.

Sulphur mushroom

Clings to decaying trees and stumps, making brown irregular shapes (in appearance it looks like wood rot), with orange and yellow growths. Eat this mushroom when young, mainly during the midsummer months.

POISONOUS FUNGI

Even more so than other types of plant, spend time familiarizing yourself with poisonous fungi types. Rely on the descriptions here as a guide to beginning your research, not as the sole method of identification.

Amanita family

These lethal fungi can kill within two or three days of ingestion. Look for a bright yellow or orange-yellow scaly cap, with a yellow flesh and white or pale yellow gills. The stem features a volva and is white and scaly. Amanita fungi generally inhabit woodland and roadsides from early summer until late autumn (fall).

Death cap

Death cap attacks the liver, with deadly consequences. It inhabits woodland in summer to autumn (fall) months. Its cap is a distinctive greenish-olive colour, and it has a pale stem, white gills and flesh, and a prominent volva.

Destroying angel

Inhabits similar locations to the death cap and has similar poisonous power. It is white all over with a scaly stem and large volva, and a sickly sweet scent.

Jack-o-lantern

A deadly fungus with saffron-yellow gill which attaches to the base of decayed tree stumps.

Fly agaric

Fly agaric is bright vermilion to orange, usually flecked with white scales. Habitat is autumnal pine and birch woods.

Panther cap

This lethal fungus likes woodland, especially woodland with a concentration of beech trees. It is brown with white flecks on the cap, and white gills and rings around the base of the stem.

TREE BARK

The inner bark of several tree species is edible, and can be eaten throughout the year, although during the summer months the nutritious sap is in higher concentrations. To get at the inner bark, first peel off a section of outer bark near the tree's bottom, and cut out the exposed inner bark. The sap or tree resin sweetens the bark, providing a good energy source, and the syrup from birch and maple trees is particularly delicious. Inner bark can be eaten raw, but boil it for easier eating and digestion. Trees with edible inner bark include maple, willow, aspen, poplar, pine, birch, slippery elm and hemlock. Note: do not eat any part of the following trees: cedar, horse chestnut, yew, laburnum, moosewood, hickory, black locust, and California laurel.

Digging up roots

Roots are often excellent sources of nutrition. To dig them up without a spade, sharpen the end of a stick into a flat 'screwdriver' shape. Use this to dig down the side of the plant, widening a hole in the earth and levering up the root.

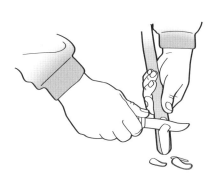

Leaden entoloma

A whitish fungus, with yellow–pink gills and a convex cap, it also has pungent smell of radish or almonds. Found mainly in beech and oak woods in the summer and autumn (fall).

EATING AND COOKING PLANTS

Even if cooking a plant, first wash it thoroughly and remove all bits of dirt and debris. Cut out any decayed parts. Boiling is the best way of cooking most plant parts. Boiling the plant matter for around 10 minutes softens the plants, and so makes them easier to digest, can remove bitter tastes (for some plants you may have to change the water several times to remove the taste) and

also destroys most harmful bacteria. Don't, however, boil for too long, as this will kill the vitamins in the plant. Generally try to cook the plant so that there is still some firmness in its flesh. For more delicate plant structures such as thin leaves, steaming is a gentler alternative to boiling. Remember, also, that the water in which you boil plants is often nutritious – drink it, do not throw it away.

When eating roots, always cook them first. Leave the skin on (unless it is very dirty), as this will contain many of the plant's nutrients. Roots can be boiled, roasted or fried. Try parboiling the root, then roasting it on hot stones until soft for a particularly tasty meal.

Pine needle tea

Pine needle tea is a nutritious survival drink. Crush up the needles to release their flavour (A), then steep in hot water for 10 minutes (B). Strain the tea through a cloth to remove the needles (C), and drink. Use two teaspoons of needles for each cup of drink.

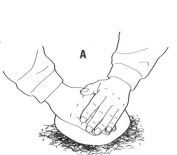

A

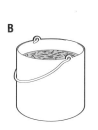

B

C

CHAPTER EIGHT

HUNTING, TRAPPING AND FISHING

In more than two-thirds of the world's natural habitats, the survivor will have to eat animals if he or she is to continue to live.

MEAT IS UNDOUBTEDLY an excellent survival food. It provides protein and fats for energy and tissue repair, and contains essential vitamins and minerals. The disadvantage of meat is that is involves catching and killing animals, both a difficult and unpleasant task for those not accustomed to it. If you have any ethical qualms about hunting, trapping and fishing, bear in mind that in a survival situation you have to live by nature's rules, not necessarily your own.

It generally takes a lot of energy to acquire animal foods, which involves hunting, fishing or constructing traps. One important rule is never to expend more energy getting the food than you receive from eating it. If your energy reserves are low, opt for fishing and trapping rather than cross-country hunting, as these demand less physical exertion. Also, put any animal you kill to full use. Mammals provide bones, skin and fur, which can be turned into various survival resources such as clothing or tools. Take special care over skin and fur. Wash and clean these – they may require boiling if infested with parasites – then dry near a fire or in the air, and use them for making clothing and shelters.

MAKING BASIC WEAPONS

If you have no commercially produced weapons available, you will have to resort to making your own to use for hunting and for killing injured or trapped animals.

Club

A solid wooden club is a useful killing tool that is easily manufactured. With the right weight and dimensions, it can even be used to kill larger mammals such as sheep and goats. Make a club from a branch about 5–6cm (2–2.5in) in diameter, preferably widening towards what will be the striking end, and about 75cm (2ft 6in) long.

Spear

Spears are made for either throwing or stabbing, and can be as simple as a hardwood pole or branch sharpened at one end. A throwing spear should be about 90cm (3ft) long, and a stabbing spear up to 180cm (6ft) long. Hold a carved point over a fire to harden it. You can make more durable points by splitting the spear shaft at the end and inserting a piece of sharp metal or bone in the split, before lashing it securely into place.

Wooden

Animal bone

When throwing a spear, put your full body weight into the cast and follow right through with the throwing arm, keeping your eyes focused hard on your target. When stabbing, lean into the thrust to supply weight and power to your movement, but not so far forward that you will fall if the spear snaps.

Split

Throwing stick

Throwing sticks are practical weapons for bringing down rabbits and squirrels. The best sticks will be slightly bent in shape, although

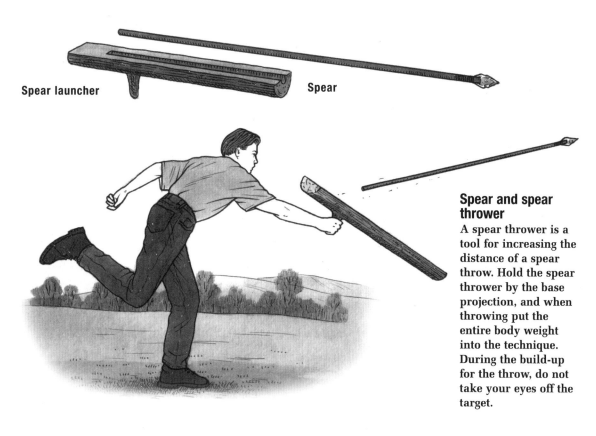

Spear launcher

Spear

Spear and spear thrower

A spear thrower is a tool for increasing the distance of a spear throw. Hold the spear thrower by the base projection, and when throwing put the entire body weight into the technique. During the build-up for the throw, do not take your eyes off the target.

a straight stick about 2ft (60cm) long with a thickened end is perfectly useable. Skim the stick on a horizontal plane to maximize the chances of hitting the target.

Stones

Stones need no construction to turn into weapons. Birds, squirrels and rabbits can be killed with stones thrown by hand power alone, as long as the stones are not too heavy and fit easily in the hand. Smooth stones give the best flight characteristics. When trying to hit birds, try throwing several stones at once in a 'shotgun' effect. You can increase the velocity and killing force of stones by launching them from a catapult or slingshot, or using them in a bola missile.

Catapult (Slingshot)

A catapult (slingshot) is simply a forked twig with a piece of elasticized material fitted between the forks. Choose a piece of wood that retains some flexibility. For example, hazel is good. For

the elasticized material, the elastic from clothes will work reasonably, but it is far better to use high-quality elastics such as surgical tubing or even rubber cut from a tyre's inner tube. Put a leather or cloth pouch in the centre to hold the projectiles. A catapult is highly accurate in practised hands, and is easily capable of killing small mammals and birds.

Slingshot (Sling)

Make a slingshot (sling) with a length of string or cord about 1.37m (4ft) long, with a patch of leather or cloth in the centre. To fire, place a stone securely in the patch, hold both ends of the string and swing the sling around in a fast circle above your head. As the projectile swings towards the target, let go of one end of the string to project the stone.

Bola

To make a bola, wrap three to six stones (each about 5cm/2in in diameter) in individual pouches of material, then tie each pouch to a piece of string about 1m (3ft) long. Gather all the ends of the strings, and knot them together very firmly. The bola is used to kill flying birds or bring down running animals. Launch it by holding the knotted ends and swinging the whole bola above your head for several revolutions before throwing it at your prey. A good bola will have significant killing force, so be careful in its use.

Bow and arrow

A well-made bow and arrow will kill sizeable prey such as deer and goats at distances of up to 100m (328ft). However, constructing an effective weapon in the wild is complicated by the lack of seasoned wood. Unseasoned wood loses its spring

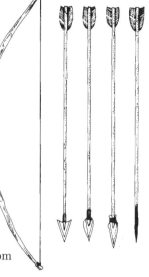

quickly, but a flexible hardwood such as yew will have reasonable durability.

The bow should be about 120cm (4ft) long. Carve it so that it is evenly weighted at both ends and that it widens in the centre to form a comfortable hand piece. Cut notches about 1.25cm (0.5in) from the bow tips to hold a string made from rawhide or any other durable cord. Sling the bow securely, but do not put it under too much tension, or the bow will have limited pull and reduced range. Rub the bow with animal fat or oil to prevent the wood from drying out.

Make arrows from hardwood shafts about 60cm (2ft) long and 6mm (0.25in) wide, with any irregularities on the surface of the wood smoothed out. Simply sharpening the wood forms

Bow and arrow construction

To make a bow, first select a suitable piece of wood of the correct length, then fashion it into the basic bow shape (A). Cut string notches at each end (B), then string the bow under tension to make the final weapon (C).

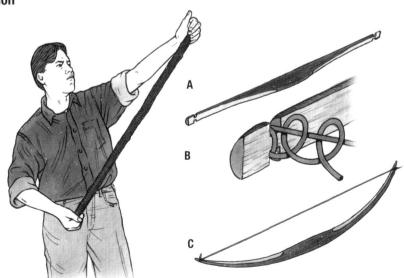

A

B

C

Hunting gun

Hunting guns are suited to different types of target. A 7.62mm (0.30in) rifle is useful for killing large game such as deer and sheep, whereas shotguns are more suited to killing birds and smaller mammals. Using the incorrect weapon or ammunition can result in a wounded animal or destroyed meat.

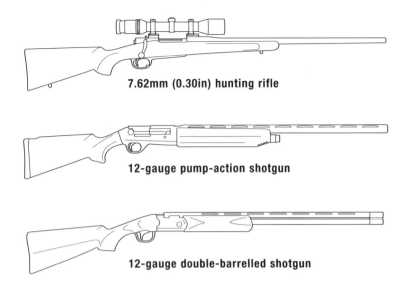

7.62mm (0.30in) hunting rifle

12-gauge pump-action shotgun

12-gauge double-barrelled shotgun

Stalking

When stalking an animal, make no abrupt movements and keep the body profile as low as possible. Keep balanced to ensure that you can freeze at any point in the stalk if the animal spots you.

The stalking crouch

The flat crawl

The crawl

Camouflage

The basic principle of camouflage is to disperse your silhouette and to avoid presenting shapes and colours which contrast with the background. Foliage is excellent for breaking up body shape, especially if camouflaged clothing is worn.

a point, although better penetration will be achieved by attaching pointed pieces of stone, bone, metal or glass. Use feathers, paper, cloth or even leaves to make flights – three equally spaced flights are optimum – and notch the blunt end of the arrow to fit into the bow string.

When firing a bow, keep the arm gripping the bow locked as you pull the bowstring back with your other hand. Pull the bowstring back to the side of your face, but be careful the string doesn't get hooked behind your ear. Line up the target with the arrow, and release the string with a natural unfurling of the fingers.

HUNTING

Hunting is probably the most complex of all survival skills, and one needing considerable practice to perfect. When hunting, strain every sense to pick up signs of animal life or a flash of movement in the vegetation. Choose your hunting times wisely – animal activity tends to intensify around first light and at dusk, especially around watering holes and feeding grounds.

The first stage of hunting is usually tracking the animal down to visual contact. The indications of a quarry's presence are known as sign, and include footprints, droppings, signs of feeding (animal bones, shelled nuts and so on), soils deposited from elsewhere, fur or feathers, burrows and nests, broken or bent vegetation, chewed bark or roots, and scratch marks on trees. A combination of several pieces of sign can let you know the animal's direction of travel, its territorial area, its dietary preferences and even

its species (if a print is clear). If following tracks, use droppings, broken vegetation and other sign to fill in gaps. Three pieces of linked sign will give you a direction of travel, probably a route of travel regularly used by the animal.

Remember that sign is affected by the passage of time. The edge of a paw or hoof print will become more crumbly over time, filling up with dirt and leaves. Faeces recently passed retain heat and scent, becoming dry and scentless with age. Flattened grass usually returns to the vertical within three or four hours of being trampled. If the entrance to a den or burrow is overgrown, it probably indicates that it is no longer occupied.

STALKING PREY

Once you make visual contact with an animal, you have to move into range to deploy your weapon. Keep downwind of the prey – the animal is likely to smell you if you stand upwind. Move as silently as possible, rolling the foot from the heel through to the toes on each step so that you can feel for sticks and breakable objects, which might give away your location. Use all available cover, and be prepared to crawl to close the distance. If the animal suddenly looks in your direction, freeze, and only move when the animal resumes its normal activity.

When the moment comes to strike, do it with deliberate, killing force. If shooting a bow or gun at a larger animal, aim at a point just behind the front shoulder. Should you wound the animal, finish it immediately with a *coup de grâce*. If the animal is dangerous, kill it by using the weapon

Water on rocks

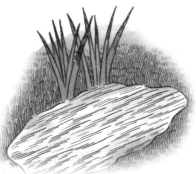

Mud on vegetation

Sand on grass

again from a distance. If it is completely disabled, slit its throat deeply either side of the windpipe with a sharp knife. For birds and small mammals, twist the head with a sharp pulling action to break its neck. Should the wounded animal run off into the bush, wait about five minutes before tracking it again following the blood trail (if you chase the animal it will keep fleeing).

Animal gait
Shown below are the four main types of animal gait. If the tracks have a slurred or erratic pattern out of the ordinary, it might indicate the animal is ill, wounded or is dragging a kill.

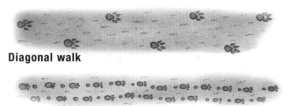

Diagonal walk

Pace

Bound

Gallop

Displacement of sign
When quarry moves from one type of surface to another, it leaves signs of its movement, such as watery prints on rocks, muddy marks on vegetation and sandy residue in grass.

TRAPPING
Trapping involves constructing and setting a mechanism that will kill or hold an animal should it upset the trigger system. The most common types of trap are snares, deadfall traps and spear traps.

Before looking at each individual type, here are some general rules to keep in mind. Avoid excessive handling of the trap, as this will leave your scent on it, and keep the trap away from campfires and foods for the same reason. Smear your hand with mud during construction to mask your scent. If your trap is scent-contaminated, try

DROPPINGS

When hunting, observe faeces to gain important information about animal species and habits:
- Carnivorous and omnivorous animals usually produce long, tapering stools
- Herbivores produce rounded dung piles matted with chewed vegetation
- Birds which eat seeds, fruit and vegetation tend to make liquid dung
- Carnivorous birds eating larger prey produce dry pellets

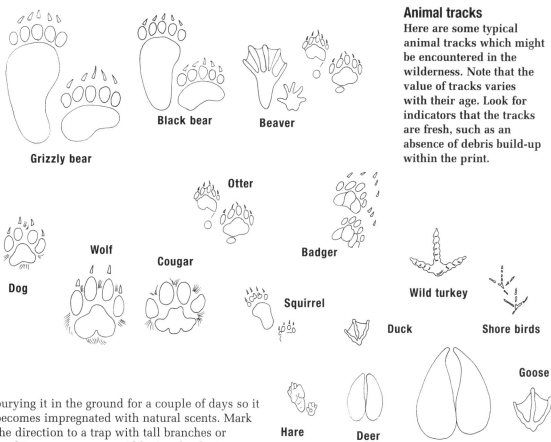

Animal tracks

Here are some typical animal tracks which might be encountered in the wilderness. Note that the value of tracks varies with their age. Look for indicators that the tracks are fresh, such as an absence of debris build-up within the print.

Grizzly bear

Black bear

Beaver

Otter

Wolf

Dog

Cougar

Badger

Squirrel

Wild turkey

Duck

Shore birds

Goose

Hare

Deer

Moose

burying it in the ground for a couple of days so it becomes impregnated with natural scents. Mark the direction to a trap with tall branches or markings on trees to avoid losing the device, something especially important in snowy conditions. Don't stand or work on the animal trail you are trapping. Instead keep to one side to make a minimal disturbance. If you have to break branches, smear the white, exposed wood with mud to camouflage your work.

SNARES

A snare is a wire or string loop that tightens around an animal when it unwittingly puts its head or a limb through the loop. Once tightened, the snare will either kill the animal by strangulation or hold the animal until you return to inspect the trap. Professional self-locking snares are a good addition to a survival kit, but they can be easily made with a piece of wire.

The crucial aspect of using a snare is positioning. Using your tracking skills, identify routes regularly used by animals, although avoid watering areas, as animals tend to be more alert

in these locations. Try placing some bait in the intended trapping site; if it disappears, the location is suitable for the trap. Place the snare a few inches off the ground with no vegetation about that might restrict the easy closing of the loop, and attach the end of the snare wire to a firmly embedded stick or branch that will hold the animal after snaring. Make a 'tunnel' out of vegetation, slightly wider than the animal's body, on the approach to the snare to channel the animal's head into the loop. Check snares regularly, otherwise the animal may escape or a predator might take the helpless catch.

There are several variations on the standard snare. One of the best is the 'twitch-up' snare. Attach the end of the snare wire to a branch bent downward under tension or with a counterweight. Another wire runs from the branch down to a

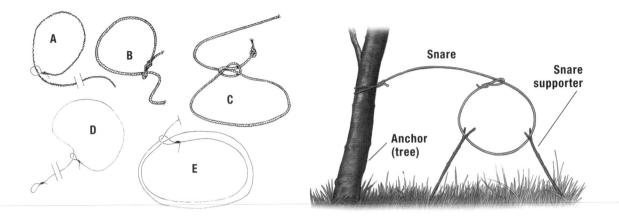

Snares

Here are shown different configurations of snare made out of wire (A, D and E) and rope (B and C). A snare should be free running, and commercial snares will often feature self-locking mechanisms.

A simple snare

This snare is anchored to a tree and elevated on two short sticks to put the snare loop at the height of an animal's head. Usually, the snare would be surrounded by foliage to disguise it.

Using snares

Snares A and B use spring tension (A) or counterweight tension (B) to lift the animal off the ground when it is snared. Examples C and D demonstrate how to position a snare, channelling an animal into the loop through use of vegetation.

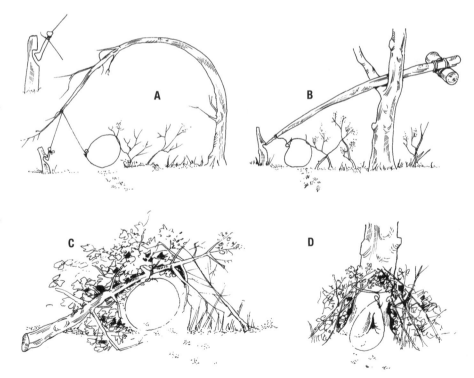

forked stick, which in turn is 'catched' into another forked stick embedded in the ground (see diagram). When the snare wire catches the animal, the two sticks are pulled apart and the branch springs upwards, suspending the animal in the air. The twitch snare reduces the risk of the animal escaping and of predators taking it.

DEADFALL TRAPS

Deadfalls kill by a falling weight – usually a heavy log or stone – activated either by trip wires or by bait. These traps are best used for medium-sized mammals such as foxes, badgers and small deer and larger ground-feeding birds such as ducks and geese. As with all traps, make sure that if you are testing out deadfalls you dismantle them completely after use to prevent injury.

For instructions on how to build some basic deadfalls, see the diagrams and illustrations in this chapter. Deadfalls need much practice to perfect, and be careful never to position yourself under the deadfall weight during construction – a falling heavy log will kill you as easily as your prey. Don't use heavy deadfalls for small prey, as

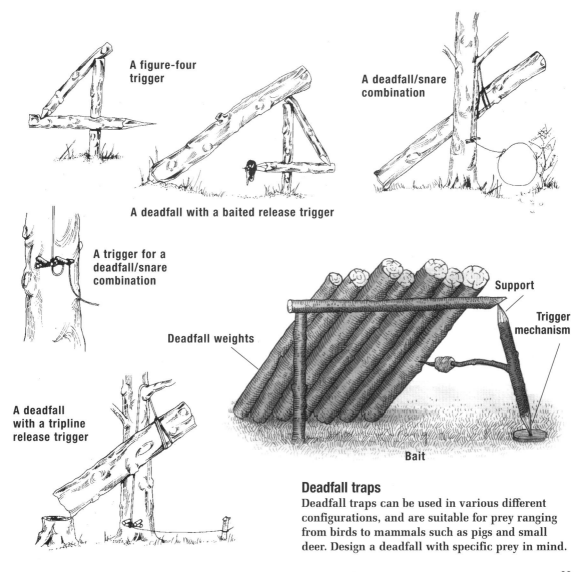

A figure-four trigger

A deadfall/snare combination

A deadfall with a baited release trigger

A trigger for a deadfall/snare combination

Deadfall weights

Support

Trigger mechanism

A deadfall with a tripline release trigger

Bait

Deadfall traps

Deadfall traps can be used in various different configurations, and are suitable for prey ranging from birds to mammals such as pigs and small deer. Design a deadfall with specific prey in mind.

Spear traps

A spear trap must sweep accurately over the tripwire or bait to ensure an accurate hit on the prey. Test the trap first, but stay well behind it to avoid injury.

either horizontal or vertical, to increase the deadliness of the spear trap. Be extremely careful, however, when setting up spear traps, as they are very dangerous. Never put yourself into the target area when the branch is under tension, and always approach the trap from behind to inspect for any snared prey.

BIRD TRAPS

Birds can be awkward animals to catch, as they possess both superb reflexes and the ability to make a vertical as well as horizontal escape. Trapping birds requires special measures. Make bird lime by boiling holly leaves and starchy grain in water until the liquid turns thick and sticky.

Spread the bird lime onto branches where birds are seen to perch – the substance will glue any landing bird to the branch. For birds that catch insects on the wing, try putting a stone in a

the weight will crush the meat and bones too severely and render them unusable. When baiting deadfalls, keep the bait well back towards the hinge of the trap. This allows for the animal's attempt to escape from the falling weight.

SPEAR TRAPS

Spear traps consist of a branch held under tension with sharpened stakes of wood attached to it. A wire runs from the end of the branch to the bait, restraining the branch against the tension and usually held in place by a stick embedded in the ground or by two interlocked notched sticks. When the animal takes the bait, it trips the wire, releases the branch and is killed by the stakes.

Spear traps should be employed to kill medium-sized to large mammals. Increase the length of the sharpened stakes according to the prey type to ensure a good kill; for killing a goat, the penetrating portion of the stake should be at least 15cm (6in) long. Targeting the sweep of the spears can be difficult. The stakes should sweep across the exact location of the bait, and having multiple stakes increases your chances of hitting the prey. Experiment with the plane of sweep,

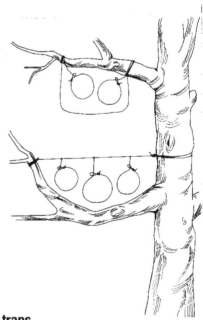

Bird traps

Bird traps can be as simple as nooses positioned along branches actively used for perching. Use fine wire to make the nooses, and ensure that the loop runs very easily to trap a light bird.

Avoid shadow on water

Crouch to avoid being seen

Fish's line of sight

piece of bait and throwing it into the air. Should the bird catch the bait, the stone will lodge in its throat and it will fall to earth. For ground-feeding birds, put fishhooks into pieces of food to achieve a similar effect.

Snaring is a more advanced method of catching birds. Bird snares must be made from very fine materials, such as horsehair or fishing line, and each snare loop should be about 1.5–2.5cm (0.5–1in) in diameter. Several of these snares can be suspended from a wire just above a water surface to catch water-skimming birds, or set on a branch to catch perching birds, the nooses facing upward. Don't be in a rush to empty a trap once one bird is caught: its flapping may well attract other birds into your trap.

Another method of catching flying birds is to tie straight lines of fishing wire across flight paths that are commonly taken by birds – flying birds may hit the wires and fall injured to the ground for your collection.

Avoiding fish's line of sight
The refraction of light through water enables a fish to see at non-line-of-sight angles over the riverbank. Stay low to avoid being seen and keep your shadow from falling on the water.

PREY TYPES
Each type of animal prey has its own different set of characteristics influencing how it is hunted or trapped. Here we will briefly look at some of the issues surrounding the most popular types of prey. Whatever the species, avoid eating any diseased animal. Signs of illness include problems in movement, disturbed behaviour, poor quality fur or skin, a distorted or discoloured head, isolation from a herd or pack, and enlarged lymph nodes in the cheeks (relevant only to larger animals, such as deer). If you are forced to eat such animals, boil the meat thoroughly and cover any cut or sore on your own body while you are preparing the meat.

COMMON PREY TYPES

Rabbits: one of the most popular survival meats. Trap by positioning a snare set outside the mouth of a warren, or kill running rabbits by hitting them with a throwing stick or bola missile. One important nutritional point is that rabbit meat takes more vitamins and minerals out of the body during digestion than it supplies. An exclusive diet of rabbit meat will therefore result in 'rabbit starvation' – you literally eat yourself to death. Always mix rabbit consumption with other foodstuffs to avoid this.

Sheep/goats: wild sheep and goats are agile,

Making fishing hooks

To make a fishing hook, cut out a section of thorny bush about 1in (2.5cm), the section having a large thorn at one end (A). Cut a notch around the circumference of the wood at the opposite end to the thorn (B) and tie the fishing line into this notch (C–F). The key point about wooden fishing hooks is that they will soften in water over time, particularly where the line is tied to the wood. Check the hook regularly for softening, and have replacements at the ready.

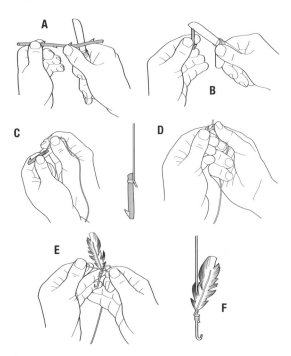

durable creatures that are difficult to catch. Kill them using a bow-and-arrow or a spear, or simply run down a sheep, take a firm hold, straddle the animal's back, pull up its head and slit its throat. Rely on snares to catch sheep and goats if you cannot get close. Avoid pursuing mountain sheep or goats unless very sure of your prey; they are sure-footed in difficult terrain, whereas you are liable either to waste energy or to injure yourself.

Wild cats: catch smaller cats with spring snares, but do not tackle big cats such as leopards and lions unless you have a gun.

Wild dogs: difficult to hunt because of exceptional senses, they can be caught with meat-baited snares. Before preparing and cooking meat from the rump, remove the anal glands by cutting around them without penetrating the membranes.

Badgers: very strong, dangerous creatures – use only powerful deadfalls, spring traps or snares. Poke any apparently dead animal with a stick when retrieving from a trap to see whether it is actually still alive.

Deer: deer are best killed with long-distance projectile weapons or spear/snare traps, as their senses usually preclude getting close. Look for chewed, stripped or deeply scratched bark or chewed twigs and buds to indicate a deer's territory. Be very careful of antlers and the animal's hind legs – they are dangerous weapons on an aggressive or wounded deer.

Squirrels: look for discarded nutshells beneath a tree, or stripped patches of bark, to indicate a squirrel's nest or feeding ground. Catch by placing snares on branches commonly used as runs, or kill when on the ground with a throwing stick, a stone or a bola missile.

Wild pigs: caution – wild pigs are large, violent creatures that can attack in packs. They are able to kill an adult human. However, they provide excellent survival nutrition through a high fat content. Signs of wild pigs include patches of soil that have been dug up and signs of bathing in muddy hollows. If the splashes of water over the side of the hole appear fresh, then the pig may have visited recently. If hunting pigs, try to catch them when they are asleep, usually around midday, when you might hear snores coming from thick undergrowth. Despatch with a violent thrust with a strong spear. Can also be caught with strong spring snares, deadfalls and pig spear traps.

Hedgehogs: pick hedgehogs up straight from the

Finding fish

Fish enjoy swimming in areas where they feel protected or where they have some respite from strong currents. The illustration indicates several locations which might provide good fishing.

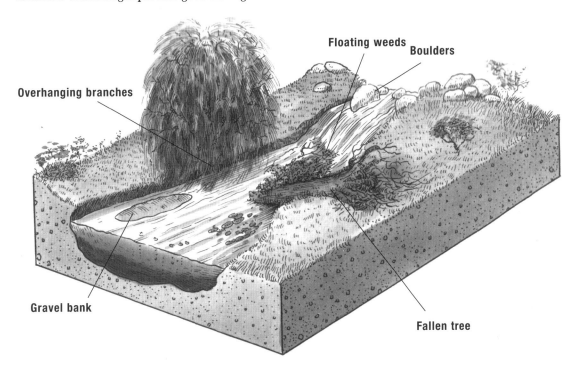

Floating weeds

Boulders

Overhanging branches

Gravel bank

Fallen tree

ground, though be careful of the sharp spines. Cook hedgehogs thoroughly to kill off parasites. Bake them in a coating of mud; the baked mud will pull off the spines when removed.

Lizards: target lizards basking in the sun on rocks or branches. Approach very stealthily from the rear, and kill them with a strike from a long stick. Avoid very large and dangerous reptiles such as alligators, crocodiles, the Gila monster and the bearded lizard.

Snakes: only attempt to kill a snake which you can positively identify as a harmless species; however, you still need to take care as even a nonpoisonous snake is capable of imparting a nasty, infectious bite. Use a forked stick to pin the snake to the ground just behind its head; kill by hitting the head with a heavy stick or cutting the head off with a machete. Beware of snakes playing dead – they will attack as you try to pick them up.

Frogs: look for frogs along the banks of rivers, ponds and streams, especially at night when their croaking gives their positions away. Dazzle them with a bright light, and hit with a stick to kill. Do not eat toads, which have poisonous skin secretions, and in the in the tropics always steer clear of extremely colourful frogs, some of which possess lethal poisons.

FISHING

Fishing is probably the best method of acquiring meat foods in a survival situation, as it places reasonably low demands on energy for potentially excellent yields. A basic understanding of fish behaviour will help increase catch numbers. Look for bubbles and ripples on the water's surface indicating a fish feeding just beneath the surface. In inland waterways, fish are attracted to shaded places. In colder weather, though, they can head for shallow sunny patches. They prefer still

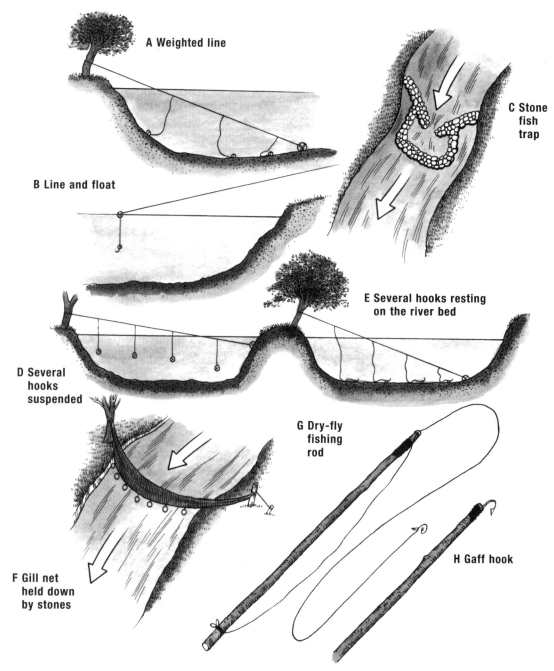

A Weighted line

C Stone fish trap

B Line and float

E Several hooks resting on the river bed

D Several hooks suspended

G Dry-fly fishing rod

F Gill net held down by stones

H Gaff hook

Fishing techniques

An innovative use of fishing lines and of terrain modifications will maximize your chances of good fishing yields. Hooks can be set to sit on the river bottom (A and E) or suspended in the water at varying levels (B and D). A stone fish trap (C) and a bill net (F) can bring especially large catches, and an improvised gaff hook (H) is useful for landing large fish on the riverbank.

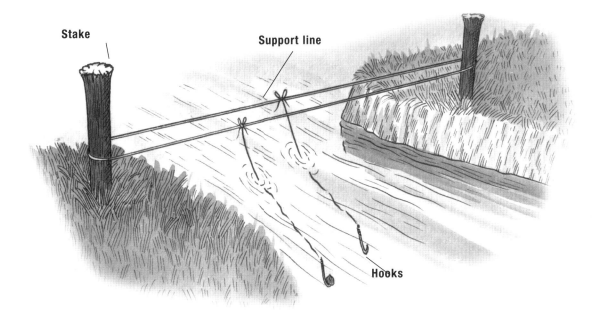

Stake

Support line

Hooks

waters found immediately downstream of objects such as large rocks or gravel banks, or on the insides of bends, which have a slower current than the outside of the bend.

Although you should have a basic set of hooks, line and split lead weights in your survival pack, there are many different options for catching fish in an emergency.

LINE FISHING

Line fishing requires nothing more than a fishing line, a hook and bait. If none of these is available, you will have to manufacture them. For fishing line, use natural grasses knotted to the required length. Improvised fishhooks can be made out of thorns, bent nails or pins, or pieces of sharp wood tied at right angles to the line. Note that any wooden hook will need to be replaced if it softens in the water after several hours. Try to match the bait with what the fish feed on normally. Easily accessible baits include worms, insects, minnows, berries, maggots or scraps of food (including meat, cheese and vegetables). Live bait gives the advantage of moving underwater, attracting the fish's attention, but fish can be curious about feathers or shiny objects such as pieces of aluminium foil and metal.

For line fishing, simply stick the bait onto the

A running line

A running line is a way of fishing while you occupy yourself with other tasks. You can fix as many hooks and line as needed, but do not overfish a water course, and check the lines regularly for any catches.

hook, and drop the hook into a place likely to contain some fish. Keep yourself well back from the bank edge if possible, and stay low. Movement on the bank scares off fish, and the refraction of light through the water enables them to see the bank side at a shallow angle. Don't let your shadow fall on the water.

For night fishing, try setting up a nightline. Take a long section of line and attach hooks at regular intervals along its length. Then tie one end of the line to a fixed object on the bank, and the other to a weight. Cast the weight into the water as far as the line will allow, and let it sink to the bottom. The nightline fishes the full depth of the water and gives multiple possibilities for catching fish. Leave it out for the entire night and draw it in at dawn to check for any fish. Remember to change the bait regularly, and do not leave the line out past daybreak – predators will steal your catch.

ANGLING

Line fishing has its limitations, and is best for catching fish feeding off insects on the water's surface. Angling is a better method for catching more elusive fish from deeper waters and requires the additional materials of a rod, floats and some weights. The rod is simply a long branch. Choose a young branch with strength but flexibility. The floats are used to indicate when a fish bites and also set the depth the hook descends below the surface. Use any buoyant material, such as cork, pieces of wood and rose hips. For weights, professional split-lead weights are obviously the best, but buttons, small stones, pieces of metal and any small heavier-than-water object will suffice in an emergency.

There are two basic weight-hook-float configurations for angling. First, the weight is placed just above the hook, which lets the hook float on the currents of the water at roughly the same depth as the weight. Secondly, the weight is set below the hook, providing a deep hook position less prone to currents.

Drop the line into places where fish are likely to be, and watch the float diligently. If the float suddenly dips below the surface, draw the rod in steadily but firmly. Another way of fishing with a rod is fly fishing. Make a brightly coloured lure out of feathers and pieces of cloth, or use a live beetle or grasshopper, and attach it to a hook without a weight. Flick the fly onto the surface of the water upstream, and allow it to float downstream. During the summer season, fish will attempt to grab the lure thinking that it is an insect.

Landing the fish will be much easier if you have some sort of net. Make a simple dip net out of water-permeable piece of fabric, such as a

GUTTING AND FILLETING FISH

Slit from the anus to behind the gills. Draw out the innards. Wash the fish. To fillet, cut off the fins and tail and cut down to the spine, but not through it. Cut around the spine, finishing behind the gills on both sides. Insert your thumb along the top of the spine, and pull it away from the flesh. The ribs should come away with the spine.

cotton T-shirt, and thread a forked sapling into the hem or seam until the forks touch at the midpoint. Make a hole in the fabric here, pull the sapling ends through and tie them firmly. Then simply tie off the neck and sleeve holes, and you have a dip net.

TRAPPING AND NETTING

Trapping and netting can provide much bigger yields than line fishing, so much so that over-fishing can be a danger in small rivers. Try never to catch more than you can eat, as you might deplete valuable sources of food for later and create a health hazard through rotting fish lying around.

An effective fishing device is the funnel trap. Make a lozenge-shaped basket from saplings with one end closed, the other open. At the open end, make a funnel pointing into the basket, then cover the body of the trap with twine or net to stop fish from escaping once caught. Place some bait at the back of the basket, and submerge the whole construction under water. The principle of the funnel trap is that the fish can swim into the basket easily, but cannot swim back out through the narrow inner spout. A similar, more basic trap

The bottle trap

The bottle trap is a quick form of basket trap, although the size of aperture of most plastic bottles means that they are only suitable for catching small fish.

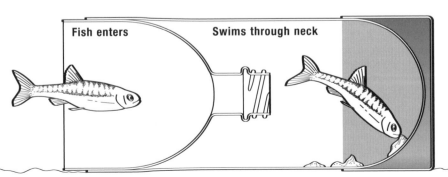

Fish enters   Swims through neck

Spiked harpoon

**Make the head of
a harpoon out of
multiple thorns (A),
set with spacing
material between
them to create a
spear head of large
diameter (B). Bind
the thorns securely
with cord (C).**

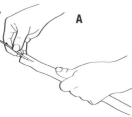
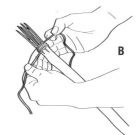
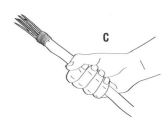

can be made by cutting a plastic bottle off at the
head, then turning the head round and inserting
it into the bottle (make sure you leave the cap off,
or the trap is useless).

NETTING

Netting is the most efficient method of catching
large numbers of fish. Make a large gill net by tying
rope horizontally between two trees, then tying the
vertical lines in to make a grid pattern. Aim to
create a mesh size of about 4cm (1.5in).

For maximum catch size, stretch the net across
the entire width of a river, setting it at a 45° angle
to the current to avoid damage to the net from
drifting objects and weighting it along the bottom
so it hangs vertically in the water. Set the net for
periods of around one hour only, otherwise the
catch could be truly excessive. To reduce the
catch yield, partially dam the river with rocks
and logs across most of its width, leaving a
narrow channel next to one bank in which you
position your net, secured in place with wooden
stakes. The dam will divert fish into the
net at the side, but in more
restrained numbers than netting
the whole river.

Both traps and nets can be
made more effective by
damming or funnelling
techniques. For the latter, build
two rock walls in a funnel shape
in the water, the wide part of
the funnel facing into the
current and the narrow part of
the funnel leading directly into
the net or trap. In tidal rivers and
estuaries, another method of

concentrating fish is to construct a semicircular
wall against the riverbank that is lower than the
water level at high tide, but higher than the water
level at low tide. When the tide goes out, fish will
be trapped in the enclosure, to be caught by
netting, line fishing or spearing.

The dip net described earlier can also be used
for fishing as well as landing fish. One peculiar
technique involves walking slowly along a river
or stream, and kicking up clouds of mud from the
riverbed. The fish swim to the surface as the mud
reduces oxygen levels in the water, whereupon
they can be scooped up using the dip net. For

Using a basket trap

**A basket trap is laborious to make, but is worth
the effort. If set in a rock channel in a fast-flowing
river, the trap can produce a large catch within
only minutes, so it should not be left unattended
for long periods.**

Spear fishing

When spear fishing, find a stable position to avoid the danger of falling into the water when you thrust. Try to put the spear tip in the water so that an entry splash does not alert the fish.

catching eels, put some fish offal (always keep the eyes and guts of a fish for subsequent fishing) or animal dung mixed with straw or bracken into the bottom of the net. Leave the net in the water overnight. The eels swim into the net for the bait, and bury themselves in the straw to feed, where they should still be found in the morning for you to collect.

SPEAR FISHING

Spearing fish can be surprisingly profitable with the right tools and technique. Construct a harpoon from a sharpened sapling or a long stick with a knife attached to the end. For a more effective multi-point harpoon, tie several sharp thorns to the end of the stick, the thorns splayed in different directions to increase the strike area.

To spear fish, find an area where large fish congregate, and enter the water slowly with your shadow falling behind you (or position yourself on the bank or water's edge). Dip the end of the spear into the water. When you are directly over a fish, thrust the spear swiftly downward to skewer it. Lift the fish out of the water, securing the fish on the spear with your free hand and transferring it to the bank.

FOOD FROM INSECTS

Insects are an unappealing but invaluable survival food, containing as they do high levels of protein. Slugs and snails are easily picked up from dewy areas. Starve the creatures for 24 hours before eating so that they excrete their internal poisons, then drop them live into boiling water, and boil them for 10 minutes before eating. Slugs are also good roasted. Do not eat snails with highly colourful shells, as they might be poisonous, and steer clear of tropical sea snails, some of which have lethal stings.

Bees and wasps can be collected for eating, as can the pupae, larvae and honey, but they require obvious caution because of stings or possible allergic reaction. Before invading a bee or wasp nest, make a very smoky fire using grasses directly beneath the nest – the smoke will kill the bees – and do this only at night when all the bees will be in the nest. Once the bees are dead, extract the honey from the nest (keep the honeycombs to provide a waterproofing wax), and prepare the bees for cooking by removing the poison sting

Shot placement on a deer

The shaded areas here represent the areas which should be targeted when deer shooting. B concentrates the shot into vital organs, while A and C hit the spinal column.

and sac, the wings and the legs. Cook by boiling or roasting. Never assault a hornet's nest, as hornets are extremely aggressive and possess far more powerful stings than bees or wasps.

Other common edible insects include ants, crickets and grasshoppers. Large numbers of ants are required to provide sustenance, and they should boiled for around six minutes to kill off any stings or poisons. Crickets and grasshoppers are a far better food source. Kill by swatting with a leafy branch, pull off the wings, antennae and legs, then roast or boil.

When hunting for insects, exercise caution. The places where many insects live – under rocks, inside the hollows of trees, under rotting wood, and so on – may also be home to scorpions, spiders and snakes that like similar conditions. Avoid any insects featuring bright colours, as they may be poisonous. This also applies to grubs found on the underside of leaves. It is best to cook all insects to kill off germs, but avoid dung-feeding insects altogether.

HANDLING MEAT FOODS
Once you have killed an animal, bleed, gut, skin and cook it as soon as possible to prevent the meat from spoiling. To bleed a typical mammal, such as sheep, slit its throat deeply from ear to ear, and allow the blood to run out, catching this nutritious fluid if you can (hang the animal up by its back legs to make catching the blood easier).

Transporting a carcass
Transport large kills such as this deer by binding the carcass to a pole and carrying it between two people. As well as bindings around the legs, tie the body so that the stomach is against the pole, otherwise the carcass will swing excessively.

Bleeding a deer
Blood is a useful survival food, providing a valuable source of nutrition when added to soups and stews. A bleeding frame such as this will ensure every drop of the fluid is caught.

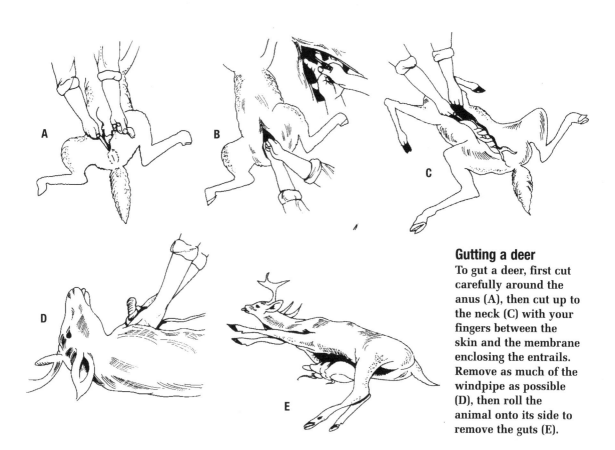

Gutting a deer
To gut a deer, first cut carefully around the anus (A), then cut up to the neck (C) with your fingers between the skin and the membrane enclosing the entrails. Remove as much of the windpipe as possible (D), then roll the animal onto its side to remove the guts (E).

Add the blood to soups and stews as a highly nutritious flavouring.

To gut the animal, lay it on its back and cut around the anus and, in male animals, the penis. Insert the first two fingers between the skin and the membrane enclosing the entrails, then run the knife, blade up, from between the fingers up to the chin, taking care to cut only the skin, not the membrane. Cut the diaphragm at the ribcage; cut the pelvic bone and remove the anus. Split the breast open and remove as much of the windpipe as possible. Turn the animal on its side and roll out the entrails.

Now you need to skin the animal. Cut up the inside of each leg to the knee and hock joints, then cut around the front legs just above the knees and around the hind legs above the hocks. Now cut completely around the neck and at the back of the ears. Next work your hands around the carcass, systematically loosening all the skin on one side, then the other. Retain the skin for making clothing and shelters.

Pigs cannot be skinned. Prepare by scorching the carcass over a fire, or immerse it in very hot water, before scraping off the pig's covering of thick hairs with a sharp knife. The animal is then ready for butchering.

Butcher an animal carcass by splitting it at any natural joint and making steaks out of thick muscular sections of meat. Keep the organ meats (offal), especially the kidneys, liver and heart, but discard anything discoloured or infected with parasites. Healthy, pink lungs can be boiled and eaten. Intestines can be turned inside out, emptied of their contents, washed and boiled to produce sausage skins into which other foods can be stuffed and cooked. The stomach can also be boiled and eaten once its contents have been emptied, but even the partly digested foods can be eaten after a thorough boiling. Keep the feet, tail and bones for making stocks (clean them well before use). Fat and blood are good for making soups more nutritious and flavourful.

Skinning a rabbit

When skinning a rabbit, do not cut too deep into the stomach cavity when making the initial incision (A and B). Grip the knife by the blade about 1cm (½in) from the tip to prevent nicking the stomach contents (C) before removing the final part of the skin (D).

PREPARING BIRDS

- Bleed the bird by slitting its throat beneath the tongue.
- Pluck the bird by pulling the feathers out with a quick motion, beginning from the chest. Submerging the bird in hot water first will make this easier, except in the case of water birds.
- Gut the bird. Cut from the neck to the tail, then pull out the innards.

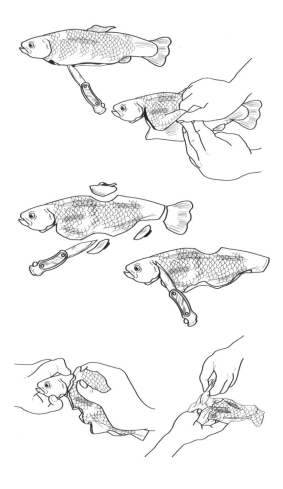

Filleting fish

By removing the guts, head and fins, the meat of a fish can often be prised off the bones to leave you with fillets. If you struggle with this, however, cook the fish whole (gutted) to avoid wasting meat.

CHAPTER NINE

SURVIVAL COOKING AND PRESERVING FOODS

Survival cooking is about making foodstuffs found in the wild both safe and palatable to eat. With a few basic techniques, surprisingly tasty and nutritious meals can be prepared.

THE TECHNIQUES OF cooking in the wild depend heavily on the nature of the environment and what types of food can be caught or gathered. Of course, the common element in cooking is fire, so make sure your shelter is, if possible, near good supplies of wood fuel. Before burning, check that the wood is not contaminated with any materials such as animal dung, which may pollute the taste of the food. Be cautious about using scarce supplies of wood for cooking in cold environments; if it is your only source of warmth, then try to find foods that can be eaten raw.

Remember what cooking is for. All cooking methods kill off much of the vitamin content of food. While it might be tasty to fry up some berries to provide a sauce for some meat, nutritionally it is far better to eat the berries raw (if safe). Cooking is therefore not always beneficial and should only be used for the following purposes (if food is hard to obtain):

- To break down tough plant or meat material to make it edible and digestible
- To kill off germs and parasites – obviously all raw meat needs cooking
- To provide body warmth in a cold environment
- To combine multiple ingredients in one meal
- To make unpalatable foods tasty
- To neutralize harmful chemicals (such as in the case of stinging nettles)

Cooking will not destroy industrial chemical contaminants, the powerful poisons present in fungi, or bacteria in decaying foodstuffs.

BASIC PRINCIPLES

If you have a fire, there are six main methods of survival cooking: boiling, frying, baking, steaming, roasting and parching. Boiling is one of the easiest to apply, and will thoroughly cook all food types. It is especially useful for breaking down tough plant matter, although it is also the cooking method most destructive of vitamin content. Be sure to drink the water used for boiling when it is cool to extract any nutrition from the water.

Roasting is done with a skewer or spit over an open fire. The important part about roasting is to make sure that the food, particularly meat, is turned continually over the heat to avoid leaving uncooked spots. Roasting is especially good for cooking whole fowls or small animals, and the meat should be set just off to one side of the fire over a receptacle to catch any dripping fat, which can be used later for frying and eating.

Baking is a good nutrition-friendly form of cooking, but one requiring you to manufacture a baking vessel or oven. Use this method for the slow cooking of meats; slow-baked meats are usually extremely tender. Frying is useful for infusing food with energy-rich fat. It requires a frying surface, such as a piece of metal or flat rock. For best results stir-fry small pieces of meat or plants in animal fats retained from earlier meals. Alternatively, put a thin layer of stock or water in the bottom of the vessel to braise the food. If cooking with oil or fat, add the meat when the oil is hot – this sears the outside of the meat and keeps it tender inside. When frying vegetables (or using any other cooking method, for that matter), cook them until they are edible but retain a crunchiness. The softer the vegetables are cooked, the more of their nutritional content is destroyed. Steaming is a gentle cooking method that preserves most of a food's nutrition. It should be used for cooking fish and leafy vegetables – it is not really effective for cooking large pieces of meat. Parching is the final cooking method. It works well with nuts and grains. Simply place them in a container or on a rock and heat slowly until they are scorched.

COOKING FIRES
Almost any type of hot fire can be used for cooking (cooler, smoky fires are suitable for food-preservation techniques – see below – but not cooking). For example, a trench fire can be used as a grill by making a wire mesh or a grid of green sticks (mature wood will catch alight) over the trench on which to place food. Make sure that any fire is up to temperature before starting to cook. The hottest point is usually when large flames die down and the wood forms itself into hot coals. Don't position food too close to a fire as it may simply char on the outside while remaining uncooked on the inside. You can check whether meat is properly cooked by driving a knife or wooden skewer into the middle of the meat and withdrawing it. If the juices run out red, it is not yet cooked. If they run clear, the food is OK to eat. Also, tentatively touch the end of a skewer. If it is hot, that means the central part of the food has been cooking.

Chapter 11 deals with basic fire making. Here we shall look at specific types of cooking fire.

HOBO STOVE
The hobo stove requires a large metal can or drum, at best something like a five-gallon metal drum. Wash out the drum first, and scrape away any potentially flammable contents. First, cut out a rectangular opening in the side of the drum, through which you can make and stoke a fire. Next, punch one or two rows of holes around the bottom circumference of the drum, several inches apart, and a couple more holes just below the top of the drum to let out smoke.

To use the hobo stove, stand it securely on the earth and light a fire inside the drum. Place a top plate over the opening of the drum (if it has already been opened). When heated, this plate can be used for frying as well as warmth.

YUKON STOVE
Dig a circular hole in the ground about 24cm (9in) across and about 30cm (1ft) deep. Then dig a channel leading down into the hole, which will be the point for starting and feeding the fire. Next, stack up rocks around the edge of the hole in a funnel shape without closing the fire channel. If possible, try to make the funnel narrow towards the middle and flare out slightly at the top. Finally, pack the funnel with clay and earth to seal it and stabilize it.

When fire is started in the Yukon stove, it produces considerable heat (feed it with sticks either through the channel or simply by dropping them down the funnel). The heat is controlled by limiting the influx of

The hobo stove
The hobo stove will provide a basic frying surface and a good source of general heat. Ensure that the drum does not have any explosive vapours or residues in it before using.

Yukon stove

The Yukon stove is capable of producing intense heat over the vent. Control the temperature of the fire by modifying the air influx through the top vent and the fire hole at the bottom.

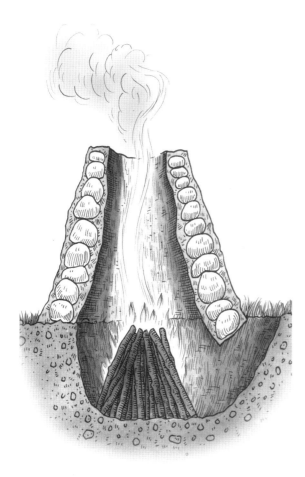

A

B

C

oxygen by partially closing the vent at the top. Place food on skewers or a grill, and position them over the vent to cook. Alternatively, wrap food in parcels of leaves and put them just inside the fire channel.

MUD OVEN

First find a metal can or other vessel to act as a fireproof pot. Dig a narrow trench, and jam the pot on its side across the gap, with a space underneath for a fire. Jam a long, thick stick

Preparing a mud oven

The mud oven is constructed by building a bank of earth over a large metal pot, using a stick to make a chimney. When constructing a mud oven, remember to leave a gap beneath the pot in which to make the fire. The mud oven is excellent for slow roasting joints of meat.

Trench fire

Making a fire in a trench means that, once the sticks have burnt down, a grill for cooking on can be made over the mouth of the trench using green saplings or, if available, a wire mesh.

upright into the ground at the base of the pot and cover the body, not the mouth, of the pot with a heavy layer of earth or clay, leaving the long stick protruding. Remove this stick to create a chimney. Build a fire under the pot in the trench. The interior of the pot will become hot enough for roasting or baking foods. Hold the lid on the pot by using a forked stick.

COOKING TOOLS

Survival cooking is made easier with a few basic cooking tools (some of these are covered in Chapter 12). An essential is a pot rod on which to hang vessels. Find a forked branch and stick it securely into the ground, forks upward. Rest a long branch through the fork, and secure one end to the ground by weighting it with heavy rocks. A vessel can be suspended over a fire from the other end of the branch. An alternative to the pot rod is the pothook. Cut out a short section of a slim tree trunk that contains several outgrowing branches. Trim off the branches to about 13cm (5in) lengths.

With the severed branches pointing upwards, the piece of wood is now suitable for hanging pots on when the hook is securely suspended from a branch using a cord. Varying the height of the pothook above the fire alters cooking time.

A rudimentary boiling pot can be made from birch bark if no metal vessel is available. Cut out a large rectangular section of bark, then roll it into a cone shape. Stitch the join into place using rawhide or plant fibres, or peg it into place with partially split sticks. This improvised pot will stand several uses as a boiling vessel. Do not let the water dry out or the container will ignite. Remember that even a hollowed-out piece of wood can be used as a cooking vessel – hang the wood over the fire and add hot rocks to the water and food, replacing them with hot ones as they cool until the food is cooked.

Steamers are relatively simple devices to make as long as you have two tin cans of different sizes. Punch several holes in the

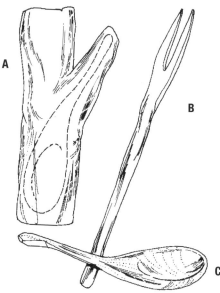

Cutlery

Simple cutlery can be made out of pieces of wood, including a pot hook (A), a fork (B) and a spoon (C). Use a sharp, strong knife to fashion these implements, and always cut away from the body.

A steam pit

A steam pit is constructed from layers of grasses laid over a platform of hot rocks and finally sealed with earth. The stick, when removed, allows water to be poured into the pit to create the steam for cooking.

smaller can and suspend it inside the larger boiling vessel using wire. If no wire is available, stand the inner can on some stones. In either case, you need to ensure that the inner can does not touch the boiling water. The inner can is your steamer. Place food inside the steamer, and put a lid over the top of the large can. Make the lid tight to build up steam pressure, but allow some steam to escape to prevent the can from exploding.

When it comes to roasting meats, you will need to make a spit that can be rotated. Stick two forked branches into the ground, one on each side of the fire. Find a long stick to act as a spit. If you are planning to roast large joints or carcasses, find a spit stick with a fork at one end to assist with

turning. To roast the meat, simply skewer it onto the spit stick, and suspend the stick across the fire on the forked branches.

For improvised skillets or frying pans, metal objects are obviously superior, and the lids of large cans are useful for this. Turning up its edge to form a lip can turn any flat piece of metal into a pan. Less ideal frying pans include a rock with a depression in it (avoid rocks with a high moisture content; these can explode when heated), coconut shells, seashells, turtle shells and half sections of bamboo.

COOKING TECHNIQUES

Basic cooking methods can be refined to improve the quality of the food produced. One excellent

Baking in mud

Mud cooking is ideal for preparing fish. Wrap the
fish first in plant material (A and B), then cover
the parcel with mud (C) and cook within a fire (D).
The mud will protect the meat while providing an
even cooking.

A

B

C

D

technique is that of cooking on hot rocks. Make
your usual campfire on a bed of rocks. When the
fire has died down entirely, brush away ash and
embers with some leafy sticks to expose the hot
rocks. Place meat or vegetables straight onto the
stones and turn frequently. Keep the pieces of
food small so that they cook thoroughly on the
rocks' residual heat.

A more sophisticated way of cooking on rocks
is to make a rock oven. Make a fire on a large pile
of rocks placed in the bottom of a pit. Again,
brush the embers off the rocks when the fire has
died down and place your food on top of the
rocks. Now cover the opening of the pit with
branches and a thick layer of earth and leaves.
The heat of the rocks is trapped inside the pit,
and will provide a cooking temperature for up to
two hours. Steam released from cooking is also

trapped to produce a pressure-cooking effect,
making the stone oven good for larger pieces of
meat or tough vegetables.

Clay or mud can be used to cook meats to
perfection. Wrap a piece of meat or fish in clay,
then wrap the clay in a 'parcel' of green leaves
and grass (the leaves and grass can be omitted if
necessary). Place these parcels directly within a
glowing fire, making sure the parcels are covered
with embers. The mud and clay stop the meat
from burning, yet get hot enough to cook the
contents. After an hour or so, remove the parcels
and crack open the clay. When the clay is removed,
it will pull off fish scales, feathers and even
hedgehog spines, leaving you with a ready-to-eat
meal. Don't cook vegetables by this method, as it
will pull off the nutritious vegetable skin.

An advanced and extremely gentle survival

cooking method is the steam pit. Dig a trench and make a platform of rocks in the bottom, and create a fire on them. Later, clear away the glowing embers, and push a long stick into the middle of the pit. Cover the rock platform with a thick layer of green grass, and place meat, wrapped tightly in a binding of leaves, into the middle. Cover the parcel of meat with another layer of grass, then spread a layer of earth over the top, filling the entire pit. Pull out the protruding stick and pour a small quantity of water into the hole. Seal the hole left by the stick. The water will turn to steam underground and cook the food to tender perfection in about an hour, with minimal loss of nutrients.

FOOD PRESERVATION
If you do manage to obtain more food than you can immediately eat, it is important to try to preserve the remainder for later. Food preserving has several different functions. It delays the

TIPS FOR COOKING AND PRESERVING

- Catch all fats dripping from meat during cooking.
- Instead of rehydrating dried foods, grind them up into a powder and add this to soups or other meals as a nutritional flavouring.
- Boil fruits to make a jelly when it cools and settles. This jelly will store for several weeks.
- Preserve fish by making pemmican. Mix flaked dried fish mixed with an equal amount of animal fat. Seal the food in a bag. Pemican is nutritious (it contains every vitamin and mineral except vitamin C) and can remain edible, in colder climates, for more than a year.
- Preserve fish or meat by salting. Smear the food with salt or, even better, store the food within layers of salt. Salting draws moisture out of the food, thus making it less habitable to mould and bacteria.

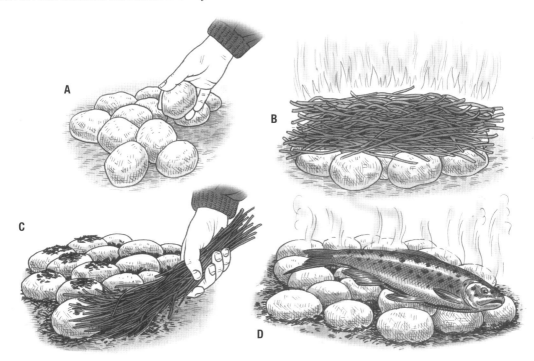

Cooking on hot rocks
Hot rocks will provide a cooking surface for some time after flames have died down. Remember to clean off ash and pieces of burnt wood using a

'brush' made of green sticks before laying the meat directly onto the rocks. Rock-cooking is suitable for fairly small fish and thin slices of meat.

Hiding a kill

Scavengers will appear shortly after an animal has been killed, particularly in tropical/desert areas. If temporarily leaving the carcass, put it up in a tree to protect it from ground scavengers.

DRYING

Moulds and bacteria thrive on moisture. Drying reduces the water content of foods to below 5 per cent of mass, so the moulds and bacteria then struggle to develop, and the food is preserved longer. As fat contains a high degree of moisture, drying is best used on low-fat foods such as fish and poultry, vegetables and fungi. If you are attempting to dry fatty meats, trim off as much fat as possible, and rub salt into remaining fatty sections to draw out moisture.

To dry food you need to, expose it to warm, dry air (if there is any damp in the air the drying will not work), preferably assisted by warm winds, which also serve to keep away insects. Place vegetables on warm rocks in the sun, and hang trimmed, thin fillets of meat over a wooden frame or simply over tree branches, but watch out for crawling insects. Maximize the food's exposure to the air, with plenty of space between each piece of food. If sunshine is not present, placing the food near the heat of an open fire will suffice. However, don't put the food so close to the fire that it cooks.

Drying can take several days to complete in the open air (some fruits can take up to 10 days), so you need to watch that animals or birds don't steal your food in the process. Keep flies away; once they have laid their eggs on the food, it becomes inedible.

Berries cannot be dried by the above method because they have watertight skins. Cut open non-segmented berries and expose the inner flesh to the air for drying. Mash segmented berries before drying, and spread the mashed berries on a hot surface until dry.

The food is finished when it is dry and brittle to the touch. Store it securely in an airtight container if possible. To rehydrate, soak the food in water for a few hours, or boil for between 30 and 60 minutes.

process of decomposition and retards the growth of germs and microorganisms. It also helps you to conserve valuable energy by reducing time spent hunting or foraging.

Most of us know basic rules of food preservation. Keep food as cool as possible, and out of direct sunlight. Avoid exposing the food to moisture, and if possible store it in an airtight container. For freshly picked foods, however, these measures will only extend the 'use-by date' by a few days. Use the techniques of drying and smoking to preserve foods for longer periods.

Drying and smoking frames

A drying and smoking frame is easy to build with just sticks and cord. For smoking frames, use green wood, which is more resistant to catching fire than dry dead wood, and try to enclose the structure with material or leafy branches in order to concentrate the smoke over the food while it is being prepared.

SMOKING

Exposing food to smoke is an intensive way of dehydrating it. Smoking not only dries food, but also leaves a waxy coating on the food's surface, which resists the absorption of moisture.

Smoking can be as simple as suspending strips or pieces of food above a smoky fire (see Chapter 11 for tips on how to generate smoke). A more systematic method is to build a smoke tepee. Take three long straight branches, and tie them together at one end to form a standing tepee. Make a platform of green branches halfway up the inside of the structure, and start a fire beneath it. When the fire is smouldering, throw on piles of leaves (preferably green). The fire will now produce a heavy smoke. Place pieces of food on the smoking platform and cover the entire tepee over with a cloth, branches or turf while leaving a small air gap for the fire. The food should be dried out after about 18 hours inside the tepee.

CHAPTER TEN

MAKING SHELTERS

Do not believe that you can do without shelter in the wild. A shelter will protect you from wind, rain, cold, sun, heat and wild animals, and help to keep up your morale.

IN THIS CHAPTER we will look at the basic types of shelter you can construct in temperate environments. Shelter types specific to tropical, desert, polar and mountainous environments are considered within the dedicated chapters. (It is worth reading these sections even if you do not intend to travel to areas such as these, to gain further ideas for shelter-building techniques in temperate climates.)

RULES FOR BUILDING SHELTERS

The first rule of shelters is, unless you are in the most predictably warm climate, always build one. Don't assume that a warm daytime temperature means a shelter is unnecessary. Even in the tropics and in the desert, it will get cold at night, and it will not be easy to construct an emergency shelter in the dark.

The second rule, but of equal importance, is to select the right spot for building the shelter. Choosing a bad location can mean the shelter is more exposed to wet, cold winds and other environmental adversities. Try to avoid choosing a site in the late afternoon/early evening after a long day's walk or march. Fatigue will probably cloud both your judgement and your building skills, and result in a shelter that is poorly located and badly constructed.

In locating a shelter, bear in mind what it is intended to protect you from, such as cold, damp, wind, snow, insects or sun. In addition, try to locate your shelter within easy access of survival essentials such as water, food sources and supplies of firewood. With these factors in mind, obey the following rules.

First, do not build a shelter on a hilltop exposed to wind and rain. However, you should be equally wary of constructing a shelter in a valley bottom or deep hollow; these could be damp and are prone to frost at night. Take advantage of the protection provided by natural features such as hillsides or rocky outcrops, and look for places where (if in colder climates) the shelter will receive a good dose of sunshine throughout the daytime. One final caution about hillside shelters is to avoid hillside terraces; these collect water draining down the hillside and are usually damp. In warm areas, try to locate shelters so that they take advantage of breezes, but don't expose the shelter to blowing sand or dust, which will steadily fill the shelter and make life fairly uncomfortable.

If you build near a river or stream, be careful that your shelter will not be in danger of flooding should there be a sudden downpour and the water level rises. Observe horizontal mud lines on the dry ground. These may indicate the high-water mark of the river so build your shelter above these lines. Also avoid building a shelter in drainage routes or in sites prone to flash floods or mudslides (such as gullies, arroyos and the like). Wherever you put your shelter, it can be a good idea to construct a runoff drainage channel gouged into the earth to divert any running water away from your shelter. Be cautious about building on spurs of land that lead to water: they are often routes to animals' watering places.

Building shelters in woodland areas has the obvious advantage of easy access to building materials, but exercise the following cautions. Look above you when choosing the site. Don't build under dead wood that could come crashing down on you during the next high wind. For the same reason, do not build under a tree containing the nest of bees, wasps or hornets. Another caution regarding trees is to avoid sheltering under a solitary tree in poor weather conditions because it could attract lightning.

Moving to shelter

If caught outdoors, build a shelter as soon as possible regardless of the climate or terrain you are in. Never sit exposed to the elements; hypo- or hyperthermia will be the likely outcomes.

Insects are a perennial problem around a camp or shelter. Avoid building a shelter near standing water, as it attracts mosquitoes, bees, wasps and hornets. Do not erect a shelter on or near an anthill, unless you want to subject yourself to a never-ending succession of bites and stings. Bear in mind that, if your shelter is too protected from wind currents, insects are likely to be more troublesome, whereas if your shelter is exposed to a steady breeze or mild wind the insect problem is reduced, as they will tend to travel on the breeze away from your shelter.

CONSTRUCTING SHELTERS

Survival shelters roughly fall into two types: improvised shelters, which usually take advantage of natural features, and shelters built from scratch. The former type is usually made hastily, although the end result can be a perfectly good shelter, whereas the latter requires more tools, knowledge and time.

The simplest form of 'shelter' is a windbreak, and is something that should be made or sought out during short rest periods. Make use of natural shelters, such as cliff overhangs, large rocky outcrops, fallen tree trunks and gradients. In open areas, sit with your back to the wind and pile your equipment behind you as a windbreak. Simple improvised shelters can be made using rocks and turf simply piled up to provide cover. For longer occupations, or for something that

Snow shelter

In snowy conditions, snow can be used to cover a lean-to shelter instead of branches – although for structural solidity, it is best to combine both materials. Perhaps surprisingly, well-packed snow has good insulating properties, as well as providing protection.

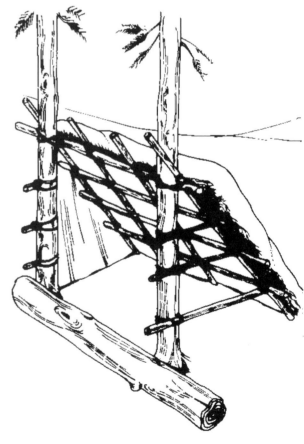

Lean-to shelter

A lean-to shelter is simply a frame propped
against a solid object and thatched with leaves.
Try to build the sloping face of the shelter facing
into the prevailing winds, tie the struts securely
with cord or plant matter, and use dense, leafy
branches for the thatching.

protects from all the elements, you will need a more substantial structure.

Construct shelters by modifying natural features of the environment you are in. Cover a natural hollow in the ground, or a scooped-out hollow on the leeward side of a fallen tree trunk, with strong branches, sticks, foliage and turf to form a fairly durable 'roof'. If you need to increase the height of the hollow, ring its edge with stones and small rocks. Stabilize this rock structure by packing the gaps in the stones with turf and foliage mixed with mud.

If sheltering in a cave, reduce any draughts by building up a windbreak over the entrance, but do not seal the cave entirely or you risk suffocation. If you light a fire in cave, locate it toward the rear, otherwise the smoke will be blown in from the front of the cave back towards you.

Making a shelter is dramatically easier if you have a tarpaulin, groundsheet or any piece of waterproof sheeting material with you. An improvised tent is made by tying a line between two trees, then throwing the sheet over the line before stretching out and securing each corner to the ground using more line and improvised pegs of wood. If no line is available, balance one end of a tree trunk or long bough in the fork of a tree, and throw the sheeting over it.

If you have time and light conditions on your side, it is worth constructing a more substantial shelter than these just described. However, it is only if you are an expert at making these that will you really gain any benefit over something more basic. An almost infinite variety of shelters can be constructed from flexible boughs or saplings, some cord and a waterproof sheet. Bend or set the wooden boughs into the shelter shape (tepee and tunnel shapes are particularly handy), tie them

A-frame shelter

An A-frame shelter, when properly constructed, will provide a warm, strong habitation. If thatching materials are not available, a large sheet of material can be used to form the outside of the shelter.

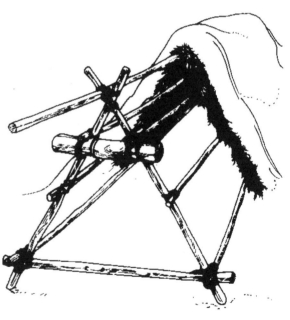

Large leaves can be used for thatching an A-frame shelter. Pack the leaves tightly to make a close, waterproof finish. Large tropical leaves are ideal for this type of shelter.

Survival shelter

A shelter should provide a place of repose, as well as being somewhere to get out of the wind and rain. Do not, however, retreat from the outside world and avoid facing your situation, but treat the shelter for what it is – a temporary survival habitation.

securely with the cord, then wrap the frame with your waterproof sheet. If you are likely to be in one location for a long time, you can even make a substantial walled shelter. Make the walls by trapping a row of thick branches between four upright logs (two at each end). Pack the gaps in the logs with a mixture of mud and foliage to improve the shelter's heat-retention properties.

Any shelter, regardless of the type, will need constant maintenance if it is to provide continuous protection against the elements. Mend any wind or rain damage immediately, and check the waterproofing regularly for any gaps. Try to keep pieces of repair material within easy access so that you don't have to travel far when any damage needs repairing.

SHELTERS AND FIRE SAFETY

Shelters built from wood and vegetation are very vulnerable to fire. Obey the following precautions:
- Build the shelter upwind of the campfire so that any hot embers and sparks are blown away from the shelter.
- Do not construct a sleeping platform too close to a fire.
- Do not allow a fire to blaze while you are sleeping.
- Never build fires within shelters.
- Ensure that nothing heavy restricts exit from the shelter, in case you have to abandon the shelter should it catch fire.

CHAPTER ELEVEN

MAKING FIRE

Fire serves many purposes in a survival situation. It not only provides warmth and the ability to cook, but it is also used for sending signals and making tools.

WHEN ATTEMPTING TO build a fire, you must pay attention to fundamental safety rules. Don't light a fire at the base of a tree, and keep the fire away from dry foliage. In woodland, clear away all debris on the ground to form a circle of bare earth at least 2m (6ft) across, and site the fire in the middle of it. Make sure that no tents or camping equipment will be caught by the flames, particularly batteries, gas stoves and flammable liquids. In windy conditions, encircle the fire with rocks; this will not only shelter the flames, but also prevent them from spreading. However, never place wet or porous rocks and stones near fires as they can explode when heated. Avoid slates and soft rocks, or any stones that crack, sound hollow or flake, for the same reason. An alternative to the rock circle is to dig a circular trench and set the fire in the bottom.

Beware of the dangers of creating poisonous fumes and of suffocation. Do not make fires in enclosed spaces without any ventilation, as you run the risk of death through carbon monoxide poisoning. Take great care when burning foam-type substances, such as is found in furniture. These can give out lethal hydrogen cyanide gas when burned. Look for fire-warning labels and make sure that there is plenty of ventilation.

TINDER, KINDLING AND FUEL

To start a fire you need three elements: tinder, kindling and fuel. Tinder is material that ignites extremely easily and is used for making the first flames. Good types of kindling are pieces of light materials that can be added to the initial flames to get the fire going and build up heat. Finally, fuel is any material that brings the fire to full temperature and sustains its heat.

Tinder must consist of light and small particles of material, usually fibrous in nature, which are absolutely dry and easy to ignite. Typical sources of tinder include shredded bark from some trees and bushes (birch and cedar are excellent choices because of their flammable resin). In addition, cotton balls or lint, dried mosses and fungi, crushed leaves and other fibres from dead plants, fine wood shavings or resin-damp wood sawdust, dry straw and grasses, and resinous sawdust work well. You can also use the dried-out linings of bird or rodent nests, lightly charred cloth, fine steel wool, powdered sap from pine trees, paper and foam rubber as tinder.

Break any tinder material down into fine particles or threads by scraping or rubbing it with

FIRE TIPS

- **Choose a sheltered site to build your fire; excessive winds will make the fire burn quickly or even put it out.**
- **If the ground is wet or covered in snow, build a platform out of green logs or stones. Cover this with a layer of earth, and build the fire on the resulting platform.**
- **Do not build a fire up against a rock. Instead, build it so that you can sit between the rock and the fire, as the rock behind you will reflect heat onto your back. If no 'reflector' is naturally available, build one out of rocks and earth.**
- **Remember to gather a good quantity of tinder, kindling and fuel in good quantities before attempting to make a flame.**
- **Put your back to the wind when lighting a fire to shelter the tinder.**
- **At night, when you are about to go to sleep, place two large, green logs against the fire to ensure that it is kept away from you and your shelter.**

a knife or rock. If the tinder is wet, dry it out in the sun or place it in a warm pocket in your clothing. In particularly wet conditions, it can be difficult to find any dry tinder. Try digging deep through the surface of trees, as the outer wood may be soaked, but the inner wood can be surprisingly dry. Your aim is to create about two fist-sized bundles of tinder. Once you have dry tinder, keep it dry by storing it in a waterproof container or bag. Outdoor adventure stores or camping suppliers sell professional tinder replacements, such as paraffin- or kerosene-soaked cotton wool, fire sticks (blocks of wood shavings impregnated with flammable chemicals), and paraffin wax blocks. With any tinder, as soon as you get a flame blow very gently on it to increase the heat enough for the addition of kindling.

Kindling is added to the ignited tinder, and raises the temperature of fire so that more substantial fuel can be added. Kindling, like tinder, must be dry, but consists of larger materials such as dry twigs about pencil thickness (resinous softwoods are good, but avoid any very green woods), pine cones and needles, and pieces of bark. If using sticks, cut small flaps of wood in the surface of the branch to improve the combustible surface area. Remember to add the kindling piece by piece to the fire, as a large pile of sticks being dumped on it will easily smother the burning tinder, forcing you to start again.

Large pieces of dry wood make the best fuel, although once the temperature of the fire is raised wet pieces of wood will quickly dry out, then ignite. Wet or green wood will produce a lot of smoke initially, so is actually a good fuel for making signals. Green wood can also be split and mixed with dry wood to be used as fuel. Try to select hardwoods, rather than softwoods. The latter will burn very quickly because of their resinous content, and you will have to be more active in finding fuel.

If there are no trees around, use any other fuels that come to hand. Twist dry grass into bunches. 'Logs' of dried peat moss or dried-out animal

Bow and drill

The bow and drill (A) is a way of speeding up the friction fire-starting method (B). As soon as hot embers begin to drop into the tinder (C), pick up the bundle and blow gently on it to encourage a flame (D and E).

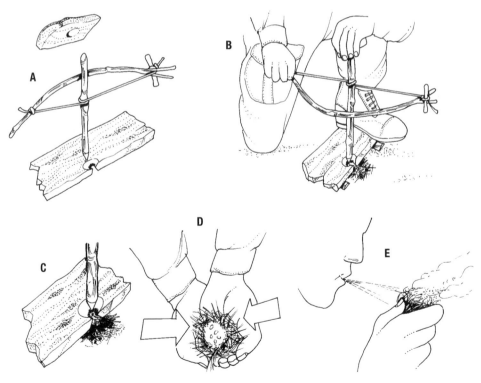

dung burn well (mix dung with dried grass and wood chips to make it burn longer). If you are in a vehicle, you will have access to several flammable liquids, including fuel, oil, antifreeze and brake fluid. Fuel is highly explosive, so mix it with sand to make it more stable. Encourage oil and antifreeze to light by adding some potassium permanganate, if you have it, to act as an accelerant. When igniting any chemical, do so with a long wick, such as a long branch with burning grasses at the end, to protect yourself from ignition flashes.

We will now look at the actual process of creating a survival fire. In all the fires and fire-making techniques listed below, open supplies of air are essential. Fires are particularly vulnerable to being smothered during the early stages of burning, but once they are well alight the air intake can be varied to produce types of fire, from hot flames burning high and bright to a smouldering low heat. Air is introduced to a fire by stoking it or by channelling a current, and air is limited by piling on more fuel or a smothering material such as wet leaves.

Hand drill ignition
Starting a fire using the hand drill requires a steady even pressure and a continuous rhythm. Give the hearth plenty of air to encourage ignition and be ready with the tinder.

Carrying fire
Carry fire by placing hot coals surrounded by tinder, then damp grass and leaves, in a can with ventilation holes (A). Alternatively, wrap tinder in bark, set it smouldering with embers (C and D), then carry the tube pointing into the breeze (B).

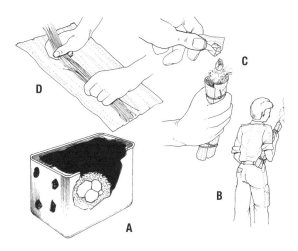

HOW TO START A FIRE
Of course, the easiest way to start a fire is with fire-making equipment. On any survival adventure, take plenty of matches stored in a watertight container. Professional waterproof matches are available, but you can waterproof standard matches by dipping the heads in melted candle wax and letting the wax harden. Simply scrape the wax off to use the match.

If matches or other methods of ignition are not available, then you must resort to one of the following methods to get a flame going.

FLINT AND STEEL
The shower of sparks produced when flint is struck with steel is enough to ignite good-quality tinder. Natural flint stone is acceptable, but man-made flint-and-steel sets are available from outdoor adventure stores. These have a magnesium alloy 'flint' and a steel striker, and produce showers of sparks.

To use a flint and steel, hold them just above the tinder, and strike the flint with the edge of the steel in a downward glance. As you do so, direct any sparks at the tinder. As soon as the tinder begins to smoulder, fan or blow it to raise a flame.

HAND DRILL

The hand drill provides method of lighting a fire by friction. Find a large, flat piece of softwood and cut a small V-shaped notch into one edge (the mouth of the V at the wood edge itself), with a small indentation at the point of the V. This will be the 'hearth'. Now get a strong hardwood stick about 61cm (2ft) long and 2.5cm (1in) thick. Sharpen one end of this stick to a point.

Place a handful of tinder beneath the V-shaped notch of the hearth, and raise the hearth up slightly using a stick so that a small air gap is left around the tinder. Secure the hearth under your knees. Now insert the sharpened point of the stick into the indentation bored into the hearth, and start rotating the stick vigorously between the palms of your hands. Apply downward pressure by working the hands from the top of the stick to the bottom, before going back to the start position and repeating as required. After time, friction generates heat in the indentation and produces smouldering coal and ash. These drop through the V-shaped notch, igniting the tinder underneath. If the embers do not drop

Fire plough

The fire plough is a fairly arduous method of fire-starting. Keep the pressure up until pieces of smoking wood are scraped up in the groove. Push these onto the tinder at the end.

Fire without matches

There are many methods of creating fire without matches, including flint and steel, a car battery, capturing the sun's rays through a magnifying glass, and putting tinder in a torch bulb fitting.

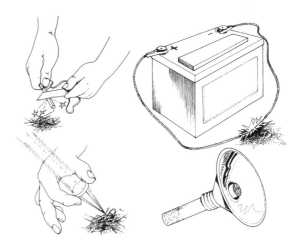

through, lift the tinder onto the hearth to make contact. As soon as the tinder is ignited, blow gently on it to fan the flames, then either remove the hearth or add kindling, or move the burning tinder into a fire construction.

Making a bow to power the stick rotation can speed up the hand-drill process. Cut a notch around the friction stick about one-third of the length down from the blunt end. Now round off the blunt end – this is the end that will fit into a socket made from a palm-sized piece of hardwood with an indentation in the middle. Lubricate the indentation with grease, oil, or soap to prevent friction wear. The bow is made from a branch just less than 1m (3ft) long and 2.5cm (1in) in diameter. Tie a piece of cord, line or any other sort of twine to both ends of the stick under tension, so that it produces a bow.

To use the bow drill, twist the bowstring once around the spindle notch. Place the sharpened end of the spindle into the hollow in the hearth. Press the socket down on the spindle's other end. Holding the bow at a right angle to the spindle, pull it backward and forward in a sawing action with long, even strokes. Keep going until smoke is produced and ignition of the tinder occurs.

Preparing a tepee fire

A tepee fire is a good basic campfire because it is easy to make, and the structure serves to encourage a good flow of air to get the flames rising. Build the fire in a square section of earth, laying a base of tinder (A) to give the fire stability. Now construct the tepee, first fixing timber in the four corners to provide the tepee shape (B). Complete the kindling structure (C), leaving an opening around the bases for tinder to be inserted. Finally, insert the tinder just outside the tepee, and push it into the structure (D). The structure offers numerous paths for the fire to work its way up.

FIRE PLOW

The fire plow is an another method of making a fire using friction. Take a piece of softwood about 30–46cm (12–18in) long. Carve a groove into the surface of the wood about 2cm (0.7in) wide and about 1cm (½in) deep, which runs the entire length of the board. Now put some tinder at one end of the groove. Rubbing the hardwood stick vigorously up and down the length of the groove will make heat. This will eventually produce flakes of wood tinder within the groove, which then ignite from the buildup of heat. As this happens, use the stick to push the burning embers to the end of the groove and onto the main tinder.

BATTERY FIRE-STARTING

Batteries can be used to ignite tinder, especially powerful car batteries if you are involved in a vehicle breakdown. Connect two pieces of insulated wire to the battery terminals, one to the positive terminal and one to the negative. If you connect the exposed ends of the wires to a piece

Types of fire

Different types of fire will produce different burn characteristics. Remember that the more open the fire's structure, the more air is introduced, and the more intensely the fire will burn.

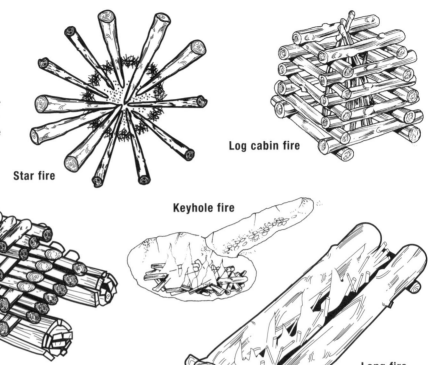

Star fire

Log cabin fire

Keyhole fire

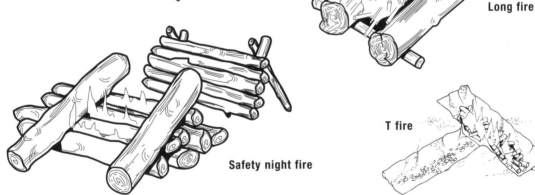

Pyramid fire

Long fire

Safety night fire

T fire

of noninsulated wire, the noninsulated wire will begin to get sufficiently hot enough to ignite kindling. Be sure to move the battery away to a safe distance once you have the fire going.

BURNING GLASS

Any sort of lens can be used to channel the sun's hot rays onto tinder to achieve ignition. For best results use a magnifying glass, a camera lens or telescope lens, or the lens of a magnifying flashlight. At worst, a convex piece of bottle glass

is also useable. Simply turn the glass into the sun and channel the rays to a single point of light. On a hot and sunny day – the only day on which this technique will really work – the tinder should quickly begin to smoulder. Blow gently on it to raise a flame, then proceed as usual.

DESIGNING THE RIGHT FIRE

There are many different types of fire, and each is suited to different purposes. (Some additional types of fire utilized for cooking are described in

Safety with a forest camp fire

When setting up a campfire, try to locate it in the middle of a large circle of cleared grass or earth, away from dry vegetation and your tent or shelter. Don't leave a fire unattended if it is burning heavily.

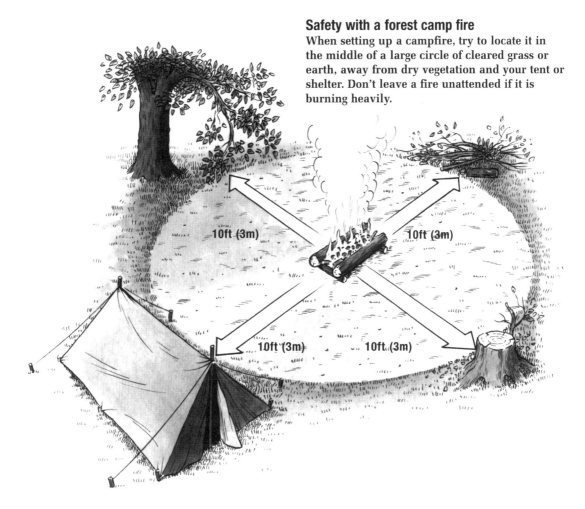

10ft (3m)

10ft (3m)

10ft (3m)

10ft (3m)

Chapter 9). One basic fire, the teepee fire, can be used for cooking and heating. Push a stick into the earth, and use it to stabilize a circle of kindling sticks formed into a shape like a teepee. Place tinder in the middle of the teepee through an opening left to provide a little wind current. Light the fire with your back to the wind, and feed the fire from the downwind side. Once the kindling is well alight, it can be collapsed and larger fuel placed on the fire.

A trench fire is ideal for use in windy conditions. Dig a trench about 30cm (12in) wide, 90cm (36in) long and 45cm (18in) deep, and line it from end to end with rocks. Build the fire on the rocks, which will radiate heat out and also protect the fire from the damp earth. The fire can be used for roasting and grilling foods across its

mouth. A variation is the 'T' fire, in which a T-shaped trench is dug. The fire is kept burning in the top part of the T, while coals are dragged out into the lower part for use in cooking.

If fires of intense heat and light are needed, build lattice fires. These are made out of logs stacked on top of one another in open lattice shapes in a pyramid configuration. The large number of air gaps in the log pile feeds the flames with a heavy current of oxygen, making a powerful fire that consumes large amounts of fuel. Reducing the size and number of air gaps will conserve fuel. If fuel conservation is an issue, try the star fire. This fire is in the centre of a 'wheel', with large pieces of fuel forming the 'spokes' (hardwood logs are best for this type of fire). The logs are pushed into the fire according to the level of heat and warmth required.

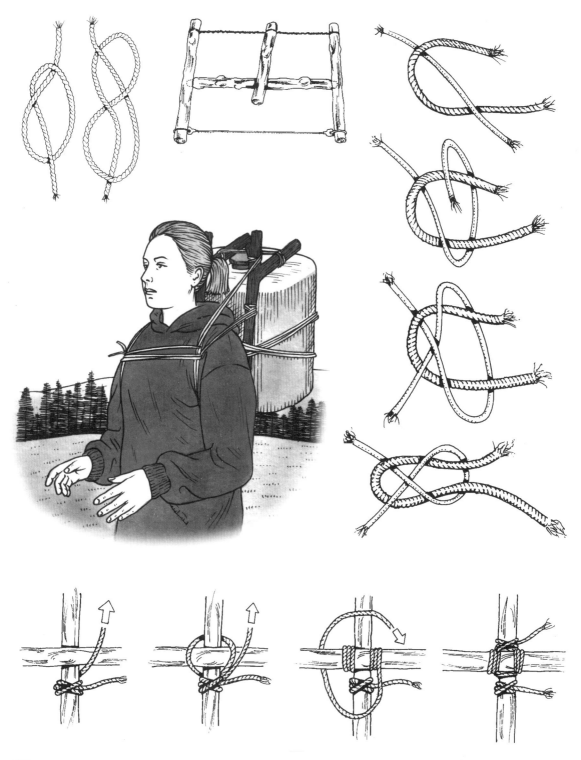

• CHAPTER TWELVE

TOOLS, ROPE AND KNOTS

Improvisation is one of the keys to survival. By making a few basic tools, and understanding the fundamentals of tying rope, the survivor can manufacture anything from shelters to snare traps.

IF YOU HAVE prepared for an outdoor adventure properly (see Chapter 4), you should have everything you need for survival in your backpack. Unfortunately, nature and unexpected emergencies have a habit of catching us unprepared. If caught without professional kit, knowing how to make a few basic tools out of natural materials will make the processes of hunting, cooking and eating, building shelter and, sometimes, extracting water, easier or at least possible.

CUTTING TOOLS

Cutting tools can be manufactured from stone, bone, glass or pieces of metal. For stone-cutting tools, choose flint, quartz, obsidian, chert or other stones with similar glassy qualities. A piece of rock already split is ideal, as the facet of the split gives itself naturally to sharpening, although check that the stone is structurally sound, with no thin fault lines. Sometimes simply smashing a lump of flint in two over a rock makes a cutting tool – the rock may shatter into sharp-edged pieces strong enough to cut wood or bone. Any small slivers of flint produced can be tied to a handle or pole to make cooking knives or spears.

For more refined edging, strike the stone with another stone at about a 45° angle, chipping the surface until a sharp edge is achieved. To produce an axe head, select a hand-sized flat stone, and scrape and chip a cutting edge, working in from both sides of the stone. Do this with soft stones or even pieces of antler or hardwood, taking a long, thick hardwood branch. To set the axe in a shaft, select a long, thick piece of hardwood and tie cord very tightly around it about 23cm (9in) from

one end. Split the wood from the tip down to the tied point. Next, set the axe head into the split, then bind the wood very firmly with twine just above the stone to hold the axe head as securely in place as possible. Always use the axe with caution, though, as the axe head is liable to fly out under inappropriate heavy-duty use.

Bone is another material that can be used for cutting tools, although it requires a little more work. A bone saw can be produced from large shoulder blades or even jawbones. Split the bone in half. Using your knife (bought or made) to cut teeth into the edge of the split results in a sharp sawing tool practical in animal butchering and for cutting softwoods. The same technique can be applied to flat bones to fashion scrapers. Do not

Knives

Improvised knives can be made out of pieces of any piece of material, including wood (A) and glass (B). Bind a sharp piece of glass or metal into a split wood handle, being certain to tie the cord extremely tightly to prevent blade slippage.

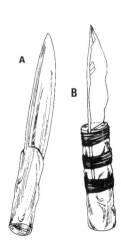

Saws

A wire saw in your survival tin/pack can be used with green saplings to make a basic hacksaw (A) or even a bucksaw (B). Cut notches into the ends of the wood to seat the saw securely.

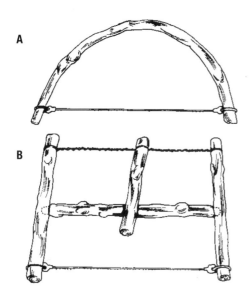

A

B

discard small bones and ribs; these can be sharpened into needles (burn an eye through the needle with a hot wire), pins and even stabbing weapons. Antlers and horns can be used for digging, gouging and hammering.

Knives and other cutting tools can also be made out of bits of junk and refuse. A piece of glass or the lids from tin cans (especially those lids made by can openers which cut inside the rim, rather than beneath), for example, can be inserted into a split stick and tied securely in place to make a sharp knife. If you find a piece of soft iron, place it on a flat, hard surface, hammer it into shape, then rub the edge on a rough-textured rock to produce a cutting edge. Tie the 'knife' onto a hardwood handle.

CAMP UTENSILS

The term 'camp utensils' mainly refers to tools that aid the process of cooking and eating. Basic cutlery, such as ladles, spoons and forks, can usually be made with tree branches, sticks and a bit of imagination. If the outline of the carved tool follows the grain, it is more water-resistant.

Bark is a good material for storage containers or even temporary cooking vessels, particularly green bark, which is waterproof and flexible (birch bark is ideal). For a simple rectangular container, cut out a large square of bark and soak its corners in water so they will be less liable to splitting when bent. After this, fold up the sides of the bark to make a lip around the edge about 5–8cm (2–3in) high, with the exterior face of the bark on the outside. Glue the joins of the container together using tree resin (from birch and pine trees especially), and hold them together while drying by using partly split sticks as grips. Finally, rubbing some pine resin on the inside of the container and allowing it to dry will waterproof it.

For holding cooking pots or drying clothes, a forked stick is a useful solution. Push the forks into the ground at an angle of 45°, secure it with rocks and prop it up at the midway point with another stick. The end of the forked stick can now be used to suspend items such as cooking pots or clothes. (For more cooking constructions see Chapter 9.)

Water-carrying frame

A simple water-carrying frame can be made from a Y-shaped framework made out of wood, using pieces of cord for straps. Pad the cords if they start to cut off circulation to the limbs.

Making a bark container
Cut out a square of bark (A), then cut the corners and fold them inwards to make a container shape (B). Glue and peg the corners (C), then paste pine resin over the container for waterproofing (D).

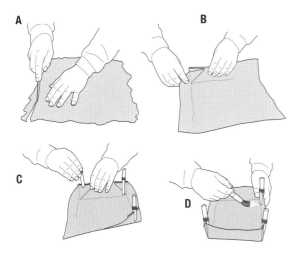

For carrying heavy objects, such as piles of firewood, over distances, try making a carrying frame. Cut a Y-shaped bough from a tree, with about 30cm (1ft) of length beneath the fork and about 1m (3ft) above the fork. The distance between the tips of the forks should be slightly wider than shoulder width. Cut notches about 8–10cm (3–4in) in from the three tips of the frame, and tie cord from each fork down to the base notch to create basic shoulder straps. Wear the frame like a rucksack, padding the cord straps to stop them from cutting into your shoulders, and tie loads onto the outside of the frame.

Reef knot
The reef knot can be tied by making a bight in one end of the rope and feeding the running end around and through this bight.

ROPES
Modern climbing and walking ropes are made from synthetic materials such as nylon, polypropylene, polyethylene, polyester and sisal. All these ropes are strong and light, and are resistant to water, insects and rot, but each has its pros and cons. Polypropylene and polyethylene, for example, are both water-resistant, but not as strong as nylon, which has a reduced breaking strength when wet. Polyester is very resistant to abrasion and performs well in wet conditions, but has little shock absorption. Sisal, which has limited resistance to abrasion and should not be used in the wet, is not recommended.

Man-made ropes are manufactured to a high standard and should be the first choice, but in an extreme emergency ropes can be made out of natural materials. Any pliable fibrous material of sufficient length and strength can make rope, and numerous strands of grasses and other plant material can be twisted or braided together for strength. Probably the strongest natural ropes are those made from animal parts, particularly tendons and rawhide. To make tendon ropes, first remove the tendons from the animal on the same day it is killed, and dry them out. Using a rock, crush the dried tendons into fibres. Moisten them,

ROPE CARE

Ropes will quickly lose their durability and break strength if mistreated. The following are important recommendations for rope care:
- Keep all rope as clean as possible, and avoid stepping on your rope or dragging it along the ground.
- Always store ropes loosely coiled. Do not leave them knotted or under tension, and do not hang them on nails.
- Do not let the rope rub against sharp implements or the edges of rock.
- Dry out wet rope by leaving it unravelled near an indirect heat source.
- Make regular rope inspections, looking for any frayed edges or split points, mildew and rot. Do not use a rope if faults are found. Cut the fault out, first binding the rope either side of the fault to prevent the rope from unravelling. Never, however, splice climbing ropes.

Joining ropes

Joining ropes can be done in numerous different ways, including the square knot (A), the single-sheet bend (B), the double sheet bend (C) and the Carrick bend. A is used for ropes of the same diameter, B for tying ropes of unequal size, C for ropes of both equal and unequal size and D for especially heavy loads or thick ropes.

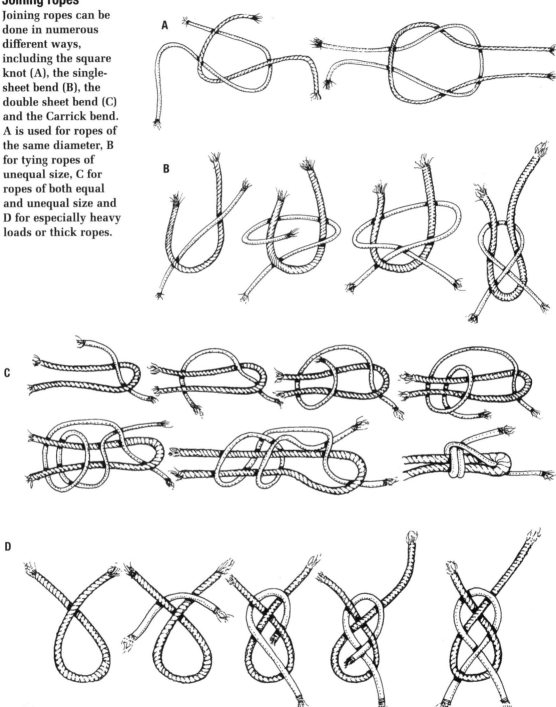

Loop making

A bowline (A) is one of the simplest and most
effective loop knots for holding equipment –
or people – in a climbing situation. To tie a
bowline, pass the running end of the rope
through the object to be fixed to the bowline
and form a loop in the standing part of rope.
Pass the running end through the loop from
underneath and around the standing part of
the rope, then back through the loop from
the top. The running end passes down the
loop, parallel to the rope coming through
loop. Then pull the knot tight.

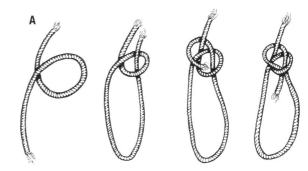

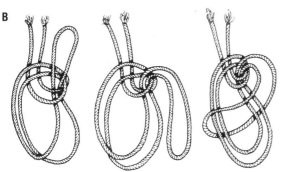

A bowline-on-a-bight (B) is a
stronger version of the bowline. It
is an easily tied knot that will not
slip. When tying, a double portion
of the rope is used to form a loop,
as in the bowline (A). The bight
end of the double loop is passed
through the loop, back down, up
around the entire length of the
knot, and tightened.

and twist or braid them into a continuous strand.
For rawhide rope, remove the skin of the animal
and clean it of all traces of fat. Spread out the skin,
then cut it into strips. Soak the strips in water for
two to four hours until they are soft and pliable,
then braid the strips together to form rope. You
can also use them singly as individual ties.

ROPE USAGE AND TERMINOLOGY

Before looking at various types of knots and
lashings, it's important to clarify the general
principles of a good knot and define terminology.
Knots should fulfil a number of requirements.
They should be secure when tied, but easy to
untie. They should be able to be tied in the
middle of a rope and when a rope is under
tension. Knots should not decrease the breaking
strength of the rope. All rope tying requires
practice. You must also make sure that you are as
proficient at untying knots as tying them in case
you have to release a knot in an emergency.

The terminology of tying rope may seem
arcane, but it will help to know a few basic terms
before moving into the descriptions.

Simple knots

The overhand knot (below left) is little use on its
own, but does form part of many other knots. The
figure-of-eight (right) is good at the end of a rope to
prevent slippage when tied to another rope.

Bight – a U-shaped bend
Hitch – a type of binding used to tie a rope to a timber or post
Running end – the free, or working, end of the rope
Standing end – the rest of the rope, apart from the running end

USEFUL KNOTS

The main text here explains the basic functions, strengths and weaknesses of the particular knots, while the referenced diagrams and captions detail the actual method of tying.

Reef knot – Useful for tying ropes together, but only if used for light work. Use the principle 'left over right and right over left' to make the knot, and make it more secure by making a half hitch with the working ends on both sides of the knot.

Figure eight (also called figure-of-eight) – Good for anchoring somebody or for tying at the end of a rope to prevent the ends from slipping through a fastening or loop in another rope. Take the running end across the front of the standing end, then twist it round and across the back. Pull the end forward, and pass it through the loop before pulling the running end tight.

Square knot – Use this for tying together two ropes of the same diameter only, and do not use it for nylon rope. Under strain, square knots draw tighter, but are easily untied by grasping the bends of the two bights and pulling them apart.

Single sheet bend – Unlike the square knot, this knot is used for tying together ropes of unequal diameter. Be aware that the knot may loosen when not under tension.

WOOD AND CARVING

The ability to carve wood is both a useful survival skill and a way of keeping the mind away from boredom. Each wood has its own distinct carving properties:
Sycamore – Soft, easily carved
Ash – A tough wood to carve into intricate patterns, but one excellent for tool handles, bows, and weapons
Beech – A hardwood, it is unsuitable for beginners or if equipped with blunt carving tools
Birch – Good carving wood, but decays easily
Hazel – Easy to carve, but also splits easily
Yew – Very hard, flexible wood good for cutlery and bowls, and also for hunting bows

Hitches

Hitches shown here include (from left to right): A – Half Hitch, Timber Hitch, and Timber Hitch and Half Hitch. B – Clove Hitch (1 and 2) and Round Turn and two half hitches. C – Rolling Hitch.

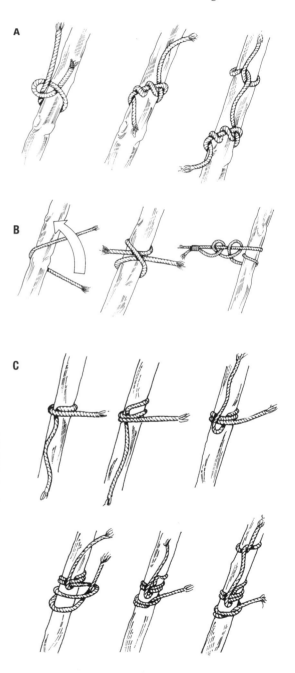

A

B

C

Double sheet bend – A useful knot for joining any ropes together, even under wet conditions, and one which will stay in place under heavy loads.

HITCHES

Hitches are used for attaching ropes to poles, posts, rings and bars, and so have applications in the construction of shelters, rafts and stretchers.

Half hitch – This is a loose hitch that is not secured. It tends to be used in making other knots or as a temporary binding.

Timber hitch – Use this to provide a tight hold on heavy poles or pieces of timber.

Clove hitch – This is a good knot for tying a rope to a pole or ring. However, the clove hitch can jam when wet and also loosen if pulled laterally. (You can overcome this problem by tying the rope at a 90° angle to its anchor point.)

Rolling hitch – Use the rolling hitch to make a nonslip fastening to a pole.

LASHINGS

Lashings are a form of knot used for binding poles and similar materials together. Consequently, lashings are useful for the construction of shelters, platforms, racks, rafts and similar structures.

Square lash – Used to tie poles or logs at right angles to one another, these make a good lash for building shelters and rafts.

Diagonal lash – This has a similar application to the square lash, but is better suited to binding two poles that do not sit at exact right angles or when the spars have to be held together under tension.

Shear lash – A general lash used for securing two or more logs together.

Lashings

A shows us the shear lash, used for tying two logs together, while B illustrates the diagonal lash for securing logs at right angles to one another. Finally, C shows the square lash, which has roughly the same purpose as the diagonal lash. Keep ropes tight during the process of tying a lash, to make a sold link.

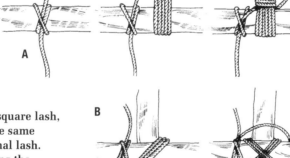
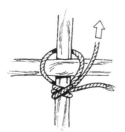
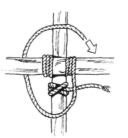
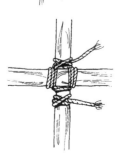
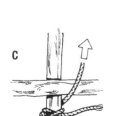

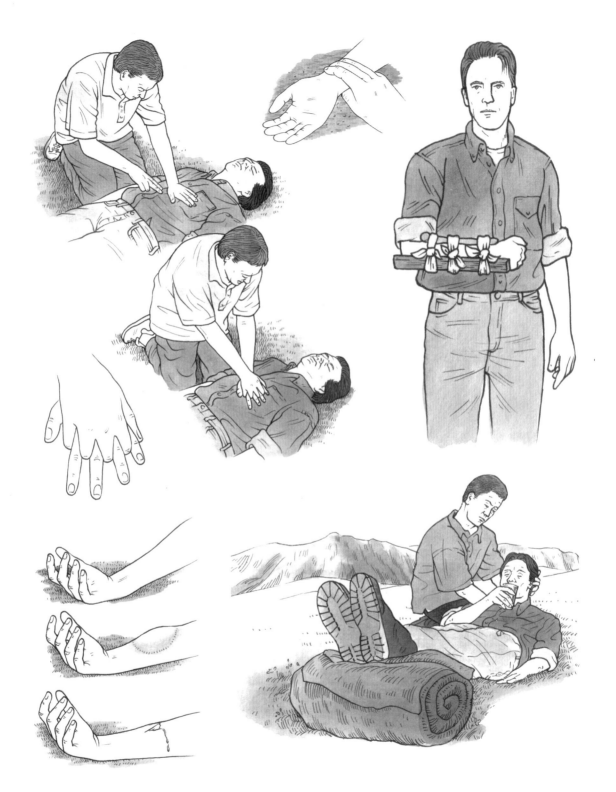

CHAPTER THIRTEEN

FIRST AID

First aid must be applied quickly and with confidence if it is to be effective. Your goal is to provide safe treatment until the injured person can be transferred to medical professionals.

YOUR FIRST ACTION in an emergency accident situation is to check for further dangers to yourself or the casualty. Before approaching the victim, look for threats such as materials that might explode, live electric cables, falling debris or approaching vehicles. If all is safe, attend to the victim. Move the casualty if he or she is in danger of further injury; otherwise stay where you are and perform an initial checkup.

CASUALTY ASSESSMENT
Your first casualty assessment should follow the ABC method which is taught to paramedics all round the world:
A = Airway
Open the casualty's mouth and check that there is nothing obstructing the throat or interfering with breathing. Typical obstructions include blood, vomit, loose teeth, the casualty's tongue or food. Clear out any loose obstructions with your fingers, or pull the tongue free from the airway.
B = Breathing
Put your cheek next to the victim's nose and mouth – listen and feel for breathing. Look at the chest to see if it is rising and falling. Place your hand on it to make sure.
C = Circulation
Check for a pulse. Place your fingers (not your thumb, which has its own pulse) against the inside of the wrist about 1cm (half an inch) in from the thumb side. Alternatively, put your fingers into the groove either side of the windpipe just beneath the angle of the jaw. The pulse should be strong and regular.

The ABC method checks that the casualty's fundamental body systems – breathing and circulation – are working. If the casualty is not breathing, you will need to deliver artificial respiration. If there is no pulse present, then cardiopulmonary resuscitation is required (see below for both techniques).

Your immediate priorities for casualty assessment and treatment are to:
- Restore breathing and heartbeat if they are absent
- Stop any bleeding
- Protect wounds and stabilize fractures or dislocations
- Treat for shock

Recovery position
The recovery position allows the casualty to breathe freely, while the head-down position ensures that any fluids in the airway will run out of the mouth, rather than form a blockage that could lead to choking.

Once you have attended to casualty's immediate needs, examine them thoroughly from top to toe. Check for any injuries you may have missed, looking for limb deformities, severe bruising, bleeding wounds, pale/bluing nails and lips (indicative of blood loss, shock or breathing difficulties), or areas of pain.

After treatment, and as long as the casualty does not have a spinal injury, roll them into the recovery position. To do this, roll him onto his front with one leg bent up at a right angle to the body. The arm on the same side should be bent outwards (with the opposite arm running down the side of the body). The face should be lying naturally to the side, with the head tilted back. This position allows drainage of any mucus and vomit out of the mouth to reduce the risk of choking. If a patient suddenly starts coughing and gurgling, try to remove fluids in the throat with a tube or straw.

It is vital that you monitor the casualty for shock. Shock sets in when the blood pressure decreases to dangerous levels and is caused by bleeding (internal and external) or loss of fluids through extreme sweating, vomiting or diarrhoea. As the volume of blood decreases in the body, vital organs such as the heart, lungs and brain are not properly oxygenated, and organ damage can result. Shock is a potentially fatal condition. Signs of shock include pale, cold and clammy skin; a rapid, weak pulse; fast, shallow breathing; and dilated pupils.

To treat shock, lay the casualty down and raise their legs about 15–20cm (6–8in) – this keeps as much remaining blood as possible circulating around the vital organs. Do not move the casualty, but reassure them and keep them warm (remove any wet clothing and replace with dry items). If the climate is cold, gently move the casualty to a shelter. If they are lying on the ground, put insulating material such as leafy boughs under the casualty to protect them from ground chill. Give only sparing sips of water to drink if the casualty is conscious and only if he or she is not suffering from abdominal wounds. Do not give food. Get the casualty to a hospital or doctor as soon as possible.

BASIC LIFE SAVING – BREATHING AND CIRCULATION

When a casualty's breathing and heartbeat have stopped, the clock is ticking. After about four minutes in this state, the casualty will start to suffer brain damage, and after 10 minutes there is

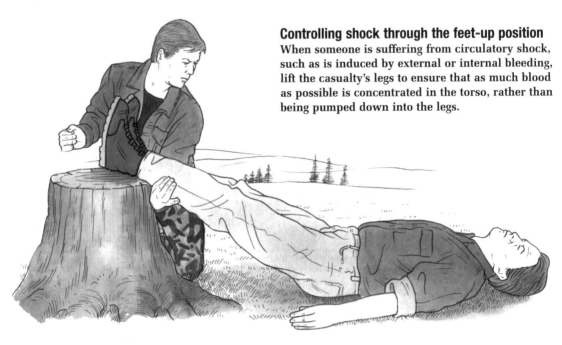

Controlling shock through the feet-up position

When someone is suffering from circulatory shock, such as is induced by external or internal bleeding, lift the casualty's legs to ensure that as much blood as possible is concentrated in the torso, rather than being pumped down into the legs.

Checking breathing and opening airway

When checking for breathing, look down the chest and listen for the breath at the same time. To open the airway, tilt the head gently backwards using two fingers held beneath the tip of the chin.

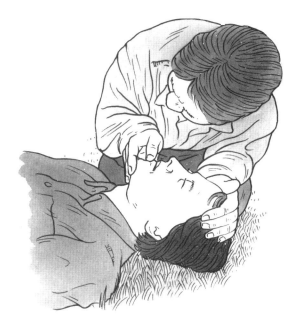

almost no chance of saving them (exceptions often occur when the casualty has been immersed in icy waters or snow).

If a patient's breathing stops (conclude this if you detect no breathing for 10 seconds), you must begin artificial respiration at once to keep his/her blood oxygenated and hopefully restart the natural breathing process.

ARTIFICIAL RESPIRATION

Put the casualty onto their back. Open the mouth and clear out any obstruction. Next, tilt the casualty's head gently backwards by placing the palm and fingers of your hand on the patient's forehead and applying firm, gentle backward pressure. At the same time, put two fingers of the other hand under the chin and lift gently upwards. This action opens up the airway. Don't use this technique if you suspect a spinal or neck injury. Instead, with your elbows on the ground, place one hand on each side of the patient's jaw and push the jaw forwards to open the airway.

Pinch the casualty's nose shut, and make a tight seal with your mouth around theirs. Make four full breaths into the casualty's mouth, watching that the chest rises when you blow and falls when you pull away between each breath. (If it doesn't rise, check that you are sealing your mouth tightly around the casualty's and that there is no obstruction in their airway. If there is an obstruction, follow the guidelines for choking, below.) After these first quick breaths, establish a rate of around 12 breaths per minute. Check every minute to see whether breathing has resumed. As soon as it does, stop the artificial respiration. If you cannot give mouth-to-mouth resuscitation for any reason (such as if the casualty has a jaw injury), close the casualty's mouth, cover it with your hand and blow into the nose instead.

When a person's breathing stops, it is often indicative that the heartbeat has also stopped.

Finding the pulse

A pulse can be located on either the wrist (A) or just to the side of the windpipe on the throat (B). The throat will usually provide a stronger pulse reading than the wrist.

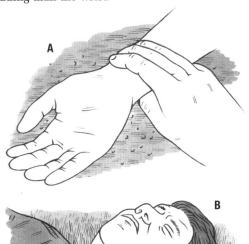

A

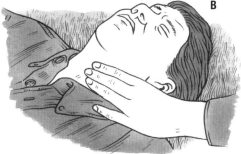

B

Check for a pulse, and if none is detected begin cardiopulmonary resuscitation.

CARDIOPULMONARY RESUSCITATION (CPR)
Cardiopulmonary resuscitation, or CPR, works by manually compressing the casualty's chest, squeezing the heart and forcing blood to circulate through the body, which in turn can restart the heart beating.

Lie the patient down on their back, and kneel by the side of the chest. Using two fingers, trace the edge of his or her ribs up to where the ribs meet the bottom of the sternum – you will feel the fingers come to a stop in the middle lower chest. Keep a finger on this spot and measure two finger widths up. Hold these fingers in place, and put the heel of your other hand just above them so that they are still touching the fingers.

The heel of the hand is now in the correct position, directly over the heart. Place your other hand over it, and knit your fingers together for stability. Lean over the casualty so that your shoulders are directly over their sternum. Push straight down to a depth of about 4cm (2in) with a strong, confident and rhythmic movement. Deliver about 80 compressions a minute and keep

Locating the heart for CPR
Move the fingers along the bottom of the ribs until you reach the sternum. Measure two finger widths up, then place the heel of your hand just above the fingertips to be in the correct location for CPR.

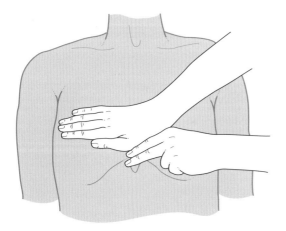

Cardiac massage
When delivering cardiac massage, first locate the right spot for the compressions (A), then link the hands together as shown (B and C) to provide a soft cushion for the thrusts.

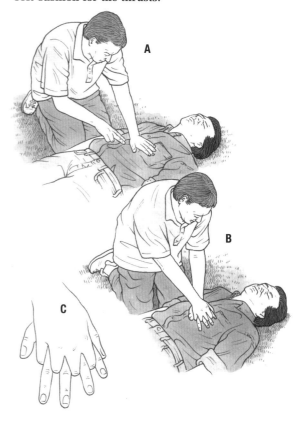

going, even though you will quickly become exhausted. Check for a pulse every minute.

When breathing and heartbeat are both stopped, you have to perform both artificial respiration and CPR. Deliver 15 chest compressions, then three breaths, and after four complete sets check for pulse and breathing. Repeat as necessary until the casualty's breathing and heartbeat are restored. This process is far easier if there are two of you working on the casualty. One should do breaths and the other compressions; switch over every few minutes. Note that for children and infants the above procedures need to be modified. On a baby or toddler, use only two fingers to make compressions to about 2.5cm (1in) depth, and speed up the rate to about 100 per minute. For older children (up to 10 years), use the same heel method as with an adult, but push only about 3.5cm (1.5in) depth at a rate of about 90–100 times per minute.

CHOKING

Choking occurs when the airway is blocked by an obstruction. If the obstruction is not quickly removed, the casualty will lose consciousness and possibly die from asphyxiation.

Indications of choking include an inability to cough or talk, gripping or pointing at the throat, extremely difficult or absent breathing, face reddening unnaturally, turning to blue in an unconscious patient.

To respond, first see if you can manually clear the obstruction with your finger. However, do not attempt to push your fingers against an object stuck at the back of the throat, as you might push it down further. If you are unable to clear the obstruction, face the

First aid for choking

While back slapping may be sufficient to assist a conscious choking casualty, if he or she is unconscious then abdominal thrusts should be delivered from a straddling position.

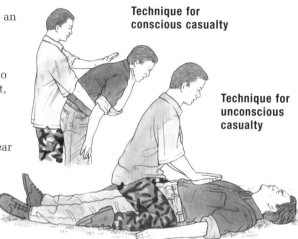

Technique for conscious casualty

Technique for unconscious casualty

Treating choking

For a choking casualty, alternate back slapping with the Heimlich manoeuvre until the blockage is cleared. For self-treatment, push the abdomen hard onto a solid object such as a tree stump.

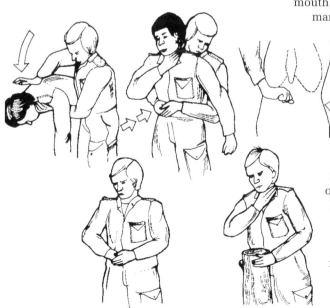

casualty's back and put the casualty's head lower than his or her chest. Strike the back sharply four times between the shoulder blades using the palm of your hand. Repeat this action two or three times. This may eject the obstruction from the mouth. If it does not, use the Heimlich manoeuvre. Stand or kneel behind the casualty, and wrap your arms around them. Make a fist of one hand, and place it at the juncture of the ribs and the waist. Place your other hand over the fist, and jerk the fist inwards and upwards four times. Hopefully the air in the lungs being forced upwards against it should push out the obstruction. Alternate the Heimlich manoeuvre with four back blows until the obstruction is released. Should the casualty become unconscious, perform the back blows with the casualty lying on their side. The Heimlich manoeuvre is modified for an unconscious person by rolling the casualty onto their back, straddling them and making abdominal thrusts straight down with the heel of the hand. When mixing back blows and the

Controlling blood loss from a limb

For severe limb bleeding, first get the casualty to lie down and raise the limb high (A), while applying pressure to the wound with a dressing (B). Bandage dressings into place over the wound until bleeding has completely stopped (C).

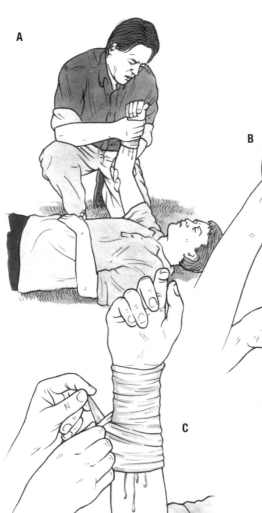

shock. To stop bleeding, use a clean pad of material and press it down on the wound. If nothing else is available, use your hand to apply the pressure, but try to make sure it is clean to avoid giving the casualty blood poisoning. Hold the pressure firmly until the clotting occurs and the bleeding ceases. If blood seeps through the dressing, leave it where it is and place another dressing on top of it.

Once the bleeding has stopped, you need to keep the wound clean and protected. First, irrigate the wound by pouring clean water across it, cleaning from the middle outwards. Don't rub or scrub the wound. If you have tweezers, gently pick out any foreign debris, but do not do this if there is any danger of restarting the bleeding. Now cover the wound with a sterile dressing (boil some improvised bandages if you do not have pre-packaged sterile dressings). Change the dressings daily, or if they start to smell bad, which is indicative of infection (an infected casualty may also complain that the wound is hot and throbbing). In the case of infection, treat by wrapping hot rocks or boiled and mashed plant products in a cloth and apply to the injury site. Never reuse dirty dressings. Clean them of matter, then boil them for 15 minutes to sterilize them. Note that if a wound is gaping, you can use adhesive tape cut into thin strips to bring the sides of the wound together. Always ensure the wound is thoroughly clean and sterile before applying the tape.

Sometimes bleeding can be extremely severe, especially when an artery is severed (you will see bright red blood spurting into the air), and more drastic action is needed. If there is a danger that the casualty is going to bleed to death quickly, a

Heimlich manoeuvre, make a sweep of the casualty's mouth after each set of the two techniques to see if the obstruction has been dislodged.

WOUNDS AND BLEEDING

Any bleeding should be stopped as quickly as possible to prevent the casualty from going into

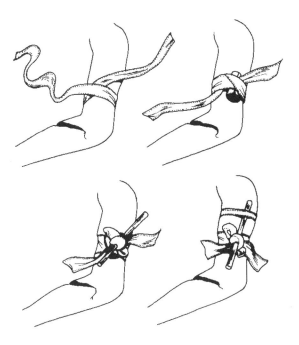

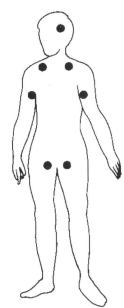

Tourniquets

Only apply a tourniquet when there is immediate danger that the casualty will quickly bleed to death. The figure represents places where major arteries can be pressed against bone with a finger as another way to control bleeding.

tourniquet might be your last resort. Tourniquets, however, can only be used for limb bleeding – nowhere else. They are dangerous to apply for two reasons. First, a tourniquet works by cutting off blood flow to a limb, and this can result in tissue damage. Secondly, if a tourniquet is kept on for a long period, when it is released toxins that have built up in the injured limb flow into the bloodstream where they can cause a potentially fatal systemic reaction.

Follow these guidelines for using a tourniquet. Use a piece of cloth about 5cm (2in) wide. Wrap the cloth several times around the upper arm or upper thigh. Tie the two ends of the cloth together in a knot. Place a stick on top of the knot, then tie a double knot over the top of the stick. Now twist the tourniquet around and around, tightening the cloth until the bleeding stops. Once the bleeding has stopped, apply dressings to the wound to encourage clotting. Release the pressure of the tourniquet frequently, and take it off as soon as bleeding is controlled.

A special type of bleeding injury is internal bleeding. Internal bleeding is usually the result of heavy impacts. These might not break the skin, but can cause damage to organs and tissues. Be observant for signs of internal bleeding when bones, particularly the thighbone, which is

surrounded by major blood vessels and tissue mass, are broken. Signs of internal bleeding are:

- Faintness
- Pale, cold and clammy skin
- Blood in the urine or stool (the stool will have a black, tarry appearance)
- Vomiting or coughing up blood
- Symptoms of circulatory shock (see above)

A person with internal bleeding needs emergency hospitalization. Before that can be delivered, treat the patient for shock.

Applying a roller bandage

Elasticated roller bandages are excellent dressings, but it is easy to apply them too tightly. Pinch the fingernails and see if blood flows back into them; if it doesn't, the bandages are too tight.

Stitching a wound

Stitching a wound is not for the faint-hearted or those people without basic medical training. Suturing should leave no pockets of blood or air in the wound, so the stitches must go down to the bottom of the wound, as well as take in equal amounts of skin on both sides of the wound.

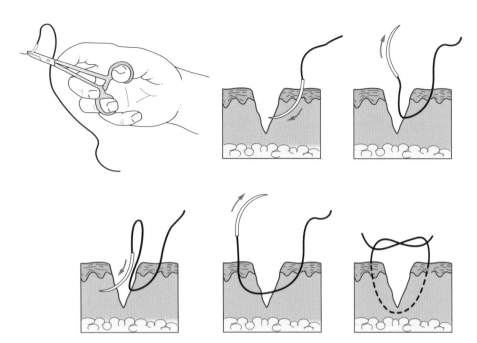

Cooling a burn

The quicker a burn is cooled, the less tissue damage will result. Keep putting cold fluids onto the injury for about 10 minutes, and cover the wound with a sterile dressing after treatment.

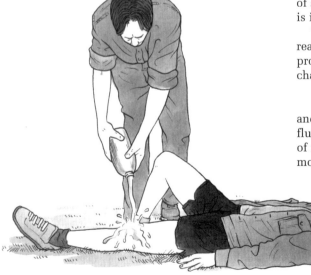

BURNS

Burns are a special type of wound and can be caused by friction, direct heat or chemicals. There are three levels, or 'degrees', of burn injury:

First degree – only involves the outermost layer of skin. Minor, non-serious burns.

Second degree – penetrates the second layer of skin, producing a red, blistered surface, which is intensely painful.

Third degree – destroys deep tissues, even reaching the bones. Third-degree burns can produce horrifying open wounds that are charred black.

The danger with burns comes from fluid loss and shock (the body will direct large amounts of fluid to the burn site for healing) and the danger of infection. While third-degree burns are the most serious burn type, the amount of body covered by any burn affects the level of urgency. So, for example, a second-degree burn over one-half of the body is more serious than a third-degree burn to a finger. To treat any burn, first submerge or drench the wound in cold (preferably slow-running) water for around 10 minutes. The heat from burns can damage tissue long after the original accident, and the water kills the heat. If clothing has stuck to the burn, simply soak the clothing. Do not attempt to pull it off the burn. Once the burn has been cooled, dress the wound with a sterile dressing. Do not put anything on the wound, including ointments, and the old advice about applying butter or lard to a burn is actually dangerous to the patient.

Change the dressing frequently, and clean the wound with water. Give the casualty plenty to drink to replace lost fluids, but reduce the intake if the urine output becomes unusually high. Treat for shock if necessary.

FRACTURES

Broken-bone injuries come in two types. An 'open' fracture occurs when the end of a broken bone pierces the skin, creating a wound that bleeds. In a 'closed' fracture, the bone is broken, but stays inside the flesh. The symptoms of a broken bone are fairly clear:

• There is an audible sound of a bone breaking

Signs of a broken limb

A broken limb will exhibit severe bruising, obvious deformity and, in the case of an open fracture, a piece of bone which has broken through the skin.

SPINAL INJURIES

Spinal injuries are a critical situation, threatening death or permanent paralysis. The following can be signs of spinal injury:
• Chronic pain in the back regardless of movement
• A noticeably deformed spinal column
• Chronic bruising or other injury over the spinal area
• Extreme tenderness over the spine
• Loss of bladder control; in men, the penis may be persistently erect
• A tingling or numb sensation in the limbs
• Paralysis, or a lack of response to stimulus (try scratching the palms of the hands or the soles of the feet ,and ask if the casualty can feel it)

A spinal injury casualty must be transferred to professional help immediately. The person administering first aid, meanwhile, should concentrate on stabilizing the injured spine so there is no further damage caused through movement. To treat the casualty:
1) Do not let them move at all.
2) Stabilize their neck by improvising a collar out of something such as a towel or magazine. Bend it around the neck. Do not move the head while doing this, nor restrict the casualty's throat. Or, if the casualty is on his or her back, place a rolled-up blanket or piece of clothing underneath and around the neck to stop sideways movement.
3) Monitor the casualty's vital signs constantly, especially if they are unconscious.

Should you have to move the casualty – something that is not recommended – get a group of people, ideally five in number, to position themselves along the length of the casualty's body and slowly lift or roll him or her onto a rigid litter or board. One person should have the dedicated job of keeping the head facing forward and naturally aligned with the shoulders. If the head is not in this position before movement, place your hands firmly over the casualty's ears and turn the head very slowly to the front without any jerking movements.

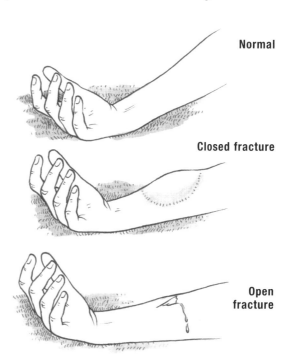

Normal

Closed fracture

Open fracture

Fracture types

Fractures come in a variety of different types. The worst to treat can be the comminuted fracture, in which the bone has been shattered into pieces rather than cleanly broken.

Simple fracture

Comminuted fracture

Open fracture

Greenstick fracture   **Closed fracture**

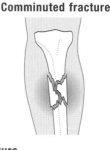

- The casualty feels the bone snap
- There is a severe pain, followed by an acute tenderness around the injury site
- A limb or joint may be noticeably deformed and will have a partial or complete loss of movement
- There may be a grating sound or sensation produced by the broken ends of the bone rubbing together
- Muscles around the injury site may go into spasm

When treating an open fracture, first stop the bleeding by applying pressure with the dressing around the exposed bone (do not press on the bone itself). Clean out any fragments of bone from the wound, and treat as described in the wounds section above. Whether you are treating open or closed fractures, check that circulation and nerve responses are still functioning in the limb. Do this by checking for a pulse at the wrist in the case of an arm break, or by seeing if the extremities are unusually cold or have gone a pink or blue colour. Another technique is to pinch the toe or fingernails hard, then release them to see if they go pink again, which would indicate that blood flow is still functioning. Check for nerve damage by pinching or scratching the toe or hand. If the casualty can feel this, nerve impulses are operating.

Fractures in which circulation or nerve impulses are severed are extremely serious, and could result in amputation, so the casualty needs to be in professional hands as soon as possible. In the interim, however, if professional treatment is not likely for some time, then you should try to restore pulse and nerve responses through applying traction. Traction is used to realign broken bones. This minimizes further tissue damage and releases the pressure on trapped nerves, veins or arteries. Do not apply traction to fractures directly at the site joints. These are best protected by being placed and supported in a position in the midpoint of their normal range of movement. To perform traction, have the casualty lie down and try to relax the muscles in the affected area. Pull gently but firmly on the broken limb, drawing it outward, then angling it back towards the original line of the bone. This process can take around 10–15 minutes. Traction can be performed on open fractures. Clean the exposed bone and wound before pulling, and don't trap any skin as the bone is moved back under the flesh.

Once traction is complete, check for nerve and pulse restoration, then splint the limb to prevent it from moving. If you have not applied traction because rescue is imminent, splint and pad the broken limb in the position in which you found it. For simple breaks such as toes and fingers,

SPRAINS

Sprains are a common complaint among outdoor pursuits enthusiasts. Treat as follows:
- **Put a cold compress on the sprain area to reduce the swelling**
- **Bandage the injured area and elevate the affected limb**
- **Give the injured limb complete rest**
- **If you sprain an ankle, but have to keep walking, keep your boot on to brace the injury and to help reduce swelling**

reset the digit, then splint it by tying or taping it to the unbroken digit next to it with a strip of wood between the fingers for support.

Splinting limbs requires any material that can be made into a rigid structure. Typical splint materials include sticks and branches, walking or ski poles, or a rolled newspaper. The splints should be long enough to reach above and below the fracture site. Place two splints alongside the injured limb, one on each side. Ensure the limb and splint are tied at four points, two above and two below the fracture, and put padding between the splint and bony or uncomfortable parts of the injured limb. For additional stability, you can tie the injured and splinted limb to an uninjured part of the body, such as a wounded leg to its healthy counterpart. After tying on the splint, check the circulation and nerve impulses in the extremities to ensure that the bandages are not too tight.

Using traction to align a broken leg
Traction relies on a steady pull then relaxation of the broken limb to realign the bones in their natural configuration, thus relieving pressure on nerves and arteries.

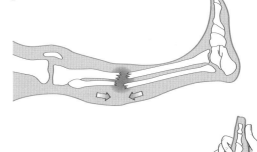

Splinting an arm and leg
Here the casualty is shown with a leg splint (below) and arm splint (at left). Note that the piece of wood provides a stabilizing structure, while the padding ensures that the broken limb is protected by cushioning.

DISLOCATIONS

Dislocations occur when a joint is displaced from its normal configuration, usually by sudden wrenching force or heavy impact. A dislocation will have many of the same symptoms and indicators as a fracture, although dislocations are confined to a joint and usually remain closed behind the skin.

Apply traction to relocate the joint in its proper place. Do this quickly, as dislocation causes increased muscle spasms and tightening around the joint, which make traction and relocation more difficult with the passage of time. Leave the injury for too long, and the casualty risks gangrene or a permanent deformity.

Traction the joints as for a fracture, before realigning it and lowering the limb steadily back into its normal joint position. Repeat this until the joint is stable and nerve impulses and evidence of circulation are confirmed. To aid recovery after relocation, apply cold packs to the injured joint, then bandage the joint into a stable position and allow it to rest until healed.

Once you have treated a fracture or dislocation, put a bandage around the limb to stabilize its movement. Specific types of bandaging are explained in the illustrations in this chapter. General principles to remember include never

Stabilizing the neck

Keep the head and neck of a spinal injury casualty as still as possible until professional help arrives. Rolled-up towels (A) or even boots (B) can be used as neck supports to prevent lateral movement.

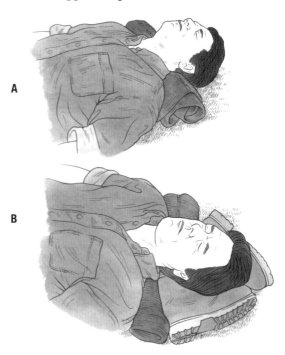

Support sling for a broken arm/elbow

Make an arm sling using a large piece of material folded into a triangular shape (A). The sling should support the arm from behind the elbow to the wrist (B). To stop the injured limb swinging around, tie a support strap across the top of the sling (C).

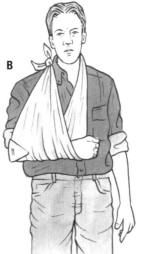

making a bandage so tight it restricts circulation; always bandaging an injured arm to the body to stop it from swinging during movement; and changing the bandage if it becomes soaked to prevent the development of skin problems.

HEAT INJURIES

Heat injuries refer to any condition induced by high environmental temperatures and direct sunlight. The commonest heat injury is sunburn, which can be treated by applying cold compresses and keeping the injured area covered with clothing to allow it to heal.

A more serious condition is dehydration caused by excessive sweating, vomiting or diarrhoea which is not compensated for by sufficient fluid intake. Dehydration produces symptoms such as cramps (caused by loss of body salts), heavy sweating and chronic thirst accompanied by sickness and dizziness. Treatment for mild dehydration is fairly simple: move the casualty somewhere cool and out of direct sunlight; loosen their clothing; give small sips of water very frequently; and allow them to rest until they feel recovered.

Heat exhaustion and heatstroke are more serious developments of dehydration. Heat exhaustion is a severe degree of dehydration and produces additional symptoms such as acute headaches, pale, clammy skin, dizziness, nausea and confusion. Treat the casualty as for dehydration, but prolong the period of rest for at least 24 hours. Watch carefully for symptoms of shock developing.

Heatstroke is a life-threatening condition in which the core temperature of the body climbs above its safe threshold of 36°–38°C (97.8°–100.4°F). Symptoms can be similar to those of heat exhaustion, but more severe in nature and combined with breathing and circulation problems. Heatstroke victims may develop a rapid, weak pulse and can start lapsing in and out of consciousness.

Your priority is to cool the casualty's body and so reduce the core temperature to safe levels. Move the victim quickly to a cool, shaded area. Strip them down to underclothes and spray or soak the whole body with water. Fan their wet body to encourage the evaporation (the water will carry away body heat as it evaporates). Or keep the casualty clothed and continually soak the clothes they are wearing with water to keep it

Treating heat exhaustion
When someone is suffering from mild heat exhaustion, get them to lie down, elevate the legs and give them frequent sips of fluids (do not allow them to gulp the water down quickly).

TIPS FOR DEALING WITH POISONING

• If the poisoning has been caused by ingested plant material, induce vomiting. Do not induce vomiting for poisoning caused by chemicals, as the chemicals can burn the throat when they are regurgitated.

• To absorb some ingested poisons, mix tea and charcoal with an equal part of milk of magnesia. The charcoal absorbs the poison and is passed out of the body.

• If poisons are inhaled, move the casualty to fresh air and loosen tight clothing around the neck and chest. Monitor for signs of respiratory failure, and give artificial respiration if necessary.

• For skin irritants, wash the affected area with soap and water.

• For chemical poisons of the skin, remove contaminated clothing, then sluice the chemicals off the skin with water. Let the water flow off the body, but don't allow it to run over other areas of skin.

For information on treating snake and insect bites, see Chapter 20. For poisoning relating to sea creatures, see Chapter 22.

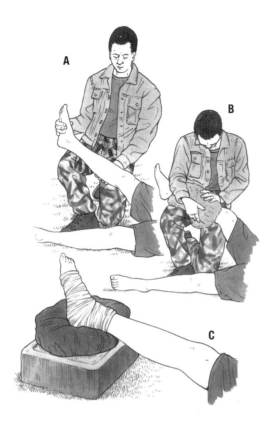

The RICE procedure

To treat a sprain or strain, rest the limb, apply an ice pack and compress to reduce swelling (B and C), then elevate the limb to reduce blood flow to the injury and further control swelling (C).

cold. If the casualty is conscious, give them sips of water to rehydrate them. A more sophisticated rehydration liquid consists of one litre (2 pints) of water into which you dissolve about half a teaspoon of salt and about eight level teaspoons of sugar. This replaces some of the vital sugars and salts lost during dehydration. Continue to monitor the casualty closely for symptoms of shock.

COLD INJURIES

Cold injuries include trench or immersion foot, frostbite and hypothermia. As with heat injuries, the important point is to treat cold injuries as early as possible before they develop into something serious. Take seriously minor symptoms such as tingling or numbness, or

excessive shivering, and watch out for patches of skin that are pale or turning blue. As soon as any symptoms of cold injury are detected, try to get to a warm, dry place, get out of wet clothing and put on dry items, and warm affected parts of the body until circulation returns.

TRENCH OR IMMERSION FOOT

Named after a condition common among soldiers in the trenches of World War I, trench foot results from the feet being kept wet and damp for long periods. The feet go pale and clammy before turning red and swollen, at which point they are vulnerable to infection and gangrene. Remove wet footwear and gently dry the injured foot. Don't massage it or you will damage the vulnerable tissue. In the early stages of trench foot, when the feet are pale, warm them gently in ambient warmth. Do not place them directly in front of a fire or other heat source, as this can lead to gangrene. At the later, swollen stage, try to keep the feet cool. Painkillers may be required. Do not massage the feet or apply direct heat or cold, such as ice. The best way of preventing trench foot is to change your socks regularly throughout the day, replacing a wet pair with dry ones.

FROSTBITE

Frostbite is the literal freezing of body tissue. The most vulnerable parts of the body include the hands and feet, and other areas exposed to the elements, such as the ears and nose. Frostbite symptoms begin with pins and needles, progressing to numbness. The skin goes white and cold before turning blue and blistered, even going black in severe cases. Body parts with severe frostbite will become rock hard as if deeply frozen.

Frostbite requires professional medical treatment, but the immediate priority is to 'thaw out' and warm up the body part with frostbite. Handle the part very carefully to avoid damaging the tissue further. Change wet clothing for dry items. If the hands are frozen, get the casualty to place them between their thighs or under their armpits to warm them through. However, for serious frostbite you may need to thaw the body part by immersing it in hand-hot water. Keep topping the water up to maintain its heat. As the thaw takes place, the casualty will experience severe pain, so administer anti-inflammatory analgesics. Do not burst any blisters that have

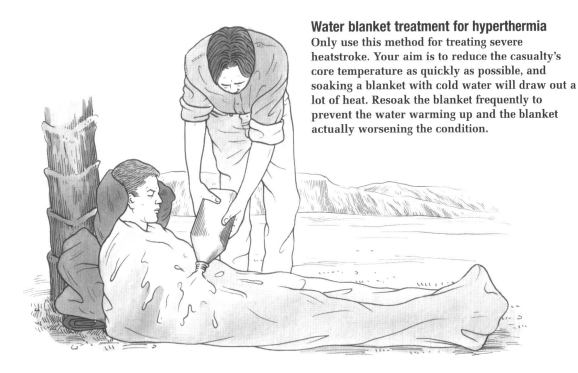

Water blanket treatment for hyperthermia
Only use this method for treating severe heatstroke. Your aim is to reduce the casualty's core temperature as quickly as possible, and soaking a blanket with cold water will draw out a lot of heat. Resoak the blanket frequently to prevent the water warming up and the blanket actually worsening the condition.

formed, and do not let the body part refreeze once it has been warmed through, as the tissue damage would be catastrophic and almost certainly lead to amputation.

HYPOTHERMIA

Hypothermia is the opposite of heatstroke, resulting from the body temperature dropping below 37°C (99°F). Symptoms will develop over time, usually beginning with psychological indicators such as dramatic mood swings, lethargy, an inability to concentrate and clumsiness. As the condition develops, the physical symptoms can include drowsiness, shallow breathing, a slow heart rate and ultimately unconsciousness and even death.

At the first signs of hypothermia, get the casualty to a sheltered, warm place and change them out of their wet clothing. Wrap them in blankets or additional clothing, or put them into a sleeping bag, and hug them to share body warmth. Give them a hot meal and hot drinks if you have them. If the casualty's hypothermia has progressed beyond this stage and they are unconscious, do not give anything by mouth. Wrap the patient up and apply warmth more

directly. A good method is to heat stones over a fire, wrap them in a towel and place them next to places where the blood flow is near the surface of the skin, such as between the thighs, the back of the neck, the pit of stomach, the armpits and the wrists. Be careful, however, not to burn the casualty. Keep the casualty still as their heart muscle will be weakened, and get rescue quickly.

WORMS AND INTESTINAL PARASITES

To prevent worm infestations, cook meat and vegetables before eating, keep food away from excrement, wash your hands after going to the toilet and stay generally clean. In the absence of specialist products, improvised worm treatments include the following:
- Eat hot chilli peppers as part of general diet.
- Dissolve four tablespoons of salt in 1 litre (34 ounces) of water, and drink. One treatment only.
- Eat one cigarette once only in a 24-hour period (note: children should not do this).
- Take two tablespoons of kerosene, once only in a 24-hour period.

CHAPTER FOURTEEN

SURVIVING NATURAL DISASTERS

While many situations arise only in a wilderness setting, natural disasters can hit anywhere. Even modern cities are vulnerable to earthquakes, storms and other extreme conditions.

NATURAL DISASTERS TEND to be unexpected, at least in the long term and to differing extents; however, modern science is becoming better and better at predicting extreme weather and geological conditions. If you live in an area at risk from a particular natural phenomenon, find out what local information resources there are monitoring local environmental activity. Tune into these sources regularly, and be prepared to go into action if the extreme event is heading your way.

FLOODING

Flooding is becoming more common as global warming increases levels of precipitation around the world. It not only occurs through heavy rains, but also when large amounts of meltwater are released from snow and ice, or if rivers or streams are suddenly diverted by mudslides.

If you live in a flood-prone area, prepare your home accordingly. Have a backflow valve fitted on your sewage system to prevent floodwater from pumping sewage up into your home. Purchase a generator-operated pump system to use for pumping out flooded basements or ground-floor rooms. Relocate your main electric circuit breaker panel at least 30cm (12in) above possible flood levels. Store bottled water and food supplies in an upper-floor room (in an emergency, fill up the bathtub with water), along with a gas-powered heating system for warmth. Make sure that the room contains bedding and waterproof

outdoor clothing for all the family. Also make sure you have a battery-powered radio, flashlight and extra batteries.

Once you receive a flood warning through your local media, act immediately. If you are outdoors and there is danger from sudden flash floods, move to high ground and don't go near open

Prepared for blackouts

In the event that you have an older electrical system, make sure that you have all that you need to change a fuse after a blackout. Keep spare fuses next to the fuse box, as well as a torch (flashlight).

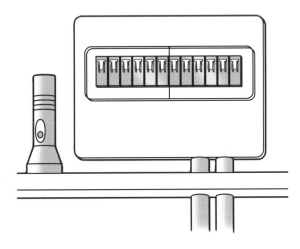

running water. Try to avoid driving if possible, particularly through hilly terrain or by the side of rivers and seas, and don't drive or wade through floodwaters. If your car breaks down, leave the vehicle if it is safe to do so and walk to higher ground. If you cannot leave the car, climb onto its roof and attempt to signal for help.

The worst-case scenario is that your car is swept away by floodwater and sinks with you in it. In this case, wind one of the car windows down a little and allow the vehicle to fill with water – if you try to get out before the car has filled the water pressure will hold the door closed. Take a deep breath just before the waters close over you, then open the door and swim to the surface. If the car has rolled over underwater, you will be disorientated. Blow out a few bubbles from your mouth and observe the direction in which they rise – that is the direction to the surface.

In cases where your home is flooded, make your way to the top of the house, collecting as many vital supplies as you can. If you have to, climb out onto the roof taking a rope with you

and tie yourselves and others to secure rooftop structures such as chimneys.

Houses are dangerous places when they have been flooded. When re-entering the building wear protective clothing. The water will be contaminated with many types of sewage, organic matter and bacteria harmful to health. Do not use electrical appliances. Wear rubber boots in case you tread on an exposed wire or appliance. Do not use any other utilities (particularly your water supply) until your local authorities have approved them. Try to clear the standing water from the home as quickly as possible, before allowing the rooms to dry out naturally. Then disinfect every surface or appliance that has been in contact with the water. Do a thorough structural check of the home also, as floodwaters can severely damage brickwork, steelwork and timber.

TORNADOES, HURRICANES AND STORMS
Hurricanes and tornadoes afflict specific parts of the world, but millions of people live within affected corridors, particularly in the middle and

Flooding while in a car
Just 60cm (2ft) of fast-flowing water can be enough to push a car along. For each 0.3m (1ft) the water rises, an additional 225kg (500lb) of lateral force is applied to the vehicle.

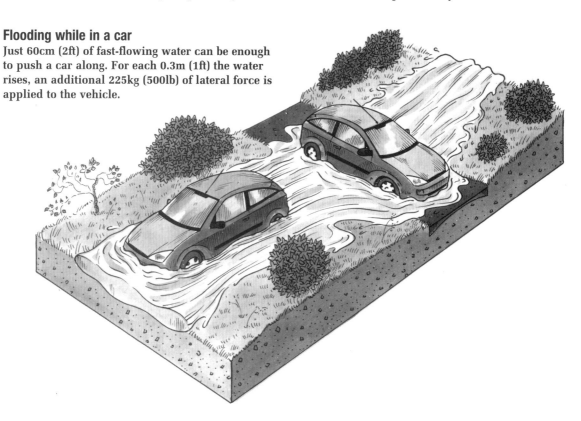

The force of water

Even small waves hitting a structure can cause damage to the foundations and brickwork, while larger waves will cause significant destruction to both foundations and the superstructure. If there is a danger of wave damage, stay on the upper floors of the house.

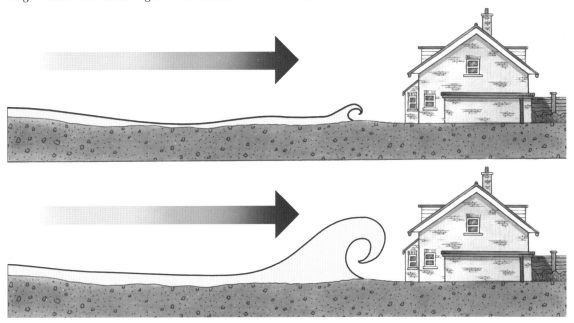

Escaping flood waters

In extreme cases of flooding, put on warm and waterproof clothing, and try to get onto the roof of a building. Take flares, mirrors or pieces of brightly coloured cloth with you to signal for help.

southern states of the United States and across the Far East. If you live in such an area, make sure your home is structurally solid with proper foundation bolts, no loose bricks, tiles or chimneys, and all woodwork and masonry in good condition. Fit hurricane shutters over windows if you live in a high-risk area, or at least have plywood boards ready that can be fitted over the windows in an emergency. Have your home checked over by an approved engineer specializing in storm-damage prevention. Gable-roofed properties are particularly vulnerable to having the roof ripped off by hurricanes, so the engineer may recommend hurricane straps that hold the roof to the walls, or extra bracing.

The response to approaching hurricanes and tornadoes is roughly the same, but with a different time scale. There is usually plenty of warning from meteorological offices about hurricanes that gives you time to prepare your home. Tornadoes can develop unexpectedly out of storm systems, though scientists are becoming better at predicting where tornado outbreaks are likely. Visible signs of tornado conditions include massive dark clouds bringing heavy rain, hailstones, strong winds and lightning. Occasionally, the air may become very still before a tornado strikes. When

one does emerge, it will form into the distinctive funnel shape (made by the dust sucked up by the winds and by condensed water droplets) and roar with a sound like a jet engine. This noise may be your only indication of a tornado during night hours. Look out for other funnel shapes dropping down from the clouds around you – tornadoes can form into groups under the right conditions.

Once a tornado or hurricane has developed,

Anatomy of a tornado

Tornadoes are created when the spiralling updraughts of a storm system create a fast, spiralling downdraught which reaches out from the cloudbase until it touches the ground.

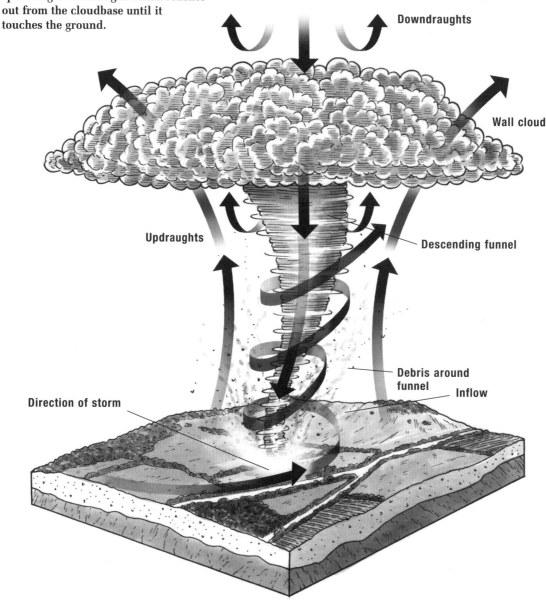

Downdraughts

Wall cloud

Updraughts

Descending funnel

Debris around funnel

Inflow

Direction of storm

Protecting yourself from a tornado
If you are caught in the debris fallout of a tornado, cover your entire head with a thick coat for protection. If the tornado comes towards you, and you can't get to shelter, lie flat in a ditch until the winds subside.

treat the situation with utmost gravity – there should be no 'storm chasing'. Tornadoes have wind speeds of up to 560km/h (350mph) and can be up to 1km (0.6 miles) wide. They are quite capable of tearing a house to pieces, and can also throw out lethal objects, some as big as entire houses, at great speed and to extreme distances. Hurricane winds tend to reach a maximum speed of up to 350km/h (200mph), but they cause damage over a much greater area and often bring massive flooding.

As soon as you see a tornado, or you receive a hurricane warning, move into a secure cellar, tornado/hurricane shelter or any lower-floor room with no external walls, and position yourself in the middle of the room away from corners and windows. Stay away from the upper floors. Take further shelter under a heavy table if necessary. Surround yourself with thick blankets and mattresses to protect against flying glass and debris. Do not open windows to 'equalize pressure' between the outside and inside of the home. Opening the windows will serve only to fill your house with high-velocity debris and give the powerful winds a route of travel. Instead, close all doors and windows, and put up storm shutters. Jam wedges under sliding doors to prevent them being lifted off.

If you have the time, clear your garden or surrounding area of any objects that may become missiles when the winds hit, particularly garden tools and loose branches. Board up the windows. If you live in a mobile home, abandon it for a permanent structure immediately.

If you are outside during the approach of a tornado or hurricane, find a cave, ditch or rocky outcrop to shelter in or under. If you are in a car, drive directly away from a tornado, but if it heads towards you, abandon the vehicle and take shelter. Be careful if you find yourself in the eye of a hurricane. The weather will go very still for a few minutes, but then the storm will return with the winds going in the opposite direction. Therefore, don't move from shelter during this period unless it is to move to a better protective location.

Once in shelter, wait for the hurricane or tornado to pass. Stay tuned to the radio for emergency advice and information – you should have with you a portable, battery-powered radio. Once the storm is over, proceed with caution. Get out of a building if you smell gas or chemical fumes, or if the structure appears unstable. Do not turn utilities back on without consulting utility companies and emergency services first. Be watchful for frayed or dangerous wiring.

HEAVY SNOW
Specific advice for survival in subzero climates is given in Chapter 18. Here we will look at urban

and vehicular scenarios for coping with heavy snowfall conditions, especially blizzards. Blizzards are heavy snowstorms with winds in excess of 56km/h (35mph) and temperatures below −6°C (20°F). The dangers of blizzards include hypothermia, frostbite and traffic accidents.

If you receive a blizzard warning, prepare your home and vehicle in advance. Have flashlights and a battery-operated radio ready, and also make sure your cell phone (mobile phone) is charged up in case landlines come down in the snow. Stock up on emergency supplies of water and nonperishable food. To help keep pathways and entrances clear, have a snow shovel and supplies of salt and sand at the ready. You should also refuel your car and check that the car's antifreeze is at the correct concentration. Put cold-weather clothing, a thick blanket, a shovel, a first-aid kit, some bottled water, a flashlight and a safety reflector in the trunk (boot) of the car.

The basic rules of surviving a blizzard are to

AVOIDING LIGHTNING STRIKES

- Avoid making yourself the tallest object or standing near the tallest object in your immediate area.
- Avoid potential conductors such as wire, metal and water.
- Get into a building or car if a lightning strike is possible.
- Stand away from others to avoid conduction through the group if anyone is struck.
- Avoid using the telephone, electrical appliances or metal objects such as ladders and taps (faucets).
- If you feel your hair stand on end – the indicator of an imminent lightning strike – jump into a shelter or drop to a crouching position straight away, keeping as low to the ground as you possibly can.
- Avoid water.

Safety when lightning threatens
When lightning is close, drop into a crouching position with as few physical contact points to the ground as possible. Never take refuge under a tree or similar tall structure, as any such feature will be an attractant for the lightning.

stay indoors and keep warm. Should you suffer a power cut, put on cold-weather clothing before you become really cold. Light candles for illumination, but never leave them unattended. A better alternative is a paraffin (kerosene) lantern, which can provide bright lighting for up to 45 hours on one filling. Eat regular meals and have hot drinks, but avoid alcohol.

Try to live in one room for maximum heat conservation. Stuff towels or newspapers in cracks under doors, and hang blankets over the windows to keep out draughts and provide extra installation. If you have a self-contained heating system, such as a paraffin (kerosene) or oil heater, use it, but only if you can provide enough ventilation – carbon monoxide poisoning is a silent killer that gives no warning. For safety, turn off the heater at night when you should be tucked up under blankets and quilts (duvets). Sleep in a hat to prevent heat loss from your head. Also be cautious about using long-forgotten fireplaces in which to make a fire. Check that the flues are not

Building damage

After a storm, flooding or powerful winds, do not enter a house if you suspect it has structural damage. Look for cracks in the masonry, broken widow frames and door jambs, and roof damage.

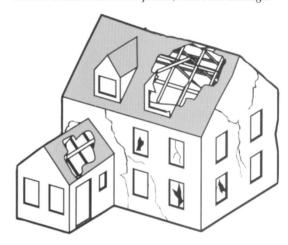

Hazards following a natural disaster

After a natural disaster, there are many hazards to be faced. Not only may local infrastructure be ruined, but also social order may temporarily collapse. In the case of forest fires, dangerous wildlife such as snakes may be forced into urban areas. Always have a stockpile of survival supplies, enough for you and your family to survive for about a week.

Keeping warm

In freezing conditions when the heating has failed, gather the family into one room and huddle together for warmth, blocking off any source of draughts. Here this family is using newspaper as an extra insulating material.

blocked, otherwise smoke and fumes will back up into the house or there could be a chimney fire.

If you are trapped inside a vehicle during a snowstorm, don't be tempted to leave it. It will be much easier for rescuers to find you if you remain in a vehicle, especially if you intermittently sound the horn, flash the lights (at night) and tie a bright piece of cloth to the antenna of the car to act as a distress signal. Each hour, run the vehicle's motor for about 10 minutes to provide a burst of heat without depleting fuel supplies dramatically. Never attempt to burn anything inside the vehicle as a heat source.

FOREST FIRES

The improper or unauthorized starting of campfires in woodland areas frequently causes forest fires. Make sure you know what you are doing when starting a campfire, especially in a dry area. Avoid lighting a fire at all in hot and windy conditions – sparks and ash will be blown into the dry brush, where the winds quickly fan them into flames. If you do light a fire, clear the ground of leaves, grasses and twigs to make a patch of bare earth at least 2m (6ft) in diameter, and build the fire in the middle of the cleared circle. If there is a lot of foliage around you, a sensible precaution is to light the fire in a trench at least 30cm (1ft) deep, or to surround the fire with large, dry stones.

Duck, cover and hold

In the case of an earthquake when you are inside a building, duck down, take cover under a solid table and hold on to one of the table legs to prevent it moving away from you.

If you see an unwanted fire developing, extinguish it with water immediately, or if water is not available use a branch with green leaves to smother it. Look also for professional fire beaters, usually consisting of a pole with a tarpaulin flap at one end, which are often provided in popular forests. When tackling or avoiding any fire, do not stand uphill of the flames, as fires burn more

Emergency water supply

Emergency water can be found in many different sources, although water from the hot-water tank and the toilet tank may need purifying before drinking. Do not drink chemically treated water.

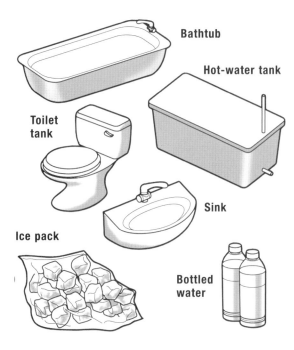

Bathtub

Hot-water tank

Toilet tank

Sink

Ice pack

Bottled water

rapidly uphill. Once a fire starts to burn out of control, get to safety as quickly as possible, moving into the wind and away from the flames. Again, avoid running uphill if possible. To guard against smoke inhalation, soak a piece of cotton material in water (avoid synthetic materials, which can melt) and wrap it around your nose and mouth. If possible, wear a long-sleeved shirt or top, and trousers rather than shorts – in natural materials such as cotton. If you have one, a cycling helmet can protect your hair from airborne burning debris.

If you are trapped by a fire, first try to find a pond, lake or river to crouch in, or at least look for shelter in rocky areas or clearings. Lie down and breathe the cooler hair close to the ground – do not stand up as superheated air above you could burn your lungs and throat, and even cause your clothes to combust. If an escape through flames is your only option, choose a section of fire that is burning low (don't try to run through

head-high flames) and which has a clear refuge a short way across the other side, usually an area which has already been burnt. Soak your clothes and hair with water if you have access to it, then run with all the speed you can straight through the flames. If your clothes catch fire, once you are safe, roll yourself on the ground to smother them.

EARTHQUAKE

If you know that you live in a zone of earthquake risk, make sure you practise or at least understand earthquake drills organized by your local authority and company. As with other types of disaster, it is also good to prepare the home for the disruption of utilities, heat and food supplies should an earthquake strike.

Earthquakes are by nature unexpected. If you are caught inside a building when an earthquake strikes, follow the 'duck, cover, hold' response. Drop down to the floor, take cover beneath a solid desk or table, and hold on to one of its legs to stop it from moving away from you. Wait there until the earthquake passes. If you live in an earthquake-prone area, it is worth investing in a large, sturdy table for protection, spacious enough to house your family beneath it during a tremor. If you can't get underneath a table, position yourself against an interior wall. Whether inside or outside a building during an earthquake, stay away from any structure likely to collapse or fall, such as exterior walls, mirrors, doorways, ornamental masonry and heavy bookcases. Keep well clear of windows or any other forms of glass sheeting which are liable to shatter from the vibrations.

Once the earthquake is over, the building you are in may be an imminent danger of collapse or fire (from broken gas mains). Listen for sounds of falling masonry, plaster, ceiling tiles or timber, and look for cracks appearing in ceilings and walls. In darkness, do not use open flames to provide illumination or you could trigger a gas explosion. If you suspect the building is about to collapse, get out quickly, avoiding the use of elevators or suspect stairways. Once outside, report the condition of the building to the building management or local fire department immediately. If a building has collapsed, do not go back inside the debris to look for survivors. Instead, inform rescue personnel exactly where you last saw any people inside the building and let the professionals handle it.

The general rule in earthquakes is to stay inside. The environment outside will be hazardous from falling debris. If you are caught outdoors, try to stand in an open area away from hazardous objects such as trees, power lines, road signs and buildings. Likewise, if you are driving, pull over to a safe location – try to avoid parking under overpasses, bridges, trees and streetlights. Stay inside the vehicle until the earthquake finishes. If a power line or telephone line falls on the car, don't get out and never try to move it manually. Once the earthquake finishes, try not to drive your car if possible, as the streets will be full of hazards. Instead wait for rescue services to get to you and provide instructions.

DROUGHT

Drought is an unusual condition in the developed world, but with global temperatures rising year on year, and the water resources of many countries stretched to the limit, it has become a more widespread possibility. The treatment of heat-related injuries is covered in Chapter 13, and advice on how to find sources of water can be found in Chapter 6.

If drought seems a future possibility, store large amounts of bottled drinking water in a cool, dark location. Try to store at least 4.5 litres (1.2 gallons) of water per person, per day, to cover a two-week period. If water supplies are suddenly cut off without time for preparation, use water contained around the house in the hot-water tank, cold-water storage tank and the cistern (not the bowl) of the toilet. Water from these locations is not designed to be drunk, so filter and purify it first before drinking. Also, gather any ice from the inside of the freezer and melt it down into water.

Some small amounts of water will be contained in water pipes around the house. To access it, turn on a tap (faucet) at the highest level in your home. This injects air into the system. Now turn on the lowest tap (faucet) in the house, and water will trickle out. Do not drink water from radiators, as this will contain harmful metallic and mineral elements, and may also be polluted with anti-limescale chemicals.

VOLCANO

Volcanic eruptions are rare events. In addition, most active volcanoes within the vicinity of urban settlements are closely monitored. If you

Volcanoes

Volcanic eruptions occur in many different types. Some will simply ooze slow-moving lava, while others will detonate with a huge explosion (as seen here). Regardless of type, put many miles between you and the eruption.

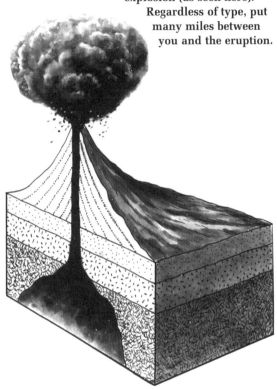

live in such as area, read any information provided by local authorities, particularly evacuation routes, the location of public shelters and any systems for casualty treatment.

Volcanoes present many varied dangers. Lava is usually the least of dangers to people, as it tends to move slowly, at about 1m (3ft) per minute. If the slope is steep and the lava emission is heavy, however, this speed can increase to 400m (1312ft) per minute, or 22km/h (14mph), which can overtake a person. Far more dangerous are the various aerial missiles flung out from volcanic explosions. Pieces of solidified and semimolten rock, some pieces weighing as much as eight tons, can be blown out to distances of 5km (3 miles). Tons of fine ash descends from the sky, threatening asphyxiation and eventually crushing buildings as it piles up.

Landslides and mudslides

Landslides and mudslides can occur after extremely heavy rainfall, when loose earth is saturated with water, or following an earthquake which has disrupted the stability of a rock face.

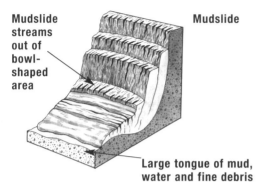

Mudslide streams out of bowl-shaped area

Mudslide

Large tongue of mud, water and fine debris

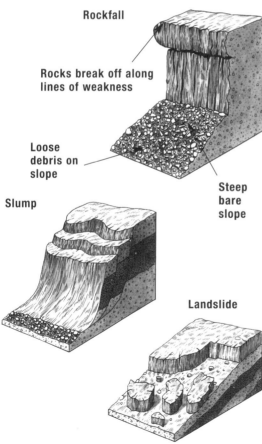

Rockfall

Rocks break off along lines of weakness

Loose debris on slope

Steep bare slope

Slump

Landslide

Most lethal of all is pyroclastic flow. This is a horrifying mixture of ash, lava fragments and superheated gas that can move at hundreds of miles per hour. To be hit by a pyroclastic flow usually means certain death, as the citizens of Pompeii discovered following the eruption of Mount Vesuvius in AD 79. Volcanoes can precipitate many secondary disasters, including flash floods, landslides and mudslides, thunderstorms and tsunamis.

Should you receive an eruption warning, you must evacuate the area immediately. Make your evacuation with great speed if you are experiencing earthquakes, which often precede volcanic eruptions. Put as much distance as you can between you and the volcano, ideally about 16km (10 miles). Plan an alternative route to use if your main escape route is blocked. If you cannot make too much distance between you and the volcano, try to get to high ground. Pyroclastic flow runs down the side of the volcano and along the floor, and may run out of steam if you are at an elevation.

One danger you will struggle to escape is falling ash. Wear protective goggles and a breathing mask, or fashion a breathing mask out of a damp cloth. Stay inside if safe, but watch for any cracks in the ceilings or walls developing, or sounds of cracking timber or masonry as the weight of volcanic ash piles up. Evacuate the building if you think collapse is imminent. If you have to walk outside, don't wear shoes with synthetic soles, as these are liable to melt on the hot roads.

Be observant for signs of landslides or mudslides. Listen out for rumbling sounds. If you are inside a building, watch for the development of structural faults or doors inexplicably sticking. Evacuate the building if it is in the path of the mudslide, but only if you have time to escape. Should you not have time to escape, follow the same type of duck, cover and hold response you would use in an earthquake. Outside, signs of an impending mudslide can be water bursting from the ground in strange places, cracks spreading across the ground and outdoor structures beginning to move. A mudslide travels fast, so don't think of trying to outrun it. Try to move out of its path to one side or head up to high ground. Avoid going up onto bridges, as mudslides are often powerful enough to bring these down. If you are caught, curl up in a ball, protect your head and hope for the best.

•CHAPTER FIFTEEN

RESCUE PROCEDURES

In a survival emergency, you need a clear plan of how to reach safety or attract a rescue. While creative thinking is important, following recommended rescue procedures is also vital.

THE FIRST STAGE in a survival emergency is to evaluate the seriousness of the threat. This is a complex equation, but if careful analysis of your situation reveals that you or other members of your group are in a danger you cannot remove without external help you need to effect a rescue plan. The rescue plan acquires more urgency if you or someone else is injured. Administering first aid is your immediate priority, followed by the need to get the casualty to professional medical care. You are faced with two choices: go and get help, or bring help to you.

USING COMMUNICATIONS
If possible, avoid making long journeys in a survival emergency. You will, or soon will be, under intense physical stress, and further journeys will place your body under increased risk of fatigue and exhaustion. Furthermore, transporting casualties across the wilderness may aggravate their condition and even endanger their lives.

If you have any sort of communications devices – VHF radio, homing beacon or satellite phone – use it to contact the emergency services directly. If in a foreign country, make sure you know in advance the telephone numbers of the emergency services and a few basic phrases to convey your situation. VHF survival radios are useful because they do not have to obtain a satellite signal, but they do have limitations. They are generally line-of-sight devices (the signals do not travel well around large obstructions) and their batteries can be quickly exhausted by repeated emergency transmissions.

For most successful use of a VHF radio, position yourself on an elevated feature overlooking the terrain, or move yourself to terrain with as few natural obstacles (trees, ragged mountain faces, large hills and so on) as possible. Alternatively, extend the aerial using any available wire. Set the radio to Channel 16 (the international Mayday channel – not to be used for any other type of broadcast), turn it to its highest power of broadcast and make a Mayday call in the following format:

Press the transmit button, pause, then say the following slowly and clearly. 'MAYDAY, MAYDAY, MAYDAY. This is …' give your name, or your vessel's name if at sea. Repeat three times. 'My position is …' State where you are either as a grid reference or as an accurate description of your location. If the latter, try to provide a distance and bearing from an easily identifiable feature. State the nature of the emergency without overdramatizing or embellishing the situation, explaining how many people are involved, and whether there are any casualties. Provide details of any injuries. Finish the broadcast by saying 'OVER', then release the transmit button and listen for a reply.

Repeat the message regularly until you receive a response. Don't use the radio unnecessarily, as repeated broadcasts at high power will soon drain the batteries.

VHF (very high frequency) radio

Global Maritime Distress and Safety System (GMDSS)

GMDSS functions when the survivor turns on an Emergency Position Indicating Radio Beacon (EPIRB). The signal is transmitted via satellite to a Marine Rescue and Coordination Centre (MRCC) within 5 minutes.

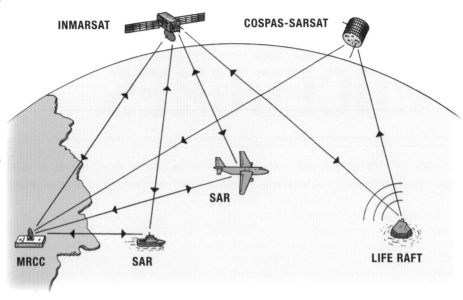

Search methods

The sweep search and square search are methods used by search parties to make their search of a land area methodical and comprehensive. These methods are most successful when the survivors remain in one position, rather than move around.

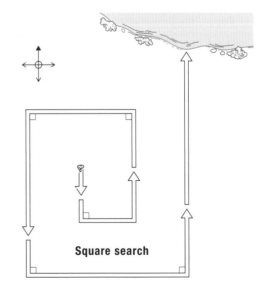

Sweep search

Square search

Important note: DO NOT issue a Mayday call unless you are in a dire emergency you cannot handle and where serious injury or loss of life is possible. Any Mayday call will mobilize major search and rescue activities, and the penalties for improper use can be severe.

GETTING HELP

If communications systems are not available, and it is unlikely that a rescue party will be sent out automatically, or that the rescue effort will come too late, then you have to go for help. When a casualty is involved and your group numbers three or more people, determine who will go for help and who will stay with the casualty. In a three-person group, one goes for help and the others stay with the casualty. If a four-person group (or more), two people should go for help, while the remainder stay with the casualty. Obviously, two-person groups present a problem.

Marking a trail

Assist search parties by leaving trail markers which indicate your direction of travel, and also alerting them to any possible dangers ahead. Dismantle signs which are no longer relevant.

This is the road

Turn to the left

Turn to the right

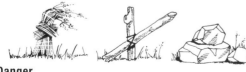

Danger

As a general rule, don't leave the casualty alone. You should have left details of your planned route and schedule with a third party, so wait until he or she activates a rescue. Even if no one is aware of your journey, try to stay put and attract the attention of others using some of the methods described below.

However, in some cases you may be compelled to go in search of rescue. If you have to, or if your are the person chosen from a group to go for help, write down the following details before you set off:

- The position of the survivors. Note down a map reference, or better still mark the position on a spare map if you have one. Ensure you mark the location accurately – take a GPS reading if possible.
- A physical description of the location, e.g. eastern ridgeline at 1800m (6000ft) on Mount X, or dry riverbed 6km (4 miles) west of village Y.
- Full details of any casualties so the correct medical services can be assigned. Note the name and age of the casualty, a description of injuries and general condition, the time of the accident, the weather conditions and any first-aid treatment given.
- The number and condition of the rest of the party, explaining what survival equipment they have and how advanced their survival skills.

UNDERSTANDING SEARCH PARTIES

Search parties follow specific search techniques designed to maximize the chances of your being found. Understanding these techniques is helpful in guiding your methods of attracting attention and knowing whether to move or not.

If the exact location of the survivors is not known, the search will begin at their last known position, from where the search party will begin a sweep of the planned or likely route. The 'sweep search' involves a line of searchers spread out at intervals abreast to maximize visual coverage. If the initial sweep search fails to find the survivors, then the search is gradually expanded into areas either side of the route.

A 'square search' is used when no planned route or even direction of travel is known. Like the sweep search, it begins around the last known position of the missing party. From here the searchers set off in one direction – here we'll say south – and walk for a fixed time measured in minutes (say, 20 minutes). At the end of this time, they turn 90° (a compass is essential for a square search) and walk east for the same period (20 minutes). Then they turn 90° again to face north and walk for twice the original time (40 minutes), then west for the same period (40 minutes). If executed correctly, the party should cover a

Morse code

The Morse code is useful for communicating across long distances. Keep a printed copy of the code in your backpack or pocket for use in emergencies.

A . _	O _ _ _	3 . . . _ _
B _ . . .	P . _ _ .	4 . . . . _
C _ . _ .	Q _ _ . _	5 . . . . .
D _ . .	R . _ .	6 _ . . . .
E .	S . . .	7 _ _ . . .
F . . _ .	T _	8 _ _ _ . .
G _ _ .	U . . _	9 _ _ _ _ .
H	V . . . _	0 _ _ _ _ _
I . .	W . _ _	
J . _ _ _	X _ . . _	
K _ . _	Y _ . _ _	
L . _ . .	Z _ _ . .	
M _ _	1 . _ _ _ _	
N _ .	2 . . _ _	

MORSE CODE SOS

A Morse code SOS is sent by nine signals: three short, three long, then three short. These signals, or any Morse code message, can be sent by a variety of means: auditory (whistle, foghorn and so on), visual (flashing torch, heliograph), and by using professional communications tools (radio with Morse keypad).

specific square of ground, and they repeat this pattern in different locations for as long as necessary. Terrain and climate dictate the distance travelled in a square search. Survivors themselves can use the sweep search and square search if they are looking for a lost member of the group, but only if this will not result in a major deviation from a planned route.

A group of survivors can help a search party in the following ways – by staying put in one location and by using signalling techniques to attract attention.

SIGNALLING
The purpose of signalling is to advertise your location over long distances. There is a range of commercially produced signalling devices, which are excellent for this purpose, the most practical being flares. Flares come in a variety of forms. Hand-held flares produce a brightly coloured smoke by day or a very harsh light by night visible up to 8km (5 miles) away. Orange smoke is the international distress signal for daytime. There are also flares that are fired up to altitude from either a purpose-designed gun or a preloaded container. They descend slowly, sometimes on a parachute, and are visible up to 40km (25 miles) away (even through adverse climatic conditions) and can lift above terrain masking.

Ideally, try to carry a mixture of flare types, such as two smoke flares, two night flares and two aerial flares. If space is tight, 'mini-flares' are available, with eight small, red flares contained in a neat waterproof package. Always follow flare instructions very carefully, holding the flare at arm's length, pointing it at the sky and standing downwind of the smoke and flame.

FIRE AND SMOKE SIGNALS
If flares are not available, a fire is a good way to create a high-visibility signal. By day you want to create a fire that produces plenty of smoke. Green boughs, oil or rubber are superb smoke manufacturers when lit, but try to create a smoke that contrasts with the terrain background. Smouldering green leaves, moss or damp wood produce white smoke, whereas rubber or oil-soaked rags produce black smoke.

Keep all fire-making materials readily accessible, preferably made up into an unlit fire and covered to keep dry, ready to light when you

CLEAR GROUND-TO-AIR SIGNALS

Modify surrounding terrain to form ground signals visible from the air:

- In snow, build up snow mounds to cast shadows. Alternatively, tramp down the snow to form letters or symbols, and fill in the contours with contrasting materials, such as twigs or branches
- In tundra areas, patterns can be made by digging trenches or gouging deep symbols into the surface of the soil
- Boulders, vegetation and seaweed can be used to form symbols in sand
- In brush-covered areas, cut out or burn (carefully) patterns in the grasses or plants
- Make sure your signals are straight and have sharp angles in contrast with nature's irregular shapes

Ground-to-air signals

Ground-to-air signals are useful for communicating with aircraft. Make the signals very visible (see feature box opposite) and, as always, remove those no longer relevant.

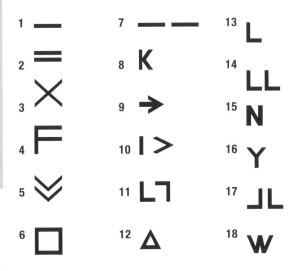

1	Need doctor – serious injuries
2	Need medical supplies
3	Unable to proceed
4	Need food and water
5	Need firearms and ammunition
6	Need map and compass
7	Need signal lamp with battery and radio
8	Indicate direction to proceed
9	Am proceeding in this direction
10	Will attempt takeoff
11	Aircraft seriously damaged
12	Probably safe to land here
13	Need food and oil
14	All well
15	No
16	Yes
17	Not understood
18	Need engineer

see a search party or ship, or hear an aircraft. Or you can simply set fire to an entire tree – pitch-bearing trees will readily burn when green, and other types of trees can be ignited by placing dry wood in the lower branches and igniting it. Select an isolated tree for this technique, otherwise you could start a forest fire.

Unless you are close to civilization, don't light the fire on the off chance someone might see it – this is a waste of material. If possible, try to coat the fire materials in some flammable accelerant, such as fuel or oil, so that you can raise a blaze almost immediately.

In terms of locating your fire, site it in open terrain if possible to maximize visibility. If you are in a forest, build the fire in a clearing where the smoke can rise into the air unhindered by foliage. Alternatively, find a river or lake, and send fires on rafts into the open water, not forgetting to anchor or tether the rafts in position. If trees or vegetation surround you, to reduce the risk of a forest or grassland fire, build earth walls around the fire. In snowy conditions, set the fire above the wet ground on a raised platform made from stones to stop it from burning down to the snow and being extinguished.

GROUND-TO-AIR SIGNALS

There are an internationally recognized set of ground-to-air signals used for communicating with a search aircraft (see the illustration above

right), and you should carry a diagram of these signals with you on any survival expedition. The signals are created from any material or terrain modification that contrasts strongly with its background. The signals need to be at least 10m (33ft) long and 3m (10ft) wide for each bar of a letter. Fluorescent-orange commercial marker panels are available, and these save the effort of gathering materials, though be aware that orange can blend into green or brown backgrounds.

You can, however, make effective ground-to-air signals in many different ways. Suitable materials

Body signals

Deliver body signals with clear, emphatic body movements. Avoid any extraneous movements which might be interpreted as signals, and be very clear about what it is that you want to happen.

Our receiver is operating   **Affirmative (yes)**   **Can proceed shortly, wait if practicable**   **Need mechanical help or parts, long delay**   **Pick us up, aircraft abandoned**

Do not attempt to land here   **Use drop message**   **All OK, do not wait**   **Negative**   **Land here (point in direction of landing)**   **Need medical assistance urgently**

include bright objects such as clothes, waterproof jackets and sleeping bags, pieces of wreckage, rocks, vegetation or marks cut into earth or snow, or indeed anything that stands out visually. Throwing shadows can also make signals. Dig a trench in soil or snow, and heap the spoil on one side to create strong shadow patterns. At night, cut a signal into the ground, pour in fuel and ignite to create a highly visible signal that will remain as charred, blackened ground in the daytime.

Locate the signals in places where they can be seen from all directions, preferably a flat, open area, and be sure to remove the symbols after rescue or if you move to another location.

BODY SIGNALS

Body signals are used to communicate over distance with rescue parties or with the crew of an aircraft that has spotted you. The illustration in this chapter shows the internationally recognized set of body signals. Make the signals with very expansive, exaggerated, clear body movements, and hold a brightly coloured rag in each hand to give the arm actions extra visual

strength. If the aircraft crew has understood your message, it will dip the aircraft's wings up and down in daylight, or make green flashes with its signal lights at night. If the pilot circles the aircraft during daylight, or makes red signal-light flashes at night, he or she has not understood your message. Once a pilot has received and understood your first message, you can transmit other messages.

REFLECTORS AND HELIOGRAPHS

Direct sunlight reflected from a highly polished metal object or a mirror can be seen for 100km (62 miles) under normal conditions and more than 160km (100 miles) in a desert environment, and so is an excellent method of signalling. An improvised reflector can be any reflective object, including hand mirrors, polished metal lids, DVDs and compact discs.

The purpose of a reflector is to flash the sun's rays towards a rescue party or search aircraft. First, catch the sunlight on the reflector and direct it onto the ground in front of you. Then, look towards your target and move the reflector so the

Using a flare

Hold flares at arm's length, and keep the flare downwind of you so that the smoke and flame do not blow across you. Keep the flare well clear of flammable structures.

Attracting attention

Make hand signals as bold as possible by holding large pieces of brightly coloured material or purpose-designed signal flags.

Signalling with a mirror

When used properly, signal mirrors have a range of between 16 and 48km (10 and 30 miles). Direct the flashes at search parties and towards flying aircraft or nearby ships.

patch of light on the ground is channelled in a straight line towards your target. Another method of using a reflector is to hold it close to your face in one hand, holding the other hand at arm's length and aimed at the target, and shining the reflected light onto the outstretched hand. When the light hits your outstretched hand, drop the hand and the beam of reflected sunlight should be aimed towards your target. Make a flashing action with the reflector by wiggling it side to side.

A heliograph is basically a professional reflector, designed for more accurate directing of the sunlight towards the target. It is a rectangular piece of metal polished to a mirror finish on both sides, with a small hole in the middle. The heliograph is held just in front of your face. With one eye closed, you sight your target through the hole. As you look into the near side of the heliograph, you will see your face with a tiny dot of light on it, where the sun is shining through the hole. Angle the heliograph so that the dot of light 'drops' into the hole, but keep the target in sight. When the dot of light disappears, the sunlight is reflected directly towards the target.

AUDITORY DISTRESS SIGNALS

Auditory signals are useful ways of attracting attention in poor visibility or night-time conditions. They include any method of producing a loud noise, such as shouting, but whistles and foghorns are particularly useful for their noise projection. A commonly used international distress signal is six long blasts of a whistle (or six flashes of a light for a visual signal) evenly spread over one minute, followed by a minute of silence, and repeated as necessary.

Distress signals

Noise signals can carry extremely well in wilderness areas, particularly at night and in still weather. Light signals are obviously suited to night-time and low-light conditions.

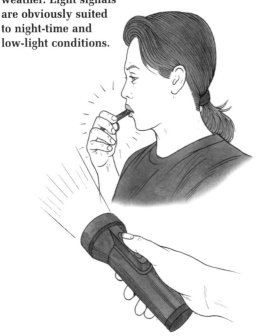

Helicopter rescue strop

When a strop is lowered to you, place it over your head and tuck it securely under your armpits. Do not hold on to the rope above your head; instead, cross your hands over your chest.

AVIATION AND RESCUE

Helicopters and light fixed-wing aircraft are now commonly used in search-and-rescue operations. Fixed-wing aircraft are unlikely to be able to stop and pick you up, but they will give an accurate relay of your position to a land-based search party or a helicopter rescue team. For helicopter rescues, you need to know the correct rescue procedures to ensure your safety and that of the helicopter crew during the rescue.

Helicopters effect rescues either by landing and picking up casualties or, in difficult terrain, by lowering a winch and hoisting the casualty on board while hovering. A landing is the preferred option, except over water where the winch is obviously more suited.

To aid the helicopter rescue, try to get yourself to a good landing zone (LZ). The LZ should ideally be about 50m (152ft) in diameter, with a clear approach from the air (ideally of around 400m/1200ft), be fairly level (a slope not greater than 1-in-10), and be free of obstructions such as telephone poles, trees, rocks and so on. Also examine the ground for large holes that could be a danger to the helicopter's landing gear. Now examine the LZ for debris. The force of a helicopter's rotor blades will send any loose material flying when it lands, so clear away as many branches, leaves and twigs as possible, and secure equipment such as tents and sleeping bags, which could be sucked into the rotor blades. In snowy conditions, try to compress the snow in the LZ by stamping on it or rolling heavy objects over it. This reduces the amount of snow drawn into the air to restrict the pilot's vision.

When a helicopter comes in to land, be very careful of its rotors (main rotor and tail rotor). Do not approach it until it has come to a halt and a crew member signals you to come forward. Never approach a helicopter from the rear – it is a blind spot for the crew and the tail rotor is unprotected. Never go down a slope to a helicopter, as the main rotor tips will be closer to the ground there.

For a winch rescue, allow the winch cable to touch the ground before you grab it so that it can discharge any static electricity into the ground, rather than you. If a member of the crew descends to you, follow his instructions to the letter. If, however, only a strop is dropped to you, place it over your head and arms, and fit it snugly under your armpits. Slide the adjusting ring down towards your chest to tighten, then give a thumbs-up sign to the winch-man to let him know you are ready. Fold your arms across your chest, or hold them down vertically at your sides. Do not raise them above your head, even to hold on to the rope, as you could slide out of the strop.

When you reach the cabin door, let the winch-man bring you in, and keep your arms in their original position. The winch-man will bring you into the helicopter and show you where to sit.

Helicopter landing zone
Although helicopters are designed for vertical landing, they still need a landing strip of a few hundred metres to allow them to make a proper approach, especially in high winds.

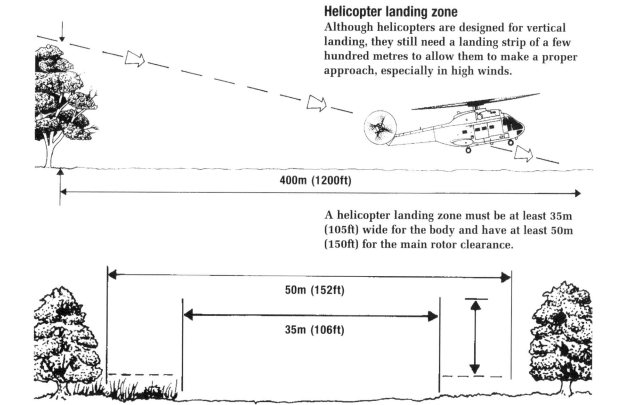

400m (1200ft)

A helicopter landing zone must be at least 35m (105ft) wide for the body and have at least 50m (150ft) for the main rotor clearance.

50m (152ft)

35m (106ft)

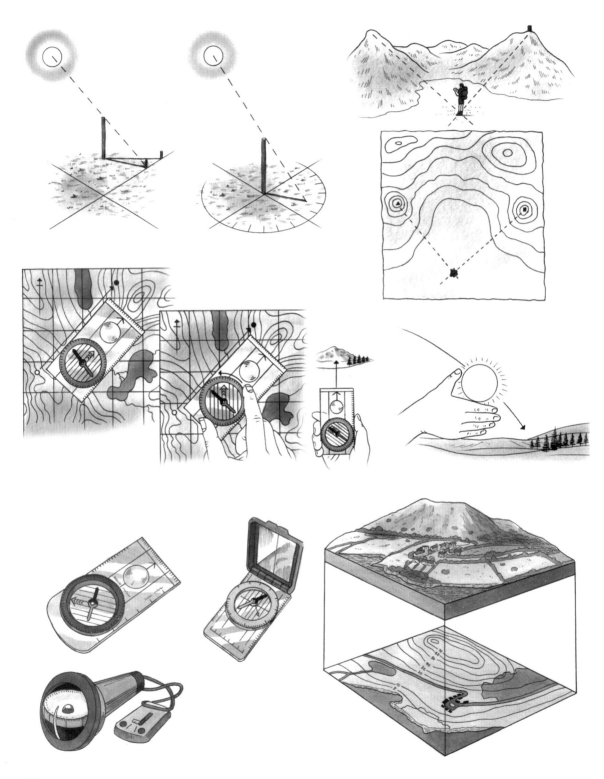

CHAPTER SIXTEEN

SURVIVAL NAVIGATION

A compass and map are the basic tools of navigation in the wilderness. When these are not available, however, nature and the skies provide other resources for finding your way.

BEFORE HEADING OFF on any outdoor activity or adventure, learn the basic techniques of navigation from an expert guide. At its simplest, accurate navigation requires nothing more than a good map and a compass. Many outdoor enthusiasts, however, are now using Global Positioning Satellite (GPS) systems. The GPS system uses a hand-held receiver to pick up signals from orbiting US satellites. The receiver uses the signals to triangulate its position and give the operator his or her precise map coordinates. More sophisticated receivers will even present a map actually showing the operator's location. It is undeniable that the GPS is an excellent piece of equipment to take into the wilderness. Yet GPS receivers are sensitive electronic tools that can be damaged or fail in an emergency. When this happens, traditional navigational skills are required.

MAPWORK

Maps are vital to understanding your place in a landscape. Choose high-quality maps produced by authoritative cartographic companies, and make sure you understand the system of symbols used by the mapmakers. Choose an appropriate scale of map. A typical outdoor map scale is 1:50,000. This means that one

Hand-held global positioning satellite (GPS) device

unit of measurement on the map represents 50,000 of the same unit on the ground. Maps will also provide a scale guide so that you can measure out distances in useful increments such as 1km (0.6 miles) or 1 mile (1.6km). If travelling through areas of dangerous terrain, get a large-scale map to provide you with as much detail as possible.

Maps represent the gradient and shape of land through contour lines. Contour lines are usually brown/orange. They connect areas of the same height, and are set at regular distances apart from one another, such as 30m (98ft). However, they will not be evenly spaced on the map – the aerial perspective of the map means that, if the land is rising at a steep gradient, the lines will be closer together, and conversely more widely spaced on shallow land.

Two further guides to landscape elevation are spot heights and trig points. Spot heights are usually shown as black spots with a figure by the side of it giving the feature's height above sea level. Trig points denote physical points of reference – usually small triangular concrete blocks – which show altitude and location, and are used in survey triangulations. On the map, trig points generally appear as black triangles.

Navigation maps are divided up into grid lines. The lines running vertically (north–south) are called 'northings', while the lines running horizontally (east–west) are called 'eastings'. Your position on the map is plotted using the grid lines to produce a six-figure number. The first three numbers consist of the eastings grid square location plus the location within the square represented by measurements of tenths, for example, 245 (square 25 plus 5 tenths – halfway – across the square). The same measurement method is repeated for northings, and, where the two points of measurement intersect, the point is represented as a six-figure number. (Refer to the illustration for a graphic explanation of this process.)

COMPASS AND MAP NAVIGATION
A Silva compass is the standard compass for outdoor compass navigation, being tough (tested from -40°C to +60°C), and accurate. The two basic procedures you need to learn are to take a directional bearing and to calculate your position from two compass readings.

To take a directional bearing, point the arrow

Navigation screens
GPS screens can present you with a large array of information.
On some models, pre-programmed mapwork is displayed along with directional arrows and map coordinates.

A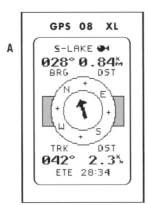

B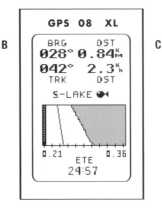

C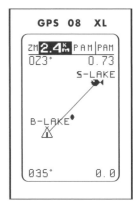

TIPS FOR SELECTING AND USING A GPS RECEIVER

- Try to get a GPS receiver with a detachable antenna. The antenna can then be elevated to get the clearest possible signal.
- Purchase a waterproof receiver. If it is not fully waterproof, waterproof cases can be brought.
- Don't leave the receiver permanently on when out in the wild, as you will quickly run the batteries down. Instead, turn it on only when you want to check your position.
- Get a receiver with parallel channels – this allows it to track and read data from 12 satellites at once. Older multiplex receivers can track only one satellite at a time, and give less reliable results in difficult terrain.
- Purchase the best receiver you can afford. Nonmapping units simply give you your coordinates, which are then manually plotted on a map. However, more expensive mapping units will actually display a map on screen with your position marked on it.

A bird's-eye view
Maps present a flat two-dimensional view of three-dimensional landscape. Learn to understand what mapwork implies in terms of real terrain, particularly relating to gradient and altitude.

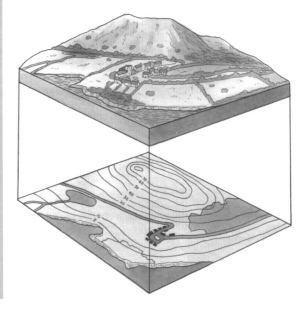

at the front of the compass in the direction you wish to go. Now turn the compass dial and place the North mark on the dial in line with the red compass needle. A black marker on the dial will be in line with the direction-of-travel arrow – this is the direction you want to travel in. Simply hold the compass in front of you, and follow the red arrow. As long as you keep the North marker lined up with the compass needle, you will keep going in the right direction.

By lining up the map's northings with the grid lines on the Silva dial, then repeating the above process, you should be able to navigate accurately between two map points. Put the straight edge of the compass (Silva compasses are rectangular) running from point A of your journey to point B. Now, turn the adjustable dial on the top of the compass until the north–south lines are parallel with the meridian lines on the map. The north arrow should be pointing to the map's north. Take the compass off the map, and turn the entire compass horizontally until the magnetic needle itself points to the north indicator on the dial and is also parallel with the north–south lines of the compass. The directional arrow on the compass will now be pointing in the direction in which you should travel.

To work out your position using a map and compass, you have to employ a process of triangulation using two prominent landmarks

visible both to the eye and on the map. Point the directional arrow on the compass at the first landmark and align the North mark on the compass to the red compass needle. Note the bearing. Now place the side of the compass on the landmark on the map and align the orientating lines in the base of the compass dial to the map's north–south grid lines, with the orientating arrow pointing north. Draw a line on the map along the compass base from the landmark. By repeating the same procedure for the second landmark, you will produce two lines

Map grid

The six-figure map reference is made up of the junction between eastings (the horizontal lines) and northings (the vertical lines), with whole squares divided into tenths for accuracy.

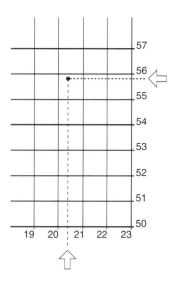

Map detail

Familiarize yourself with the map's symbols, and try to plot your route of travel to allow you accessible passage to civilization if you get into trouble at any point.

TYPICAL MAP SYMBOLS

⊹	Church with tower	≖	Bridge
●	Church with spire	⌐	Golf course
■	Building	⋀	Campsite
⬟	Built-up area	⤨	Picnic area
▬	Main road	△	Triangulation pillar
⌇	Minor road	⚡	Windmill or water pump
∿	Stream	⌰	Radio tower
(	Public telephone	P	Post office

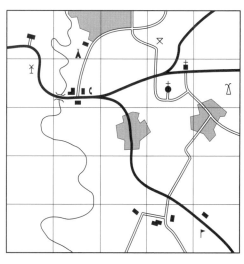

on the map, and your position will be where these two lines intersect.

If you are moving across an area where there are no visible landmarks (such as an Arctic landscape) or where landmarks are obscured (such as in dense forest), you will have to work out your position using 'dead reckoning'. Dead reckoning basically involves estimating distance travelled in time and plotting any changes in bearing. First work out your average pace – the

Contour lines

Contour lines represent the gradient of terrain. The more closely packed the contour lines (B), the steeper the gradient; if the lines are widely spaced (A), they indicate land of shallow gradient. (C) shows a rise with a variable gradient.

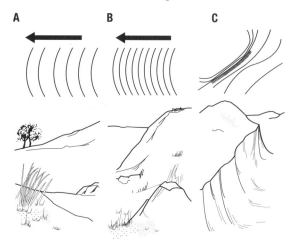

TIPS FOR READING CONTOUR LINES

- If contour lines are widely spaced, the slope is gentle. If narrow, the slope is steep.
- An absence of contour lines means that the ground is level.
- If several contour lines gather together into a single line, this means that there is a vertical cliff
- Concentric contour lines with increasing height imply a hill or mountain.
- V-shaped contour lines imply a sharp spur of land or a V-shaped valley. U-shaped contour lines imply the same, albeit with more rounded shape.

average pace is 60–70 double paces per 32m (100ft) on flat easy ground – and use this to estimate distance travelled. For example, as long as you know your start position, if you travel at 4.8km/h (3mph) for 20 minutes at a bearing of 045°, then turn 090° to the right and travel at the same speed for another half an hour, then you can plot roughly where you are on the map. Dead reckoning requires you to keep an accurate account of time, bearing and estimated distance, and you should regularly transfer these details to the map. Remember that dead reckoning is a rough system of calculation and is affected by everything from the gradient of the land to minute deviations in your course owing to strong winds. Be particularly careful not to overestimate distance covered on steep or difficult ground.

Although a map and a compass are the basic recommended tools of navigation, in a survival emergency these may not be readily available. In these circumstances, you will have to resort to ancient methods of navigation using nature and celestial bodies. Although these are not as accurate as compass methods, they can give you vital directional information.

Cross-section

Map contour lines essentially give a cross-section of landscape features. Pay close attention to the altitude figures which straddle each contour line, and make sure you can operate at that altitude.

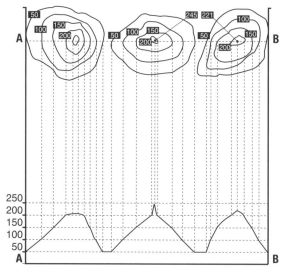

NAVIGATION USING THE SUN

Because the sun rises predictably in the east and sets in the west wherever you are on the Earth, it is the most elemental navigational aid. At midday in the northern hemisphere, the sun is due south, and due north in the southern hemisphere. If you

Types of compass

Compasses can be purchased in a wide variety of configurations. Only purchase those which are durable, waterproof and have dials which are easy to read, even in low-light conditions.

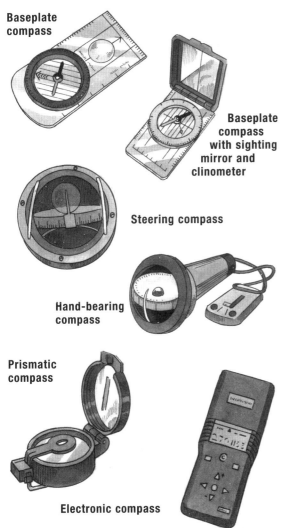

Baseplate compass

Baseplate compass with sighting mirror and clinometer

Steering compass

Hand-bearing compass

Prismatic compass

Electronic compass

are almost on the Equator, the midday sun will be straight above you, and is then a confusing navigational aid.

However, because of the tilt in the Earth's axis, the point on the eastern horizon where the sun rises each day varies with the seasons. In winter in the northern hemisphere, around the time of the winter solstice (around 21 December), the sunrise is at its farthest south, but rises to an exact easterly position by the time of the spring equinox (around 21 March). It then moves to its maximum northerly position at the summer solstice (around 21 Jun). After this high point, it begins to move south again, being exact east at the autumn equinox (around 21 September).

In the southern hemisphere, the winter solstice is on 21 June, when the easterly sun is at its farthest north. Around 21 September – the southern hemisphere's spring equinox – the sun rises exactly due east and thereafter moves to maximum south by the summer solstice (around 21 December). Around 21 March, the sunrise is exactly due east again. Remember that these rules for both the northern and southern hemispheres affect how the sun sets as well.

As well as the sun itself, the shadows it casts are useful navigational tools. To draw out an accurate east–west line, put a stick about 1m (3ft) high into the ground (the taller the stick, the more accurate the line). Clear the ground around the stick of any debris and tall grasses, and attempt to smooth over irregular ground shapes. Observe where the shadow falls, and mark the tip of the shadow with a stone. Wait about 15 minutes, then mark the tip of the shadow again with another stone. Scrape a straight mark in the soil between the two stones and you have your east–west line. Bisecting this line will give you north–south orientation.

The shadow lines can also help you to tell the time. If you place the stick at the intersection of the east–west line and the north–south line, the west part of the east–west line shows 06:00 and the east part 18:00. The north–south line becomes the noon line, and the shadow of the stick becomes the hour hand.

An analogue watch (one with hands) is another useful improvised navigational aid. The technique of reading direction using a watch varies slightly according to whether you are in the northern or southern hemisphere. For both,

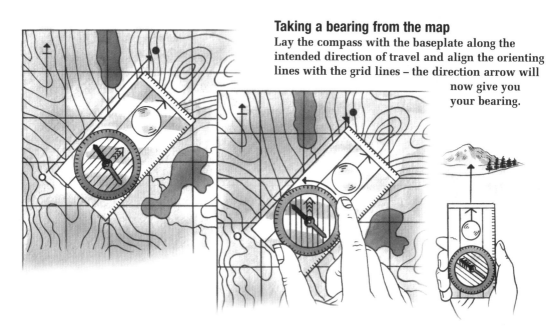

Taking a bearing from the map
Lay the compass with the baseplate along the intended direction of travel and align the orienting lines with the grid lines – the direction arrow will now give you your bearing.

set the watch to true local time – do not incorporate any daylight-saving additions or subtractions. Now hold the watch face flat. If in the northern hemisphere, point the hour hand towards the sun and bisect the angle between the hour hand and the 12 o'clock mark on the watch face. This direction is south, except before 06:00

and after 18:00, when it will indicate north. To make a reading in the southern hemisphere, point the 12 o'clock mark itself at the sun, then bisect the angle between mark and the hour hand to find north, or south before 06:00 and after 18:00. If you have a digital watch, simply draw out an analogue representation of the time on a piece of paper or on the ground, and make the usual calculation.

NAVIGATION USING THE STARS AND MOON
Stars have been used for navigation for centuries, but require knowledge of constellations and clear skies to use. In the northern hemisphere, the easiest constellation to identify is the Big Dipper (known as the Plough in the United Kingdom), part of the constellation called Ursa Major, or the Great Bear (see illustration). The two outer stars on the cup of the Big Dipper (called Dubhe and Merak) align themselves with a single isolated star. This is Polaris, the Pole (North) Star, which gives you a permanent point of reference for geographic north. If you can't see the Big Dipper, Cassiopeia also directs you to Polaris. Cassiopeia is a W- or M-shaped constellation, depending on which way you are looking at it. It lies on the opposite side of Polaris from the Big Dipper. Picture a straight line joining the tips of the two outside arms of the W (or M), then

Following a compass course
When following a compass course, turn your whole body with the compass held out in front of you until the direction arrow is on the correct bearing. Check your course regularly.

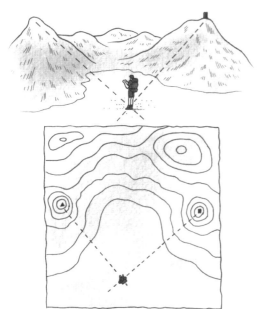

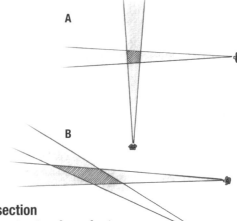

Resection

Resection involves plotting your position using two visible landmarks and a compass. Choose landmarks about 90° apart if possible (A), as these give less margin for error than landmarks at narrow angles (B).

Watch navigation

An analogue watch can be used for navigation. In the northern hemisphere, point the hour hand at the sun and bisect the angle between it and 12 o'clock to find south. In the southern hemisphere, point the 12 o'clock mark at the sun and bisect the angle between the mark and the hour hand to find north.

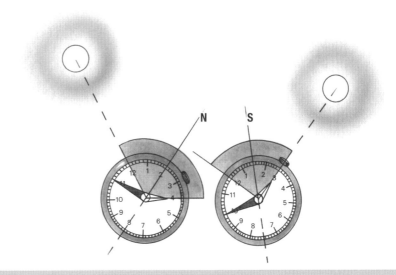

MOON NAVIGATION

In addition to stars, the moon can provide navigational guidance. The illumination on the surface of the moon alters as it turns relation to the sun. If, therefore, the moon rises at dusk just after the sun has set, the illuminated face will be pointing west. Conversely, after midnight, the illuminated face will be looking east.

When looking at a quarter moon, draw an imaginary line through the 'horns' of the moon down to the horizon – the place where the line touches the horizon is due north in the northern hemisphere, due south in the southern hemisphere.

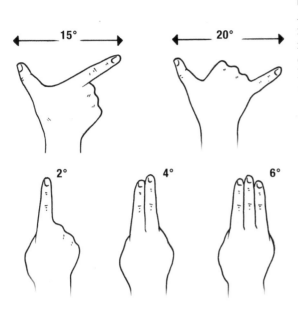

Estimating angles by eye

Angles can be estimated using the hand as illustrated here. Angle estimation has applications for distance calculations, but is also used to calculate sunset times. Held between sun and horizon, each finger's width represents around 15 minutes of available sunlight.

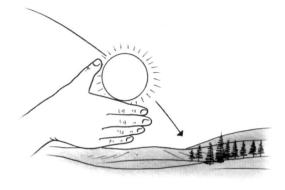

Time and direction by shadow

Casting a shadow using a stick embedded in the ground can provide you with both direction information (using time-elapse plotting) and, once you have your compass points, time information.

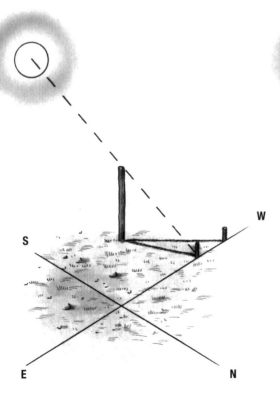

ESTIMATING ANGLES & DISTANCES

Angles and distances can be estimated using some simple techniques and a bit of mathematics. To calculate your distance to the horizon, know that from a position 2m (6ft) above level ground the horizon will be about 6km (3.3 miles) away. If your eyes are about 1m (3ft) above ground or water level, the horizon is just under 4km (2.5 miles) away. The higher you stand above ground level, obviously, the more distant the horizon becomes. Viewing from 20m (60ft) above sea level the horizon is 17km (10 miles) distant.

You can also use angles to estimate distance. A finger or thumb held up at arm's length covers an angle of roughly 2°. A clenched fist covers around 8°, your splayed thumb and forefinger 15°, and your hand span from thumb to little finger 20°. Estimate your distance from an object of known width or height, or from two objects if you know the distance between them (in metres/feet), using the following formula: width or separation in metres (or feet) / 100 x angle = distance away in miles.

For example, you are heading towards a mountain you know is 1.6km (1 mile/5280ft) in width at the base. If you hold your hand out at arm's length, three finger widths blot out the mountain base, indicating an angle of coverage of 6°. Now apply the formula above: 5280 / 100 x 6 = 8.8. It tells you that you still have 14.16km (8.8 miles) to go.

imagine a line at right angles to this one which is about 4½ times the span of the W (or M) in length. This again should point you to Polaris. By locating Polaris, you can either follow it directly or choose another star on the bearing you want and follow that instead. If you do the latter, check your course every 30 minutes, as other stars rotate around the Pole (North) Star at 15° per hour. Keep selecting new stars to guide you on the right course.

In the southern hemisphere, it is the Southern Cross that provides one of the clearest navigational markers. The Southern Cross contains five stars in a cruciform pattern. When the Southern Cross is standing vertically the sky, south is directly below the bottom star. If the Southern Cross is at an angle, multiply the longest axis of the cross by 4.5, which brings you to an imaginary point above the horizon. Direct south will be immediately below the point.

Another distinctive southern hemisphere constellation is Orion. Orion's most noticeable feature is its straight 'belt' of three stars spaced evenly in a straight line. Orion rises almost exactly due east and sets almost exactly due west. As Orion sets below the horizon, the point at which the belt disappears out of sight is due west.

Although well-known constellations are helpful to navigation, any star in the sky can give you a point of reference. Sit yourself down in one position and set your eyes on two fixed points on the ground in the distance. Pick a star and monitor its movement in relation to the fixed points for about 15 to 20 minutes. The direction the star moves in will tell you which direction you're looking in. Interpret the star's movements according to the following rules:

Northern hemisphere
Rising – the star is in the east
Falling – the star is in the west
Left – the star is in the north
Right – the star is in the south

Southern hemisphere
Rising – the star is in the west
Falling – the star is in the east
Left – the star is in the south
Right – the star is in the north

NAVIGATING FROM NATURE
Survival navigation entails a high degree of awareness of the natural environment. Nature may not be as accurate as map and compass, but certain observed features may give you good indication of the compass points.

If you are planning a trip to an unfamiliar area, you should find out as much as possible about any natural direction indicators. Research the flow direction of the main rivers in the area. Learn the 'grain' of the country. In which direction does the coastline run? Familiarize yourself with the prevailing winds in the area. As an example, the ridges and valleys of the Appalachian Mountains of Virginia and West Virginia generally run from the southwest to the northeast. So, if you are following a major valley there, and reading other signs from the sun and stars, then you will have a good idea of your direction. When visiting a mountainous area, or in polar climates, there are other clues around you. Look at the way the snow has been sculpted by the prevailing winds or the way that ice crystals build up on the upwind faces of rocks. If you know the direction of the prevailing winds in the region, these features show directional information. The same rule applies to sand dunes in desert environments, although sand dunes are prone to more variation. Transverse dunes, which occur in areas with a large amount of sand, set themselves perpendicular to the wind, with a long, gently slope facing into the wind, and a steep downwind slope. In arid areas with thin sand, the dunes tend to align themselves parallel to the prevailing wind. In other areas, prevailing winds tend to sculpt trees and bushes along the route of airflow, particularly around coastal areas. On Britain's exposed westerly coasts, for example, the trees are bent over to the northeast by the constant pushing of the strong southwesterly winds.

Plants can provide some very general indications of direction. Be careful when reading these signs, however, as the direction of plant growth is affected by many different factors, such as soil conditions and the availability of water. Flowers tend to grow toward the point of strongest sunlight, so will often face towards the south (in the northern hemisphere) or north (in the southern hemisphere). Similarly, the foliage of trees flourishes most abundantly on the sunny side. The

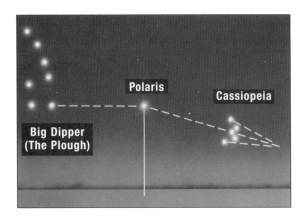

Pole (north) star

The Pole (North) Star is a true guide to north, and is set between the Big Dipper (Plough) and Cassiopeia. Using the Big Dipper is probably the easiest way to locate the Pole (North) Star, simply by drawing an imaginary line through the constellation as here.

rings of tree stumps will be more densely packed on the south side (in the northern hemisphere) because the bark usually stretches more on this face. In mountainous areas in the northern hemisphere, south-facing slopes will have a greater density and variation of vegetation growing on them, whereas the north-facing slopes will tend to be more barren. In addition, in springtime the north-facing slopes tend to be the last ones to keep the remnants of winter snow and ice.

The Southern Cross

The Southern Cross (below) is a distinctive constellation with two 'trailing' stars out to the east and a dark nebula (known as the 'Coalsack') just off to one side. When stood upright in the sky (left), the main axis of the cross points to the geographic south.

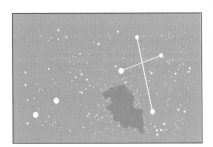

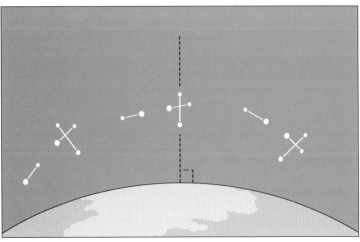

Bracketing

Mentally 'bracket' your campsite with identifiable features so that, if on your return journey you get lost, arrival at one of the features will let you know in which direction you should head.

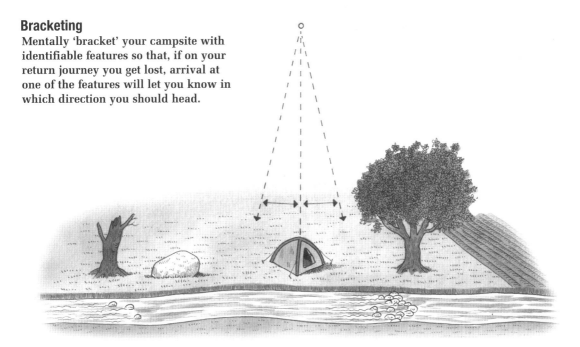

While it is true that moss tends to grow on the darker side of a tree or rock, where the moisture on which it lives is more protected from the harsh noonday sunlight, be very careful about making directional decisions on this basis. Moss chooses its growing sites for many different reasons, including the presence of certain bacteria, minerals and foods, and these locations are not always adverse to midday sunlight. If reading moss indicators, use them only in combination with other signs.

There are certain plants that give very definite directions. In North America, the pilotweed (*Silphium laciniatum*), also known as the compass plant, aligns its leaves in a north–south direction. The compass barrel cactus (*Ferocactus cylindraeus*), which is found in northern Mexico and in the southwestern states of the United States grows faster on its shady side, and ends up slanted towards the south.

The way animals behave rarely suggests direction with any degree of surety, with a few exceptions. At sea, flocks of sea birds flying overhead at dusk are usually heading to roost on the coast or the nearest island. Interestingly, in northern Australia, termite mounds are always oriented with their long axis running north–south.

IMPROVISED COMPASS

To make an improvised compass, you need to magnetize a needle of iron or steel (only ferrous metals will do) first. The best choice of needle is likely to be a sewing needle or pin, but a needle can be improvised from a paper clip or even the metal clip from a pen lid. To magnetize the needle, stroke it in one direction only with a magnet – you can often find one of these in the loudspeaker or headphones of a radio set. If a magnet isn't available, stroking the needle with nylon, silk or a piece of stone will still produce a magnetization, although it will be weaker. Alternatively, connect a piece of wire to a battery, and wrap the wire in a coil around the needle to produce a strong magnetic pull. Whatever method you use, re-magnetize the needle at least two or three times every day to strengthen it.

For the compass itself, float the magnetized needle in water on top of a leaf, piece of paper, piece of bark, or any material that is light and floats. The container for the compass should be nonferrous, such as a plastic cup or an aluminium mess tin. The needle should steadily turn until it settles, pointing north. Never use a compass near appliances that produce magnetic fields, particularly cars or stereos.

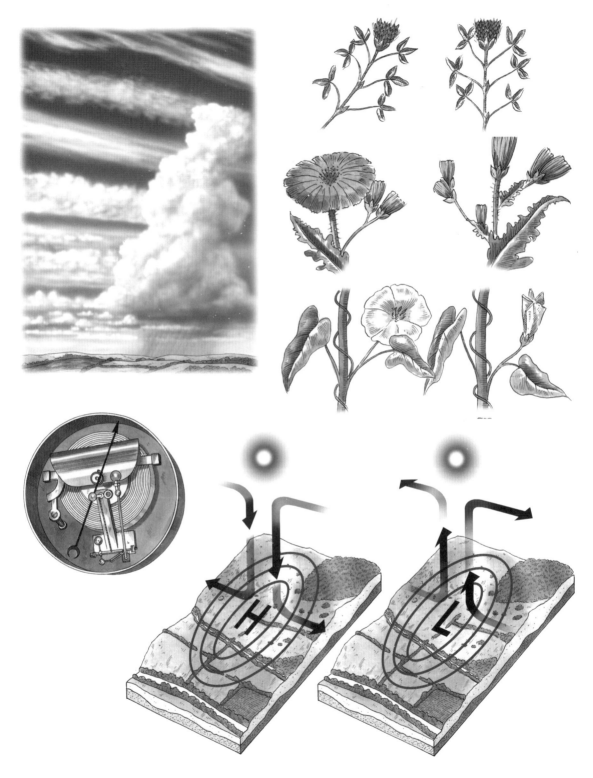

•CHAPTER SEVENTEEN

PREDICTING THE WEATHER

Forecasting the weather helps you to make more informed survival decisions, and modern technology can now determine future weather conditions with a high degree of accuracy.

WHENEVER YOU ARE heading for an outdoor activity, gain as much information as you can about future weather conditions. The most obvious place to gain this information is from professional weather forecasts available on television, on the radio, in newspapers and on the Internet. When interpreting weather forecasts, assimilate every fact into your planning. If you are heading out on water or up a mountain, closely observe wind speed and any storm fronts that might be brewing. Take the wind direction into account – this will give you information about sheltered places for your route planning, and also give you a crude navigational tool should you get lost. If travelling in the tropics or desert areas, observe not only maximum daylight temperatures, but also night-time ones, and pack clothing accordingly. If the weather forecast provides them, note the humidity levels. Very high humidity (around 90 per cent) combined with high temperatures is a recipe for heat exhaustion, so plan to take plenty of water and schedule many rest stops into your trip.

The important things to consider in weather forecasts are the isobars. Isobars are drawn between points of equal pressure. When the isobars are closely spaced, they indicate low-pressure systems, which usually bring strong winds and rain. Conversely, when the isobars are widely spaced, they are associated with high-pressure systems and clear weather. Compare these symbols to temperature figures, and plan clothing requirements slightly in excess of the extremes given. For example, if the weather forecast predicts a temperature of 4°C (39.2°F), pack clothing for subzero temperatures because

the wind-chill will significantly push down the still-air temperature.

Treat all weather forecasts with some caution, particularly as they attempt to predict weather in the long term. Generally, in temperate zones, anything beyond five days will have questionable accuracy. Weather systems tend to be much more predictable in Equatorial, arctic and tropical environments. If there are professional ranger services operating at your destination, telephone them first for local weather information.

THE TOOLS OF PREDICTION

Forecasts are your main weather predicting tool, so take a small radio with you into the wilderness (if you are going on an extended trip) for listening to weather forecasts. Alternatively, many cell (mobile) phone services offer a weather text service in which the forecast is texted to your telephone every day.

Apart from relying on others for weather information, there are several tools that can help in your own predictions. For example, a change in air pressure can indicate a change in the weather. High pressure generally brings clear skies and fair weather, and low pressure brings wet and stormy weather. A mercury barometer measures air pressure in inches of mercury. A column of mercury is contained in a sealed tube. Higher air pressure forces the mercury up higher in the tube, while lower air pressure allows the mercury to drop. A gauge running up the side of the tube will often provide an indication of what type of weather system is associated with the level of air pressure.

Dry and wet bulb thermometers

The dry and wet bulb thermometer can be used in tandem to determine relative humidity by comparing the difference in temperature readings (see main text).

Dry bulb

Wet bulb

The other basic piece of weather kit is a mercury thermometer, which works on the same basis as the barometer, but provides temperature information only. Knowing the temperature can be useful for adjusting clothing. If you are exercising hard, for example, you may not realize that temperatures have actually plummeted to freezing levels and that you will need warmer clothing when you stop moving.

Thermometers can also be used to find out humidity levels. A comparison of a dry bulb thermometer reading and a wet bulb thermometer reading is used to determine relative humidity. This gives a measure of the water evaporation present in the air compared to the amount of water evaporation needed to saturate the air at that temperature. Take a temperature reading using a dry bulb thermometer, then take another reading using a web bulb thermometer (also known as a hygrometer). This latter type of thermometer features a damp muslin bag covering its bulb.

World climate zones

Some world regions, such as the deserts and the polar regions, have very predictable climate conditions. By contrast, temperate zones can be even more dangerous because unpredictable weather patterns can catch people out when they are not properly dressed or equipped.

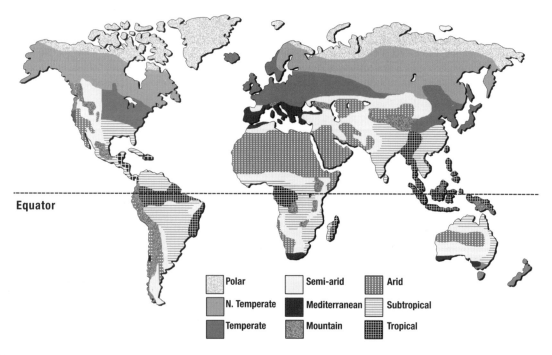

Equator

Polar	Semi-arid	Arid
N. Temperate	Mediterranean	Subtropical
Temperate	Mountain	Tropical

It is used for measuring how much the air is saturated in water evaporation. The difference in measurements between the two thermometers yields a percentage describing relative humidity. If both thermometers show the same temperature, the relative humidity is 100 per cent.

Instead of carrying an individual thermometer, barometer and hygrometer (an implement for measuring humidity), modern electronic weather stations combine all three, and can be little more than hand-held size.

NATURAL INDICATORS
If technological systems of forecasting are not available, you will have to take your clues about future weather from the skies and the natural world around you. Plants are generally sensitive to the weather, particularly changes in humidity levels. Approaching storms often cause plants to open their pores in readiness, releasing a distinctive musty scent. Pine cones are more finely

Aneroid barometer
The aneroid barometer functions via a vacuum-filled capsule which is compressed by a rise in air pressure and expands when air pressure falls. These changes are linked to a dial for reading.

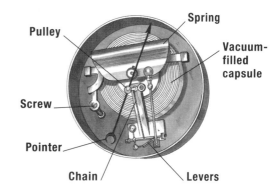

Formation of high- and low-pressure areas
High-pressure weather systems are formed when air cools and sinks, and are usually associated with fine weather. Low-pressure systems evolve as air warms and rises, this producing atmospheric instability and cloud formation.

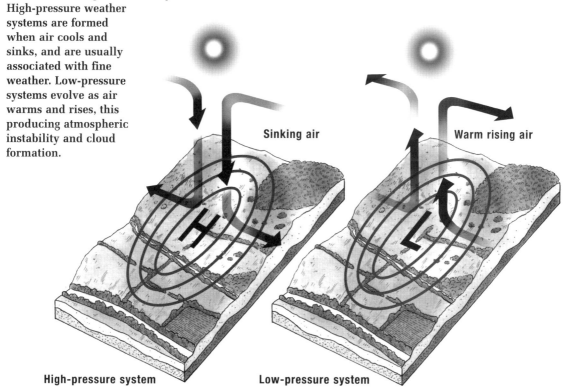

Types of cloud

Clouds are the best elements to observe for predicting the weather. Generally, the lower, thicker and darker the cloud base, the greater the likelihood of poor weather, the towering anvil-headed cumulonimbus bringing the worst weather conditions.

A. Cirrus
B. Cirrocumulus
C. Cirrostratus
D. Altocumulus
E. Altostratus
F. Stratocumulus
G. Nimbostratus
H. Cumulus
I. Stratus
J. Anvil Head
K. Cumulonimbus
L. Rain, hail and squall winds

attuned to humidity changes, closing their scales as the air becomes more humid with the onset of wet weather, and opening them on the approach of fine weather as the air dries out. Other plants demonstrate similar responses to airborne water evaporation. Clover, chicory, shamrocks and morning glories close their petals or leaves as humidity levels increase, and the silver maple turns up its leaves in expectation of rain.

The way animals behave can provide some clues about weather developments. Herding animals tend to respond to drops in air pressure (and approaching rain) by moving to lower ground, gathering together, and – if the weather is likely to be very bad – lying down on the ground. Bear in mind, however, that they might do this up to two days before the rain actually arrives. Ants sometimes build up earth around entrances to their colony to prevent rain from flooding their nest. When bees are observed heading back to their hives in the daytime, it is also believed to suggest the imminent arrival of rain.

Be cautious about reading the animal and plant signs with too much certainty – many different

THE BEAUFORT SCALE

BEAUFORT NUMBER	SPEED (MPH)	SPEED (KM/H)	DESCRIPTION	EFFECTS ON LAND
0	< 1	< 1	calm	calm; smoke rises vertically
1	2–3	1–5	light air	smoke drift indicates wind direction; vanes do not move
2	4–7	6–11	light breeze	wind felt on face; leaves rustle; vanes begin to move
3	8–12	12–19	gentle breeze	leaves, small twigs in constant motion; light flags extended
4	13–18	20–29	moderate breeze	dust, leaves and loose paper raised up; small branches move
5	19–24	30–38	fresh breeze	small trees in leaf begin to sway
6	25–31	39–51	strong breeze	large tree branches in motion; whistling heard in utility wires
7	32–38	52–61	near gale	whole trees in motion; resistance felt in walking against wind
8	39–46	62–74	gale	twigs and small branches broken off trees
9	47–54	75–86	strong gale	slight structural damage occurs; slate or tiles blown from roofs
10	55–63	87–101	whole gale	seldom experienced on land; trees broken; structural damage occurs
11	64–74	102–120	storm	very rarely experienced on land; usually brings widespread damage
12	> 74	> 120	hurricane force	violent; widespread destruction

factors can affect the way animals and plants behave. However, these signs can give you a general hint at what weather is approaching.

One well-known piece of weather folklore is: 'Red sky at night, shepherd's delight. Red sky in morning, shepherd's warning.' This aphorism is substantially accurate. The sky appears red due to dust particles in dry air. In western Europe, for instance, weather systems generally move from west to east. Therefore, a red sunrise indicates dry weather moving away to the east, with rain approaching from the west, while a red sunset suggests dry weather will come from the west during the night and next day.

CLOUD TYPES

The clouds above you denote what weather conditions will prevail throughout the day with a high degree of certainty. The following are the principal cloud types divided according to their respective altitudes.

HIGH CLOUD 5,485–13,715m (18,000–45,000ft)
Cirrus (Ci)

Description: delicate, wispy and thin white cloud, transparent to the sun. Variable in shape, appearing as streaks, curves or tufts. Cirrus is the first to glow and the last to dim at sunrise and sunset, respectively. At night cirrus will diffuse starlight.
Implications: generally indicates changing

weather. If accompanied by lower cumulus clouds and followed by cirrostratus, suggests the approach of a rain-bearing, low-pressure system. For a more accurate idea of the weather, face into the wind so that cumulus clouds are moving straight over your head. Now study the relation of cirrus to cumulus clouds. In the northern hemisphere, if the cirrus is approaching from your left, the weather will become clearer and drier. If the cirrus approaches from the right, expect rain. The reverse situation applies in the southern hemisphere.

Cirrocumulus (Cc)

Description: set lower than cirrus. Appears as regular, tufted cloudlets or streaks, with a dappled or rippled appearance. Can blot out dimmer stars at night.
Implications: generally associated with dry weather. If it thickens, turns grey and drops lower in the sky, however, expect rain.

Cirrostratus (Cs)

Description: white, milky, thin white veil of cloud. Can mix with cirrus to form parallel bands across the sky. When seen through cirrostratus, the sun and the moon have a 'halo' effect.
Implications: suggests a change in weather. Like cirrocumulus, watch for the cloud lowering and thickening – expect rain within 24 hours.

MID CLOUD 2440–5485m (8000–18,000ft)
Altocumulus (Ac)
Description: small, flattened, round cloudlets, grey on the underside. Gathers in loose, disorganized formations, with blue sky often visible between. Sometimes appears as sweeping bands of cloud, rolling like waves. Can be strong enough to blot out sunlight. Creates spectacular displays of colour when caught by early or late sunlight.

Plant weather indicators

The illustrated plant types all respond to changes in the levels of air humidity, often folding up their petals or leaves in humid conditions to protect their seeds from possible rainfall.

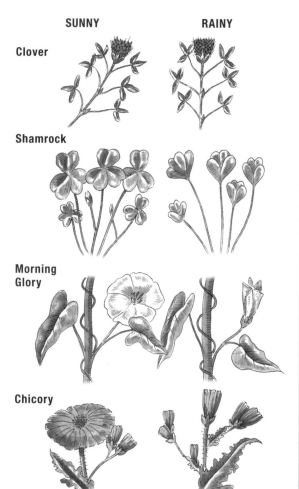

SUNNY   RAINY

Clover

Shamrock

Morning
Glory

Chicory

Implications: If cloud lowers and thickens, expect short, thundery showers. If altocumulus grows taller with a 'turreted' appearance, expect more substantial thunderstorms.

Altostratus (As)
Description: A fibrous and thicker version of cirrostratus. Diffuses light from the stars and, when thick enough, can reduce sun and moon to a blurred light.
Implications: if lowers, thickens and darkens, or if low-level gray 'scud' cloud forms below it, heavy, prolonged rain or snow is on its way, probably arriving in a few hours.

LOW CLOUD 0–2440m (0–8000ft)
Stratocumulus (Sc)
Description: soft, globular white cloud appearing in regular layers, lines, waves or long patches. Often has a grey underside. Waves might join together to form a uniform overcast sky, softer and more regular in formation than stratus. Occasionally this appears as parallel rolls of cloud with blue sky visible between them; this is known as roll cumulus.
Implications: Stratocumulus tends to clear at night, bringing good weather.

Stratus (S)
Description: very low cloud almost like fog, only about 150–610m (500–2000ft) at its base. Forms a continuous layer of cloud unless broken up by strong winds.

PREDICTING RAIN

- A grey and overcast morning usually means rain later, especially if the winds are increasing or the low cloud has not lifted by midday.
- Rings of curly hair tend to tighten with impending rain.
- Approaching rain can induce additional stiffness and pain in the joints of arthritis sufferers.
- Wooden handles tighten up when rain is about to arrive.
- Smoke rises more turbulently as rain approaches.
- Sounds travel further just before rain, as noise is able to move more efficiently through moisture-soaked air.

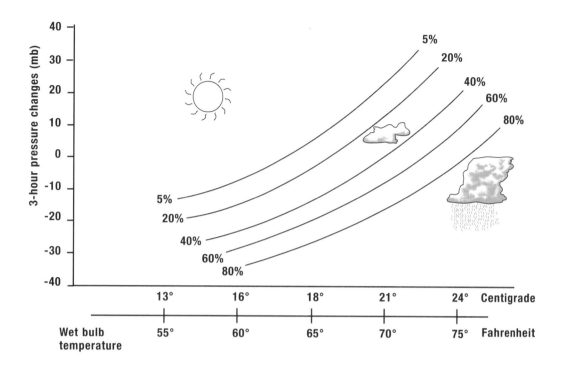

Thunderstorm probability

A high wet bulb thermometer reading and a drop in barometric pressure together indicate an increased probability of a thunderstorm.

Implications: Usually implies wet weather, particularly if combined with strong winds.

Nimbostratus (Ns)
Description: uniform, dark grey layer that blocks daylight. Its base can reach down to sea level or up to 1220m (4000ft), but is more commonly around 150–610m (500–2000ft). Can form the underside of nimbostratus or cumulonimbus systems, and is usually seen as part of a major low-pressure system.
Implications: usually brings continuous, steady rain or snow, especially if it darkens with low, scudding clouds beneath its base.

Cumulus (Cu)
Description: Classic white, 'fluffy' clouds, with a convoluted shadowed surface and domed tops. Varies considerably in size, from small 'cotton wool' tufts to huge cumulonimbus thunderclouds. Implications: can be part of fine weather systems, although if base flattens and greys, implies approaching rains and storms.

Cumulonimbus (Cb)
Description: mountainous, flat-bottomed cumulus clouds that stretch to high altitudes, often forming a towering anvil shape of dark, threatening colour. Implications: heavy, blustery rainfall and showers and possible thunderstorm conditions. Can produce hail and snow.

APPROACHING BAD WEATHER
Using the information about clouds provided above, it is possible to spot the signs of an approaching rain-filled low-pressure system. Look for dark cumulus clouds massing in the sky combined with cirrus at high levels, or a dark haze of cirrostratus and below it nimbostratus. As these clouds move over you, visibility will deteriorate with strengthening, blustery winds and increasing rainfall. As the cold front passes, the steady rainfall will lighten into showers, while visibility and temperature will improve.

•CHAPTER EIGHTEEN

POLAR CLIMATES

True polar environments are probably the most hostile climates on Earth. Food and shelter-building materials are scarce, travel is fraught and subzero temperatures can kill in hours.

TRUE POLAR REGIONS lie between 66° latitude and the North and South poles, and have icy climates. They are absolutely unforgiving landscapes. In the Antarctic, temperatures are commonly in the region of –43° C (–45°F) and average wind speeds are 70km/h (44mph). However, speeds of up to 177km/h (110mph) have been recorded. The ice sheet reflects back 80 per cent of the warmth of the sun. The Arctic is just as inhospitable. Even though summertime temperatures in the lower latitudes can reach 18°C (65°F), they plummet to around –56°C (–81°F) in the winter, and much lower in the ice zones, which rarely climb above freezing point. Both these environments are incredibly barren, featuring almost no vegetation and few animals.

Most of us are unlikely to find ourselves in such extreme environments. Yet polar conditions can prevail almost anywhere in the world. Blizzard conditions have been recorded in Equatorial zones in the Middle East, and seasonal snow climates (between 35° and 70° northern latitude) prevail in much of the northern hemisphere. Snowy climates are more environmentally varied than ice climates. These include coniferous forests, freshwater lakes, swamps and tundra, which experience temperatures ranging from 16°–21°C (60°–70°F) in the summer and winter to –9°–4°C (15°–25°F) and below in the winter, usually accompanied by heavy snowfall.

HEALTH AND HYGIENE
The main danger in any subzero environment is without doubt from the cold. Freezing still-air temperatures combined with a high wind-chill factor can precipitate frostbite and hypothermia within hours, even minutes. Wind chill is the lethal ingredient. A wind of 32km/h (20mph)

will push a temperature of –14°C (5°F) down to –34°C (–30°F), and can freeze exposed human flesh in around 60 seconds.

The treatments for cold-related injuries are contained in Chapter 13, but prevention is always better than cure. You should be wearing the appropriate clothing (see Chapter 2). This includes multiple layers of thermal clothing with the head, hands and feet all protected, and an outer covering of garments that are both windproof and waterproof. Keep covered up, but, if you are sweating and start to overheat, loosen or remove some clothing to avoid the sweat building up, then freezing when you stop moving. It is especially important that you keep garments clean, as dirt and grease reduce their insulating properties by clogging up the air spaces. Ensure clothing is not so tight that it restricts circulation.

Watch out for all the signs of Arctic illnesses: frostbite, hypothermia, trench foot, sunburn and sunblindness. To prevent frostbite, hypothermia and trench foot, always wear proper clothing and dry it out if it gets wet. Make sure that the feet and hands especially are kept dry. Wrinkle your facial muscles to stop stiff patches forming on your face. Bend and flex the toes and fingers to maintain circulation. Look out for patches of white, waxy skin forming, and keep these patches dry and warm. Try not to expose bare flesh outdoors – dress and undress in your sleeping bag. Do not touch metal with your bare hands, as the freezing steel will burn your skin and pull it off. When entering shelter, brush the snow off your clothes before you go inside to keep the interior of the shelter dry.

Take care if you are very tired, rest if you are sick and be aware of the risks of dehydration. Freezing climates are actually very dry climates – there is little airborne moisture present. If you

The Arctic

The Arctic is actually a frozen ocean. Some of the more peripheral Arctic areas have extremely changeable climates ranging from –43°C (–43°F) in the winter to 43°C (110°F) in the summer.

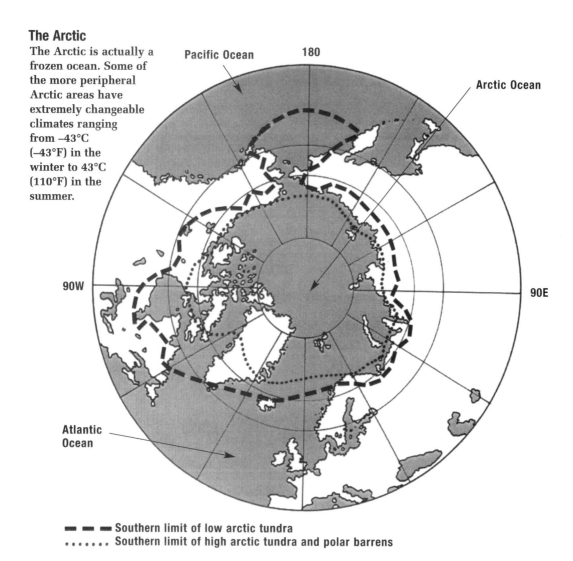

— — — Southern limit of low arctic tundra
······· Southern limit of high arctic tundra and polar barrens

exert yourself, you can easily dehydrate, leaving yourself exposed to hypothermia. If your urine is dark yellow and you feel drowsy or are suffering from headaches, rest and drink plenty of liquids (but not alcohol).

Sunburn can be acute in polar environments because the ultraviolet rays of the sun are intensified when reflected off the snow and ice. Apply high-factor sunscreen to all exposed areas of the face, especially the nose, lips and eyelids. Snowblindness is another danger caused by the same phenomenon, and produces red, watering, sore eyes accompanied by intense headaches. To

prevent snowblindness, wear high-quality sunglasses or at worst improvise a pair of goggles out of cardboard or tree bark. Smearing streaks of charcoal underneath the eyes also helps against snowblindness. If you are affected, rest your eyes until they recover, ideally in a dark place.

Hygiene is very important. Living in subzero climates means that clothes are worn for long periods of time, and neglected hygiene can result in infections and increased risk of hypothermia through dirty clothes. Change socks and wash feet daily, or at least massage and dry your feet. Wash your groin and armpit areas every few days, and

Preventing snowblindness

Simple improvised snow goggles make from a piece of cloth or even bark will help to prevent the onset of snowblindness.

Smearing charcoal stripes under the eyes will also help.

change underwear at minimum twice a week. If you haven't a change of underwear, then at least air the items for a couple of hours. Keep your teeth clean, and if you have no toothbrush use a clean piece of cloth wrapped around a finger or the end of a twig chewed into a pulp.

MOVEMENT

Movement through polar terrain is especially hazardous. The following are just some of the problems you might face.

- In blizzard conditions 'whiteouts' can occur when land and sky merge into one uniform sheet with no visible landmarks. Do not travel in whiteout conditions, as you will lose all sense of direction (people have been lost and died only yards from their shelters in these conditions). The snowfall also obliterates your tracks, making it harder to retrace your steps.
- Navigation by compass is difficult in far north or south latitudes, as pronounced magnetic variations affect the compass readings.
- Short daylight conditions in the winter mean less time for navigation, shelter construction and food gathering. Use every minute of the

daylight hours – always be dressed and ready for sunrise.

- Polar landscapes are constantly shifting, even in summertime. Therefore you may come across large features such as lakes and rivers not marked on any map.
- Ice sheets can give way and you can fall into freezing water. When walking across frozen lakes or rivers, use a pole to probe the strength of the ice ahead of you. If you do fall in, get onto land with great speed and roll in the snow to absorb excess water. Then get to shelter and into dry clothes before you start to freeze.

These are just problems associated with winter conditions. Polar landscapes present other problems in the summertime, including clouds of

Falling through ice

If you fall through ice, try to claw your way out using knives, ice picks or ski poles to get adhesion on the slippery ice. Once out, strip off your wet clothes, and dry out quickly.

Human chain for ice rescue

If attempting to rescue someone who has fallen through ice, one person should lay flat across the ice to spread his weight while another person holds on to his ankles for safety. As the trapped person is pulled to safety, she should slide across the fractured ice to safety without standing up.

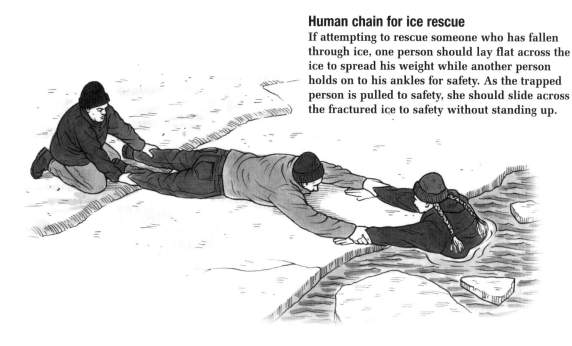

aggressive insects and treacherous bogs, swamps and standing water, which are all difficult to cross. Streams and rivers become pounding currents from the injection of meltwater.

Only travel in polar terrain if you have to for essential survival tasks, such as collecting food, water, firewood or shelter materials. If travelling through deep, soft snow, manufacture a set of snowshoes out of saplings. Bend and tie a piece of willow (or other flexible wood) into a frame, fitting in wooden crosspieces. Then use some rawhide or cord to make straps for the toe and heel (see illustration).

When you leave your camp, make an indicator of your direction for rescue crews or other members of your party. Fashion a large arrow in the snow, making it as high as you can so that it throws a shadow visible from the air. Build further signals along your route as you change direction. These will also help you to get back to camp if you become lost.

Choose your route of travel carefully. Avoid dangerous and wet terrain such as bogs or ice flows, but try to follow a waterway if possible. The waterway will provide you with fish and fluids, as well as the many other animals that visit the water to drink and waterside edible plants. Most settlements are built alongside rivers or streams, so following a watercourse maximizes your chance of rescue. Don't be tempted to build a raft and try to sail the river – northern rivers are fast, cold and dangerous.

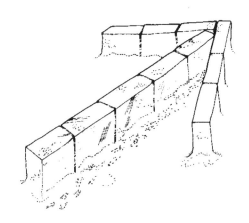

Snow signals

Rectangular blocks of snow can be used to build up snow signals on the ground for rescuers. The advantage of snow blocks is that they can be used again to make different signals.

Take special care when moving across ice fields. Plates of ice shift and crush together, suddenly pushing up ridges of ice at steep angles, while opening up gaps into the freezing seawater in other places. Be especially wary of being stranded on a sheet of ice that is breaking away and floating out to sea.

Compasses tend to be unreliable near the poles, so rely on natural systems of navigation (see Chapter 16). The clouds can provide some navigational information. Clouds appear black underneath when they are above over open water, timber or snow-free ground, but white over the sea ice and snowfields. Don't use icebergs or distant sea landmarks to get your bearings, as they will change position. It is worth remembering that during the springtime thaw migrating wildfowl fly towards land, while most seabirds fly out to sea during the day and return at night.

SHELTER

The type of shelter you build depends on what the environment makes available. If you are in a forest area, build the shelters described in Chapter 10, with some variations. Spruce trees make ideal shelters in thick snow. Dig out the snow around the base of the tree so that the lower branches of the tree form a canopy above you. Line the dugout with spruce branches for insulation from the ground. Alternatively, make a frame from willow branches (either as a lean-to or an independent structure) and cover the frame with clumps of earth and snow.

If, however, you are surrounded by little but snow and ice, then you need to make snow shelters. For these you need to cut blocks of snow around 45 x 50cm (18 x 20in) long and 10–20cm (4–8 in)thick using a saw knife, snow knife, shovel or machine. Cut snow blocks from deep

Making snowshoes

A simple pair of snowshoes begins with a sapling (A) shaped into a frame (B and C), with cross-members fitted (D) and cord (E) used to tie the shoes over the boots.

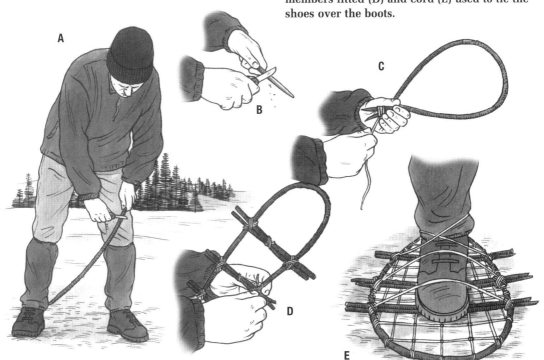

drifts that have an even, firm structure, and no hollow or softer layers. Never set your cutting tool down in the snow because it is liable to get lost. The main types of snow shelter are the moulded dome shelter, the snow cave, the trench shelter and the igloo.

MOULDED DOME SHELTER

Make a large pile of wooden boughs or any other material and cover with a sheet, such as a groundsheet. Then cover the groundsheet with snow, leaving a gap for an entrance to the shelter. When the snow has hardened, remove the wooden boughs from inside the snow cave, then gently pull out the sheet, hopefully leaving a freestanding snow shelter with an entrance. Tie up a small bundle of sticks to make an entrance block, or use your backpack.

SNOW CAVE

Burrow a small tunnel into the side of a deep snowdrift to a depth of about 1m (3ft). From the

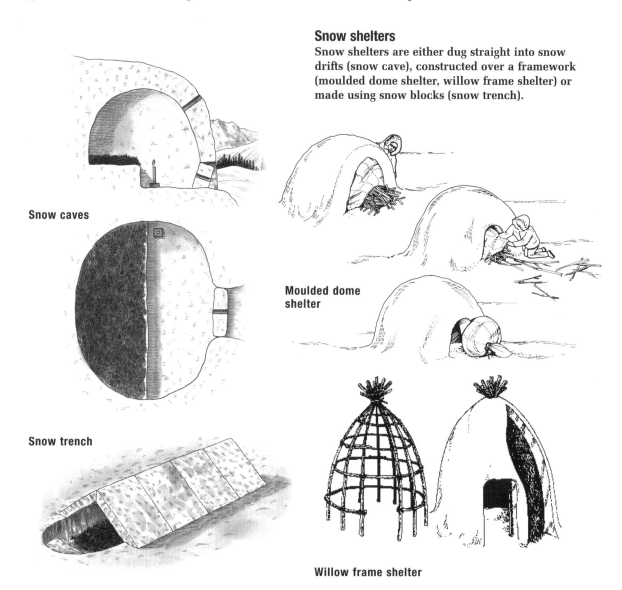

Snow shelters

Snow shelters are either dug straight into snow drifts (snow cave), constructed over a framework (moulded dome shelter, willow frame shelter) or made using snow blocks (snow trench).

Snow caves

Moulded dome shelter

Snow trench

Willow frame shelter

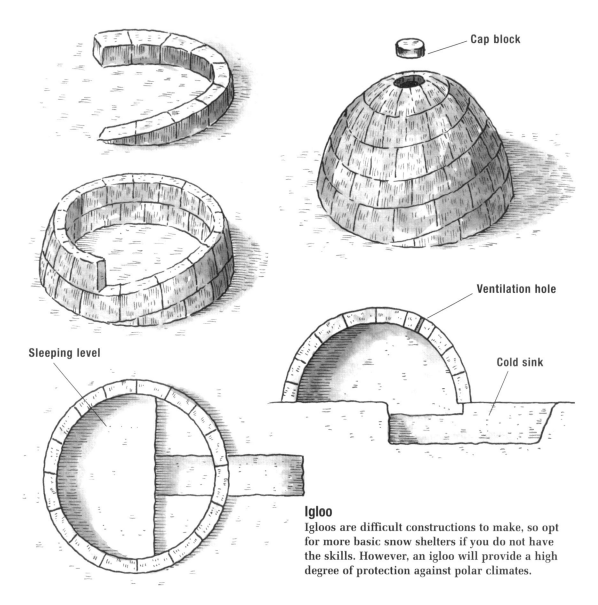

Cap block

Ventilation hole

Cold sink

Sleeping level

Igloo
Igloos are difficult constructions to make, so opt for more basic snow shelters if you do not have the skills. However, an igloo will provide a high degree of protection against polar climates.

end of this tunnel, cut out other tunnels to the right and left – these will form your living space and must be at right angles to the tunnel entrance to be protected from wind currents. Bore at least two ventilation holes in the roof at different locations. Vary the heights of the living-space tunnels, and make all the roofs rounded for extra strength and to ensure meltwater runs down the sides, rather than dripping onto you. Sleep in the higher, warmest sections of the snow cave (always

remember that heat rises), and cook and store equipment in the lowest sections. Block the entrance with a stick bundle, backpack, poncho or snow block to retain warmth.

TRENCH SHELTER
Build up snow blocks in a snowdrift in a rectangular pattern to form a trench long enough to accommodate you and your sleeping bag in a lying position, and rising to about 1m (3ft) high.

Put more blocks over the top to form a roof, making the inside of the roof blocks slightly curved. Bore a ventilation hole in the roof. The trench shelter is only temporary accommodation until you can make something more substantial.

IGLOO

Draw a circle about 2.5–3m (7–10ft) in diameter on the snow. This will be the inside diameter of the igloo. Cut around 12 snow blocks, and begin stacking them around the line. Make sure the blocks lean inwards and that the end joints of each snow block have faces radial to the middle of the igloo. Now cut more snow blocks and build the igloo wall up higher, bevelling the tops of the

blocks so that the igloo curves in towards the middle. A small hole should remain in the middle of what is now a roof. Put a fitted disc of snow – known as a 'key block' – into this hole, juggling it into position from the inside. Finally, construct an entrance tunnel leading into the igloo. Pack any gaps between the blocks with powdery snow and leave to harden (keep checking the outside condition of the igloo, particularly in high winds), and push through one or two ventilation holes. Inside the igloo, make a platform of snow for sleeping on (insulated with branches, of course). Place your cooking stove near to the entrance so that it is well ventilated, and force sticks into the wall on which to hang utensils and clothes.

SHELTER RULES

Whatever shelter you build in polar regions, observe the following rules.
- Always cover the floor of snow shelters with insulating material, such as boughs, dry grasses, and moss.
- Build your shelter as near to sources of fire fuel as possible.
- Avoid building shelters on the lee side of cliffs – snowslides might bury your shelter.
- Limit the number of entrances you build; the more you have, the more heat is lost.
- Store firearms outside. Storing them inside encourages condensation to build up on the barrel and in the action, causing either rust or, if it freezes, weapon malfunction. (Always check the end of the barrel before use; a plug of ice could cause the gun to explode on firing.)
- Make a latrine area outside. If the weather is too extreme to venture out, either dig an additional latrine tunnel extending out from your snow cave, or urinate into tin cans and defecate onto snow blocks that are then thrown outside.
- If your sleeping bag gets wet, knock off any frost, then dry it near a fire.
- Check regularly that the shelter's ventilation holes are not blocked with snow, and chip off any coatings of ice – ice reduces your shelter's insulating properties.
- Do not allow excessive amounts of snow to build up on your shelter. The weight may cause the structure to collapse.

FIRE IN POLAR CLIMATES

Fire is a vital ingredient of polar survival. The principles of making a fire are discussed in Chapter 11, but there are additional considerations in a polar climate. The major problem in ice and snow environments is finding materials you can burn. Vegetation is often scarce, and any woods are usually soaked with snow.

If you are in a vehicle, use anything combustible. Drain the oil from the sump (oil pan) while the vehicle is warm, as the oil will congeal in the engine if left to go too cold and will not run out from the sump. Leave fuel in the tank. Oil and water can be combined to form a very hot flame. Hang one can of oil and one can of water above a metal plate or stone, and puncture a small hole in the bottom of each. Plug the hole with wooden pegs, but loosen them so that the cans slowly drip their contents at a rate of one drop of oil to three or four of water. When

MAKING FIRE IN POLAR CONDITIONS

- Always build a fire reflector behind you out of logs, stones or turf to maximize warmth.
- Heat stones in the fire, and place them around the shelter for extra warmth.
- Stockpile firewood at every opportunity to reduce the amount of time spent outside.
- Try to gather hardwoods because these will burn for longer. Build your fire with minimal air gaps to limit fuel consumption.

Polar fires

In snowy conditions, build fires on log platforms so that the snow does not extinguish the flames. To cope with extreme polar winds, site the fire behind a shelter or in a pit.

Base for signal fire

Enclosed fire

Pit fire

ignited, this mixture will burn ferociously. If you have been involved in a plane crash in arctic conditions, salvage any flammable materials such as seating, paper or aviation fuel. Aviation fuel may have soaked into the ground – collect the fuel-soaked earth and use it for fire blocks.

To find wood in icy climates, search seashores regularly for driftwood. In many subarctic regions, however, woods that can be burned are usually available. Try to find resinous woods. These will burn even when wet, and include birch, juniper, willow and pine. Cut the bark into thin strips for kindling. The Casiope plant provides another excellent fuel – look for a low-lying (10–30cm/4–12in high), heather-like evergreen plant with tiny leaves and white, bell-shaped flowers. If wood is almost entirely unavailable, animal fat, especially whale and seal blubber, is an excellent fuel for both heating and cooking. When butchering a seal, cut away any fat and store it for later use.

Always remember to construct your fire on top of a platform of stones in snowy or icy conditions to prevent meltwater from extinguishing it.

FINDING WATER

Water is abundant in polar climates in the form of snow and ice. Always melt the snow and ice down to water before drinking it, as eating them when frozen can accelerate hypothermia, cause tissue damage to the mouth and lips, and create stomach disorders. Water from clean snow and ice does not usually need to be filtered and purified, though do so if they are taken from coastal areas – they may contain harmful marine microorganisms. If cutting ice from icebergs to use as water, use only old sea ice that has a blue or black coloration and a crumbly texture. Old ice has lost its salt content, whereas new ice, which has a white, hard and glassy appearance, is full of salt. Cut ice from the landward side of the iceberg, as the side facing the sea will be coated in salty sea spray. Remember the following advice if you do take ice from icebergs. Only use icebergs that have lodged themselves securely ashore; do not approach moving icebergs. Watch out for falling ice blocks above you as you cut into the surface.

To melt snow or ice, either heat it in a container or make a melting machine. A melting machine is a tepee-like structure constructed from three branches or poles tied together at the top. Hanging in the middle of the frame is a bag of porous material holding the snow and ice with a container beneath it. By making a fire near the melting machine, the snow and ice melt, and drip through the cloth into the container.

During arctic summers in tundra and forested areas, water can usually be found in rivers, streams and lakes. Filter the water to remove vegetation and sediment, and let it stand in a container to separate out any silt.

Store any water you collect in a plastic rather than metal bottle, as metal containers can split

Water maker

A basic device for melting snow and ice to water consists of a wooden tepee frame with a bag of material tied between the struts. The bag is filled with snow and a fire built to the side, and the meltwater drips through the cloth into a container.

Snow melter

The snow melter is an ideal way of melting large blocks of ice and snow. Light a fire under an angled rock platform, and place the ice on top of the platform when the rock is hot. Create a channel with stones to direct the meltwater into a container.

should the water inside freeze and expand. Whatever the container, do not fill it to the top to allow the forming ice room to expand. Put the water bottle in an inside coat pocket to stop it from freezing again.

PLANT FOOD

Although vegetation is sparse in ice climates, snow climates have several different varieties of edible plants. They also have a few poisonous varieties, which obviously need to be avoided. These include water hemlock/spotted cowsbane, monkshood, spring larkspur, false hellesbore, wild lupine and baneberry (which has red and white berries with a deceptively appetizing appearance). Learn to identify these plants, and avoid them at all costs.

EDIBLE ARCTIC/NORTHERN PLANTS

Arctic willow: has rounded, shiny leaves and yellow catkins. Eat the young shoots, leaves, inner bark and roots (peeled).

Bearberry: the entire plant is edible after cooking. Look for a plant that spreads over the ground like a mat, with tough evergreen leaves, pink or white flowers and red berries.

Black spruce: like the red spruce (see below), except smaller and with shorter needles. The young shoots are edible raw or cooked, and the inner bark can be eaten after it has been boiled. Use the needles to make tea.

Iceland moss: a leathery plant with straplike branches, it form mats up to 10cm (4in) high. All parts are edible after several hours of soaking and then boiling.

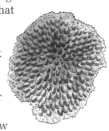

Labrador tea: an evergreen shrub growing to 30–90cm (1–3ft) with narrow leaves that are whitish or grey underneath, it has white flowers. As the name suggests, its leaves can be boiled for a nutritious tea.

Red spruce: grows to 23m (70ft) high with yellow-green needles and hairy twigs. Boil the inner bark of the red spruce to eat, or eat young shoots raw or cooked.

Reindeer moss: a lichen growing 5–10cm (2–4in) high, it forms large clumps with branches that resemble reindeer antlers. The whole plant is edible after soaking and boiling.

Rock tripes: round growths that are greyish or brownish, and resembling blisters, these are found attached to rocks. Soak and boil all parts to eat.

Salmonberry: a plant with purple-red flowers and red or yellow berries, it looks like a small raspberry plant. The raw berries are edible.

ANIMAL FOOD

The dangers of movement through arctic landscapes can make hunting animals perilous. However, killing and eating animals is essential because the sparse vegetation will not provide sufficient sustenance on its own.

When tracking in polar terrain, you do have the advantage of being able to see animal tracks clearly defined in the snow. Equally, however, the animals can see you, and camouflage is a problem because the terrain is often flat and the white background makes it difficult to hide. Use snowbanks when tracking creatures or, ideally, wear pure white arctic camouflage clothing.

Many polar land animals are large and dangerous creatures, and are best killed with a hunting rifle of large calibre (7.62mm/0.3in plus) firing high-velocity rounds. Good maintenance of a firearm is essential in subzero climates. Don't over-oil the weapon, as the oil may congeal in the freezing temperatures and seize up the mechanism. Check that firing pins, ejector systems, bolts, barrels and gas-pistons (if you have a semiautomatic weapon) are free from frost and ice before using. Don't take a gun straight into a warm environment after being outside, as condensation will build up in the mechanism, eventually causing rust and malfunction.

Bears are the most dangerous creatures you will encounter in arctic climes, and should only be tackled with a gun owing to their power and size. They are formidable hunters on land and in water, and will defend territory and cubs with aggression. Shoot from a distance through a telescopic sight, and have more ammunition ready (preferably loaded in a magazine) in case the wounded bear charges you. To eat polar bear, boil muscle meat to kill *Trichinosis* parasites. Never eat the animal's liver because it contains lethal concentrations of vitamin A.

Thankfully, there are many other animals living on the ice and snow which are less dangerous and easier to catch and kill. However, hunting in polar conditions requires the full range of improvised weaponry, so you should at least manufacture a bow-and-arrow, a spear, a throwing stick and some snares.

SEALS
Track down the young pups in particular, which are born between March and June, and have limited movement. Both pups and adults are easily killed with a heavy blow to the head from a club. To track adults, approach downwind while they are sleeping or wait by breathing holes in the ice. The seal will return to the hole about once every 7–15 minutes to snatch a breath, at which point it can be clubbed and dragged out onto the ice with a hook. Save the seal blubber for fires. As with polar bears, avoid eating the poisonous livers.

SMALL MAMMALS
Subarctic and arctic small mammals include lemmings, arctic hares, stoats, mink, weasels and squirrels, and you can use snares and deadfalls to catch them. Bait the snares with small pieces of meat and position them outside burrows or along runs. Marmots are found in mountainous arctic areas, with burrows marked by large patches of orange lichen outside the entrance. Squirrels tend to inhabit tundra

Arctic fox

Shrew

areas, sticking to ravines and riverbanks for cover. Try to wear gloves when skinning arctic rodents, otherwise you may contract tularemia disease by touching the animal's flesh with your bare hands. Also remember, do not subsist entirely on a diet of rabbit or hare, you will end up starving yourself by depleting your body of nutrients.

GRAZING ANIMALS
Subarctic forested regions are inhabited by several species of grazing animal, including reindeer, caribou, musk ox, elk, goats and sheep. These animals can be large and dangerous, particularly those with antlers, so try to kill with a gun or a bow and arrow. Most grazing animals have acute senses and need to be stalked. Approach them from downwind while their heads are lowered during feeding. Caribou, however, have a natural curiosity, and may even walk over to inspect a flag being waved on a stick. Failing that, crawl up to the caribou on all fours. Be careful, however, that a wolf stalking caribou does not mistake you for prey.

FOXES
Arctic foxes are small, with a body length of only up to 55cm (22in). These animals are well camouflaged by seasonal changes in coat colour and have superb senses. For these reasons, it is necessary to kill them by trapping them, rather than by hunting them. Place snares at the mouths of rabbit or hare burrows, which the fox will visit when hunting, or across the mouth of the fox's burrow itself. Arctic foxes often follow polar bears, hoping to scavenge the bear's kills.

BIRDS
Northern forests and tundra have many birds, usually in the form of water birds such as cranes, geese, swans and ducks, although there are also other types including ptarmigans and grouse. Many – particularly ptarmigans and grouse – are 'tame' and easy to approach. Simply try walking up to one slowly and casually, and killing it with

Ptarmigan

with marine life, including arctic cod and tom cod, eelpout, sculpin, grayling, trout, salmon and crayfish, all to be caught using the fishing methods outlined in Chapter 8. The eggs of the salmon, herring and freshwater sturgeon are safe to eat, but those of the sculpin are not. If you are unsure of a fish type, eat only the main meat.

Shellfish are also in abundance in polar waters, but both catching and eating them requires caution. Be very careful of slipping when probing icy arctic shorelines alone, as the shock of sudden submersion in the water can knock you unconscious. Do not eat dead shellfish (live mussels should close when touched or tapped); shellfish that are tightly shut and do not open after they have been boiled for 5–15 minutes; and shellfish that are not covered at high tide. Avoid the black mussel in areas of snow and ice, as they can be very poisonous. If you have no choice but to eat them, take them only from deep offshore inlets, and eat only the white meat. King crabs come close to the shore in spring and can be caught with a line.

a club or throwing stick. During the summer many arctic birds moult feathers, becoming flightless for two to three weeks.

Whatever animal you kill, do not waste a scrap of flesh or bone. Remove the fur carefully and use it for clothing (you must bleed and gut the animal immediately, before it freezes). Store fat for fuel, and bones and antlers for tools. Preserve any meat you do not eat. Cut any unused meat into joints or cubes, and suspend it above the ground to allow the subzero temperatures to freeze it, while keeping it out of the reach of scavengers and well away from where you sleep. Once it is frozen, wrap the meat up in bags or store in containers.

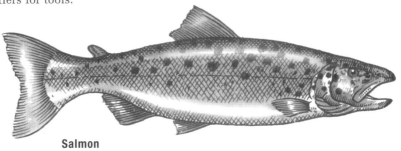

Salmon

Another preservation method which is well suited to the arctic is to soak the food in a brine solution and then dry it. You can make the brine solution by filling a container with seawater, then boiling it. Keep topping the water up as it evaporates, to concentrate the salt solution. After a few refills, stop the boiling and allow the brine to cool. Soak the strips of meat in the solution, then dry them in the air.

FISHING

Fish is probably the most accessible source of meat in a polar climate if you don not have a gun. Arctic and subarctic rivers and seas are teeming

ICE FISHING

To fish through frozen lakes, first cut a hole in the ice over deep water. Make a pennant from cloth or paper, and tie it to a light stick that is shorter than the diameter of the hole. Now tie another stick to the first. This stick should be longer than the diameter of the hole and must be secured at right angles to the first stick. Fasten the fishing line to the other end of the flagpole, and rest the long stick across the hole. When a fish takes the bait, the flagpole will be jerked upright.

CHAPTER NINETEEN

MOUNTAIN SURVIVAL

Mountains are truly dangerous places for the unwary and inexperienced. Terrain, climate and gradient hamper even the simplest processes of movement.

MOUNTAIN EXPLORATION SHOULD be attempted only by, or take place in the company of, very experienced climbers or explorers. Their very location and inaccessibility mean that mountains are unusual places for people to find themselves unwittingly thrust into survival situations. However, with the growth of adventure sports, particularly skiing and snowboarding, more and more people are facing mountain dangers each year. This chapter will provide the fundamentals of mountain survival, but sophisticated climbing or mountaineering techniques must be learned directly from an instructor.

CLIMATE AND TERRAIN

Mountainous terrain varies dramatically in nature depending upon where the mountain is located, its altitude and the local geological conditions. Mountains are as diverse as an arid lump of rock in the American Midwest, to a snow-laden massif in the Himalayas. Generally speaking, mountains are split into two levels: above and below the snow line. Below the snow line, a wide variety of terrain is often found, including loose stones and rocky debris (known as scree), grassy slopes, forested areas and firm ground. The gradients can be shallower than further up the mountain. In a temperate region, mountains follow a fairly standard evolution in ascent below the snow line: deciduous trees, then evergreen coniferous forest, then barren slopes with almost no vegetation. Above the snow line, the conditions are far more barren and extreme, with heavy snow and ice coverings, as well as extreme winds.

Mountainous terrain presents many dangers. Snow and ice are dangerous not only because they threaten a slip and fall, but also because they bring avalanches and tumbling slabs of ice, and obscure handholds and lethal crevasses. On snow-free mountains, falling rocks are a real danger, particularly on scree slopes and across crumbling ridgelines. Other climbers usually cause rock falls, but heavy rain and extreme temperature changes can also bring them on. Wet or smooth stones, or those covered in grass or moss, are slippery and treacherous. Mountain soil can also be extremely loose and prone to giving way underfoot without warning.

Mountain weather conditions are equally hazardous. Even in the course of a single hour, the weather can change quickly from pleasant sunshine to driving rain or snowstorms. Mountains attract three main weather elements: severe cold, high winds and rain (which turns into snow in freezing, high-altitude conditions). These elements form a life-threatening trinity: the rain or snow soaks the individual, then the wind and cold sucks the heat from his or her body.

Air temperature drops with increasing altitude at a rate of about 0.5°–1°C for every 328ft (100m). (For survival purposes, remember that the side of the mountain facing the Equator in temperate regions is significantly warmer than that on the opposite side.) The chill of the wind, however, drives the actual temperatures much lower, even on the sunniest days. Mountain winds are the most powerful on summits and across ridges because wind speed generally increases with height. Wind places a major drain on energy as you try to stay

Rain-shadow effect

The windward slope of a mountain tends to attract
higher levels of precipitation as moist air rises
up the mountain side to form rain clouds.
The leeward side of the mountain
subsequently suffers from a rain-shadow
effect, the descending air being drier
and less prone to severe winds.

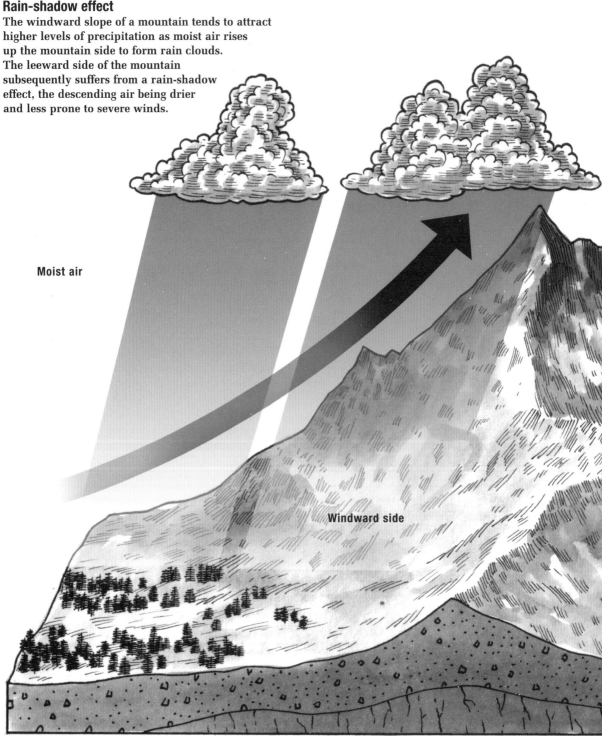

Moist air

Windward side

balanced and it also brings unhelpful precipitation. Weather systems rise up the mountain slopes, cooling as they do so and producing rain, sleet or snow depending on the air temperature. On the leeward slope, rain is reduced. The inclement environment of mountains produces a range of adverse weather effects, including dense fog, whiteouts and storms.

EQUIPMENT

There is a huge range of specialist mountaineering equipment available, but for basic backpacking requirements the following are essential.

WALKING AND CLIMBING ROPES

Walking ropes are used for light climbing duties, fording rivers, and for making a physical link with one another in low-visibility conditions. A walking rope has a breaking strain of around 907kg (2000lb). A climber weighing 82kg (180lb) falling 30m (82ft) will exert a 1038kg (2288lb) force on the rope when he or she is brought up, so walking ropes are not suited to vertical climbing. Proper climbing ropes should have a breaking strain of 1900kg (4200lb), although in the absence of climbing ropes, two walking ropes can be used together as a double rope.

ICE AXE

An ice axe is used for support, stability, braking during falls, digging, and probing the conditions of snow and ice. It consists of a head (adze and pick), a shaft, and a spike. The shaft should have a rubberized cover to aid grip and a leash at the end of the shaft to help you keep hold of the axe should you drop it.

WALKING POLES

A telescopic walking pole (or a pair of them) is an excellent tool to enable safe movement and energy conservation. Research has shown that using a pair of poles for the duration of an eight-hour walk relieves pressure upon the knees and legs of 250 tons. Walking poles also enable greater stability when crossing uneven or rubble-strewn ground.

ASSORTED ANCHORS

There is a range of devices that are extremely useful for setting anchor points when crossing difficult mountainous terrain, and for use in climbing techniques such as belaying and

Dry air

Rain shadow

Leeward side

abseiling (rappelling). A reputable mountaineering supplier should equip you with a selection of the most useful. They can make sure that you have anchors suited to the type of terrain you will be travelling in and, most importantly, teach you how to use them correctly.

CARABINERS
Carabiners are lightweight metal links which are used as connectors between climbers, ropes and pieces of equipment, and like anchors come a huge variety of strengths, configurations and methods of operation. Get expert advice before purchasing (be particularly sure that you understand operational differences between locking and unlocking carabiners), and equip yourself with a minimum of 20 carabiners of different types.

MOUNTAIN MOVEMENT
Walking around mountains requires conscious technique. Inefficient movement results in wasted energy, fatigue and the greater likelihood of accidents. If the mountain is free of snow, or you are below the snow line, walk with small steps at a steady pace, placing the sole of the boot flat on the ground and keeping the body weight balanced over the feet.

On steep gradients, traversing is often a better option than walking straight up. Traversing is simply a zigzag movement up the slope that allows the legs to avoid the full stress

Atmospheric pressure change
The chart below shows how atmospheric pressure drops with the increase in altitude. Altitude sickness tends to begin occurring at altitudes above 2400m (8000ft).

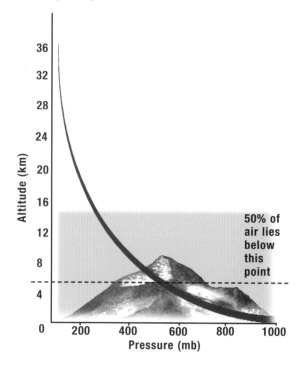

50% of air lies below this point

of the incline. Turn at the end of each traverse by stepping off in the new direction with the uphill foot. This eliminates the risk of losing your balance by preventing you from having to cross your feet. For short stretches of direct uphill travel, keep your toes pointed outwards (known as the 'herringbone step') for greater stability. During descents, keep your back straight (do not lean forwards) and your knees bent, with your weight centred. For walking on grassy slopes, place your foot on the upper side of each tussock, as the ground is usually more level there and the tussock can provide some foot support (although don't rely on it). When descending, it is best to traverse.

Rocky slopes provide a number of challenges and dangers. Do not kick rocks, as you are likely to start a dangerous rockfall. Nor should you jump, as the ground is likely to give way beneath your feet as you land. Keep your heel down, and

LIGHTNING

Lightning strikes are a threat in mountain environments. Here are some precautions to take to lessen the risk.
- If caught in a thunderstorm, avoid summits, vertical cliffs (remember that even standing under an overhang will not protect you from a strike), exposed ridges, lone trees, pinnacles, and gullies with running water.
- Leave wet ropes and metal equipment at least 15m (50ft) from your shelter.
- Sit with your knees drawn up against your chest. This is the best position for surviving earth currents, where the lightning conducts out from the point of impact to other conducting objects.

always watch where you put every foot. Step on top of and on the uphill side of each rock; if you slip, the rock beneath may brace your foot and arrest your slide. If the gradient requires you to use your hands as well, try to keep three points of contact with the rock at all times. Remove any rings you are wearing in case your fingers get jammed in cracks and are injured or torn off.

For ascending scree slopes, kick in with the toe of your upper foot to make a step. When descending, walk down the slope with your feet in a slightly pigeon-toed position using a short step. Always take frequent rest stops to renew your mental and physical strength.

MOVEMENT ACROSS SNOW AND ICE

Movement through thick snow is an exhausting process, one best avoided if at all possible. Assess the type of snow terrain with which you are faced. Early-morning snow is the most stable after low night-time temperatures have hardened it. Snow on south-facing and west-facing slopes has a hardened surface late in the day after the

surface has been exposed to the sun, then refrozen. East-facing and north-facing slopes are frequently soft and unstable. Slopes darkened by rocks or uprooted trees and vegetation provide more stable footing.

If you have to, rope all members of the group together for safety, and those behind the leader can walk in his or her foot imprints (change the leader frequently so that he or she doesn't become exhausted). Travel in single file or in echelon formation. When travelling upwards in deep snow, traversing is the easiest option. Kick the toe into the snow to make a solid footing – don't attempt to walk on the slippery surface of hard snow. Walk slowly in small, even steps. Ideally you should be wearing crampons (spiked iron plates that clamp onto your boots) for maximum grip.

When descending a snow slope, thrust the heel of your boot hard into the snow to make a flat step. On hard snow, this action may require some force. If the slope is very steep, face the slope and go down backwards step by step, using the toe of the boot rather than the heel and maintaining an

Mountain lands

Mountainous areas constitute a small percentage of the Earth's land mass. Major concentrations are down the eastern side of the Americas, parts of

southern Europe and the Balkans, and in Central and northeastern Asia. Almost every country, however, has its own mountainous terrain.

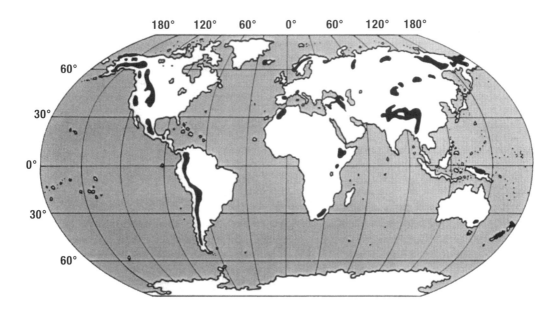

Braking using an ice axe

The braking procedure using an ice axe involves flipping onto your front, gripping the ice axe diagonally across your body. Dig the axe pick into snow, pushing down with full body weight.

ARRESTING A FALL

If you slip on ice or snow, the technique for arresting your fall alters depending on whether or not you have an ice axe:

WITHOUT AN ICE AXE:

• Dig into the snow using your arms, feet, hands and legs to slow acceleration and bring you to a stop.

• Alternatively, roll on your front, push out from the slope with your arms and dig in with your toes.

WITH AN ICE AXE:

• Drive the shaft vertically into the slope. Keep hold of it with one hand near the base, and drive the toes into the snow to get a foothold.

• On harder snow, brake yourself by forcing the pick of the ice axe into the snow. One hand should be on the head of the axe and the other on the shaft. The adze of the axe is pushed into the hollow just below the collarbone. Force the pick down into the slope by pushing down with your arm and shoulder. Pressure should be on the axe and on the knees, with feet raised.

anchor with an ice axe (the ice axe should be used as an anchor for all snow and ice walking).

Try to avoid crossing crevasses if at all possible, although you can sometimes jump over narrow crevasses. If you choose to do this, take off all bulky clothing and equipment before you jump, and pack down the snow at the edge of the crevasse to make a solid takeoff point. Make sure you know for certain where the opposite edge of the crevasse really is before making the jump. As you land on the other side, fall forwards and dig into the ground with the ice axe. Remember, also, crevasses are not always visible, so keep an eye

open for irregularities in the snow, such as dark patches or dips, which may be covering a crevasse.

Exercise extreme caution if forced to use a snow bridge across a crevasse. Using their ice axe, the lead person should probe the immediate area closely, checking that the snow is both deep and

Braking positions
To brake yourself during a slide, either adopt a spread-eagled position, digging in with your heels (A), or push yourself off the slope as shown in (B) – this latter position drives all your weight onto your toes, which then act as brakes.

strong. Rope up the lightest member of the team and send them across first. If the bridge holds, send everyone else over one at a time, walking in the tracks made by the first person. Cross narrow or weak bridges by slithering on your stomach, distributing the body weight over a broader area.

Should the worst happen and someone falls into a crevasse, the rest of the team should drop backwards and down on their haunches, digging their heels into the snow to arrest the fall. Pass a rope down with a loop in it so the suspended person can put a foot in it and therefore prevent his rope from asphyxiating him. Pull the victim out of the crevasse as quickly as possible, as temperatures down there will be like a deep-freeze.

GLACIERS

Glaciers are expansive rivers or sheets of ice that move across a mountain or through a valley. Snow accumulates on top of the glacier and is itself turned into glacial ice with time. Glaciers also pick up crushed rock, known as moraine, and deposit it in ridges along the side (lateral moraine), along the middle (medial moraine) and at the end of the glacier (terminal moraine). Glaciers are dangerous geological features. Their surfaces can be brittle and weak, with crevasses

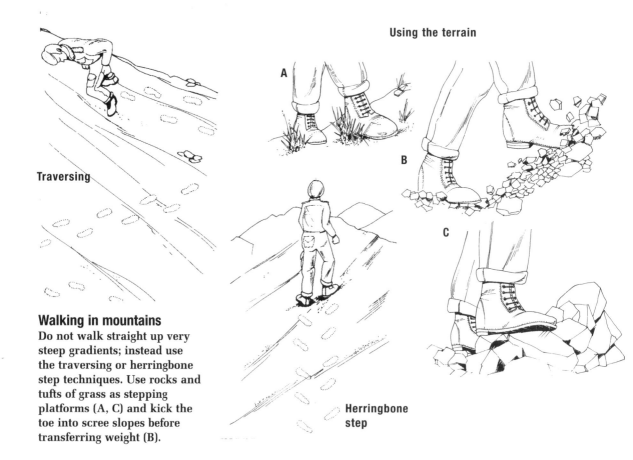

Traversing

Using the terrain

A

B

C

Walking in mountains
Do not walk straight up very steep gradients; instead use the traversing or herringbone step techniques. Use rocks and tufts of grass as stepping platforms (A, C) and kick the toe into scree slopes before transferring weight (B).

Herringbone step

and glacial streams running just beneath the ice. These same streams may run on the surface, creating a lethal and almost frictionless surface. Moraines are also dangerous, their material being loose and difficult to cross.

When crossing a glacier, all group members should be roped together and walking in single file, stepping in the leader's footsteps. Early morning crossings are best – higher temperatures later in the day will turn more ice to meltwater. In especially icy conditions, or if a glacier is heavily crevassed, lateral and medial moraines can provide the best routes of travel, particularly if composed of larger blocks of stone. Exercise extreme care when crossing a glacial surface stream because the bed and undercut banks are usually made up of hard, smooth ice that offers no secure footing. Watch out for areas where the glacier gets steeper or bends, as these are often unstable locations.

AVALANCHES
The threat of avalanches needs to be taken very seriously. The lives of numerous winter sports enthusiasts are carried off each year by this phenomenon. Avalanches can occur at any time of the year (though are most common in winter), and are caused when surface snow slides over a harder base layer of snow or ice, or smooth ground. Wet snow is the more dangerous type, as water acts a lubricant while making the snow denser and heavier, and more likely to slide. If you can make a snowball out of the snow, it is quite wet; if your gloves are dripping wet from handling the snow, it is very wet.

The best way to protect yourself against avalanches is a careful reading of the landscape and climate to alert you to danger areas so that you can avoid them. The following are typical factors in the origins of an avalanche:

Ground surface: avalanches are common on

Safe **Safe if wind has eroded snow** **Safe** **Dangerous** **Moderately dangerous** **Safe**

Wind direction

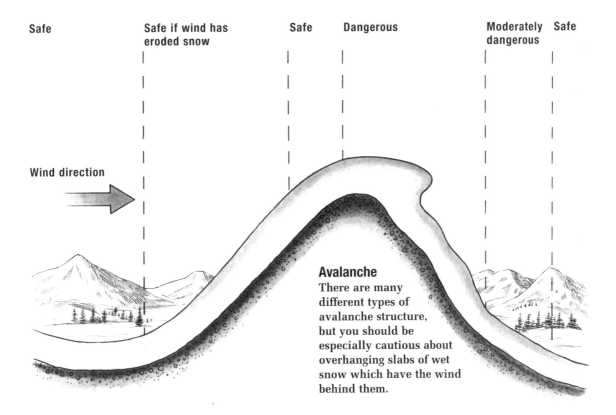

Avalanche
There are many different types of avalanche structure, but you should be especially cautious about overhanging slabs of wet snow which have the wind behind them.

smooth, grassy slopes or hard rock surfaces because these have less arresting friction. In contrast, areas strewn with trees and large rocks are generally low risk. An area that has suffered an avalanche is likely to suffer one again.

Gradient: slopes of between 20° and 50° are most likely to have an avalanche, and the steeper the gradient, the more the danger.

Slope profile: slab avalanches are more likely to occur on convex slopes because of the angle and gravitational pull. In winter, north-facing slopes are more prone to snow slides, whereas in summer south-facing slopes are vulnerable. Leeward slopes are hazardous because snow is blown into large drifts. If the surface snow is not attached to the snow underneath, a slab avalanche can occur. Although windward slopes generally have less snow, they can be prone to avalanches in warm temperatures (when the snow becomes wetter).

Cornices: cornices are overhanging masses of snow forming on the crests of ridges or any angled feature. A cornice can break off and trigger an avalanche.

Snow type: loose snow underneath compacted snow increases the risk of avalanche, as the loose snow forms a fluid base over which the hard snow can run. Check the underlying snow with a stick to gauge its quality. If you prod the snow with the axe shaft and notice sudden softening in resistance beneath the surface, there is an avalanche danger. Light snow and dry snow also increase the risk of avalanche, as does a sudden heavy snowfall that doesn't have time to settle and become stable.

Winds: wind speeds of more than 25km/h (15mph) increase the danger of an avalanche.

Temperature: subzero temperatures, sudden and extreme temperature changes (especially between day and night) and the warmer temperatures of spring can all heighten the likelihood of avalanches.

Direct indicators: look for signs of earlier avalanches, such as trees that have been pushed over rocks that have been scattered. Snowballs tumbling downhill or sliding snow are direct indicators of a possible impending avalanche.

Types of avalanche

Wet slab avalanches are the result of snow mixed with water. Hard slab avalanches are formed by huge chunks of snow which break off from a wind-compacted sheet. Soft slab avalanches consist of powdered snow.

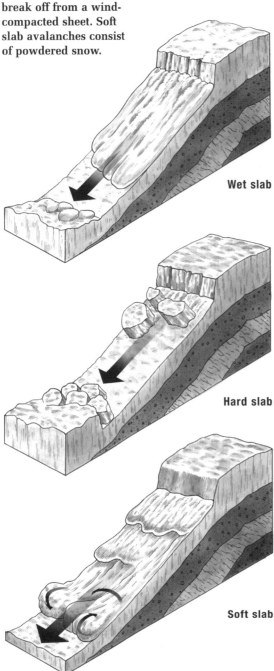

Wet slab

Hard slab

Soft slab

Be wary if the snow sounds hollow underfoot. If long cracks start to run through the surface of the snow, a slab avalanche is actually beginning.

If you are crossing an avalanche danger zone the team should be roped together. One person at a time should cross, travelling as high up the slope as possible (crossing lower down means you'll be hit by more snow if an avalanche does run), aiming to disturb the ground as little as possible. Moving between protective features, such as large rocks, increases your survivability.

SURVIVING AN AVALANCHE

If caught in an avalanche, remove your backpack and skis immediately if possible. Once it hits, try to move towards the peripheries of the avalanche (which have less force) by rolling or making a backstroke swimming action – this keeps your back to the avalanche blast and stops your head being driven down into the snow. Keep your mouth tightly shut, and if powdery snow threatens to block your nose and mouth cover them with clothing. Remember that the avalanche is stronger than you are. If you are truly caught by one, wait until it settles before you try to rescue yourself. If the worst happens and you are buried, your goal is naturally to get to the surface. Clear a breathing space in front of your face and don't

ICE AND SNOW ANCHORS

Above the snow line, vegetation anchors are almost entirely absent and rock anchors may be covered completely with snow. Anchors can, however, be manufactured from snow and ice.
ICE ANCHOR:
Cut a mushroom-shaped anchor in a solid piece of ice. It should have a diameter of at least 40cm (18in) and a depth of at least 15cm (6in). Test the bollard under strain, and if it shows any signs of cracking make a new bollard.
SNOW ANCHOR:
Snow anchors should be at least 30cm (1ft) deep and from 1m (40in) wide in hard snow to 3m (10ft) in soft. The big problem with snow anchors is that ropes cut easily into the soft material. To prevent this, put packing material such as clothing or even backpacks between the rope and the anchor to stop the rope from slicing into the snow.

Avalanche protection

Areas with a high avalanche risk often take precautions, which include avalanche walls to shore up snow accumulation, rakes, fences, wedges and forest to slow avalanche flow, avalanche gullies to channel an avalanche and deflectors to protect habitations.

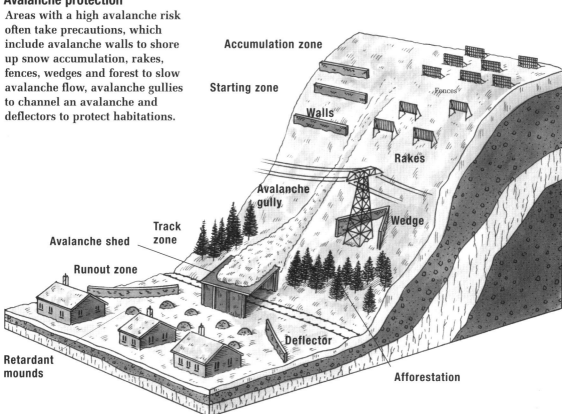

expend valuable air by shouting for help. Disorientation from being tumbled in the snow, combined with the pitch black, can mean you don't know the direction to the surface. To find out, allow some spittle to drip freely from your mouth – the direction in which the spittle drips is the opposite direction to the surface. Now dig slowly and methodically towards the surface, resisting panic, until you break free.

Rescuing someone else buried by an avalanche is not easy. There may be some distance between where they were hit and where they are actually buried. First, mark the person's position where the avalanche hit. Work downwards from this point to try to find the place of burial (a trail of personal belongings may indicate the direction in which the person was swept) probing gently through the snow with the ice axe shaft (or any other means). The more people who can be involved in the search the better, but do not go for

assistance that is more than 15 minutes away – the person buried is likely to suffocate in that time. On finding the victim, dig them free and immediately clear their mouth and airways of snow. Give artificial respiration if they are not breathing (see Chapter 13), even before fully removing them from the snow.

CLIMBING TECHNIQUES

Climbing techniques cannot be learned from a book, but you can acquire knowledge of some basic climbing methods through reading, which will provide a clear advantage to survival in mountainous terrain. If climbing in rocky or steep terrain without a rope (a bad idea), face the cliff and move only one foot and hand at a time, ensuring a good hold before moving your body weight. Avoid spread-eagled positions; keep your weight centred and let your legs take the strain. If climbing up vertical fissures, place your back

Avalanche survival

When caught by an avalanche, if possible 'swim' to safety by thrashing the arms in a crawl stroke to stay on the surface. If you are submerged, thrash your arms and legs as the avalanche slows to create a breathing space for when movement stops.

against one surface, and wedge your legs across the gap on the other.

When climbing using ropes, the techniques of belaying and abseiling (rappelling) are useful tools for controlled ascents and descents. Belaying is a way for two or more climbers to secure an ascent. One person, known as the belayer, first finds an anchor point (see below) and ties the rope securely to it using a figure-eight knot. He or she then passes the climbing rope over his or her head and down to just above the hips (but not the waist), making a twist around the arm closest to the anchor (known as the dead arm) and taking up the slack. Long sleeves and gloves must be worn to protect against friction burns. The climber then attaches the rope around the waist with a bowline and climbs, while the belayer secures their ascent and pays out or pulls in rope (rope feeding is

MOUNTAIN RESCUE CODES

The following codes are internationally recognized mountain rescue signals and can be transmitted by auditory (whistle or foghorn) or visual (flare, heliograph, flashlight) methods:

SOS SIGNAL
Auditory: three short blasts, three long blasts, three short blasts (repeat after a one-minute interval).
Visual: three short flashes, three long flashes, three short flashes (repeat after a one-minute interval). A red flare also means SOS.

'HELP NEEDED' SIGNAL
Auditory: six blasts in quick succession (repeat after a one-minute interval).
Visual: six flashes in quick succession (repeat after a one-minute interval). A red flare can also be used.

'MESSAGE UNDERSTOOD' SIGNAL
Auditory: three blasts in quick succession (repeat after a one-minute interval).
Visual: three flashes in quick succession (repeat after a one-minute interval). A white flare also means the message has been understood.

'RETURN TO BASE' SIGNAL
Auditory: prolonged series of blasts.
Visual: prolonged series of flashes. A green flare can also be used.

Rescue search

Searching for avalanche victims should follow a methodical procedure. Search downwards from the last position where the person was seen, using discarded pieces of equipment and clothing as further directional guidance. Speed the search up by using several people in an evenly spread line.

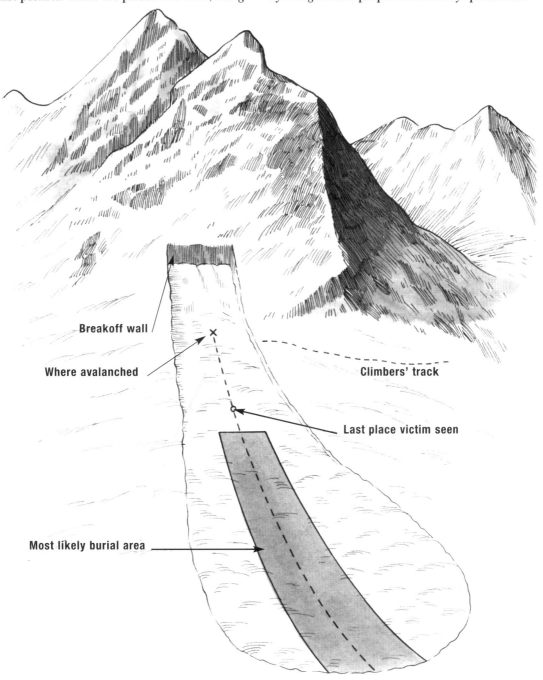

Breakoff wall

Where avalanched

Climbers' track

Last place victim seen

Most likely burial area

Belaying

Belaying is a way of climbing for two or more people using ropes. The belayer (the person who feeds out the rope) should be firmly anchored to a solid structure and must lay the rope out to run freely through the braking knot. The skill of belaying is to not let too much slack develop nor take up the slack too quickly (therefore throwing the climber off balance).

Abseiling

When abseiling, make sure you lean out from the rockface at a 45 degree angle and keep the legs spread about shoulder width apart for stability. Brake by leaning back and facing straight into the rockface. Make sure that no bare skin is in contact with the rope, or friction burns will result.

Figure-eight loop

Manharness hitch

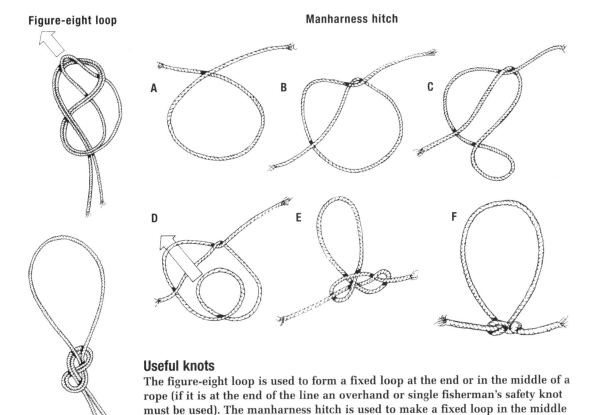

Useful knots

The figure-eight loop is used to form a fixed loop at the end or in the middle of a rope (if it is at the end of the line an overhand or single fisherman's safety knot must be used). The manharness hitch is used to make a fixed loop in the middle of a line, and can be used as an anchor loop or foothold.

only done with the live hand). The belayer and climber should always keep in a straight line with one another. If possible, the belayer should adopt a sitting position, bracing the legs against a solid surface with the rope running around the hips. Should the climber fall, the belayer brings their dead hand across the front of the body and braces for the impact.

Abseiling (rappelling) is a solo technique for a safe descent, although it requires practice under expert supervision to master. As with belaying, the first stage is to find an anchor point, ideally above the ledge on which you are standing, so that the rope does not rub on the ledge as you descend. Double the rope around it, ensuring that the other end of the rope reaches your intended destination (tie two ropes together if you need a longer drop). The abseil (rappel) point should allow the rope to run around it when one end is pulled from below to free the rope. Check the area around the anchor

point carefully. The rope should not run against any sharp rock that could cut through it, nor should it be allowed to run through narrow cracks in case it gets jammed in where you cannot retrieve it. Remove any loose rocks because the rope may dislodge them to fall on you or others.

To make the abseiling (rappelling) action, the climber first faces the anchor point, straddles the rope, then pulls it round the upper left thigh from behind, diagonally across the chest, and back over the right shoulder. (Note: all instructions can be reversed to the other side of the body if preferred.) The rope is held by the 'braking hand' on the same side of the hip that the rope crosses; the braking hand is kept low and facing slightly sideways.

Now walk slowly backwards off the ledge, using the lower hand, never the upper, to control braking. Descend smoothly and slowly, feeding the rope through your hands and taking small

Seat harness

To tie a seat harness, keep the midpoint on the hip, cross the ends of the tape in front of the body and tie three overhand wraps where the tapes cross (A). From the front to the rear bring the ends of the tape between the legs, around the legs and then secure with a hitch (B). Bring both ends around to the front and cross the tape again. Then bring the tape to the opposite side of the brake hand and tie a square knot (C).

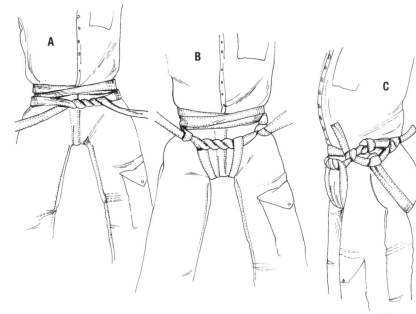

steps. Don't allow yourself to swing side to side, as this may cut the rope against a rock edge. Once at the bottom, you should be able to retrieve the rope by gently pulling and whipping it.

Anchors are the vital safety ingredient in both belaying and abseiling (rappelling), and must be chosen wisely. Two or more anchor points can be a wise precaution, as long as the system doesn't interfere with rope retrieval. The anchor is either a fixed natural feature or can be manufactured using what is known as a chock stone. A chock stone is a stone wedged firmly into a crack in the rock, around which a sling can be fastened. Chock stones take experience to use and select properly, so for general use fixed anchors are better. Spikes of rock are ideal, and trees are also good, although be cautious if they are set in rocky or loose soil – the tree could easily uproot. Rock bollards – large pieces of rock with angled surfaces to prevent rope slippage – are also useable as long as the rope is secure and the bollard will not dislodge under strain. As well as natural anchors, you can use artificial anchors: chocks (metal wedges that fit into cracks) and pitons (metal spikes that can be driven into a crevice to secure a rope).

EMERGENCY PROCEDURES

In a mountain emergency, your priorities are

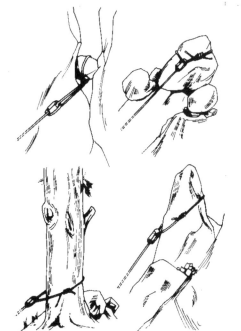

Anchor points

Anchor points need to be selected carefully. Test an anchor's strength prior to hanging your full weight on it, and ensure that the anchor has no sharp edges which will cut through the rope.

simple: head downwards to reduce exposure to high-altitude weather conditions. Down in the valleys, you are also more likely to find civilization and rescue. Before moving off, spend time reconnoitring the terrain. Do not move at night or in conditions of poor visibility, as you could injure yourself or make bad decisions. Look for viable routes down to the mountain floor, avoiding difficult climbs, gullies (which have a higher risk of rock falls) or areas of loose and precipitous terrain. Ideally, try to locate and use paths worn by other climbers or walkers. Work your way around to the lee of the mountain, out of the wind and with lower precipitation levels than the windward side.

The worst-case scenario for mountain survival is if you lose, or do not possess in the first place, a tent or similar shelter to protect yourself from the elements. Beneath the snow line, there should be enough woodland to find shelter-building materials, but above the snow line there will be almost nothing. Here the best response is to dig out a snow cave (of the type discussed in Chapter 18), as this will shelter you from the lethal

mountain winds. If conditions and materials allow, build a fire when possible, and use fire reflectors to provide all-round warmth. Whatever shelter you choose to build, don't allow yourself to forget the need to get off the mountain and down into the valleys as quickly as possible.

As well as sheltering materials, mountains are also low on food sources on their higher slopes (the lower slopes will often have many of the plant and animal foods associated with temperate climates – see Chapters 7 and 8). Mountain goats and sheep sometimes live on the upper slopes, but their agility and excellent senses make them difficult to catch unless you have a gun. If you do have a gun, don't shoot the creatures on narrow ledges where they might tumble off and fall out of reach. As always, make your goal getting down into the valleys – the lower you go, the more plant and animal food you will find. Finding water, however, is usually not a problem in mountains. Rainwater often courses down through natural channels, or settles in rock bowls, and melted snow and ice can be drunk when melted without the need for purification.

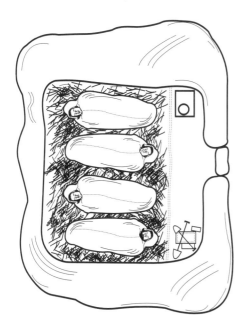

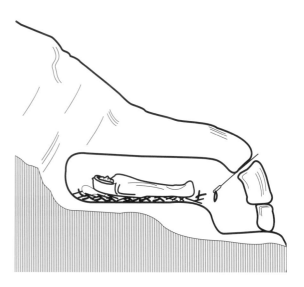

Mountain snow cave
Mountain snow caves can be built into ledges or recesses where snow drifts have formed. Cut deep into the snow to form a central chamber and, if

there is any vegetation available, use it to make an insulating platform. Seal the door with a snow block or rucksack, but leave some ventilation.

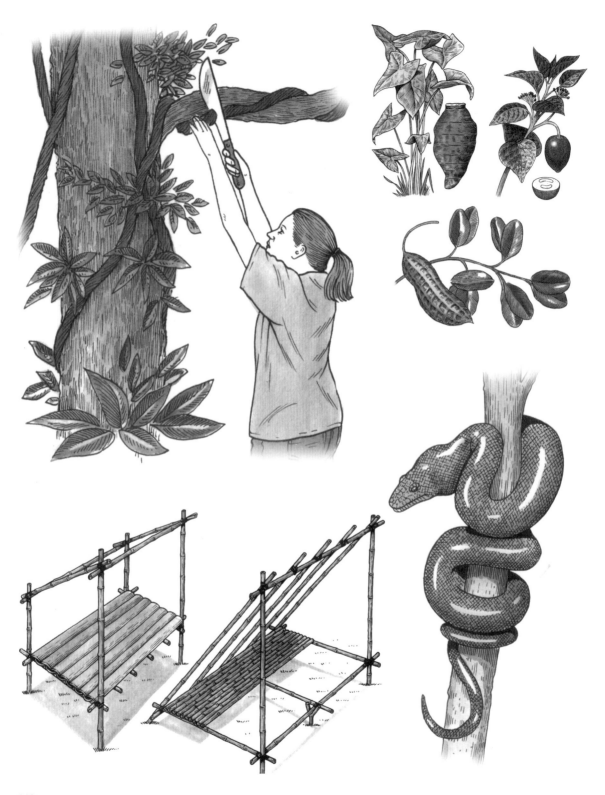

• CHAPTER TWENTY

TROPICAL SURVIVAL

Tropical regions usually offer the survivor many sources of food, water and shelter. Yet the climate and abundance of dangerous creatures mean the tropics remain hostile places.

TROPICAL ENVIRONMENTS ARE usually classified according to five categories: rainforest, semi-evergreen seasonal forest, tropical scrub and thorn forest, tropical savannah, and swamps. While each of these environments has its own specific terrain and weather conditions, tropical environments are unified by several distinct factors. High temperatures are combined with oppressive humidity and a generally heavy rainfall that occurs either year round or in seasonal movements. There is a marked dry season of reduced rainfall and a monsoon season of continuous heavy downpours persisting for days or even weeks.

Tropical days and nights are of equal length. In jungle areas, the lush foliage is extremely thick, and in rainforests it forms itself into a canopy high above the ground, creating almost twilight conditions below. Animal and insect life in the tropics exists in greater density and variety than anywhere else on Earth, creating a fascinating biophysical environment, but one full of dangers for humans.

Tropical regions are prone to powerful weather forces such as hurricanes, cyclones and typhoons. These tend to originate over the oceans, then move inland to cause widespread destruction.

JUNGLE MOVEMENT

Moving through the jungle is a frustrating and painful business. Sharp thorns and thick vegetation both reduce visibility and inflict constant minor injuries. Insects, high humidity and extreme temperatures add to the misery.

Jungle movement is made easier by basic items of practical equipment. A machete should be a standard part of your kit, to cut through vegetation, make shelters, collect firewood, build rafts and even prepare food. When hacking at

vegetation, cut at an oblique angle to the stems of the plants, as cutting at right angles is largely ineffective and can result in the blade getting stuck in the foliage. A compass is needed to maintain a bearing, as visibility is reduced to a matter of yards in dense jungle unless you can reach high ground. For the nights, pack a hammock and some mosquito netting so that you can quickly create a comfortable and protected sleeping environment.

Only travel through the jungle during the daylight, as the night is a particularly dangerous period. Try to follow human or animal trails to make the going easier, but watch out for animal traps left along the trails by local people. In particular, do not follow a trail with a rope barrier or grass net across it, as there is probably an animal trap beyond. You also need to be wary of where animal trails might lead you to – they could take you deeper into the jungle.

Try to avoid walking through dense thickets and swamps, and make your way carefully

THE MONSOON

Monsoons occur in India, Myanmar (Burma) and Southeast Asia. Monsoons are not only associated with heavy rainfall. Between November and April runs the 'dry monsoon', during which time northern winds from Central Asia produce sparse, intermittent rainfall and much fine weather. By contrast, between May and October the 'wet monsoon' is brought in on southern winds from the Bay of Bengal, resulting in heavy, often torrential rain that lasts for days or weeks at a time. It is the alternation of high rainfall and intense sunlight that gives the tropics its lush vegetation.

around thorn bushes. If you have to walk straight through dense vegetation, maintain a rhythm with the machete to clear a path, and move slowly and cautiously, using your upper body at an angle to push vegetation aside, rather than walk flat into it. Don't grab onto plants to help pull you over obstacles; many tropical plants contain irritants or spiked surfaces. Never use your hands or feet to push aside thick foliage as you may disturb snakes, spiders, ants or any of the number of tropical creatures inhabiting the branches. Use a stick first to probe the ground.

Following the lines of ridges and rivers can aid jungle travel. Ridges often have less vegetation covering them which, combined with their altitude, makes visibility and navigation easier (hence game trails are often found along ridges). However, tropical ridges can be crumbling and may run alongside dangerous ravines, crevices and cliffs, so exercise caution. The banks of rivers and streams can make for better going, and following a waterway will help you to navigate, offer you plentiful supplies of fish and increase your chances of finding civilization. If a river has a mild current, rafting down it is one way of making good progress. Avoid negotiating

waterways that are swampy or excessively overgrown, or have powerful currents.

Try to stay out of the water itself, as tropical waters usually contain leeches, parasites and dangerous fish or reptiles. Also, do not use river trails at night, as during the hours of darkness they tend to be used by wild animals.

CLOTHING TIPS FOR THE TROPICS

- Wear clothing made of strong materials to protect the body against thorns, vegetation, insects and leeches. Always check clothing and boots for insects before putting them on.
- Always keep one set of clothing wrapped up in waterproof bags to change into for the night. Daytime clothes will become soaked with sweat and are unlikely to dry out because of the humidity.
- Buy strong jungle boots and always wear them when moving. Do not wear leather boots because they will rot in the harsh tropical climate.
- Wash out clothes at every opportunity. Bacteria grow rapidly in tropical climates, and unhygienic clothing can soon produce skin diseases.

Tropical rainforests

Tropical rainforests are concentrated in relatively few areas of the Earth, and constant deforestation by humans means that these areas are shrinking at an alarming rate each year.

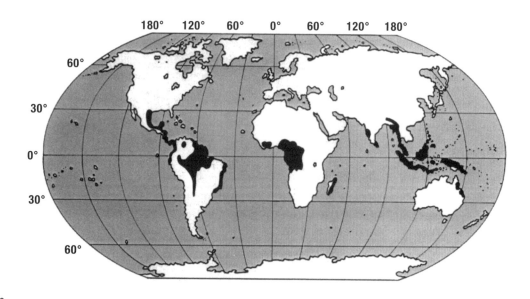

Should you need to cross a stream, first select a safe place you can enter the water from. Select a point away from rapid, rocky or deep waters. Ideally the waters should come no higher than your waist, although the final deciding factor should be the strength of the current. Check that you are able to climb out on the opposite bank, preferably crossing to an area of shallow sand or shingle banks. Note that you should cross a river at a 45° angle to lessen the impact of current, so pick your exit point accordingly. When crossing any river, use a long stick held downstream of your body to brace yourself against the riverbed and provide you with

River crossing

Using a loop of rope to make a river crossing ensures that the person in the water is fully enclosed by the line for both the initial and subsequent crossings.

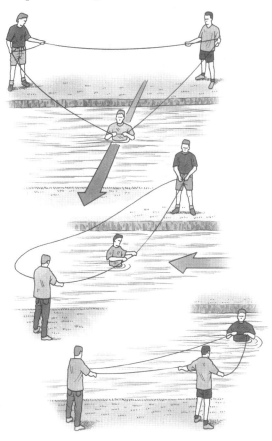

QUICKSAND

Quicksand is commonly found along tropical rivers and on flat shores. Should you find yourself sinking into quicksand, don't struggle because this will only make you sink more quickly. Smoothly adopt a spread-eagled position on your back. This helps to disperse your body weight and stop you from sinking. Now make swimming actions to move yourself out of the quicksand, or get companions to throw you a lifeline. Spread out, and swim or pull along the surface to reach firm ground.

three points of stability instead of the two offered by your legs. Also, never cross a river with a pack fully strapped to your back. If necessary, make a small raft of sticks and float the backpack across.

When trying to get your bearings in the jungle, first attempt to work out where you are. Move to high ground (or climb a prominent tree if you can do it safely) and take note of rivers and other landmarks you can use to get your bearings. Now set a compass bearing and follow it, although jungle undergrowth will inevitably mean many deviations. Keep checking your position in relation to a prominent landmark, and once you have passed that landmark select another to keep you on course. In very dense jungle, mark your trail as you walk with notches cut in trees, or piles of stones. These will enable you to find your way back to camp or your starting point if necessary.

CAMPS AND SHELTERS

Aim to begin constructing your camp and shelter at least an hour before sunset, as darkness comes quickly in the tropics. Regardless of the warm tropical temperatures, never sleep on the ground, as insects and possibly snakes looking for somewhere warm to sleep will plague you. Instead, make a raised shelter either on a platform or by setting up a hammock. Follow all the usual rules for locating a shelter (see Chapter 10). Look up and check for any dead wood, coconuts or insect nests directly above that might come crashing down on you. Ensure that rivers or streams nearby will not endanger you if they flood owing to a sudden downpour. Clear away as much underbrush and dead vegetation as possible around your campsite to reduce insects, remove

Shelters

The tropics has plentiful materials for shelter
building. In jungle areas, always ensure the main
platform of the shelter is built above the jungle
floor to prevent insect infestation.

Paraplatform shelter

Platform shelters

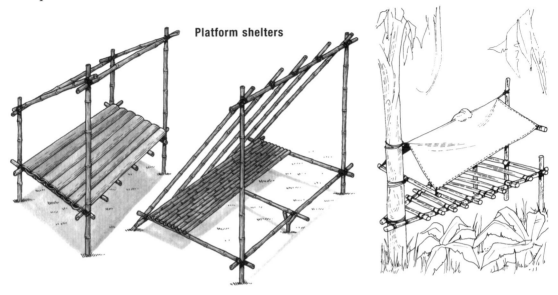

Process for building a seashore shelter

Hammock

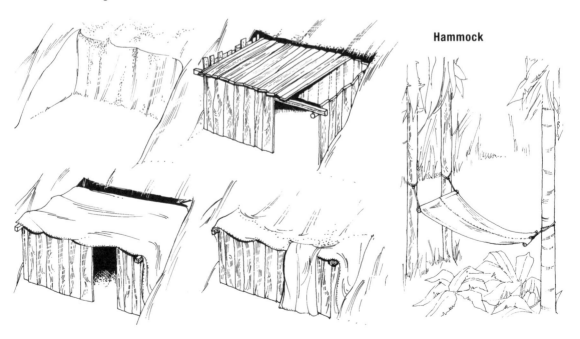

hiding places for snakes and make you more visible to rescue aircraft.

The jungle will provide you with all the materials you need to build a shelter. Bamboo shafts can be used to make any structural part of the shelter, from pole supports to roofing, and frames of sticks or bamboo can be thatched with large leaves (such as palm or atap leaves) or elephant grass. To build a basic platform shelter, find four trees set in roughly a rectangular shape. Now cut two strong poles or two shafts of bamboo, and tie these parallel to each other between the trees above the floor level (if you are in the swamp area, make sure the platform is higher than the visible high-tide mark on surrounding trees). Lay cross pieces between the two poles to make the sleeping platform (cover it with leaves and branches to make a 'mattress'), and construct a secondary sloped platform higher up to act as a roof. You can use split bamboo to make roofing: cut the stem in half and lay pieces alternately to interlock with each other. You can also flatten split bamboo and use it for lining walls or shelving. Exercise caution when using bamboo; it produces very sharp edges and splinters when cut, and can often spring up at speed when cut under tension.

A platform shelter is one of the more advanced tropical dwellings, but use your imagination to construct lean-to, A-frame or any other type of shelter that suits the environment. Two excellent pieces of kit to have with you are a hammock and a tarpaulin. Simply sling the hammock between two trees, then make a roof above you using the tarpaulin thrown over a piece of rope also tied between the two trees, with stabilizing lines running from each corner of the tarpaulin to open it out. In this way, a simple but functional shelter can be erected in minutes.

FINDING WATER
The tropics usually contain plentiful supplies of surface water such as streams, ponds and rivers. Simply collect it, filter it and purify it to drink, observing all cautions about dangerous water sources outlined in Chapter 6. (The purification process is made more important by the fact that in many tropical regions streams and rivers are used as toilets.) If a stream is flowing fast and has a stone and sand bed, the water is usually of good quality, but you must still boil it as a precaution.

Bamboo
Bamboo sections will often contain water suitable for drinking. Tap the bamboo and listen for water, then cut out a section and drink from the open end if the water appears clean.

Banana stump
Cutting down a banana tree will produce a stump which, when scooped out and formed into a bowl, will steadily fill with water.

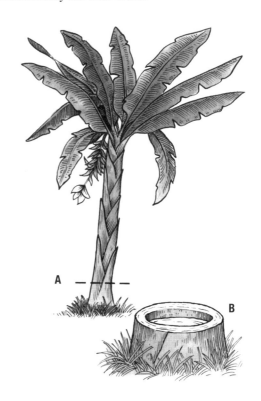

Tropical plant life can be another good source of water, as many plants are designed by nature to capture and retain water. The bromeliad plant of South America, for example, stores water at the point where their leaves gather together at the base. Pitcher plants feature a leaf structure like a cup, which fills with water to trap and digest insects. The traveller's tree, which is much like a palm, can hold up to 2 litres (3.5 pints) of water at the intersection of the leaf stalks. Look for water in hollow sections of stems or leaves, Y- or cup-shaped plants, and cracks and hollows, and be guided by mosquitoes, flies and ants concentrating over a particular plant. Filter and purify any water taken from plants.

Green bamboo frequently contains water.

The pitcher plant

Pitcher plants are structurally designed to capture water, and some of the larger specimens can hold up to 4 litres (one gallon). However, always filter and purify any water taken from this plant.

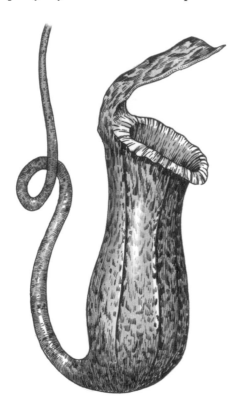

Shake the stem and listen for water sloshing inside. Either cut out the section containing the water or cut off the top of the plant and bend it over to allow the water to run out into a container. You can drink the water if it is clean-looking, but purify it if it is brown or black or has any discoloration.

Banana plants and coconuts are two other excellent sources of water. To obtain water from a banana plant, cut out the inner section of a stump to make a natural bowl – water will seep into the bowl and fill it up. Coconuts, of course, supply coconut milk, which can be drunk without purification. Tap a small hole into the coconut using a sharp stone or knife as a chisel, and drink straight from the hole.

A classic tropical water source is the common vine, although some species of vines are poisonous. Don't drink from vines that have a white, milky sap. Rub some of the fluid on the inside of your wrist before drinking to see if you get an allergic reaction. To access water in a vine, cut off a piece of vine with your machete, making the cut as high up as you can reach. Then cut off the bottom few inches of the severed section, and water will begin to flow out. If it stops, chop off more of the plant to get the flow going again.

JUNGLE FOOD – ANIMALS

Animals are in unsurpassed abundance in the tropics, with the fauna ranging from almost microscopic insects to elephants and giraffes, depending on the region. The natural place for your hunting is along game trails, where you can trap hedgehogs, porcupines, anteaters, mice, wild pigs, deer, wild cattle, squirrels, rats and monkeys, among other creatures. Do not place traps along routes frequented by human beings, for obvious reasons.

When hunting in the jungle, use your hearing as much as your eyesight. Target your prey from the noises it makes by standing silently and angling your head from side to side until you pinpoint the sound, then acquire the animal visually. When looking at a creature in low light conditions, look at the silhouette of the animal rather than its central mass, as peripheral vision is stronger than direct vision at night. If shooting the animal, you will need to aim a little low to allow for this phenomenon.

Certain tropical mammals provide an excellent

Water from a vine

Chop off a section of vine about 1.5m (5ft) long, then chop off a few inches from the bottom of the section. Water will begin to drip out of the bottom, which can be caught in a container.

meal. The tapir, which is similar to a pig, is often found sleeping in thick, swampy undergrowth and can be killed in a stealthy surprise attack with a spear, club or heavy stone. The chevrotain, or mousedeer, is a tiny, sensitive creature susceptible to the old hunter's trick of lamping – shine a bright flashlight into its eyes in the dark and it will stand rooted to the spot. Step straight forward and kill it with a club. The capybara is a large and very tasty amphibious rodent that can be tracked by following its webbed, muddy footprints and listening for its grunting, squealing calls. Try to kill it on the bank with a projectile weapon before it can slip into the water and dive. Wild pigs are a dangerous prey, but can be killed with spear traps along trails. One point to

MAKING A BLOWPIPE

- Find a piece of hollow reed or bamboo, or drill a hole through a piece of straight-grained wood about 2m (6.5ft) long and about 15cm (6in) in diameter.
- Make darts from the split leaf stalks of trees such as the arenga palm, wrapping a dart made from a large thorn to the same diameter as the tube of the blowpipe.
- Coat the dart with a poison – indigenous tropical hunters often use the poisonous sap of the ipol tree (*Antiaris toxicaria*), which can kill a large mammal in minutes by inducing heart failure.

remember is that peccaries (a type of wild pig) have unpalatable musk glands located 10cm (4in) up from the tail on the spine, which must be removed (cut around them) before the animal is eaten.

Finally, monkeys are a good source of meat, but only small varieties should be tackled as larger chimpanzees or gorillas can be lethal adversaries. Place traps along common primate trails (spear traps baited with fruit are excellent), or kill the monkey in a tree using a gun, bow and arrow, or blowpipe.

It is important to remember that many tropical animals are in fact endangered species. Never kill any animal in the tropics unless you are in an emergency survival situation with a realistic danger of starvation.

Apart from mammals, the tropics' abundant species of birds and lizards will form a large part of a tropical diet, as will larger insect types such as grubs, grasshoppers and crickets. Grubs can be split and roasted it over a fire. When eating grasshoppers and crickets, be sure to remove the wings and legs before cooking and eating. Many tropical frogs are also edible, but avoid any with a brightly coloured and/or malodorous skin, as they can be lethally poisonous. Termites can be collected in volume by pushing a long, thin stick into the side of a mud termite nest, and withdrawing it – aggressive termites will have their jaws clamped on the stick. Or, smash off a piece of the nest with a stone and drop it into water, letting the termites float out to the surface for collection. They are tasty and nutritious creatures and can be eaten raw or cooked by almost any method. Remove the wings and legs before eating them.

Despite their dangers (see below), snakes should be considered a food. Kill a snake with either a blow to the head with a long club or by pinning it to the ground just behind the head before cutting the head off with a machete.

A far easier source of meat obtainable in the tropics is fish. Fishing techniques are outlined in Chapter 8, but some additional methods are available in the tropics. There is a poison called rotenone contained in certain tropical plants which, when extracted and thrown into water, will kill any fish in the vicinity. The seeds of the barringtonia, *Anamirta cocculus* and *Croton tiglium*, and the roots of the *Derris eliptica*, all contain this poison. Simply grind up the respective plant part, mix with water, and leave the mixture to stand overnight. The next day, tip the poisonous compound into a pond or river with a slow current, and dead fish will soon float to the surface of the water.

Fishing in coastal regions can provide good supplies of fish, crab, lobster, crayfish, and octopus, but take special precautions. Never walk barefoot in the water – coral will cut your feet to pieces, or you will acquire needles in your feet from sponges and sea urchins. Slide your feet along the muddy or sandy bottoms of rivers and

Pigs and monkeys
Wild pigs and monkeys are both edible jungle animals and are eaten by indiginous peoples throughout the world.

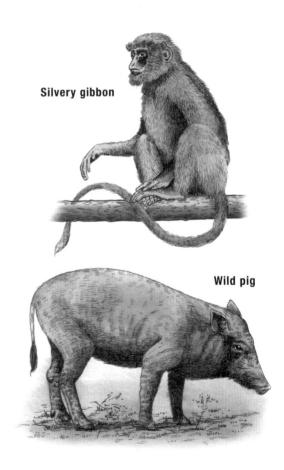

Silvery gibbon

Wild pig

TROPICAL DISEASES

These are typical tropical diseases, listed with symptoms, method of transmission and basic treatment, including prescribed drugs.

When dealing with any tropical disease, you should get the victim to a hospital rather than attempt self-treatment.

BILHARZIA – disease of bowel or bladder. Transmitted by microscopic fluke or worm, passing into body through infected drinking water or broken skin. Treatment: fluids, rest, niridazole.

AMEBIC DYSENTERY – chronic illness producing fatigue, general illness, and bloody stools. Transmitted by ingesting contaminated water and uncooked food. Treatment: fluids, rest, flagyl.

MALARIA – potentially fatal febrile illness transmitted by mosquitoes. Treatment: quinine, paludrine and darapryn.

DENGUE FEVER – transmitted by insects. Produces headaches, joint pain and rashes for up to seven days, then abates leaving the casualty with immunity.

YELLOW FEVER – insect-borne disease producing vomiting, pains, fever and constipation. Treatment: rest and general care.

TYPHUS – transmitted by lice or rat fleas, it is potentially fatal. Symptoms include vomiting, headache, nausea, rash, fever and coma. Treatment: professional medical attention.

seashores to avoid stepping on stingrays or other sharp-spiked animals.

Any food caught in the tropics will decay rapidly if not eaten immediately or preserved. For preservation, rely on smoking, as drying in the open air is practically impossible in the humid atmosphere. In addition, the smoke will keep insects away from both you and the food.

ANIMAL THREATS

The tropics are full of dangerous animals, but most can be avoided by using common sense. The following are typical tropical animal dangers:

Big cats

Big cats such as tigers, jaguars and leopards are rarely a problem, as they rightly fear humans more than we fear them. Normally only sick, old or wounded creatures will attempt attacks on people. If there are any reports of such attacks in an area, stay away from long grass, from where big cats will usually spring an ambush. If you inadvertently corner a big cat, simply back away slowly without making any threatening movements, and allow the cat to escape.

Crocodiles and alligators

Crocodiles and alligators attack prey at the water's edges, approaching silently across the surface before leaping out and dragging the animal, or human, into the water. Give groups of alligators or crocodiles a wide berth, and if you are at the water's edge have another person on dedicated lookout – little more than the eyes will be visible as the creature glides in to attack. Swimming in seemingly tranquil pools is not a good idea. When walking in tropical waters, avoid thrashing around, as this attracts crocodiles and alligators. If chased by a crocodile, ignore the advice to zigzag. Sprint with all the speed you can and attempt to climb quickly up a tree.

Hippopotami

In the African subcontinent, the hippopotamus is actually the most dangerous animal, killing more people than the combined human fatalities from spiders, snakes and big cats. Hippos are massive, aggressive creatures with fearsome tusks and unpredictable temperaments. Do not pilot any sort of boat through a concentration of hippos.

Arachnids

Although there are notable exceptions, such as the black widow and funnelweb spiders, and the buthids scorpions, most poisonous arachnids are rarely capable of killing a healthy adult (the fatalities tend to occur in the very young and very old). Scorpions like to sleep in dark, protected spaces so, to avoid getting bitten or stung, knock out your boots and clothing and pack every morning before getting dressed. Do not touch spider webs. If looking under rocks or logs or in rodent holes, use a long stick to probe. Never use your hand.

DANGEROUS FISH

The South American piranha is the most famous dangerous fish in inland tropical waters. Piranhas grow up to 50cm (20in) long and attack living creatures and strip dead ones with razor-sharp teeth. They are most dangerous when water levels drop during the dry season, so avoid entering the water in areas of piranha activity at these times. A fish of much mythology is the Amazonian candiru. Although it is only about 2.5cm (1in) long, the candiru can, very rarely, swim up the urethra of a person urinating in the water, then become stuck there because of its dorsal spine. Avoid urinating in water.

Boomslang

SNAKES

Snakes are another reason you should wear strong boots when moving through the jungle. Tropical areas contain high concentrations of snakes, and many – such as vipers, cobras, tropical rattlesnakes, mambas and boomslangs – are justifiably feared for their lethal poisons. Snakebites are best prevented rather than cured. Do not antagonize any snake; most will have little interest in attacking you unless you threaten or hurt them. Be careful not to step on a snake, particularly when stepping over logs and stones, and watch that a snake is not coiled around a branch when you go through foliage. Use sticks, not your hands, to inspect under logs and stones. Always check bedding, clothes and backpacks before putting them on in the morning.

If a snake bites someone, do not panic. Before the snake escapes, check what type of it is, or if you do not know remember features such as markings, size and colour so that you can give this information to medics. Get the victim to sit down and try to relax – panic will accelerate the heartbeat and pump the poison more quickly through the bloodstream. Immediately wash the bite area with soap and water. If the snake is venomous, the symptoms will depend on the snake type, but can range from a small

bleeding wound with bruising to failure of the respiratory, cardiac or nervous systems.

Do not attempt to suck out the poison, as this endangers you as well as the casualty. Unless you have specific antivenoms and the knowledge to use them, focus all your efforts on getting the victim into the hands of medical professionals. Monitor them for signs of shock or cardiac/respiratory failure, and treat accordingly. Tie a tight bandage around a bitten limb above the bite to delay the poison circulating around the body. This bandage must not, however, cut off the circulation entirely, as this will possibly endanger the victim more than the bite. You can check the circulation by pinching and releasing the fingernails or toenails to see if the blood flows back in.

Note that some cobras can spit poison as well as bite. If the poison gets into your eyes or an open cut, wash out the wound immediately with water or even, in an emergency, with urine.

Mamba

INSECTS

Insects are actually the most dangerous creatures in the tropics, carrying diseases that cause widespread illness and death. Malaria, for example, is distributed by the anopheles mosquito and kills around 12 million people globally each year. Mosquitoes, combined with the multitude of other tropical insects, can make life a misery for the survivor.

Take sensible precautions to avoid insect bites and stings. Make sure you camp well away from swampy areas, which are perfect breeding grounds for insects. Keep your skin covered with clothing, particularly during the hours of the night, and apply insect repellent to any areas of skin left bare. Always wear your boots, as these will protect you from ticks, chiggers and ants. Also do a thorough inspection of your body each day to check you are not carrying any ticks, leeches or other parasites.

The following is advice on handling specific insect species.

Ticks

Ticks live in grassy areas and can attach themselves firmly to your skin using their powerful jaws. (Also be careful of ticks jumping onto you from an animal carcass.) If they are on your clothing, brush them off. Check your skin each day, and if you find a tick attached do not attempt to pull it off – it will leave its head parts inside your skin and cause infection. Instead, cover it with Vaseline, heavy oil or tree sap (this cuts off its air), then, when the tick opens its jaws, pull it off, gripping as close to the mouth as possible. Alternatively, applying direct heat, alcohol or fuel can make them drop off.

Fleas

Fleas will attempt to burrow under your toenails or skin to lay their eggs. Regular immersion bathing should kill off fleas. Scrape off any attached fleas with a sharp, sterilized knife, taking care not to cut the skin.

Mites

Mites generally inhabit earthen banks, tall grass and stream banks. Mites can be washed off, but prevent their proliferation by maintaining a clean shelter and campsite. Burn off any long grasses, and do not lie or sit on the bare ground.

Protective clothing for insect gathering

When collecting insects, particularly of the flying and stinging variety, cover the entire head with netting, wear gloves and place elastic bands around the trouser ankles.

Bees, wasps and hornets

Avoid making your shelter near nests of bees, wasps or hornets. Prevent any attacks from a swarm by standing still – wasps tend to attack moving targets. If you are attacked, run through thick foliage to break up the insects' flight patterns. If you are stung, remove the sting straight away – scrape it out with a fingernail or knife, but do not squeeze the poison sac. Wash the injury area and use cold compresses to reduce pain and swelling. This advice applies to all insect bites.

Centipedes and millipedes

Although most centipedes and millipedes are harmless, some can give powerful bites or have irritating hairs. Brush them off the skin, swiping in the direction they are walking.

Ants

Never make a camp or shelter near a nest of ants. Watch out for collections of biting ants moving across foliage (especially around mangrove trees) or for ant column in movement along the jungle floor.

Leeches

Leeches are aquatic creatures that can drop onto your skin, latch onto you with a painless bite and feed on your blood, dropping off when they are finished. Check your body for leeches after passing through water or moving through wet foliage by the side of a watercourse. Remove leeches by applying salt, alcohol, the burning tip of a cigarette or stick, nicotine or raw lime. Do not attempt to pull one off because it will leave its head parts inside your skin and cause infection.

Mosquitoes

In areas where mosquito infestation is acute, wear a mosquito head net to protect the face and neck, and sleep under a mosquito net. If you have no net, improvise one or cover exposed skin with mud. Keep a smoky fire burning at night. Tuck your trouser legs into your socks and your shirt sleeves into gloves. Generously cover all exposed skin with insect repellent, and steer clear of swampy areas, where mosquitoes breed.

JUNGLE FOOD – PLANTS

The tropics are full of plant food. Be clear about your identification process, however, as there are some highly poisonous plant varieties. The plants listed below do not grow in all tropical areas. Observe the rules for plant identification and testing outlined in Chapter 7 – the descriptions below are intended as an initial guide only.

The following of the best tropical plants for use as food, although there are many more.

Coconut

Eat the white flesh inside the coconut, and drink its nutritious milk. The section from which the leaves protrude, known as the 'cabbage', can be cooked and eaten.

Citrus fruit trees

The tropics have several varieties of citrus fruit trees, including passion fruit, guava, pomelo and rambutan. Look for tough, evergreen leaves and accompanying small white-to-purple flowers. The round, segmented fruit may have a leathery skin.

Bamboo

Bamboo

You can eat the young shoots (up to around 0.3m/1ft in height) raw or cooked, although avoid or cut off the fine, black hairs along the edge of the leaves. Boil bamboo seeds to eat.

Yams

Yams tend to grow in light forest and clearings. The classic yam (there are several varieties) features a squared vine with two rows of heart-shaped leaves growing on opposite sides of the vine. Yams provide edible tubers, although these must first be cooked to kill off poisons.

Wild yam

Papaya

The papaya has green or yellow fruits growing in clusters under the leaves. The tree itself reaches up to 6m (20ft) in height with large rough-edged leaves clustered at the top. Papayas should be peeled before eating.

Banana and plantain

You can eat banana and plantain fruits either raw or cooked. The flowers, rootstocks and leaf sheaths can usually be boiled and eaten as well.

Plantain

Bignay

A shiny, evergreen shrub with small, round red or black fruit, which can be eaten raw or jellied.

Breadfruit

Breadfruit

A tree bearing large, round, green fruit. Bake, boil or fry the fruit whole or in slices, and boil or roast the seeds to eat.

Mango

A delicious oval fruit that can be eaten raw, the mango grows on trees throughout the tropics.

Nipa palm

Nipa palms have long leaves that collect at the base to form a diminutive trunk. Their flower stalks and seeds are edible.

Papaya (pawpaw)

The fruit of the papaya tree can be eaten either raw or cooked, and grows directly from the trunk. The fruit turns yellow when ripe.

Rattan palm

Rattan palm

This is a climbing plant with a creamy white flower. You can eat the stem tips and palm heart roasted or raw.

Sago palm

A short palm tree with long, arching leaves, it grows by the side of tropical waterways, lakes and ponds. The pith of the tree produces sago. Cook the sago before eating.

Sweetsop

A small tree with a lumpy fruit, which can be eaten raw.

Taro

Taro

Plant growing to about 0.5–1m (2–3ft) high with heart-shaped leaves. Eat the roots, young leaves, and stalks, either boiled or roasted. If boiling, change the water several times to get rid of any extracted poisons.

Water lily

An aquatic plant with edible seeds and roots. Boil or roast the plant parts to eat.

Wild rice

A tall grass found growing in and around wet environments. Access the 'rice' by collecting the husks, then threshing and winnowing them to leave the grain. Boil or roast the grain, which can then be ground into flour.

PREVENTING DISEASE AND ILLNESS

Tropical conditions are perfect for the incubation and proliferation of serious diseases. Your first and most important step to preventing illnesses such as typhus and yellow fever is to have all relevant vaccinations before taking a trip to the tropics. Visit your doctor at least six months in advance of travel, as some courses of vaccination may have to be ordered in or administered over a period of several weeks.

Once in the tropics, put into practice all the insect-avoidance measures outlined above because insects and parasites are primary vehicles for disease transmission. Purify all the water you

Edible tropical plants and fruits

Wild figs, manioc and peanuts will together provide vitamins and, in the case of peanuts, good supplies of fat. Supplemented with meat, these plants can form the basis of a survival diet.

Wild figs

Manioc

Edible roots

Peanut

drink, and try to avoid eating plant foods that you haven't peeled or cooked yourself. Avoid local dairy produce.

Tropical watercourses are disease hotbeds, full of parasitic creatures, so don't enter rivers and streams unless absolutely necessary. If you do go into the water, keep your shoes and some clothes on. Put waterproof bandages over any wounds, no matter how small (many parasites are almost microscopic). It is imperative that you cover any open sores or wounds with waterproof bandages to protect against parasite intrusion. Always wear something on your feet to avoid puncture injuries, whether in or out of water. If you are injured, keep the wound as clean as possible, regularly changing the dressing and applying antibiotic ointment (unless the injury is a burn). Try to have some antibiotics in your medical bag (as long as you know how to use them) in case you or another member of your group gets an infected wound or systemic infection.

It is essential that you pay particular attention to cleanliness in the tropics. Your flesh, especially in sweaty parts of the body such as armpits,

groin, feet and thighs, is vulnerable to 'jungle rot' in very hot and humid conditions. Here, bacteria breeds on the damp flesh, which actually starts to soften and decay resulting in maceration, where the skin softens and begins to decay. Wash regularly in purified water, and allow your body to air itself as often as possible.

Heat exhaustion is a constant problem when trying to function in the tropics. At very high temperatures of above 35°C (95°F), your body relies almost entirely on sweat evaporation to achieve cooling. However, the humidity of the jungle means that the air is already saturated with water, so the sweat is unable to evaporate and cool the body. It just runs off instead, allowing heat exhaustion to set in. General treatments for heatstroke are found in Chapter 13, but in the tropics you can help to prevent the condition by properly acclimatizing over a period of around two weeks. Slowly increase your activity levels over the period to strengthen the body so it can operate in the heat. Drink at least half a litre (one pint) of water every two hours when in the jungle, and maintain a regular salt intake.

Poisonous tropical plants and fruits

The tropics is replete with highly poisonous plant types. Do not eat anything which you cannot positively identify or which you have not proven as safe through the Universal Edibility Test.

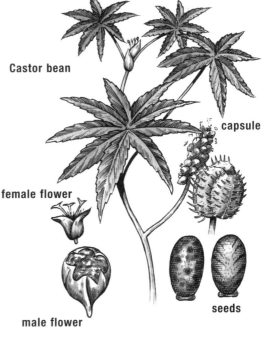

Castor bean

capsule

female flower

male flower

seeds

Physic nut

Strychnine tree

Section of fruit

POISONOUS TROPICAL PLANTS

Research the following plant types and avoid them. Apply the Universal Edibility Test (see Chapter 7) to any plant you cannot positively identify.

nettle trees	strychnine tree
physic nut	cowhage
duchesnia	pangi
castor bean	white mangrove
water hemlock	lantana
manchineel	poison sumacs
rosary pea	

CHAPTER TWENTY-ONE

SURVIVAL IN THE DESERT

Desert survival is, above all, concerned with finding water and making shelter. With midday temperatures of around 54.4°C (130°F) in some deserts, death by dehydration can be rapid.

WE TEND TO associate the word 'desert' with the sandy expanses of regions such as the Sahara, but deserts can be surprisingly diverse environments. Some deserts contain large amounts of vegetation. The Gobi desert, for instance, features grass and scrub coverage over three-quarters of its expanse of 1,040,000 square km (400,000 square miles) and has mainly gravel instead of sand. Even the sand bowls of the Libyan and Saharan deserts become surprisingly luxuriant after the annual rains, which trigger buried seeds and bring apparently dried-out plants into flower.

Acknowledging seasonal rains, the unifying quality of all deserts is aridity and a rainfall of less than 25.4cm (10in) per year. Some deserts actually receive far less rain than this. The Atacama Desert in northern Chile, for example, has around 10cm (4in) of rain each year, and has been known to go for several years without rainfall. To add to the dearth of water in desert environments, the heat of the sun means that evaporation exceeds precipitation, producing an arid landscape, usually with sparse vegetation and only the hardiest and most ingenious of animals.

TEMPERATURES AND RAINFALL
The other characteristic of the desert is scorching temperatures, although in the Gobi Desert winter temperatures can drop to −10°C (−50°F). Even the hottest Equatorial deserts have been known to experience exceptional wintry conditions – frosts may occur in the winter months – but the desert's clear skies, absence of shade and tropical location generally create blistering daytime temperatures of up to 55°C (131°F) in the shade. Temperatures at night can be surprisingly chilly, especially on elevated plateaux, and may even drop below freezing as the desert soil releases its heat.

When rainfall does occur in the desert, it is often in huge volumes and flash floods are common, particularly around rocky plateau deserts, such as the Golan Heights. Because desert soil is loose and dusty, the rains cut out canyons and wadis over time, which are both dangerous to negotiate as well as being good sources of water.

The landscape of deserts varies according to region, altitude, winds and levels of precipitation. In sandy deserts, the sand dunes can be up to 300m (1000ft) high and 24km (15 miles) long. Rocky deserts are often mountainous, and feature high-altitude plateaux where the temperatures are usually cooler and even experience snowfall. Salt marshes are very inhospitable desert terrain. Created by alkaline deposits left in the wake of water evaporation, they are usually incredibly hot, desolate and water-free zones. Most deserts will, thankfully, contain wadis (dry riverbeds) and oases where water can usually be found.

Desert heat and winds can create some particularly hostile weather phenomena. Sand and dust storms are common, and can reduce visibility to zero and in severe cases, even bury vehicles and shelters. For people, sandstorms are desperately uncomfortable. Sand fills the mouth, nostrils and ears, making navigation almost impossible. Navigation is also impaired by mirages created from the refraction of light through heated air. Mirages not only create the appearance of water where there is none, but also create problems in estimating distances and identifying landmarks.

Desert regions

Desert regions mainly straddle the Equatorial lines, although some deserts are to be found as far south as Argentina. All are characterized by extreme aridity and high temperatures.

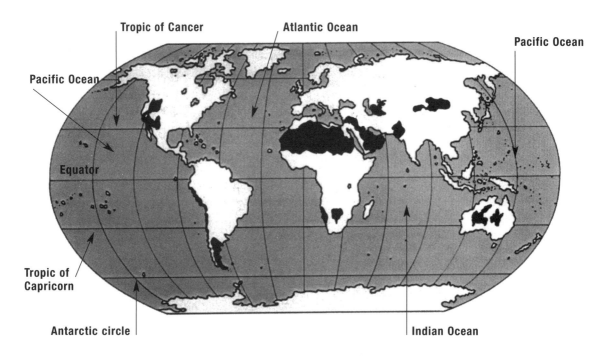

Deserts are typically places with extremely low human populations, but manmade features are found there. Ancient stone-built ruins still litter many deserts, and provide ideal shelter. Roads, pipelines and irrigation canals may also be in evidence, and can lead you to civilization, although such features might stretch for hundreds of miles. Look for trails cut by nomadic tribespeople, as these will usually lead to oases at intervals of around 32–64km (20–40 miles).

WATER

Finding water is the primary consideration in the desert. Even if you rest in the shade, without water you will be dead in three days at a temperature of 48°C (120°F), and even in moderate desert temperatures two weeks of survival would be unlikely without adequate water supplies. If you rest throughout the day, you will still need 4 litres (one gallon) of water every 24 hours to meet your body's basic fluid requirements; if you are exercising hard, then around 12 litres (2.5 gallons) will be more appropriate. Remember that with no water at all, you will probably drop dead from dehydration before you could walk 8km (5 miles) in desert temperatures. Always take more water than you think you need into the desert. You will not be able to carry enough if you go on foot, so vehicular travel is recommended. Try to find out where watercourses, wells and oases are located before you set out.

Obey all the principles of water conservation outlined in Chapter 6. In particular, refrain from eating fatty or high-protein foods. You should not eat at all in any climate if you have a daily ration of only 0.5 litres (17 ounces) of water. Find some kind of shelter as soon as possible, and sit out the daytime heat, using night for movement and tasks. One of those tasks should be hunting for natural sources of water.

Water is undeniably scarce in the desert, but it can still be found. First look at the terrain for any places in which rainwater might have collected,

Dry riverbed

When digging for water in a dry riverbed, dig on the outside of the bends, as this is usually the last place from which the water evaporated, and so is more likely to have water beneath the surface.

Dig here

Dig here

including caves, the base of valleys, gullies, cliffs and canyons, and rocky outcrops, where water may have collected in crevices and holes. Watch for converging animal tracks, trails of animal dung or patterns of bird flight, as the creatures could well be heading for a watering hole. Fresh green vegetation is an excellent sign of water being present, either as open water or as underground water. Palm trees, for example, indicate water within 0.6–0.9m (2–3ft) of the surface. Cottonwood and willow trees suggest a deeper water table, about 3–3.6m (10–12ft) beneath the surface. Certain trees, including the common sage, greasewood and cactus, do not indicate a predictable water table, so do not waste much energy digging beneath them.

Certain plants will actually contain water within them. The inner flesh of the barrel cactus is rich in fluid. Cut into the middle, and squeeze the fluid out of the mashed pulp. The leaf stems of other desert plants, such as pigweed, contain water. Date palms and the baobab tree have water in the trunk (the baobab collects it only in the rainy season), which will ooze out when a branch is cut off near the base or the trunk itself is cut. The lobes and fruit of the prickly pear plant contain water, as does the bark of the saxaul tree. Access this by pressing large quantities of the bark. In the arid Australian outback, the

Desert water sources

Several key desert water sources are represented here: an oasis, a well and a dried-up riverbed. The palm trees are a good indicator of subterranean water.

Water from a dry riverbed

African bushmen are known to extract water from a dry river bed by inserting a long hollow reed into the earth and sucking hard. After around 10 minutes, water may begin to flow up the reed.

bloodwood desert oak and water tree have water-rich roots that can be cut open and sucked.

If no water can be found on the surface or in plants, try to tap into underground water. Dry lakebeds will often contain water beneath – dig down into the bed on the outside of a bend (this will have been the last place from which water evaporated). Should the ground become wet, stop digging and let the hole fill up with water.

In addition to the above, you can utilize the solar still and transpiration bag techniques for extracting water as described in Chapter 6. Dew can also be collected in appreciable quantities off some desert plants, and if you find muddy soil soak a cloth in it and wring out the water into a container. Also look out for gathering rain clouds and be prepared to catch water in a tarpaulin or any other large containers you can improvise. If it is raining in the distance, head in that direction for water.

CLOTHING

Following rules about clothing is just as important in the desert as it is in polar conditions. An improperly covered body will be exposed to sunburn, sunblindness, insects, dehydration and heat exhaustion. During the hot hours of daytime, wear loose trousers and a long-sleeved shirt to protect the skin. Wear a wide-brimmed hat at all times to shield the head from the intense sunlight. A further sensible precaution is to wear a cloth neckpiece over the back of the neck, an area particularly sensitive to burning and overheating. Make sure that all your clothing is loose, as the still air trapped between your body and the clothes makes a cool insulating layer between you and the outside sun. White or light-coloured clothing is best. If possible, manufacture a long, loose robe in the style seen in North Africa and the Middle East. Take off your clothing and boots only in shaded areas or at night.

Water from a barrel cactus

By cutting the top off a barrel cactus (A), mashing the pulp inside (B) and inserting a straw, a decent drink of water can be obtained (C). Cutting through the tough plant can be difficult, so do this only if other water sources are unavailable and then only in the cool evenings to reduce sweating.

Keep your boots on at all times during the day, as burned feet will give you problems in walking, and walking barefoot will leave you open to animal bites and stings. Knock the sand out of your boots regularly, as the buildup will be abrasive and cause open wounds and blisters. If heat is penetrating up through the soles of your boots or shoes, improvise an insole to add a further layer of heat protection.

Your eyes and face are particularly vulnerable to sunburn and glare, especially in sandy deserts where the sunlight is reflected back off the sand. Wear high-quality sunglasses at all times. If you do not have sunglasses, make a headdress by wrapping a protective cloth, preferably white, around your face, cutting two slits for vision.

FOOD
Food is admittedly scarce in the desert, but can be found in a select group of plants and also in desert wildlife. In terms of plant food, there is a key group of plants to look out for:

Protective headwear
This Arab-style headdress is ideal for desert survival. It protects the skull and the back of the neck against the sun, while a face cloth prevents sand inhalation and a burnt nose and cheeks.

Improvised goggles
The sun can damage the eyes as much as the skin. Improvise sunglasses by cutting slits in a piece of material (A) or a cutout section of tree bark (B), and use a cord to fit the 'glasses' around the head.

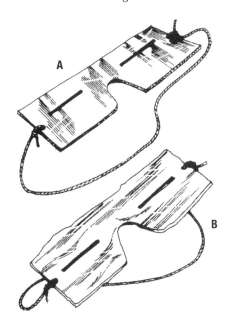

Agave
The agave is common to deserts throughout the Americas and the Caribbean, and it provides edible flowers and flower buds, both of which must be cooked before consumption.

Edible desert plants

The baobab, prickly pear and carob are common desert foods. They are good sources of vitamins and fibre, and the prickly pear and the baobab can both be tapped for water, the prickly pear from its stem and the baobab from its roots.

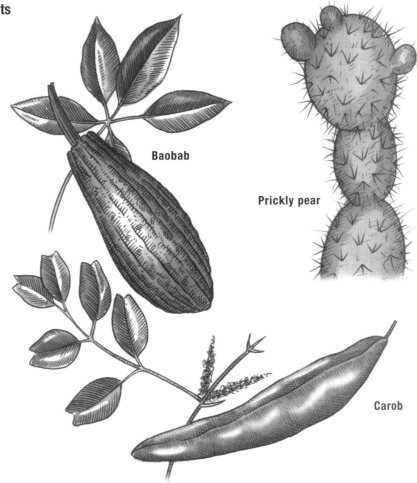

Baobab

Prickly pear

Carob

Fig tree
Description: tree with tough evergreen leaves. Found in Syrian and European deserts.
Eating notes: produces fruits that are edible when ripe (coloration will be green, red or black).

Carob
Description: tree with shiny, evergreen leaves that grow in groups of two or three to each stem.
Eating notes: edible pulp extracted from seedpods. Seeds can also be ground and cooked as porridge.

Acacia
Description: thorny tree with small leaves and rounded flower heads of white, pink or yellow flowers.
Eating notes: cook the seeds, young leaves and shoots to eat. Roots provide water.

Baobab
Description: large tree with massive bulbous trunk up to 9m (30ft) in diameter.
Eating notes: eat fruit and seeds raw, but boil young leaves. Roots provide water.

Date palm
Description: tall palm tree which has long, arching leaves.
Eating notes: fruit can be eaten raw, and the tree sap can be boiled into a sugar.

Grass
Most desert grasses can be eaten. Cook and eat

the white stem that is exposed when the grass is pulled from the ground.

Mescal
Description: made up of strong, spiky leaves that project from the ground. From the middle of the leaf comes a tall, branching flower stalk.
Eating notes: boil the stalk to eat.

Wild gourd
Description: a plant similar to a vine, which creeps along the ground and produces brown fruits.
Eating notes: fruit is edible, although unripe fruit does need boiling. Young leaves and seeds are edible when cooked (use boiling and roasting, respectively). Stems and shoots contain water – chew to access it.

Wild gourd

Carrion flower
Description: plant like a cactus with large, hairy flowers that have five petals, which emit an unpleasant stench of rotting meat.
Eating notes: stems can be tapped for water.

Prickly pear
Description: Large, padded plant with jointed sections covered with spines, which produces yellow or red flowers and fruits. Beware: African spurges have a very similar appearance, but contain a poisonous milky sap.
Eating notes: young pads can be eaten when cooked. Fruits are edible raw. The stem contains water.

Drawing out a rabbit
Make a fire outside a rabbit warren, and waft the smoke into the entrance. When the smoke forces the rabbit to emerge, strike it with a stick. Alternatively, position a snare wire around the hole.

Most desert animals are edible, but not all are easy to catch. (For the fundamentals of hunting and trapping, see Chapter 8.) Don't attempt to catch big cats or large antelope unless you have a powerful rifle, one which you know how to use. For most large animals, target just above the shoulder of the front leg to hit vital organs. Do not attempt to take a shot at the head because at range the bullet is liable to cause a terrible wound to the animal's strong skull, but not actually kill it. For smaller or young antelope, watering holes are good places to attack, although watch you yourself do not become prey to a big cat out hunting.

More viable desert animal foods include rabbits, rodents, snakes, lizards and birds. One innovative but dangerous method of hunting desert rabbits is to make a fire in a section of heavy grass or sagebrush, and look for a precooked rabbit once the fire has gone out (you may also find rats, mice and lizards). Lay snare traps for birds, especially around the site of carcasses where birds congregate to scavenge.

Insects are a readily accessible desert food. They, like you, are attracted to water and shade, so look under rocks, pieces of bark, in caves and in holes. Use a stick, not your hands, to inspect these places, otherwise you may be bitten by a sheltering scorpion, spider or snake. Attract insects at night with a small light. Bear in mind that insect larva usually make good eating. Always cook desert insects before eating to kill off bacteria and parasites, and remember to remove the wings and legs of grasshoppers and crickets. See Chapter 20 for more tips on tropical insects as a food source.

DANGERS

A lack of water and the extreme heat are by far the most severe threats in the desert. However, there are dangers in the flora and fauna of which you should be aware (see Chapter 20 again for instruction on handling dangerous animals). Poisonous varieties of snakes, spiders and scorpions abound in the desert conditions. Stay covered, wear your boots at all times and shake out your clothing and boots in the morning before dressing. Check your sleeping bag thoroughly before you get into it at night in case a scorpion has sheltered inside. Avoid siting your shelter or camp near insect nests, and obey all the usual

RABIES

Rabies is a lethal disease transmitted by the bite of infected animal, often a dog or fox. Do not fuss or attempt to feed local dogs in tropical or desert areas. Steer clear of violent, staggering animals that are foaming at the mouth because this indicates a rabies infection, and the animal may attack without provocation. If an animal you suspect might have rabies bites you, clean the bite vigorously with soap and water. Then apply a disinfectant and get to a hospital immediately. There is a treatment for rabies, but it must be applied within 24–48 hours to work. Should someone else have advanced rabies, tie him or her down, and do not go near them. If they die – which they almost certainly will do – do not handle the body or attempt to bury it.

anti-insect measures – cover yourself with net while you sleep, and don't sleep or sit on bare ground (particularly in grassland areas.)

Desert areas contain two particularly nasty varieties of lizard. The gila monster grows to around 45cm (18in) long, with a powerful, stocky body and a bright yellow pattern to its skin. The beaded lizard is somewhat larger with a more slender tail and darker coloration. Both lizards have poisonous bites equivalent to a venomous snake. They are not confrontational,

Locusts as food

Locusts are a good source of protein in the desert. Kill by striking them with a leafy branch and remember to remove the legs and wings before cooking and eating them.

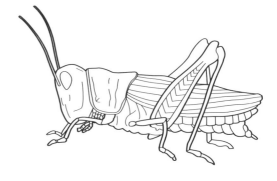

Water trap for termites

The termite trap consists of a smooth-sided pot, half-filled with water, buried up to its rim in the ground and covered with a board propped up on four stones. Termites crawl under the board for shelter and fall into the water, where they are trapped for later collection.

however, and as long as you do not corner one they should not bother you.

Take extra care not to be injured on thorns or cactus spines, as any wound will become infected quickly in the desert. If you are scratched, treat the injury as a bleeding wound (see Chapter 13), and wash and clean it thoroughly. Protect the injury with a dressing to prevent flies and other insects from landing on it.

Termites

Termites come in several types: the 'sexual' termite has wings and can reproduce, whereas the wingless 'non-sexual' and worker termites cannot reproduce. All make excellent food.

'Sexual' termite

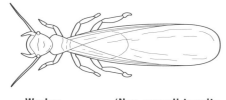

Worker

'Non-sexual' termite

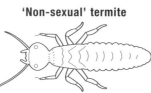

HEALTH

Your health priority in the desert is to avoid dehydration and heatstroke (see Chapter 13 for first aid for heat-related illnesses). Concentrate on staying out of direct sunlight, and don't take sweat-soaked clothing off, as it will help to keep you cool. Maintain a good intake of fluids throughout the day. If you suffer from sunburn, apply rehydrating creams, and treat sore eyes with rest in a dark place if possible, or tie a damp bandage lightly around the eyes.

Another threat to health comes from insect-borne diseases, such as malaria, sandfly fever, typhus and plague. As explained in Chapter 20, ensure that you have all your relevant vaccinations before you travel to foreign climes. Also pay special attention to basic hygiene. Wash your hands before eating and after going to the toilet, and keep human waste at a distance from your camp – bury all excrement and garbage in deep holes. Keep cooking utensils clean, and don't let flies settle on your food. Try to have a full-body wash every two or three days. No matter how slight the injury, clean it and protect it with an adhesive bandage.

NAVIGATION AND MOVEMENT

At all costs, avoid walking without purpose or direction in the desert. Desert movement should be planned around places of shade and water, and should aim towards rescue if you're in a survival situation. Travel only in the evening,

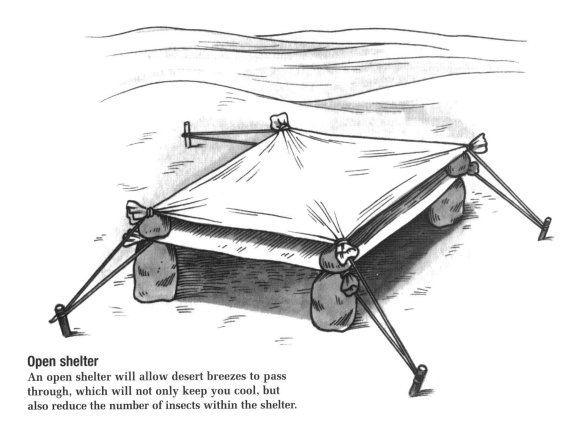

Open shelter

An open shelter will allow desert breezes to pass through, which will not only keep you cool, but also reduce the number of insects within the shelter.

night or early morning to avoid exposure to the midday sun. Don't attempt to walk through very difficult terrain such as sand dunes and rocky areas, as this will probably result in unnecessary and avoidable fatigue or injury.

To navigate around desert terrain, try to follow defined routes such as roads, coastlines, trails and any route that indicates the passage of people. Be careful about overestimating how far you can travel in a day. The heat haze in deserts makes landmarks appear closer than they really are. As a general rule, multiply your distance estimation by three to get an accurate picture of how far you will need to travel.

Compass navigation is the best method of accurately steering around the desert. But do not follow a compass bearing blindly if it leads you into more inhospitable terrain. If you do not have a compass, move between clear landmarks to avoid wandering off course, making sure that you choose a second landmark aligned with your course of direction before you reach the first. Stars are

Scorpion

There are two families of scorpions: the Buthids and the Scorpionids. The 500 species of Buthids are small in size, but include the most poisonous scorpion types. The Scorpionids are larger, but are rarely dangerous.

Underground shelter
An underground shelter will provide good protection in the desert. The airspace in the roof forms an insulating layer of still air to keep the shelter cool. Be vigilant for snakes and scorpions, which may be attracted to the shelter to get out of the daytime heat and sun.

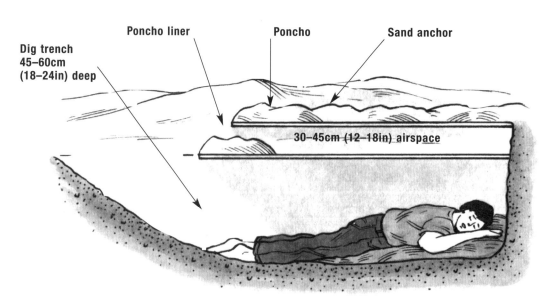

Dig trench 45–60cm (18–24in) deep

Poncho liner

Poncho

Sand anchor

30–45cm (12–18in) airspace

usually very clear in the skies of an open desert, so use them for guidance at night (see Chapter 16). If you know the direction of the prevailing winds, you can use these to navigate also.

A sandstorm will be a severe obstacle to movement, so sit it out before attempting to travel farther. Rest with your back to the wind, and cover your face with a cloth. Before the sandstorm strikes (you will see the sand massing in the sky), mark your direction of travel with a long stick or by any other means. When the sandstorm is over, this means that you'll be able to pick up your bearing even though the sand deposits will have altered the landscape.

SHELTER
Desert shelters are vital for protecting you from the aggressive elements, but they need not be complex constructions. Natural shelters in desert areas are usually limited to shaded cliffs, the lee sides of hills, dunes or rock formations. But in rocky areas some cool natural caves might be found. Exercise caution when entering a cave. Desert animals, including snakes and rats, could

be in there as well, using the cave as a refuge from the desert heat. As a precaution, don't venture too deeply into the cave.

If you have to build a shelter, do so in the cooler hours of the day, and try to locate the shelter near firewood and water to cut down on your walking time. Locate it away from sloping areas at risk of rock falls, and be aware that in the rainy season low-lying ground may be prone to flash floods. It is a good idea to site your shelter where it will catch breezes to help keep you cool and carry insects away from you.

Construct a shelter out of any vegetation you find, but if you have a large sheet of material, preferably of light colour, you can make some excellent desert shelters. In rocky areas, anchor one edge of the material to an outcrop with loose rocks, then stretch the sheet out and anchor the other edge to the floor to make a shaded area underneath. In areas where there is no rock, pile up sand or earth to form one side of the shelter. Material shelters are greatly improved if you can make two layers of material with a gap for air between. The gap forms a section of still air, which insulates against the heat of the sun.

Emergency desert shelters

During the daytime desert heat, use any materials available to create shade. Here a dinghy has been used as a shelter – the air trapped inside acts as an insulating layer.

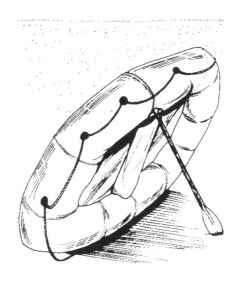

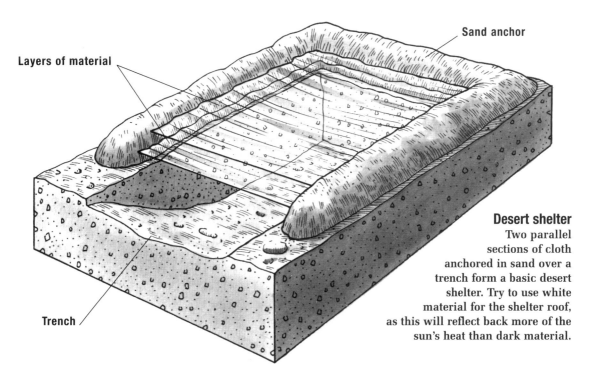

Layers of material

Sand anchor

Trench

Desert shelter
Two parallel sections of cloth anchored in sand over a trench form a basic desert shelter. Try to use white material for the shelter roof, as this will reflect back more of the sun's heat than dark material.

• CHAPTER TWENTY-TWO

SURVIVAL AT SEA

The planet Earth is nearly three-quarters covered by water, yet human beings are never more out of their element than when lost at sea.

THE INITIAL CHALLENGE of survival at sea is how to prevent yourself from drowning. If you can survive the first few minutes of an emergency at sea, the principle dangers are hypothermia or heatstroke (depending on where you are), and lack of water and food.

ABANDONING SHIP

When a ship is sinking, your priority is to get as far away from it as possible before it goes beneath the waves. A sinking vessel, if it is a large craft, creates a powerful downward suction as it fills with water that will pull you under the water and possibly drown you if you are still in the vicinity.

At the first sign that the ship is going to sink, and at the command of the ship's captain, immediately put on warm wool clothing, waterproofs, hats and gloves. Put your life jacket on over the top, but don't inflate it yet, as it will hinder your movement around the boat. Although the clothes will get soaked in the water, they will still provide you with some insulation, and you can dry them out aboard a life raft. Also, clothes will trap some air and give buoyancy. Other items to collect if possible include a flashlight (torch), some foodstuffs and any pieces of survival kit such as flares, equipment for sending signals and navigational tools. However, do not weigh yourself down so that you are incapable of swimming.

Try to get into a life raft that is launched from the side of the ship. (If this is not possible, and you have to jump into the water, first throw something that floats into the water that you can grab onto.) Step off the side of the boat, keeping your body straight, gripping your nose and pulling your arms and elbows tight into the side of your body – if you leave them out at the side they will be wrenched on impact. Do not inflate your life jacket until you are actually in the water.

When you hit the water, swim immediately to your floating object or to a life raft. If there is burning oil on the surface of the water, swim around it, or, if that is impossible, deflate your life jacket and swim underneath it, surfacing where you see patches of clear water.

Abandoning ship through burning fuel
When jumping overboard into a sea covered with burning oil, jump into a clear patch of sea, then swim underwater to a safe spot. Do not inflate your life jacket before jumping in.

SURVIVAL IN THE WATER

If you are not in a life raft, your immediate dangers are drowning and hypothermia. Try to relax your body – a relaxed body is more buoyant than a tense one. If you haven't got a life jacket, try to conserve your energy by periodically floating on the surface of the water with your arms and legs outstretched. Alternatively, float face down on the surface with your arms outstretched and your legs pointing towards the bottom, raising your head occasionally to draw breath.

Your swimming technique in the sea should be adapted to the conditions and your energy levels. In rough seas, breaststroke is best and is ideal for swimming underwater. The dog paddle is a good technique for use when you are clothed or wearing a life jacket. Use sidestroke or backstroke to provide muscular relief when you need to.

Launching a life raft

On abandoning ship, throw the lift raft canister overboard to leeward, having attached the static line to the toe rail. Throw the canister to a clear spot away from any debris.

Draw in the static line until it stops paying out, then give the line a sharp tug to initiate the CO_2 inflation mechanism.

Allow the raft to inflate fully (it should take about 30 seconds), then load your survival gear inside before climbing aboard and casting off.

Crouching position

The crouching position is a technique of energy conservation. Periodically, let the body and hands go limp in the water, and float for as long as you can hold your breath, relaxing your muscles. Bring the arms upwards to return your body to the upright position.

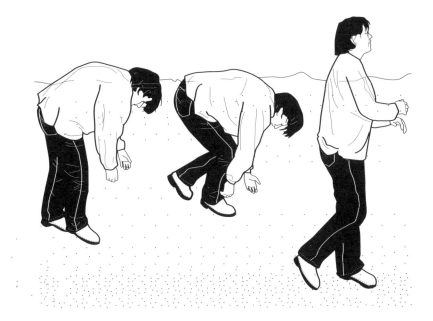

To lessen the risk of hypothermia, if you're wearing a life jacket, adopt the Heat Escape Lessening Posture (HELP) position by raising as much of your torso out of the water as possible. Try to keep your head dry at all times, as much body heat is lost through it. Huddle together with other survivors in the water to share body heat. Remember, though, that in cold waters hypothermia will set in if you do not get out of the water into a raft or onto dry land – that should be your overriding goal.

Swimming ashore on a coastline can be a dangerous moment, as you are at risk from large waves dashing you against rocks or pulling you beneath the water. Focus on where you want to land, avoiding areas of exploding waves and aiming towards places where the water rushes onto the rocks in a smooth flow. Swim into shore in the troughs between waves (swim under or through large waves as they pass over you) to control your speed. Then, to land, catch a single small wave and ride into shore with your feet facing forwards, swimming only with your hands.

SURVIVAL IN A LIFE RAFT

If you are in a life raft and the sinking of your boat was reported, you are likely to be rescued fairly quickly. However, if your position is unknown, you could be at danger of death from

HELP posture

The Heat Escape Lessening Posture (HELP) reduces body heat loss by keeping as much of the torso as possible out the water, pushing the arms against a flotation device to achieve lift.

dehydration or starvation at sea before help arrives. Make sure that you look after your raft, checking for and repairing any damage both before and during the emergency.

When you first get aboard, check over what supplies are available, including navigation and signalling equipment, water rations (or the means to make drinking water, such as desalination equipment), and food supplies. Read through any instructions that are contained in the boat relating to the equipment.

Ration out food among the members of the boat, and set a strict daily ration of water. Salvage any useful materials floating from the wreck, as

Life raft and contents

Aboard larger vessels, the contents of a life raft can have a nasty habit of going missing. Inspect the raft regularly, ticking off everything against a checklist and replacing missing items.

A. **Sea anchor**
B. **Paddles**
C. **First-aid kit**
D. **Fishing line and hooks**
E. **Bellows**
F. **Quoit and line**
G. **Survival leaflets**
H. **Bailer**
I. **Repair kit, flares, stopper, sponge, knife**
J. **Water, can openers, cup and seasickness pills**
K. **Torch (flashlight), batteries and bulb**
L. **Resealing lids**

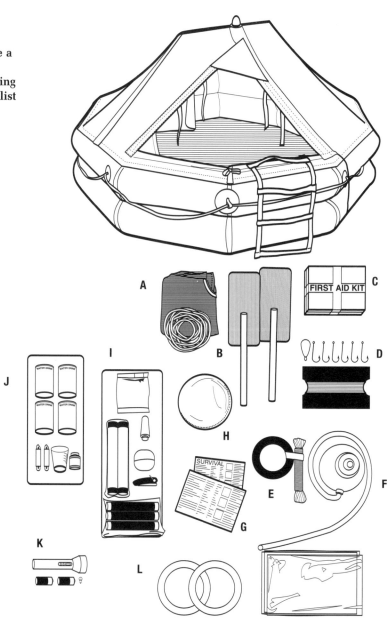

Improvised float
Tie the ankles of the trousers tight together then, holding the trousers by the waistband or belt, swipe them over your head to fill with air. Hook the tied ankles behind your neck to form a rudimentary flotation device.

Floating together
When floating in a group, tie yourselves together so that you do not float apart, and also tie a link to your grab bag so that it does not get lost in heavy waves.

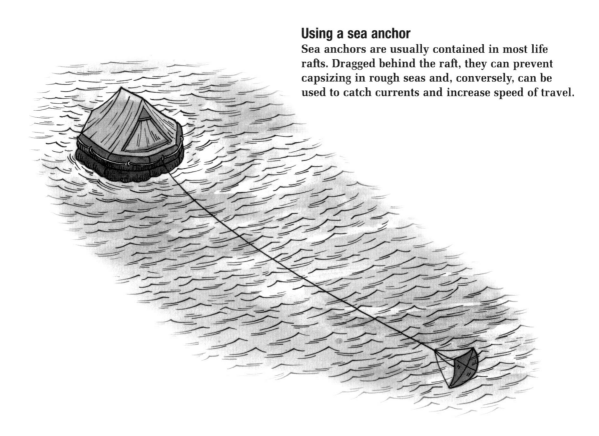

Using a sea anchor
Sea anchors are usually contained in most life rafts. Dragged behind the raft, they can prevent capsizing in rough seas and, conversely, can be used to catch currents and increase speed of travel.

long as their weight will not make the boat unstable. High-quality life rafts will often have a sea anchor that drags in the water and resists currents. Unless you are within easy access of land, use this anchor to keep you within the vicinity of the wreck, as you will stand more chance of being rescued.

In terms of your immediate wellbeing, treat any casualties aboard the raft with first aid. Then guard against hypothermia by stripping off wet clothing and allowing it to dry out before putting it back on. Huddle together for extra warmth. In tropical climates, if your raft does not have a cover, make one out of any material available to shelter you from the sun.

A serious situation occurs if the life raft capsizes. When you first get into the raft, attach one person to it with a line so that, if it does capsize, the raft does not float away. To right the dinghy, grab hold of the righting line, put your feet against the hull of the boat and pull to bring the raft upright.

Exercise caution when landing the raft on a shoreline. Avoid rocky, dangerous sections of coastline, coral reefs and areas where there are strong surface currents. Do not attempt to land at night or if bright sunlight is shining directly in your eyes. If possible, choose shallow, sloping beaches for landing zones. In icy climates, aim for large stable ice floes. Use oars and paddles if you have them, and adjust the sea anchor to prevent the sea from throwing the stern around and keep the raft pointed towards the shore. Allow the waves to carry you into shore; only when the raft is grounded should you jump out.

MOVEMENT AND SIGNALS
As a general rule, try to stay around the place where your ship sank for up to 72 hours, particularly if you are in busy shipping lanes or if you have sent an SOS. After several days, or if you did not send an SOS, try to reach land.

Unless you paddle constantly – which you will not have energy to do – your movement will be

Righting a dinghy

To right a capsized dinghy, take hold of the lanyard, place your feet on the side of the craft,

then lean backwards while pulling to flip the dinghy over.

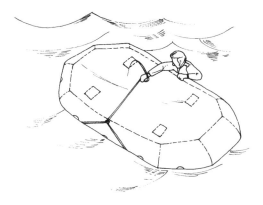

dictated by winds and currents. This can be to your advantage. Make a basic sail, or erect one if the raft has one onboard, to accelerate your pace – currents alone will only push you at around 8km/h (5mph). Winds blow in an easterly direction in tropical areas, the so-called trade winds, and from the west in higher latitudes.

Look for the following signs of land to guide your direction.

- Large, still cumulus clouds usually indicate land beneath them.
- In the tropics, clouds that are light green on the underside tend to be hovering above a coastal coral reef.
- Deep seawater is dark green or dark blue, but lightens the closer you get to the shore. Muddy streaks in the water may have come from the mouth of a coastal river.

Using your VHF radio

A VHF radio will have ship-to-ship range of about 16–24km (10–15 miles). If you make contact, remember to keep the radio on an agreed channel so that a rescuer can communicate with you when required.

- Drifting vegetation might indicate land nearby.
- Groups of birds flying in the late afternoon are usually returning to land.

If you are unable to make land, then you should try to attract rescue. If your life raft contains a

Reverse osmosis pump
A reverse osmosis pump will convert seawater to fresh drinking water just by pumping the handle, and so is an essential piece of maritime kit.

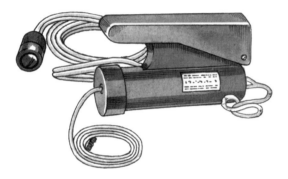

Smoke canisters
Smoke canisters are an excellent way of attracting rescue in daylight conditions, although only use a canister if there is a realistic chance of being spotted by a passing ship or aircraft.

radio transmitter, it should be preset to Mayday frequencies. Make transmissions one or two times every hour, but be careful of causing the batteries to run down by using it unnecessarily.

Sending a signal at sea is helped by the flatness of the seascape, so flares and reflected-sunlight signals can be seen over very long distances. Launch flares whenever you see another boat or an aircraft, but hold the flares high above the raft to launch them to avoid the risk of an onboard fire. Dye markers are another excellent way of sending a signal to attract attention. When added to the water, they create a large, brightly coloured patch on the surface that can be seen by ships and aircraft. However, they can only be used in the daytime and have a working duration of about three hours.

WATER
The first rule of finding water at sea is never to drink seawater and never drink urine. Desalinated seawater, however, is perfectly drinkable, and most modern life rafts will contain chemical desalination kits. Follow the instructions on the kit, which are usually a simple matter of dropping tablets into a container of seawater. If your raft does not contain a kit, then you may be

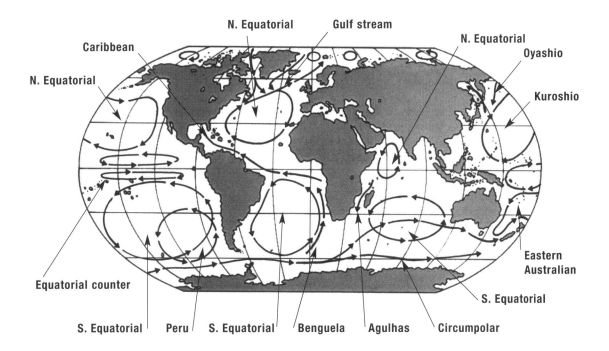

Ocean currents

Understanding ocean currents is an essential piece of research before embarking on any maritime trip. If lost at sea, knowledge of these currents will help you to make informed navigational decisions.

able to desalinate water by using a solar still.

To do this, fill a large container with a few inches of seawater. Put a smaller empty container in the middle of the larger without allowing seawater to flow into it. Stretch a plastic sheet over the large container, making an airtight contact, and weight the sheet in the middle so that it dips over the smaller container. Put the still in the sun, and as the seawater is warmed it will evaporate – leaving the salt particles behind – before condensing on the underside of the plastic and dripping down into the central container as fresh water.

Solar stills can give imperfect results, so your best option for accessing fresh water is to catch rainwater at every opportunity. Set up as many open containers as possible to collect the water, steadying them with heavy objects to stop them from falling over with the rocking of the boat.

Solar still
A solar still can be made on a boat using two containers and a plastic sheet. The water source is rags soaked with seawater.

TYPES OF EDIBLE SEAWEED

Kelp – thin, wavy, olive-green or brown fronds clinging to submerged rocks
Irish moss – tough and leathery seaweed that becomes crisp and shrinks when dried
Dulse – short stem with dark-red fronds expanding outwards into a fan shape
Laver – purplish to red, it has smooth, shiny fronds

FOOD

Fish will obviously be your main food source at sea. The subject of fishing is covered in detail in Chapter 8, but angling and netting will be the only two methods reasonably practicable in open seas. You can fish in any section of the ocean, but there are some signs that indicate where fish are concentrated. Look for seabirds attacking sections of water, as this usually implies a shoal of fish beneath. Similarly, a concentration of seals, dolphins or sharks is another indicator.

Another emergency seafood is plankton. Plankton is essentially clouds of minute plants and animals that drift around the oceans. Individually they are too small to eat, but caught in bulk using a fine-mesh net or cloth they can provide a good supply of protein, carbohydrates and fats. Before you eat plankton, search through it and remove all jellyfish tentacles, spiny creatures or plants, or plankton that is gelatinous (this has a high saltwater content). Eat plankton only in small quantities, as the presence of so many marine organisms can give you diarrhoea.

Seabirds can also be eaten if necessary. If your boat has a mast, set a line of nooses along it as explained in Chapter 8, or trail lines in the water set with baited hooks. You may even find that birds will simply land on your craft feet away from you, and can be killed with a blow from a club.

Plant foods in the ocean are few and far between, but seaweed is to be found both around shorelines and in deep waters. Seaweed should be eaten in moderation, as its mineral-rich content can have a laxative effect. Boil seaweed before eating it. Coastal regions will also feature mussels clinging to rocks (see Chapter 18 for cautions about eating mussels), and crabs can be found under seaweed and in rocky areas.

MAKING RAFTS

On occasion, the survivor must head out into water to either improve his or her chances of

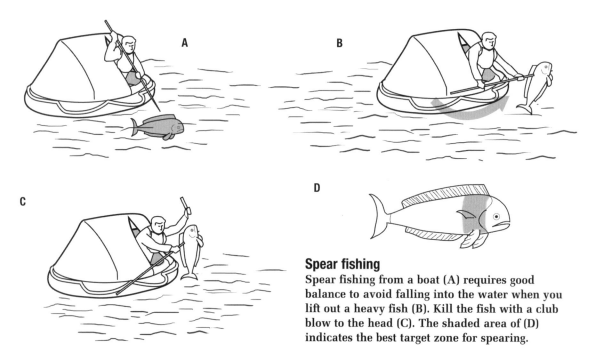

Spear fishing

Spear fishing from a boat (A) requires good balance to avoid falling into the water when you lift out a heavy fish (B). Kill the fish with a club blow to the head (C). The shaded area of (D) indicates the best target zone for spearing.

rescue, transfer between landmasses (particularly islands) or to fish. If no professional craft is available, then a raft must be made. This is an advanced skill, and you should test each boat you make in safe, still waters before putting out to sea.

ONE-PERSON RAFTS

The crudest one-person rafts are the log flotation raft and vegetation raft. The log flotation raft is nothing more than two spaced logs tied parallel to each other with cord, the 'pilot' sitting with the legs over one log and the back braced against the other. This raft is designed primarily to prevent drowning. A vegetation raft is a buoyancy aid consisting of any bag of material stuffed with plants and tied.

LOG RAFT

Log rafts are the most energy intensive to make, but are also the most seaworthy when finished and can take more than one person. The easiest log raft to make is the lashed log raft, for which you will need long pieces of cord. First lay two long thick poles on the ground parallel with one another. Lay logs on top of these crossways, knocking them tightly together to form a square raft shape. Now put two more thick poles over the top of the logs, mirroring the poles on the bottom of the craft. Tie each set of stakes to each other on both sides, so that the poles now grip the logs between in a 'sandwich' structure. Notch the ends of the gripper bars to stop the ropes from slipping, and if you have the tools cut running notches along the logs for the poles to sit in to make the whole structure more secure.

Construct a deck from poles on top of the raft, and use paddles to power it. Remember to tie the paddles to the raft with a line to prevent you from losing them.

Rafts

Rafts are constructed according to the availability of materials, tools and skills. The brush raft requires a sheet of material, vegetation and rope, while the log raft requires heavy logs and some engineering talent.

A more sophisticated version of the latter is the bush raft, which can support up to 105kg (250lb) of weight if properly made. Spread a large poncho on the ground, and pile up fresh green vegetation (A) in the middle to a height of about 46cm (18in). Now tie two strong branches together into an X shape and place on top of the brush stack. Pull the poncho sides up around the brush and tie the ropes diagonally from corner to corner and from side to side (B). Roll the bundle into the centre of a second large piece of material, so that it is facing downwards (C). Now tie the second piece of material around the whole structure to complete the raft.

Brush raft

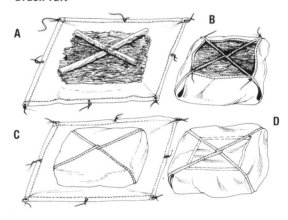

Log flotation

Lashed Log raft

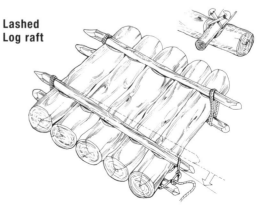

Poisonous fish

The sea has a bewildering variety of poisonous animal life. As a general rule, do not approach any highly coloured, spiky or aggressive-looking marine creatures.

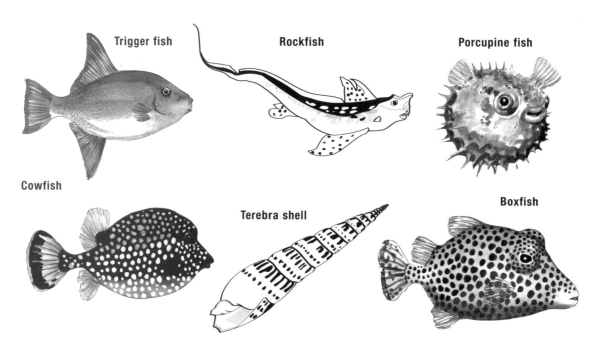

Trigger fish

Rockfish

Porcupine fish

Cowfish

Terebra shell

Boxfish

DANGEROUS CREATURES

Of all the many dangerous creatures in the world's seas and oceans, sharks are generally the most feared, although shark attacks on humans are actually very rare. Taking some basic precautions can usually prevent shark attacks. If you are on a raft, try not to dump rubbish, body wastes, fish parts, and blood overboard in large quantities, as sharks are scavengers and will come from long distances, attracted by the potential food. Don't dangle your feet or arms in the water. Try not to fish when sharks are in the area, and if they approach your raft fend them off with sharp pokes from an oar or pole.

If you're in the water in the presence of sharks, the situation is far more serious. Stay still and quiet, and if you have to swim do so with strong regular strokes that the shark will not confuse with the disordered movements of a wounded or sick fish. Urinate in very short bursts to disperse its scent, and throw faeces a long way from you. If a shark does swim in to investigate or attack you, try to fight it by gouging its snout, gills or eyes with a knife or any strong, pointed object. When you are in a group in the water, bunch together for mutual protection.

Although sharks receive a lot of bad press, there are many more equally or more dangerous creatures in the water. Killer whales, for example, will kill almost any large creature swimming in the sea and will hunt in packs of up to 40 mammals. If killer whales are in the area, get out of the water, and do not stand or swim near typical killer whale prey, such as penguins and seals.

Barracuda are another predatory animal (confined to tropical and subtropical seas). They are attracted to bright objects and blood, and will attack in large groups. As with sharks, do not enter the water if you have any bleeding injuries, and do not swim with any bright objects.

Although sharks, killer whales and barracuda are undoubtedly fearsome predators, the most dangerous creatures in the oceans are actually poisonous fish and other smaller creatures. Never attempt to catch and eat brightly coloured fish, especially those with bristles or spines, and large

JELLYFISH STINGS

Jellyfish stings vary considerably in their severity. While most common jellyfish deliver a sting roughly the same power as a bee sting, some of the large varieties such as the sea wasp can kill an adult in just 30 seconds (though three hours is more usual). Swim around any jellyfish in the water (this process is aided by wearing a snorkelling mask for visibility) and get ashore quickly. Do not touch dead jellyfish, as they are still capable of stinging. If you are stung, use a piece of clothing, the back of a knife or seaweed to clean off any stinging cells. Don't rub them as this will spread the pain – use a scraping movement. Some of the stinging action can be counteracted by applying soap, lemon juice, baking powder or urine, but monitor a victim for signs of shock and systemic poisoning (see Chapter 13).

teeth. Also avoid fish with mouths shaped like parrot beaks. In coastal waters, keep your shoes on in the water to avoid treading on lethally poisonous fish such as a stonefish, and use a long stick to inspect rocky areas. Never put your hands into any rocky holes underwater, as vicious moray eels or an octopus may populate them. The moray eel will clamp its teeth on with such ferocity that you have to cut its head off to release the grip. If you are bitten by either of these creatures, treat the injury as a bleeding wound, apply cold packs to reduce swelling and, in the case of the octopus, monitor the casualty closely for shock. Some types of octopus, such as the blue-ringed octopus found off eastern Australia, have highly venomous, potentially fatal bites. Clean any venomous bites with plenty of fresh water, and avoid touching the injury with your bare flesh.

Marine snails and slugs are another acute danger around coastal regions. These animals have barbs that can inject lethal poisons into anyone who treads on them or disturbs them. The venom can induce catastrophic body failure, including complete muscular paralysis, coma and death. Try applying hot packs to alleviate some of the pain at the injury site, and be ready to deliver CPR. Beyond this, there is little you can do, and you should try to get the victim to a hospital as quickly as possible.

Defending against shark attack

Watch a circling shark constantly (A). If it circles in tightening patterns, swim away with strong motions (B), turning towards it if it makes an attack approach. Attempt to kick its nose (C) to ward it off, or scream and slap the water to scare the shark (D).

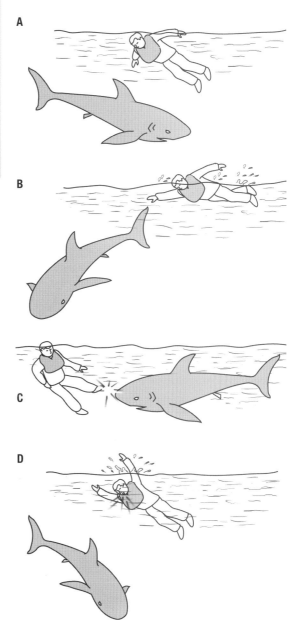

A

B

C

D

CHAPTER TWENTY-THREE

DEFENDING YOURSELF

The fundamental rule of defending yourself is fight only if you have to. Fights have dangerous, unpredictable outcomes, and should always be your last resort.

OUR CHANCES OF being assaulted have unfortunately risen over the past two decades, particularly if we live in urban areas. Domestic incidents still account for a major percentage of violent crime, but there has been a worrying climb in almost all other forms of violent attack, including rape, casual assault, armed assault, muggings and female-on-female violence (female conviction rates for violent offences rose by 55 per cent in the 1990s). Yet we cannot live in fear. While training ourselves to fight back physically is an important and useful tool, we will also see in this chapter that preventive measures will dramatically reduce our chances of being attacked at all.

RECOGNIZING IMPENDING VIOLENCE

The first layer of defending yourself is to be aware of violent people and to avoid them at all costs. Some will give obvious clues to aggression, such as threatening conduct, whereas others will attempt to conceal their intentions to unleash a surprise attack.

In public places, particularly in bars and nightclubs where alcohol is available, look for any signs of developing violence and get yourself away from the area. Stay away from obviously intoxicated and rowdy groups of young men between the ages of 18 and 30, the category of individual most likely to commit violent assault. If you are a man, avoid competition with other men (unless they are the closest of friends) for the attention of females. Watch out for verbal arguments breaking out, the sound of shattering glass or aggressive eye contact between strangers.

Do not assume that a fight between others does not involve you. Violence in another part of a room has a nasty habit of spreading and sucking in onlookers. Never become involved with domestic arguments or incidents, as it is not uncommon for both the arguing parties to then turn on the arbiter. The basic rule is, once you see signs of violence developing, get away. If you are in a crowded bar or nightclub and it is difficult to get out, tell the bouncers or doormen. Describe what's happening, identify the individuals involved and let them take over.

The trigger for actual violence can be as minor as accidentally knocking over someone's drink, and you should be one the lookout for the following clues that a person intends physical aggression. The impending attacker may:
- make bold and defiant direct eye contact, often at close range
- close up the distance between the two of you
- let fly with a string of short threatening questions such as, 'What are you looking at?', usually punctuated with expletives
- make threatening body gestures, including aggressive finger pointing, head thrusting and opening out the arms to expand their presence
- shorten verbal threats to single syllables (such as repeating 'yeah' or 'c'mon') in the immediate moments before attack. Usually this stage is accompanied by the attacker adopting a fight position
- struggle to control their breathing as adrenaline pumps through their body. Watch particularly if he or she takes a sudden deep breath, as this is often a sign that they are launching an attack.

Your choices when confronted by such individual are fight or flight.

Violent posturing

Signs of impending violence can take many forms, including staring, finger beckoning and outright preparation for a fight. If someone approaches you with these signals, attempt to stop them with firm language, but also put yourself into a guard position.

DEFUSING ATTACKERS

In situations where an aggressive individual faces you, try not to show any signs of weakness – this is what the attacker wants and will give him or her confidence that a physical assault will pay off. Stand up to your full height, lift your face upwards and adopt a strong, steady but unthreatening facial expression. Speak slowly and clearly, breathing deeply from your abdomen while tensing the diaphragm to reduce nervous tremble in your voice.

Now try to defuse or control the situation without violence. State clearly but without fear that you do not want to fight, and if possible lighten the situation by making the aggressor laugh, meeting him at his own level of humour. Although you should not appear weak, do not be afraid of losing face. Say you will go to another bar – this will elevate the aggressor's stature in front of his friends and give him a sense of victory without violence.

Should the rational approach not work, you may have to resort to reciprocal intimidation and threat (though still remember your goal is to avoid violence). Change your posture to make it clear that if you are attacked you will fight back with a pathological commitment. Being mildly intimidating won't work. If the aggressor states he wants to fight, accept his offer with menace, but challenge him individually, not his group of friends. State that you want to fight him alone, and suggest he is a coward if he does not accept. Without the backing of his friends, he might climb down. Always watch, however, that while you are arguing the group is not circling around you to position themselves for an attack. Keep moving so you can see everybody positioned to the front.

Alternatively, pretend that you are bordering on psychopathic. Make violent and gratuitous verbal threats, screaming wildly and even dribbling saliva. It sounds extreme, but the attacker may believe that he's in serious danger of being damaged if he attacks you, and he may back down. Try giving the aggressor a hard shove to the chest that throws him backward. Then shout, 'Stay there.' Strangely, the shock of the push and the shout may make him comply with your order, or at the very least give you an opportunity to escape.

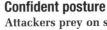

Distancing

Try to maintain a safe distance from a potential assailant, but be prepared to move to close range if it comes to an actual fight, stepping to the side of an opponent rather than straight into his blows.

Confident posture

Attackers prey on signs of weakness, so do not display any. Pull yourself up to your full height, walk athletically and confidently, and maintain strong eye contact if directly threatened.

The unfortunate implication of meeting threat with threat is that the aggressor may follow through and accept your invitation to fight. Only use the intimidation approach if the rational one has failed, and be prepared for actual violence.

SAFETY ON THE STREETS

The chances of your being exposed to violence at all dramatically decrease with some basic common-sense precautions. First, do not go into any place or district with a reputation for violence or criminal activity. In an unfamiliar town or city, ask a local or a police officer to identify the high-risk areas. Steer clear of events, usually sports events, which have a reputation for large and violent crowds. The police will usually attempt to steer the crowds between the sports ground and public transportation, so avoid any routes in between, and try not to use public transportation on the day of the event.

Watch where you are walking at all times. Avoid dark or deserted side roads, alleyways,

streets bordered by wasteland or bushes, or derelict areas. At night, avoid parkland (public parks) or streets with a high density of bars (unless you are purposely going there). Position yourself correctly on the pavement (sidewalk), walking close to the curb to spot potential ambushes from doorways. Always face oncoming traffic so you can deal with attacks launched from vehicles (a common strategy applied by rapists is to drive up behind the victim and literally drag them into the vehicle). Give the corners of streets a wide berth, and cross over to the other side of the road if you are approaching aggressive or intoxicated individuals. Don't make eye contact; just keep walking in a confident manner.

STREET CRIME

Street crime may or may not involve violence. Pickpockets, for example, use covert methods of theft and tend to avoid violent confrontation. Unfortunately, however, violent street crime is on the rise, partly because of increased drug use in the past 20 years.

The best way to avoid getting mugged in the street is not to display your wealth. Do not wear expensive jewellery on the streets, and split your money between several pockets so that you do not display large amounts of cash when paying for goods in shops. Make sure briefcases and handbags are securely carried using a long strap going over the shoulder to defeat bag-snatchers.

Only visit ATM machines to draw cash out during the daytime in busy streets, and go to another machine if you see undesirable characters in the vicinity. Try, if possible, to vary the times and directions you use for routine journeys, as some street criminals may be relying on you to be at a certain place at a certain time. Walk with

Dangerous areas

The alleyway pictured below has many danger points, apart from the two suspicious men. The doorway to the left could hide an attacker, as could the overhanging tree up ahead. The steps would make a fast escape difficult.

Parking lots

Inner-city parking lots are ideal places for surprise assaults, as they present many places to hide and give the attacker quick escape routes into the streets around them.

Assault and attacks

Muggers will attempt to use surprise to spring an attack. In the distraction assault here, the attacker gets his victim to look at her watch before pulling a knife. In the pincer attack, one person keeps the victim occupied, while the other attacker circles around for the actual assault.

Distraction assault

Pincer attack

someone if possible; criminals tend to select isolated individuals as the victims.

If someone approaches you on the sidewalk, observe him or her carefully. Thieves often wear baseball caps and hooded jackets to conceal their face and hair against identification. The assailant will generally look tense and may even shiver slightly with nerves. Look at their hands – if one is pressed unnaturally against the body or held in a jacket pocket, they may be holding a knife. Watch the hands at all times.

Try to put distance between you and the suspicious individual by crossing the road or entering into a store or office. If he follows you, and you can't get away, deliver a firm verbal warning such as 'Stop there. Don't come near me.' Should you have misjudged the situation, an apology will cost you nothing. If individual keeps coming towards you, be prepared to fight.

Cunning street criminals will often use deception techniques to set up a robbery. They may approach you first and ask you the time or for directions, then strike while you are distracted. Street criminals frequently work in pairs or packs – one person will approach you from the front and distract you, while a second attacker comes at you from behind. Watch all suspicious individuals using your peripheral vision, and be particularly wary if approached by a group that splits up when it draws close to you.

The final rule of street crime is that, if you are surprised and threatened with any sort of weapons, hand over your wallet or jewellery without question. It is not worth getting killed for items that can be replaced.

RAPE ATTACKS

Rape is a hideous crime in which sexual assault is often accompanied by other forms of physical violence, even murder. This type of attack is usually committed by people known to the victim – boyfriends, friends, even relatives – rather than complete strangers, so measures against rape must be in place at all times.

In relationships, set clear sexual boundaries, and be prepared to enforce them with firm verbal instructions if the partner attempts to cross those boundaries. Tell them that unwanted sexual intercourse constitutes rape – just the word itself may sober up amorous men. If you ever invite a man to your home (this is not advisable if you do not know him well), be clear about what you intend to happen. Should the man become sexually aggressive and will not leave, go straight to a friend's house and phone the police. Be cautious that a man is not misreading any flirtatious signals you are sending out, particularly if he is drinking alcohol, which tends to fuel unrealistic fantasies. Also avoid drinking excessively, as this can lead to your overstepping your own boundaries. If a person's sexual advances become unwelcome, break off the interaction and move to another place. Only meet people you do not know in public places, and always accompanied by a friend. Never travel alone in a car with a man you do not know well, especially one who has made heavy sexual advances towards you in the past.

If someone you do not know offers to buy you a drink, watch them do so. Check that they do not put a so-called 'date rape' drug into your glass. The drug rohypnol is a sedative that can incapacitate you for several hours and leave you unable to remember anything that happened, and it is not the only one with this effect. If you have to go to the restroom, have a friend guard your glass or finish the drink before going. If you start to feel drowsy or dizzy, tell a friend, and instruct him or her not to let the person you suspect may have drugged your drink take you home.

Social rapists of the type described above differ somewhat from predatory rapists. Predatory rapists will usually attack by ambush, assaulting the victim in sheltered or dark places such as parks, city gardens, or stretches of wasteland, or may pull the victim into a car or van. The measures for avoiding this sort of person are largely the same as avoiding street criminals and violent people, with some differences. You are very vulnerable when entering a vehicle, so as soon as you are inside lock the doors before doing

Concealed knife

When approached by a suspicious character, look closely for an arm held unnaturally by the side of the body with the fingers of the hand cupped upwards, as he may be concealing a knife.

DEFENDING FROM THE GROUND

At all costs, try to stay on your feet when fighting. Use small shuffling steps to move around, and do not cross your legs over when moving. If you do end up on the floor, curl up and cover your head with your arms. Drive your legs out at your opponent's shins, knees and groin until you can buy enough time to leap quickly to your feet and resume the fight standing up.

Keeping a distance

By raising your hands up in an open-handed protective guard (you needn't even make it look like a guard, see bottom picture), you can control the distance between you and your opponent, while also being ready to fight.

anything else. Avoid dark areas of the street or city parks, especially at night. Carry a rape alarm along with you, and have your finger ready on the button in case you are attacked.

Look strong at all times and, if attacked, fight. Rapists almost always want a compliant victim, not a victim who is fighting with every ounce of strength. Rapists' assurances of 'Do what I want and you won't get hurt' count for nothing – just the very act of rape means that you will get hurt. Also, many rapists follow the sexual act with another act of violence.

PHYSICAL SELF-DEFENCE

Violence is ugly and unpredictable. Only attack if you believe violence is inevitable, or if you are already being assaulted. Don't be afraid to hit first – the person who lands the first solid blow

Ground defence

Should you find yourself on the ground, kick out with your legs at the attacker's shins, knees and groin. Try to buy yourself a few seconds in which to get to your feet and resume the fight in a standing position.

will often win the fight. Equally, don't be afraid to hit hard. Remember that you are trying to inflict such pain on your attacker that agony and injury will defeat them. Don't hold back power from your blows. If you are worried about the law, bear in mind the old expression, 'It is better to be judged by twelve than carried by six.' Keep fighting until your opponent is emphatically stopped.

In terms of techniques for defending yourself there are some general rules. Adopt a guard position the very second you are threatened. For a right-handed person, step forwards with the left leg (do the opposite if left-handed), and angle the body at 45° to your opponent, raising your open hands up to the front to create a protective zone. The open hands will appear unthreatening and seem part of your reasoning process, but can be easily converted to fists the second the fight kicks off. During the fight, focus your eyes on the opponent's sternum so that your peripheral vision can monitor every limb movement.

Generally speaking, unless you are a first-rate martial artist, avoid using complex locking techniques or blocking movements. These tend

Group attacks

The only policy when dealing with a group attack is to try to attack first, and keep hitting every target of opportunity. Move about constantly to break up the opponents' attack patterns.

not to work if you're not entirely competent or if your opponent is very strong or intoxicated (alcohol reduces the pain response on which locking techniques rely). Instead, defend yourself by moving out the way of incoming attacks, pulling your head backwards or to the side of punches, and jumping diagonally away from kicks as the kick builds up pace. During a fight, your fists should be raised and held either side of your jaw to protect your face from punches. Always return to your guard position after performing any technique.

VULNERABLE POINTS

In combat it is not only how hard you hit, but also where you hit that determines the outcome of the fight. Human bodies are resilient things, especially around the muscular and bony areas. What you must target are those areas which have no muscular covering and which are acutely painful or vulnerable to harm if struck hard. The fundamental vulnerable points are:

- Eyes – scratch or poke to induce temporary (or possibly permanent) loss of sight
- Nose – strike hard and without hesitation to break the nose or induce watering eyes, which temporarily blind the opponent
- Ears – tear them with a clawing hand, or even bite them
- Jaw – striking anywhere along the line of the jaw can result in a knockout punch or a broken jaw – the supreme boxer's target
- Throat – punching, poking or chopping the

GROUP ATTACKS

Tips for handling attacks by groups:
- Attack the group's leader (usually the most verbal member), and take him out with a powerful attack before the others can join in.
- Constantly move around so that the attackers cannot coordinate themselves.
- Stand in the entrance to a narrow alleyway or door so you can take the attackers one at a time.
- Improvise a weapon to improve your chances, such as a knuckle duster made by inserting your keys between your fingers.
- Fight ferociously, hitting every target of opportunity that presents itself.

throat should only be done in the most dangerous circumstances, as a heavy blow to the windpipe or the nerves, arteries and veins running up the throat can be fatal. However, it is a very effective target, producing either a choking pain or unconsciousness. The throat is also vulnerable to strangleholds using the forearm to compress it. Remember that, if the jugular veins either side of the throat are compressed, the person will lose consciousness in around 30 seconds and die in around two minutes if the pressure is maintained (which it should not be)

- Chest – strike the solar plexus to 'wind' the

opponent. Attack the floating ribs (the lowest pair of ribs, not connected to the breastbone), which are easily broken

- Joints – apply locking techniques to joints, if you are an expert, to control the opponent. Kick knee joints to damage the kneecap, and twist back fingers either to break them or to control the opponent
- Groin – kick the testicles to produce pain, nausea and sometimes unconsciousness. Kick them from underneath rather than in front to make a solid contact
- Kidneys – attack the lower back with hook punches to produce chronic pain

Targeting

The points illustrated are good places to attack in a fight. Target selection must be done with care, however, as points such as the throat and spine can result in a fatality if severely damaged.

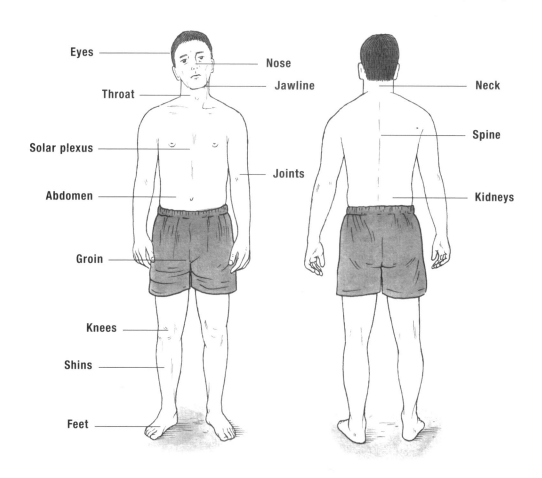

- Shins – kick the shins with heavy boots, or scrape the side of your shoe down them if you are being gripped from behind. Both techniques produce sickening pain
- Feet – stamp on the feet to crush the toes and break the bones of the foot.

HAND TECHNIQUES

Above all, fights are won with punching techniques. First, make a solid fist by curling the fingers tightly into the palm of the hand, then squeezing the fingers between the thumb and the little finger (keep the thumb pulled well back to avoid it being damaged when punching). Your

Fighting guard

In a fight, be sure to maintain a good guard throughout, with the fists raised (ideally held by the side of the chin), the body angled to present a small target and the knees bent to aid fast foot movement.

striking point is the two largest knuckles, and when punching try to keep the back of the hand level with the top of the forearm to distribute the force of the blow straight through the arm for power and your own safety. When performing any punch, keep the arm relaxed as it flies through the air, as relaxed muscle moves faster than tense muscle. When the punch connects, however, push all your body weight into the technique by tensing every muscle, and pushing the hip on the side of the punching arm suddenly forwards. If you weigh only 44kg (98lb), your punch should have 44kg (98lb) of force behind it, more than enough to knock out even a large assailant. Also, aim to punch into your target; don't simply strike the surface. Imagine you are actually punching, or kicking for that matter, a point about 7cm (3in) inside the opponent's body, and hold the technique there for a split second to allow full transfer of energy.

There are several different types of punch you can use, all of which should be delivered from the guard position stated above, with the left hand farther forward than your right (if you're right-handed). The jab punch is a fast technique using the front hand. Simply drive the left fist (in this case) straight into the target, pushing the left side of the body sharply forwards on impact, while twisting the fist palm downwards to 'screw' the fist into the target.

The cross punch is a decisive weapon delivered with the rear hand. For a right-handed fighter, standing with the left foot forward; the right fist is punched into the target and the right hip and right shoulder driven forwards at the moment on impact. If the hip, shoulder and punch all coordinate as one, the effects can be devastating. Try to get all the different elements to lock together in a single moment, and also lift the left foot slightly off the ground and push forwards with the right foot to attain further body-weight transference.

Hook punches are swinging techniques good for hitting the side of the jaw or for punching at close ranges. The hook also has the advantage that it attacks the opponent from a blind spot if executed properly. To throw a hook, swing the fist in a semicircular trajectory following the arc of the punch with your hip to add body weight. Keep the palm of the punching hand facing towards you so that the knuckles, not the little

Punches and strikes

The key point with any striking technique is to transfer the full body weight behind the blow, otherwise the technique is unlikely to be effective and will leave you open to counterattack.

Cross punch

Twist punch

Elbow

Upper cut

Eye strike

Kicking

The front snap kick is the easiest kick to master. Do not kick the opponent like a football, but rather bring the knee up high and thrust the foot into the target.

Front snap kick

Lean hard into the side-thrust kick, otherwise you risk being knocked over by the kick. Target area is the groin or abdomen.

Side-thrust kick

Roundhouse kick

The roundhouse kick derives most of its power through the rotation of the body, and requires practice to master. Don't be tempted to kick high on the body; instead aim for the groin, thighs, knees or shins.

finger, connect with the target. Hooks are most powerful when thrown from the rear hand, as with a crossing technique.

Finally, uppercut punches resemble the hook, but are swung vertically upwards to hit the opponent's chin from beneath, rather than from the side. Push the hook upwards in a straight vertical line and on impact thrust upwards with the feet and the hip behind the punching arm. Keep the fist facing towards you, and bend your knees before delivering it, pushing them straight on impact to increase the upward force.

When practising punches, shoot them out straight from your guard without making any buildup movements, such as shaking the fist, pulling it back, inhaling a sharp intake of breath, or shuffling your steps to get the range – all these will give your intentions away. Keep your face blank, and don't give your opponent any clues about what is coming. Just send the fist out straight into a clearly defined vulnerable point. Stare at this point hard during the technique to increase the accuracy.

Note that at very close ranges punches may not work, so convert all the above techniques into elbow strikes. Swing the point of the elbow around like a hook or upwards like an uppercut straight at the opponent's head or ribs. These are very powerful attacks and can easily crack bones.

KICKING TECHNIQUES

Kicking techniques can be used before punching range is closed, and if accurate they can win a fight. Realistic kicking techniques are different from the ones used in martial arts movies. Whereas martial artists easily kick to the head, in reality you should never kick above the waist. By keeping your kicks low, they will be fast, they won't be caught and you stand less chance of being knocked off balance. Low kicks can target the shins, knees and groin.

The basic kicking technique is the front snap kick, which is usually performed with the rear leg, although the front leg can be used for a faster, albeit less powerful, attack. In one smooth, powerful action, lift the knee of the kicking leg high to the front (both knees should be bent at the beginning of this attack). Whip the foot out powerfully into the target, striking with the ball of the foot or, if in strong shoes or boots, the toecap. Keep your body level throughout the

technique, as any bobbing up and down will take away energy from the forward thrust. The whole technique should be delivered in a fast whipping action, not a heavy push, and aimed to deliver a stunning pain. Practise kicking a heavy punching bag so that you become used to striking a target without losing your balance.

The side-thrust kick is a more complex technique used to thrust your opponent away from you. It is a difficult kick to master, and only use it if you have been trained in it under a competent instructor. Lift the knee of the kicking leg to the front in the same way as for a front snap kick, then use the force of the lift to twist through 90° and thrust the leg out sideways into the target. The impact point is the sole of the foot or the heel. Roll the hip of the kicking leg over to provide body-weight transference. Lean into the kick to prevent yourself from being knocked over backwards by the impact. When using the side-thrust kick, you need to keep your body as upright as possible. This will prevent you from overbalancing. This kick is an excellent weapon for attacking the knees.

The final kick in your repertoire should be the roundhouse kick, which involves a circular motion to attack the opponent from the side. Lift the knee of the kicking leg high to the side of the body, holding the knee and foot almost parallel to the ground, while spinning your body through 90°. At the moment when the point of the knee is aligned with the target, whip out the lower leg and strike the opponent with either the ball of the foot or your shinbone. Targets for the roundhouse kick are the knee, thighs and abdomen, and such a kick executed well can generate enormous power. As with the thrust kick, keep the body upright, and, as soon as you have struck the target, retract the kick back down to the floor immediately and recover your balance.

For close-range combat, the knees can be used as weapons instead of the feet. Apply the knee lift preparation used for the front snap kick and roundhouse kick as weapons in themselves – either thrust the knee into the opponent's groin or abdomen, or swing it from the side into the kidney area or thighs.

CLOSE-RANGE COMBAT

Most fights end up at grappling distance. Generally, a fight begins with a brief exchange of

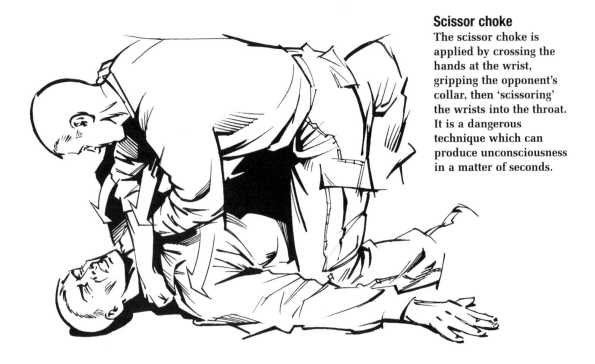

Scissor choke
The scissor choke is applied by crossing the hands at the wrist, gripping the opponent's collar, then 'scissoring' the wrists into the throat. It is a dangerous technique which can produce unconsciousness in a matter of seconds.

blows and kicks before the distance is closed and the fighters pull themselves to the ground. The person with grappling skills will usually come out on top in such a situation.

The objectives of grappling are either to restrain the attacker by locking a joint into a painful position or to apply a chokehold until they either submit or pass out. Locks and chokeholds take considerable practice to perfect, and a programme of judo or jujitsu is the best training.

LOCKS
Locks rely on pushing a joint against its natural range of movement and locking it into that position to induce pain and compliance. Locking techniques are difficult because they require technical skill and powerful body strength, particularly when used against a strong opponent or one who is high on drink or drugs, and will not respond to the pain of the lock.

A classic arm lock is as follows. If the opponent grabs your collar with his right hand, grip it strongly with your right hand and spin around in a counterclockwise direction. As you come around, put your left arm forearm against the opponent's elbow joint, and push hard to lock

the opponent's arm straight. Keep the pressure up and force the opponent downward to his knees, then onto his front. Once he is in that position, kneel on his elbow joint to securely lock him into place.

If you are unable to lock an arm, the finger joints make far easier targets – simply grab a finger and twist or bend it against its natural movement, either breaking the finger or twisting the opponent's arm over his shoulder, then pushing him to the floor. Finger attacks are a good way breaking out of someone's grip if they are attempting to strangle you or have gripped you around the waist.

BASIC THROW
A grappling technique can usually be converted into a throwing technique. For instance, grab onto your opponent's collar or his sleeves, and with great speed step diagonally forwards with the right leg, passing it around the back of the opponent's right leg and putting your right hip against the back of his thigh. By pushing hard with the hands, while driving the hip upwards, the opponent will be thrown backwards over your right leg with considerable power. As soon as he

Chokeholds

To escape from a chokehold, pull down on the choking arm to relieve the pressure, then either crush the testicles in a grip or make a powerful punch to the groin.

hits the floor, apply a locking, punching, stamping or kicking technique before he can recover – it may not sound like fair play, but your objective is to stop the fight before he can recover and attack again. When using any throwing technique, keep your upper body as upright as possible at all times to prevent yourself from being dragged down with your own technique.

CHOKEHOLDS

A chokehold is a compression grip applied around the opponent's throat. The technique will result in the opponent submitting, being injured or losing consciousness, so must be performed only in dangerous circumstances. A choke is applied using either the wrist or forearm as a pressure point. From the front, try the following 'scissor choke'. Cross your hands at the wrist and grab the opponent's

Leg sweeps

Rear leg sweep

Front leg sweep

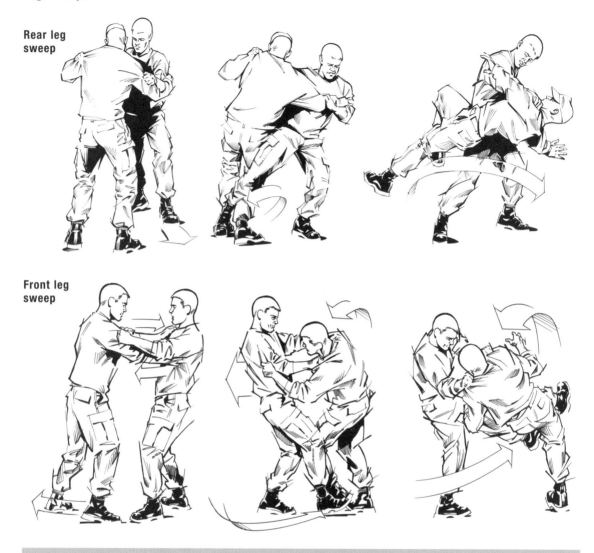

LEG SWEEPS

Sweeps are used to pull an opponent's legs from under him and throw him to the floor. A basic sweep is performed as follows:

- Hook the instep of your foot around the back of one of your opponent's legs. While doing this make a feint jab to the opponent's head to distract him from what is going on down below.

- Pull and lift your foot at the same time, sweeping the opponent's leg off the floor and across the front of his body. If performed correctly and with commitment, this will force the opponent to lose their balance and fall to the floor.
- Turn the sweep into a throw by grabbing the opponent's collar and throwing his shoulders in the opposite direction to the sweep.

collar – this technique will only work if the opponent is wearing strong clothing around the throat, such as a denim or leather jacket. Now push the elbows outwards, resulting in your wrists cutting into the sides of the opponent's throat. Combine this grip with knee attacks into the opponent's groin to limit his response options. If the opponent starts kicking you, move him from side to side to keep him off balance.

To apply a chokehold from the rear, hook your right arm around his throat, and place your right hand in the crook of your left elbow. Curl your left hand up around the back of the opponent's head, and squeeze your arms powerfully together. Your right forearm should now press into your opponent's throat. Walk backwards while doing the technique to throw the opponent off his feet and cause his whole body weight to drop into the stranglehold. Remember that this is a dangerous technique and, as with all chokeholds, should be released as soon as the opponent loses consciousness or clearly submits.

ATTACKS WITH A KNIFE

An attacker holding a knife has the advantage no matter how skilled you are. If he is just demanding money or valuables, simply hand them over. However, if he is attacking you with the knife, attempt the following:

- Strike at low targets beneath the attacker's waist using aggressive kicking techniques.
- Wrap your jacket or another piece of clothing around your front forearm. Use this to swipe away the knife attacks and, as soon as there is an opening, make a very violent attack to the throat, eyes or jaw to try to put down the opponent.
- Try to find a stick or club, and attack the elbow joint and wrist of the arm holding the knife. Keep the stick resting on your shoulder when not attacking so the opponent cannot grab it. If the opponent's head is exposed at any moment, hit it as hard as you can with the stick.

Fighting a knifed attacker
When facing a knife-wielding attacker, make low, long-distance kicks to the knees, or at close range go for fight-stopping targets such as the eyes or throat. Wrap a coat around your arm and swipe away the attacks.

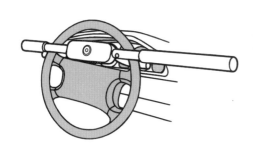

CHAPTER TWENTY-FOUR

SAFETY ON THE ROADS

As traffic density increases, roads are rapidly becoming the places in which we are in greatest danger, not only from automobile accidents, but also from violent carjacking.

THE FIRST AND most important stage in being safe on the roads is developing a safe driving style. Aggressive and inconsiderate driving is as much a danger to you as it is to others, and must be curbed. Avoid the following habits.

- 'Tailgating' other vehicles. Maintain an appropriate braking distance according to your speed.
- Breaking the speed limits, particularly in urban residential areas. Bear in mind, however, that the highest percentage of road fatalities occur on rural roads and involve only one vehicle, the most common cause of accidents being losing control on a bend at excessive speed.
- Overtaking into oncoming traffic on roads where you feel there is sufficient width to do so. You are likely to end up in a head-on collision.
- Overtaking lines of traffic when in a hurry. You may find there is not enough room to slip back into the traffic and end up trapped on the wrong side of the road.

Instead of such dangerous practices, foster a habit of responsible driving, giving other vehicles plenty of space, never overtaking unless the road ahead is totally clear, braking in plenty of time, controlling your speed and being vigilant in observation. Most crucially, don't drive for long periods without taking frequent rest breaks. Accidents caused through fatigue, including drivers literally falling asleep at the wheel, are among the top causes of road traffic accidents, yet they are easily prevented. Get out of the car at least every 90 minutes, walk around, eat and have some water or soft drinks. If you are very tired – especially if your eyes start to roll involuntarily – stop at the first available place that is safe for parking and get 15 minutes sleep in the car. This will refresh you enough to continue your journey safely.

ROAD TRAFFIC ACCIDENTS

Your first priority in any road traffic accident is to ensure your own safety. If your vehicle is involved, get out of it immediately in case it catches fire, and find a safe place at the side of

VEHICLE MAINTENANCE

To keep your vehicle safe, learn to perform basic maintenance work and have your car serviced annually by reputable mechanic. You should:

- check tyre pressure, including on the spare tyre, at least once every two weeks
- know how to replenish or change the oil, and know what type of oil your car needs
- know how to change a wheel
- have the brakes and wheel alignment checked about every six months
- check coolant levels at least once every two weeks
- know how to replace the bulbs in the headlights, signals (indicators) and brake lights
- have the brakes, cooling system, timing chain or cam belt, catalytic converter, and exhaust system checked at least annually by a professional mechanic.

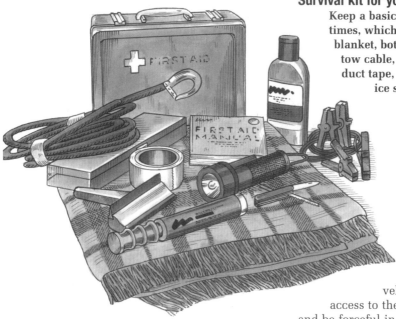

Survival kit for your car

Keep a basic survival kit in your car at all times, which should include a first-aid kit, blanket, bottled water, torch (flashlight), tow cable, jump leads, knife, tool kit, duct tape, spare fanbelt, footpump and ice scraper.

traffic, and turn on their emergency flashing hazard lights. Also put out warning cones or triangles, if you have them, about 25m (82ft) before the accident scene. If a car cannot be moved, the driver and passengers should remain in the vehicle with seat belts fastened until help arrives. Move any vehicles that might be restricting access to the scene by the rescue services, and be forceful in instructing people who are driving slowly by to have a look to get out of the way.

In an accident where there are casualties, make an immediate assessment of their condition using the principles outlined in Chapter 13. Look for anyone who may be trapped either under or

the road to sit and wait to be rescued. If you are trapped in the vehicle, try to smash a window using a heavy object or, at worst, your elbow wrapped in cloth. Get into the habit of carrying a hammer designed for the purpose of smashing car windshields. These should also feature a cutting mechanism to slice through the seat belt if it is trapping you into the seat.

Regardless of whether it is you or others involved in the accident, first phone for rescue (or flag someone else down to do it for you) and assess the accident area for immediate dangers. Look for hazards such as vehicles likely to roll or move, or spilt fuel. Check if trucks or tankers are displaying chemical or radiological hazard warning signs. Warn anyone smoking around the scene that they could start a fire and tell them to put the cigarette out immediately. Check if any vehicles are in contact with power lines or electricity cables. Beware of and watch out for vehicles heading at speed towards the scene of the accident (a problem common at accidents that have occurred in heavy fog).

If you see dangers, clear everybody away from the area. Get drivers to move their cars to the side of the road, out of the way of oncoming

ACCIDENT HANDLING

At the scene of an accident, if the area is safe and the casualties are being attended to, take down the following details to assist the police, emergency services, or insurance companies with their response:

- The name, address and phone number of every driver or witness involved
- The driving license number and insurance company details of each driver, including the insurance policy number if possible
- A description of each car – make sure you write down the make, model, colour and license plate
- If you have a camera, take multiple pictures of the scene from various angles.

Following an accident, always contact your insurance company immediately after the event and follow their instructions.

TYPICAL CRASH INJURIES

SIDE IMPACT: Fractured leg and arm on side of impact; fractured pelvis; shoulder/upper-arm injuries; head injuries
REAR IMPACT: Spinal and neck injuries (especially whiplash); facial injuries
HIGH-SPEED FRONTAL IMPACT: Multiple fractures; internal bleeding; head and spinal injuries; multiple lacerations; impacted pelvis; crushed lower limbs (occur when the dashboard is compressed onto the victim's lap and legs)
ROLL-OVER ACCIDENT: Depending on the severity of the roll, this accident can produce similar injuries to a high-speed impact. Children often worst affected in a roll-over
MOTORCYCLE ACCIDENT: Leg and arm fractures (particularly around the wrist and ankle); head injuries; internal bleeding; severe bleeding wounds
PEDESTRIAN ACCIDENT: Depending on the type of vehicle: side impact injuries; multiple fractures; head and spinal injuries; crushing injuries; traumatic amputation

Safety when removing a helmet

Do not remove the helmet of an injured motorcylist or cyclist unless you have to deliver CPR. If you do have to administer CPR, one person should stabilize the head and neck, while another inches the helmet off slowly.

VEHICLE FIRES

Petrol (gasoline) is a highly explosive and volatile substance, and any type of vehicle fire is extremely serious. Thankfully, vehicle fires in well-maintained cars are rare, but there are various points and warning signs to be aware of. Check all gaskets, hoses and pipes for leaks, and monitor the electrical system for any faulty wiring or sparking. Make sure your catalytic converter is properly maintained. Catalytic converters reach extremely high temperatures when the car is running, and can ignite if faulty. Also check that no fuel is leaking from the tank, which can drip down onto the hot exhaust pipe, and take the car to an engineer if the fuel consumption seems excessively high. Check that exhaust pipes have no rust holes, cracks or broken joints, as these can drip fuel and start a fire in dry grass that can spread to the vehicle. Damaged exhaust pipes will often produce a distinct 'putt putt' sound, particularly when accelerating, and may even leak fumes into the inside of the vehicle.

inside a vehicle, but be very careful if you insert your head through a broken window that you do not cut yourself on shards of glass or sharp pieces of metal. Treat any casualties you find with first aid, but only move them or the vehicle if there is an immediate danger from fire, explosion and so on, or if you cannot deliver lifesaving first aid in their current position. Never remove the helmet of a motorcyclist or cyclist unless you have to perform CPR. Also, do not wrench open a car door as the casualty may be impaled or trapped on the twisted door metal. Particularly in rural areas, you should also check in and over roadside walls, hedges and ditches to see if anybody has been catapulted from the vehicle away from the apparent accident scene.

Try to control any panic developing at the accident scene. Comfort casualties verbally, and do not allow shocked or injured persons to wander away from the scene. Wrap casualties or traumatized people in clothing or blankets to help keep them warm and reduce shock symptoms. Remember to check whether people are simply psychologically shocked or are actually going into circulatory shock (see Chapter 13).

If you are unfortunate enough to be in a vehicle that catches fire – usually indicated by smoke pouring out from under the hood – first pull smoothly and calmly over to the side of the road, avoiding sudden braking. Put on your flashing hazard lights to warn other drivers you are in trouble. Once you have stopped, turn off the engine and get out of the car. If you have a

Improvised stretcher

Coats stretched between two poles will make a basic emergency stretcher. However, do not move casualties at the scene of a road traffic accident unless their lives are in serious danger should you not do so.

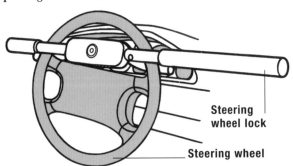

fire extinguisher, poke its nozzle through the front grille and spray the engine area thoroughly. Do not attempt to inspect the fire by opening the bonnet (hood), as the influx of oxygen could make the flames explode in your face. Now stand away from the vehicle at a safe distance – at least 20m (66ft) – and call emergency services. Give other people in the vicinity clear verbal instructions to stay away from the vehicle.

PROTECTING YOUR VEHICLE FROM CRIME

A poorly maintained vehicle is a hazard to you and others. Not only might it break down, but it could leave you stranded in inhospitable wilderness or urban settings as well. It is therefore imperative to keep your car in good working order. In addition, you must also maintain or improve the vehicle's security features to protect you from criminal activity.

In terms of security, first fit secure door locks, if you don't have them already. The exposed end of the lock just beneath the window should be straight, not T-shaped. The straight type prevents a thief or attacker from gaining a firm grip if they are trying to get into the vehicle. Ideally your car should have central locking, which allows you to secure all points of access into the vehicle with one click. Get into the habit of locking the car the moment you are sitting in it – attackers will often strike at the moment you have just sat down, while your attention is focused on putting the keys in the ignition.

A further deterrent to car thieves is a steering-wheel lock. Although most modern cars come with internal steering locks, these do not have the visual deterrence factor of an external lock, and in any case many car thieves are able to snap them using leverage on the steering wheel. Some steering-wheel locks also have a connecting arm that clamps the gearstick, providing a further layer of protection.

Anti-theft devices

Steering-wheel and pedal-jack locks can be overcome by determined criminals, but most will not want the extra effort and will look for easier pickings elsewhere.

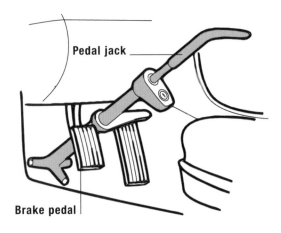

Steering wheel lock

Steering wheel

Pedal jack

Brake pedal

To prevent the car from actually being started by criminals, a range of security measures is available. Obviously, never leave your car running with the keys in it, or nip into a store with the car doors open. Many thefts from and of cars occur in supermarkets when people are returning their carts after unloading the shopping, leaving the car unlocked. Cars can be fitted with ignition systems that can only be operated with the designated electronically coded key, and also a fuel cut-off device is available which prevents the flow of petrol (gas) once the fuel in the petrol line is used. Protect against the criminals attempting to override these systems by fitting a secondary bonnet (hood) lock. A secondary boot (trunk) lock, or a lockable guard plate over the main lock, is also beneficial to protect valuables.

Follow basic anti-theft precautions by never leaving anything of value on display in the car interior, regardless of whether you think a criminal will be interested in the item or not. Try to fit a car radio/stereo with a detachable front panel that can be taken with you when you leave the car – this will make it worthless to the criminal. Also, never leave any system of identification on your car key, otherwise a criminal will be able to steal the keys and either find your vehicle or head for your home.

Finally, for emergencies on the road, keep the following items with you at all times: a first-aid kit, a freestanding torch (flashlight) with an adjustable light so you can have your hands free when performing maintenance tasks, electrical tape, a fix-a-flat tyre kit, bottled water and reflective emergency triangles.

SAFETY FROM CRIME
Awareness is your greatest asset when driving around urban areas. Criminals employ sophisticated tactics to force drivers to stop, at which point the driver is either assaulted or robbed, or becomes a victim of a carjacking. Watch pedestrians carefully. Occasionally, criminals position themselves in the middle of the road, pretending to sell flowers or newspapers, or offering to wash windows. Never stop for such people, and turn away anyone who attempts to wash your windows at a set of traffic lights. Keep your doors locked and your windows rolled up at all times. If you are asked for directions from a pedestrian, give them from behind the window

glass; however, if you have the least suspicion about the pedestrian's intentions, drive away immediately. A useful addition to your car are little stick-on mirrors that fit onto the main side mirrors, which enable you to see down the side of the car. Fit them on both sides of the vehicle so that you can see if anybody is creeping up on you from a blind spot.

Another common criminal ruse is to pretend to be in a brokendown vehicle. When you stop to offer help, a robbery is sprung. Generally, do not offer assistance unless you are entirely sure that the need for help is genuine. If you are really concerned about the breakdown, call the police and give them a map reference and directions to the breakdown so that they can handle it.

Be aware of the 'bump-and-rob' tactics also employed by criminals. Here the criminals purposely drive a car into the back of yours. As

Night-time parking
At night, try to park your car in well-lit, public areas (preferably areas with security patrols) which are as close to your destination as possible.

Parking safety
Do not park your car next to or between large obstructions, as such a position makes an ambush easier when you enter or exit the vehicle.

you get out of your car to confront the driver, you are robbed or your car is stolen. Such robberies are often accompanied by violence, with guns and knives employed to gain your compliance. If you are hit from behind, stay seated in your vehicle and immediately call the police using a mobile (cellular) phone. Do not step out of the car if apparent bystanders approach you with offers of help, and keep all the doors locked and windows rolled up. If you have a telephone with you, stay inside the vehicle and exchange any insurance details through the glass before driving off. If the person who bumped you is a criminal, he or she is unlikely to stay around that long.

You are most in danger when parking the vehicle, especially in isolated or large city car parking lots. Think about where you are parking; if you are parking in the day, bear in mind how safe the position will be like if you are returning to the car at night. Try to position your vehicle in full view of public movement in well-lit places, away from alleyways. Steer clear of shadowy corners or areas where there is thick foliage – both could hide attackers – and do not park between two vans or trucks for the same reason. Parking in front of open businesses is a good precaution, as

you can run inside if threatened. When using large municipal parking lots, select ones that are well used, with closed-circuit cameras, and operated by attendants.

If you are concerned about safety, ask friends or coworkers to walk you to your vehicle and ensure you get there safely. When you are alone, however, walk towards the vehicle looking strong and confident to deter attackers (most attackers prey on weakness). Always leave and approach your car with extreme caution, remaining alert and watchful, and checking the car carefully before entering it, in case anyone may be hiding around, underneath or even inside the vehicle. Have your car key at the ready, and if you have remote door opening open the car a few seconds before you get to it. Once inside the car, lock the doors immediately.

PLANNING JOURNEYS
Plan journeys in advance to help you avoid criminal trouble. Steer clear of areas plagued with violence. Read your local newspaper and learn where gang activity and crime hotspots are concentrated. If you are in a strange city and you don't know where these areas are, ask a police

officer to mark them on a map for you. When passing through a dangerous area, do so by the most direct route, sticking to main roads rather than side streets where you will have to stop frequently for stop signs and traffic lights. If the road has multiple lanes, drive in the middle lane (if the law allows) to make it more difficult for pedestrians to approach the vehicle. Generally avoid going into dead-end roads or streets that run through derelict areas, particularly streets in abandoned docks or along waterfronts.

Should you be followed by another car, stay calm and use a mobile (cellular) phone to telephone the police. If you do not have a phone, either drive directly to the nearest police station or, if you do not know where this is, drive into a drive-by fast-food establishment and ask them to phone the police.

GPS system
A GPS (global positioning system) device is a useful navigational tool for car travel. The better receivers can be programmed to give you directions throughout your journey.

Carjacking

ATM machines are a common destination for carjackings, as the attackers will get both your money and your vehicle. Hand the keys over without a struggle when faced by weapons.

CARJACKING

Carjacking is becoming a major problem. As modern vehicles are fitted with ever more advanced security systems, criminals often do not have the technological know-how to break into them and start the ignition. As an alternative, they simply steal the car while the occupants are driving it.

Many of the precautions outlined above concerning security and safe driving will protect you from carjacking attempts. In addition, keep the doors locked and windows rolled up, plan safe journeys and don't park in risky areas. Be aware that you need to come to a stop for the carjackers to attack, so the following are vulnerable locations:

- Drive-through ATM machines
- Parking areas, particularly around ticket machines
- Traffic intersections, particularly those controlled by stop signs or traffic lights, and motorway (freeway) exit and entry ramps
- Self-service petrol (gas) stations or car washes

In the event that you are the victim of a carjacking attempt, remember that the carjacker is most likely just interested in your vehicle. If the carjacker has a gun, do not protest – simply get out of the vehicle and let them take it away. Don't be tempted to drive off at speed, as you are liable to crash the vehicle (at which point you will be subject to the carjacker's anger) or be hit by gunfire. Once on the street, get away from the immediate area quickly, find a telephone and call the police. Try to find a safe place to wait for the police to arrive, such as a business or inside a store. When the police arrive, given them the full details concerning your vehicle and also a description of what the carjacker looked like. Include details such as the carjacker's gender, race, age, hair and eye details, distinguishing features, and clothing.

Avoiding dangerous routes

If possible, do not take your car through areas known for crime or gang activity. If you do have to drive through such areas, stick to free-moving highways (motorways), keep windows up and doors locked, and make sure you have plenty of petrol (gas) in the fuel tank.

ROAD RAGE

Road rage is a fairly modern phenomenon in which drivers explode with anger at what they see as the inconsiderate or annoying driving of others. Road-rage incidents are not predictable – everything from someone being overtaken by another driver to major road traffic accidents can elicit a road-rage response. While many road-rage outbursts are simply verbal, an unfortunate percentage involve physical violence, and in some cases murder.

Your first response to an enraged driver should be to try to calm the situation down. Without winding the windows down or getting out the car, make a clear apology. One suggestion from police departments and experts is a keep a sign in the car on which is written the word 'Sorry'. You can hold this up to a driver in another car without having to get close, and research has shown that the anger of most enraged drivers will subside when they see this message.

If a furious driver gets out of his or her car and begin shouting at you through the window, call the police on your mobile (cellular) phone. Do not try to rationalize with the driver; in this enraged state he or she is only likely to get angrier. Never get angry yourself, as this will signal to the other driver that you want to meet violence with violence. When the enraged driver finally breaks off their tirade, let them get into their car and drive off. Wait for several minutes to let them get some distance from you, then make sure you are calm enough to drive before proceeding.

Road rage

Road rage serves little purpose. Take deep breaths when you start to feel your anger rising; if it looks set to get out of control, pull the car over and sit still and quietly until the aggression subsides.

Aggressive drivers

If an aggressive driver gets out of his car and approaches yours, do not get out. Instead, lock all doors and communicate through closed windows. Let the aggressor get back in his car and drive off.

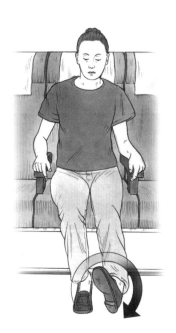

CHAPTER TWENTY-FIVE

SAFETY ON PUBLIC TRANSPORTATION

We can all take safety for granted on board an aircraft or train. The chances of an accident are admittedly rare, but simple preparations could save your life if the worst happens.

THE FIRST ORDER of business for surviving during travel on public transportation is to stay alert and to be mindful of escape routes, safety measures and other resources at your disposal that could save lives in an emergency.

RAIL TRAVEL
Collisions and derailment
Strict procedures and advanced command-and-control technologies make the possibility of a disaster somewhat remote on modern railroads and on the trains operating on them. However, because of a train's mass and the speeds with which it travels, a collision or derailment delivers a huge amount of kinetic energy to the carriages and passengers. It is important to be aware of the location of the nearest carriage exits and be ready to get yourself and others out in the event of a crisis. Never kick your shoes off on long journeys in case you have to move fast.

As is the case with all survival situations, be aware of signs of danger and react promptly to them. While a collision may occur without warning, a derailment can produce several advance signals, including sudden braking, violent rocking or shaking, the sound of an impact, and the train beginning to pitch over. Passengers, baggage and other materials may be thrown around, along with the passengers themselves. Immediately, pull a thick coat over your head and your upper body to protect against flying objects, and push your head down towards your knees with both arms covering your head. Stay in this position until the train has come to a stop. When the train has come to rest, look for the nearest door out. If it is not possible to use a door to escape, the windows may be loosened or kicked out to allow you to climb to safety. Watch out for broken glass and twisted metal, as these pieces of wreckage could cause injury.

If a collision or derailment occurs while travelling on an underground (subway) line or tram, be aware that one of the rails beneath the train may be electrified, carrying more than 700 volts. Identify this electrified rail ahead of time; it should be visible from the platform before the train arrives. In an accident it may be safest, if you are uninjured, to remain in the carriage until

In a train crash
In the event of a train crash, do not exit the train unless there is a fire, as there is the danger that you might be electrocuted on the line or from hanging overhead cables.

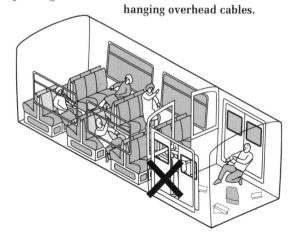

professional help comes to rescue the passengers. If you must escape from the train wreckage because of fire or another hazard, avoid or, if you must, jump clear over the electrified rail and move away from the accident site towards the nearest tunnel or track exit.

Fire

A diesel locomotive's fuel can spill and catch fire during a collision or derailment. Surviving fire in a train wreck requires similar procedures to surviving fire in other settings. Stay low in case there is danger of smoke inhalation. Move as far from the site of the fire as possible. If the fire occurs while trapped aboard the train, avoid

Basic precautions

Try not to display valuables on a train, especially laptop computers, as you will become a magnet for muggers. When carrying a laptop, use the shoulder strap worn diagonally across the body.

opening interior doors – the onrush of air could cause the fire suddenly to explode or spread. If you really have to open a door, touch it first, checking to see if it is hot; if it is, there is probably a fire on the other side and you have to find another way out. Shut all the doors between you and the fire, and use luggage to break open a window and escape, being careful to avoid injury when jumping down from the carriage. Wrap layers of clothing around yourself for protection against the glass. Get well away from the train, as fuel fires may occur on the ground surrounding the accident site.

Travel security precautions on trains

A crowded train presents an ideal opportunity for an active pickpocket or for a robbery or assault to occur, as the victim may have less chance to detect the perpetrator in the crowd. The crowd also may increase the chances for the criminal to escape by masking his movements or obstructing his apprehension. As always, make sure that you hide any anything worth stealing. Conceal all

Train awareness

Try to sit near an exit on a subway or train. Should any aggressive or intoxicated individuals enter your carriage, casually exit the train at the next stop and get into another carriage.

valuables such as wallets, money or jewellery. Purses (handbags) and backpacks should be closed with a zipper or other positive measure, and held or strapped securely in front of your body. On quiet late-night trains, avoid using your laptop computer – it will be a magnet for criminals. Also, try not to use a mobile (cellular) phone, another desirable object.

To guard against train crime, stay as close as possible to an exit, remain alert and avoid distractions. Do not fall asleep – a gift for a competent thief. As you enter a train, be vigilant for danger signs – suspicious or intoxicated persons, trains packed tight with people or, conversely, empty platforms, especially late at night. Think carefully before committing to board a train, watch those getting on and off, and be alert for sudden jostling or grabbing, or other violent conduct. Be aware of other passengers and whether they exhibit evident signs of mental instability or violent temper – move to another section of the train at the first opportunity.

Stay equally alert when you get off the train, and if you suspect you are being followed go straight to a guard and ask them to contact the police, if necessary. Never wait for a train on a deserted part of the platform.

Sleeping on a train

Try to avoid sleeping on trains. Not only is a sleeping passenger a target for pickpockets, but he or she is also vulnerable to attack, as a sleepy individual is rarely capable of a defence.

Platform safety

On subway platforms, avoid isolating yourself at far ends of the platform. Stay away from anyone loitering near the exits, and stand close to the wall so no one can move up behind you unseen.

Air travel

Travelling by commercial aircraft is one of the safest modes of transportation from the standpoint of technical reliability and personal security. While dramatic when they occur, air crashes are rare events considering the enormous amount of air traffic moving around the globe every hour of every day. Modern jet carriers offer rigorously tested aerodynamic performance, high-technology control systems, continual tracking and air-to-ground communications, and the aircrews have accumulated thousands of hours of flight time. Today passengers are screened with extra thoroughness, given the heightened state of global security following the September 11, 2001 terrorist attacks in the United States. Probably no other form of public transportation ensures as complete a vetting of passengers.

Should an aircraft crash, the chances of passenger survival are, however, slim. A straight-on high-speed impact against the ground has rarely, if ever, produced survivors, but crash landings – where the pilot retains some degree of control over the aircraft – certainly have. Surviving a plane crash requires some of the same precautions taken before a rail disaster. Be aware of your surroundings and note the nearest escape routes. On a commercial carrier, the flight crew will tell you the location of exits, in-flight

Turbulence

Modern airliners can cope with levels of turbulence most of us will never experience. Don't panic, stay in your seat with your seat belt fastened and know that the turbulence will pass.

safety procedures, and the process of donning an oxygen mask in the event the cabin loses air pressure. Listen to this briefing, no matter how many times you have flown before. In the event of a crash landing, adopt the crash position with your head down and covered by your arms. Once the aircraft comes to a stop, try not to panic and move quickly to the exits. If smoke is obscuring your vision, the aircraft will usually have direction lights that come on at floor level. Follow the flight crew's instructions for exiting the aircraft, which can vary slightly according to the model of the plane.

Turbulence during the flight

Short of crashing, there are several other dangers accompanying air flight. A plane may encounter air turbulence during the flight, even when the weather is bright and sunny. Air currents move invisibly across the Earth and it may be difficult for the pilot or weather radar systems on the ground to predict the location and force of rough air. Turbulence can occur with almost no warning, ranging from a light bump to violent shaking of the plane and loss of altitude, causing sensations not unlike those experienced during a roller-coaster ride. When it is very severe it can throw passengers bodily into the air if they are not wearing a seat belt, causing injury and, on very rare occasions, death. Most turbulence is minor,

but it is recommended that you remain seated with your seat belt on. Choose periods of smooth flight to move around the cabin for exercise or a restroom break, but return to your seat the moment things get rough again. During turbulence, overhead baggage stowage may present a hazard if it is not secured; always ensure the compartments near your seat are securely closed before takeoff and during the flight.

An important thing to remember when experiencing turbulence is the aircraft has been engineered to withstand much more severe buffeting than is likely to be encountered during the flight. Remain calm; try to reassure the passengers near you if they seem agitated by the turbulence.

Air rage

Even with stringent security checks, not every potentially disruptive or violent passenger will be screened out. The airline industry has adopted the term 'air rage' to refer to the aggressive conduct that may be associated with excessive consumption of alcohol or mental instability.

Locating exits

On an air flight, pay attention to where the nearest exist is. In an emergency, however, do not make a move for the exit while the aircraft is still in motion – wait until it has come to a complete stop.

As is the case with boarding a train, be aware of your fellow passengers before you get on the plane. Be alert for signs of trouble such as drunkenness, aggression or excessively impolite conduct during the check-in process. Many passengers betray signs that give some warning of their behaviour, even while still on the ground. If you suspect that one of the passengers may pose a threat to an otherwise uneventful flight, discreetly notify the authorities. Once aboard, be vigilant for stressed or irate conduct, and other signs that may emerge in passengers, especially during a frustrating situation such as a delay in takeoff.

Never attempt to take the situation into your own hands. The flight crew are extensively trained to handle air rage. Discreetly notify the flight attendants of any suspicious behaviour. However, in situations when a passenger truly goes berserk and attempts to smash windows or open a flight door, be prepared to lend your strength if the flight crew needs it. Attempt to pin the passenger down so that the crew can apply handcuffs or other restraining devices.

Health considerations

Avoid flying if you are ill or recuperating from an illness, particularly those of the upper respiratory system. The air pressure inside the aircraft and the effects of high altitude may turn a minor cold into a serious health problem. Also avoid flying if you are recovering from surgery, particularly from a heart complaint. Always make the flight crew aware of any special health conditions. At the time you book your ticket, tell the airline of any allergies you have so that they can check the content of in-flight meals and snacks, and arrange different food for you if necessary.

Another serious health risk is from deep vein thrombosis, or DVT. This occurs when blood clots form in the deep veins of the legs. A clot can then circulate to the heart or the vessels that supply oxygen from the lungs. The result is that the oxygen supply to the body can be cut off, a condition known as 'pulmonary embolism'. Warning signs of this potentially lethal condition are reduced circulation, chest pain and shortness of breath. One cause of DVT is the restricted legroom and relatively cramped conditions of most airline passenger cabins. To prevent DVT, move regularly and flex the lower limbs in order to create muscle contractions that keep the deep vein blood flowing back to the heart. Simply exercising your muscles during a flight greatly reduces your chances of becoming ill as a result of a circulatory disorder.

Avoiding deep vein thrombosis (DVT)

On long-haul air flights, avoid crossing your legs, as this hinders free circulation and increases the risk of DVT. Instead, stretch the legs out as much as possible and perform regular exercises, such as circling the ankles and pulling the knees up to the chest.

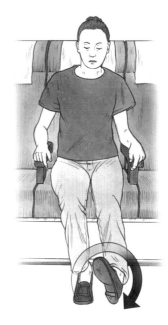

CHAPTER TWENTY-SIX

SURVIVING IN THE HOME ENVIRONMENT

More accidents happen in the home than in any other environment. Although the home is a place of refuge, it is also full of hazards and is a potential magnet for criminal activity.

SAFETY AWARENESS IN the home is as critical as survival awareness in the wilderness. Be constantly vigilant for any possible dangers in either the physical structure of your home or dangers from objects that you store within your living space.

HAZARDOUS CHEMICALS

Homes are generally full of hazardous substances. The most common of these substances are household cleaning products or chemicals used for home improvements (DIY). Examples include ammonia, bleach, paint, rust treatments, drain cleaners, pesticides, solvents and fuel.

Store all such products appropriately in a secure, preferably locked, cupboard – this is especially vital if children live in or visit the house – or ideally in an external outbuilding. Make sure that the cupboards where you store cleaning products have childproof locks. If the chemicals are releasing vapours, provide the storage area with plentiful ventilation to prevent a dangerous buildup of gases. If the chemicals are explosive, buy a metal cabinet in which to contain them.

Keep any chemicals away from sources of direct heat. Never smoke around dangerous chemicals, and check the packaging of the products regularly to ensure that there are no leaks. These points apply particularly to metal containers under pressure, such as aerosol cans. Do not place these in direct sunlight as they could explode, and keep them away from damp

so that the metal does not rust and weaken. Do not store dangerous chemicals in general household containers; there is always the risk of confusion. Once you have finished a container of chemicals, treat the empty container with caution, as it may still contain flammable vapour or residues. Throw all such containers away safely and with regard to the environment. Never dispose of them, especially aerosol cans, on a bonfire.

Hazardous materials

Ensure all hazardous materials are clearly labelled (replace any faded or torn labels). Always store them according to instructions and well away from the reach of children.

Smoke alarms

Smoke alarms are inexpensive and save lives. Regularly test every smoke alarm (they feature a test button on the outer shell), and replace the batteries as necessary.

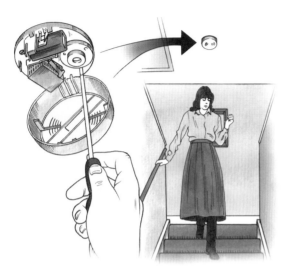

Extinguishing a pan fire

Smother pan fires by throwing a damp towel over them – never throw water on the pan. Leave the pan covered for at least half an hour – otherwise it could reignite when exposed to the air.

Should any dangerous chemicals be spilled, soak them up with cat litter, sand or sawdust first, then scoop up the solid matter with a spade straight into heavy-duty plastic garbage bags and transfer them into the external trash can.

One final point to remember is that mixing certain chemicals can set off violent reactions. In particular, avoid mixing chlorine bleach with ammonia – both used in cleaning products – because they will produce a highly toxic chlorine gas. Always read warning labels on hazardous substances, and store them separately from other chemicals in the house.

FIRE PREVENTION AND RESPONSE

Most home fires are preventable. The three classic causes of house fires are electrical faults, carelessly discarded cigarettes or fires that occur during cooking.

When using any electrical appliance, never overload the plug or an extension cord (cable). This can happen if you have too many machines plugged into one electrical outlet. Keep the outlet free from clutter, especially paper, which could ignite if the socket overheats. Don't leave extension cords (cables) running where people can trip over them. Always turn off and unplug any appliance that feels unnaturally hot or starts to smoke or spark.

Pay particular attention to the quality of heaters. Ensure that heaters, as well as open fires and their chimneys, are serviced annually. This will also guard against the danger of faulty heaters emitting poisonous carbon monoxide fumes. Keep heaters at least 1m (3ft) away from flammable items such as clothing, paper or curtains.

Cigarette fires are simply avoided by stubbing out cigarettes thoroughly in a

STORING FIREARMS

If you have firearms in the home, store them wisely. Never have them in a place which is easily accessible to children – hundreds die each year from firearms accidents throughout the United States. Store the gun in an approved gun safe, which should in turn be bolted to a solid structure such as a brick wall or floor joist. Store the ammunition separately in a heavy-duty safe. If you ever suffer a house fire, tell the attending fire officers immediately where ammunition is located so that they can take due precautions. Children should not know any combinations for gun or ammunition safes, and as an extra layer of safety fit every firearm with a trigger lock. As a final precaution, teach your children all about gun safety. However, never underestimate how curiosity can override common sense.

Gun safety

Fitting a gun with a trigger lock and storing it in a gun safe will help prevent it falling into the wrong hands. This includes children, of whom thousands are injured or killed each year through gun accidents.

proper ashtray. Never smoke if you are very tired or have been drinking, as you could fall asleep, drop the cigarette and cause a fire on the furniture. To avoid accidentally starting a fire in the kitchen, never overfill deep-fat fryers or pans. Should a pan catch fire, do not throw water onto

it or carry it outside – this will make the flames explode in your face. Instead, wet a towel, wring it out and throw it over the pan to smother the flames. Don't take the towel off for at least an hour.

All homes should be fitted with smoke alarms, which are available from any hardware store,

Door security

The doorway on the left is attractive for criminals, as it has plenty of hiding places on the approach and is shaded and poorly lit. The open and brightly lit doorway on the right gives a criminal no hiding places.

department store or supermarket. Install at least one alarm on every floor of your home, and check once a month that they are working, replacing the batteries if necessary. Replace the entire unit after 10 years. Your home should also feature an accessible fire extinguisher and a sturdy rope or chain ladder, which can be hung out of upper-floor windows to make an escape.

Should the worst happen and a fire breaks out in your home, immediately get yourself and your family outside, and phone the emergency services. If flames and heat are building around you, drop to the floor where the air is cooler and cleaner (heat rises). Smoke is the real killer in almost all house fires, so staying close to the floor puts you below most of the toxic fumes. Putting a damp cloth over your nose and mouth will help filter out some toxins. If the flames trap you, get everyone in a single room, close the door and pack clothes around any cracks to keep out fumes. Open a window and try to attract help. If you are on the second floor of a house and the fire services might arrive too late, throw cushioning materials such as mattresses and clothes onto the ground beneath a window, then hang out of the window and drop to the ground. By hanging out the window first, you bring your feet much closer to the ground and lessen your speed and impact on landing.

Every occupant in the home should know his or her escape route, planned from where he or she sleeps. Test out these escape routes in a family fire drill on a regular basis.

SECURITY FEATURES
Home security is a major concern, especially as most countries in the developed world have seen a significant increase in house burglary over recent decades. Many criminals will approach your house from behind, so never leave a ladder outside your home and cut away any vegetation that either extends to your upstairs windows or creates shadows and hiding places in your garden or backyard. Fit locking gates to side alleyways, and plant thorn bushes around external fences to deter criminals from climbing over. Cover any approach routes to the house with gravel materials, such as small-gauge granite rock, that makes a noise when walked on.

Security lighting should provide a further layer of protection around your home. Motion-sensing

Double entry doors
Make double doors secure by fitting heavy-duty slide bolts to the non-active door. Make sure these bolts slide into deep recesses in the door frame.

active door

slide bolt

inactive door

slide bolt

lights are ideal. They automatically turn on when anything moves within range of the sensor and both save you electricity and act as a deterrent to a criminal suddenly caught in a powerful beam. Some more sophisticated detectors work by triggering an alarm when changes in infrared energy levels are sensed as an intruder moves into a protected area.

The following are the most crucial points relating specifically to the security of the physical structure of your home, and concern door and window security.

Doors

- Install solid wood or plastic doors with toughened glass. If the door glass is not reinforced, fit a double-cylinder lock to prevent it from being opened by someone reaching in from the outside.
- Ensure that the doorframe and doorjamb are tightly fitting and that the doorframe is properly sealed to the wall.
- All doors, including back doors, should be fitted with peephole viewers and overhead illumination so that you can scrutinize visitors before opening the door.
- Doors must feature quality five-pin mortise deadlocks made of hacksaw-resistant metals and extending at least 2.5cm (1in) into the frame of the door. Don't just rely on spring-loaded latches, as these can be forced open with a screwdriver.
- Add additional bolts to a door at the top and the bottom. Multiple locks make it very difficult for someone to kick a door open, and the spread of bolts distributes the impact along the entire length of the doorjamb.

Deadbolt lock

Hinge bolts

Patio doors

- Ensure patio doors are made from high-impact materials with fully welded joints and a steel-reinforced outer frame.
- There should be deadlocks at both the top and bottom of the doors.
- Fit an antilift device (most criminals simply crowbar patio doors from their tracks). This can be simply a block of wood jammed in the door slide, but professionally produced versions are far better.
- Arrange your home so valuable items are not easily visible through the patio doors.
- Connect the patio doors directly to the household alarm system.

Patio door lock

Windows

- If affordable, replace conventional glass with toughened tempered glass or polycarbonate.
- Install locks on all windows (or replace old ones), and keep them locked at all times when the window is not deliberately opened.
- If a window is in a particularly vulnerable location, fit a metal grille over it or metal shutters that can be pulled down when required.
- Connect all the windows to the household alarm system.

Window lock

Alarm systems are excellent additions to your household security, but come in a bewildering range of setups and prices. However, the basic system consists of a control panel and a chain of sensors placed around the property. The sensors trigger the alarm through either detecting motion or by reacting to a door or window being forced open. Once triggered, the alarm system will either set off a deafening audible alarm and/or send out a security alert to a monitoring company who then call the police. Simply having the alarm box on the outside of your house will usually be enough to deter most criminals.

There are three zones of your home that should be protected by an alarm system of some kind. First, there is the outer perimeter of your property which extends up to the boundaries of your property. The garden or backyard is not usually protected by an alarm system, although security lighting of the type described above should be installed. After the perimeter, the outer shell of the house – which includes all doors and windows – should be connected to the alarm system using a direct trigger system (usually magnetic contacts which, when broken, trigger the alarm). Finally, motion detectors that will trigger the alarm if someone actually makes it inside can protect the rooms inside the house.

The final point about burglar alarms is to make sure that they cannot be tampered with. Good-quality alarms come with systems to bypass the main electricity circuit if the criminal cuts off your power or if there is a general power cut or blackout. Also, mount the exterior siren as high as possible in a steel box on an outside wall where it cannot be easily tampered with.

DETERRENTS

There are various other purchases that can deter a criminal from attempting to break into your home. The most companionable is a dog. Dogs are one of the surest deterrents against home intruders, although that should never be the sole reason you purchase an animal. If loved and cherished, a dog will usually be committed to protecting the home and your family, but if it is neglected it can become an aggressive nuisance. Make sure that the dog is socialized with other dogs, children and adults when it is still a puppy, and invest time in training the dog so it becomes manageable and obedient. If you do not buy a puppy but an adult dog, check that it has come from a reputable breeder, who will have invested time socializing the creature. Never leave any dog alone with small children.

Be cautious about buying a dog with a tough reputation. Such animals, including Dobermanns, German shepherds (Alsatians), Rottweilers and bull terriers, need to be very firmly controlled and can, under certain circumstances, be very dangerous indeed. They must be trained under the guidance of an expert dog handler. Almost

Home burglar alarm

Your burglar alarm should have both perimeter sensors and internal sensors, with every window and door directly connected to the main control box (which should be located by the front door).

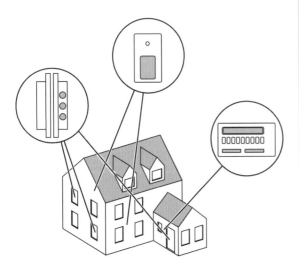

any breed of dog barking ferociously will deter a burglar. Remember that criminals are looking for the house that is easiest to break into and rob. Anything that might make the job more complicated or draw unwanted attention will usually force a criminal to look elsewhere.

Almost all house burglaries are performed when the occupants are out. Set one or two interior lights on automatic timers to come on while the house is empty, and you can even set televisions and radios to come on using the same devices, adding an auditory as well as a visual deterrent. However, don't let interior illumination expose the contents of your home. Use illumination in tandem with blinds, curtains or shutters to prevent the criminal from looking in. Also, avoid illuminating valuables in display cases or setting valuables near windows.

Silly mistakes can leave you vulnerable to theft. When you go away on vacation, cancel milk and newspaper deliveries beforehand, so that newspapers and milk do not pile up on your doorstep and advertise your absence. Get a neighbour to push any unsolicited mail through the letterbox or to take your mail into your house for you while you are away. Never hide a spare set of keys outside your home to us in case you are locked out, as criminals have a good sense of where to look for spare keys. Instead, leave spare keys with neighbours.

A SAFE ROOM

A safe room is a secure location within your home, usually leading off the master bedroom, which can be occupied and sealed in the event of a break-in. The room should have the following features:
- A solid metal-cored door fitted with deadlocks operated from the inside (usually electronically, but with manual override)
- A failsafe system of ventilation, ideally an open-grid vent to the outside world
- A telephone line to the outside world and a cellular (mobile) phone
- A fire extinguisher
- A fully packed first-aid kit, including stocks of any prescription medications required by any family member
- Plenty of bottled water and canned/packaged foods

DEALING WITH INTRUDERS

The first principle of defeating intruders is not to let them into your home. Be vigilant for any strange activity outside your house, such as an individual loitering and peering into windows, or anyone sitting in a vehicle outside your home seemingly without reason. Make a note of what the people look like, and the license plate number of the car, and notify the police.

Never open the front door to strangers or unexpected callers – check them out first through the spy hole. If they claim to be from an official organization, ask them to pass their identification papers through to you. Telephone a head office number for confirmation. If they are legitimate visitors, they won't mind you doing this. Make this precaution even with visiting police officers if you are suspicious.

Should you arrive home to find the door open, or a window smashed, never go inside. Get to the nearest telephone and call the police. Stay at a

Security dogs

Although the Rottweiler here is a powerful guard dog, almost any dog has security benefits. Their barking will alert you to intruders, as well as deterring the intruders themselves.

Checking visitors

Check visitors through a spy hole before opening the door – don't just rely on the door chain. If you are in any doubt as to the visitor's identity, get him or her to put an ID through the mailbox, and make a brief phone check with the listed company.

friend's house or keep at a safe distance until police help is at hand. Never enter your property until police have inspected it.

The worst-case scenario occurs if you are inside the house at the time of a break-in. Try to leave the property quickly and call police. If you cannot get out, telephone the police from an internal phone and stress that a break-in is in progress. Preferably do this from a room you can lock yourself into. The police should be there within minutes. Stay silent unless detected.

Don't attempt to fight the intruder, unless, of course, your life is in danger. If the intruder directly confronts you, be cooperative and let them get away. Or, look for your first opportunity to escape. Try telling the intruder that all you want to do is leave the house. If they become aggressive, you may have to fight back (see Chapter 23) or smash a window and scream out that you need help. If you can, try to remember as many details as possible about the intruder so that you can help with the police investigation later.

CHAPTER TWENTY-SEVEN

SURVIVING TERRORISM

Terrorism affects every nation on Earth. Being vigilant and prepared for terrorist attack is important, as is never overstating the threat.

THE STRATEGIC APPLICATION of terrorist violence changed markedly during the late twentieth century. Large numbers of casualties and the creation of horrific scenes for live broadcast have become important goals of the terrorist. This is different from earlier examples of modern terrorism, which concentrated on material destruction, targeted assassination, disruption of infrastructure and commerce, and social collapse as first considerations.

The terrorist of an earlier era sought to bring about anarchy or revolution through violence. Similar goals remain in the stated, long-term objectives of organizations such as the Levantine group Hamas and the pan-Asian network known as al Qaeda. But the sinister intimacy of televised terror as an attention-getting device has immediate and lasting impact on a broad cross-section of today's societies. Consequently, attacks played out in the arena of 24-hour headline news programmes have grown increasingly dramatic, and horrific.

TARGETS

Terrorism has generally served dual purposes. From one perspective, the actions of a terrorist – whether these take the form of assassinations, taking hostages, bombing or other attacks – are aimed at raising awareness for a political cause and using public outrage to lobby governments to get results. From another perspective, terrorists may view their attacks as military action against officials or government institutions directly opposed to their political objectives.

Persons or organizations under threat from terrorism may be viewed in two categories: high-

value targets – such as political and military leaders – and targets of opportunity, including bystanders whose deaths or injury serve to raise the dramatic impact of an attack without being directly tied to the attack's primary motivation.

Most of the world's population is concentrated in urban environments, and as such these are the places where the terrorist tends to strike at both categories of targets. Urban settings provide a

WORLD TERRORISM

On September 11, 2001 the United States suffered the worst terrorist atrocity in history, as nearly 3000 people were killed when four airliners were turned into flying bombs to attack the World Trade Center and the Pentagon. Despite this horrific event, the United States actually stands as one of the world's safest places in terms of terrorism, at least in crude numbers of incidents. Terrorist attacks in Israel, for instance, have occurred at a rate of one or two a week, with enormous impact on the social and cultural life of the nation. Overall, the worldwide occurrence of terrorism is declining since it peaked in the 1970s and 1980s. In 1986, there were 897 terrorist attacks globally, falling to 666 in 1987, 427 in 1993, and 321 terrorist attacks in 1994. (Data: US State Department) However, casualty figures from the individual attacks have risen. In the 1970s, property bombings accounted for 70 per cent of terrorist assaults and direct targeting of people 30 per cent. Today the reverse is true, as terrorists seek to capitalize on public fear and horror.

Terrorist bombing – targeting

Unfortunately, social venues are the most common targets for bombings. Watch out for any isolated individuals depositing bags in public places or who are wearing incongruous, heavy clothing (they could be a potential suicide bomber).

high density of targets, most within easy access, and the logistical infrastructure necessary to plan, develop, execute and recover from an attack. Urban environments also offer the terrorist the best chance of maximizing casualties.

For the terrorist, urban targets are selected according to different considerations. Individual civilians are rarely targets, although the family members of significant target groups may be at risk. Government officials, corporate executives or members of the military are more likely to be targets, particularly those with a key role in relation to foreign policy. Such has been the case with attacks by insurgents in Colombia, and those of the Basque separatist group, ETA, in Spain. Business leaders with international trade links or who handle government contracts are also vulnerable targets both as hostages and for assassination.

Personnel employed by firms doing business internationally, as well as the workers at target sites – such as power plants and refineries – may also be targets. As the kidnap and murder of Daniel Pearl in Karachi, Pakistan, in the winter of 2002 demonstrated, journalists working in fields of political analysis or foreign correspondence are also targets. Political activists directly or indirectly opposed to the politics or cause of the terrorist organization are also in danger.

Public places are often selected for bomb attacks to maximize casualties. Places with heavy foot traffic and large concentrations of bystanders – such as bus and train stations, shopping districts, nightclubs and outdoor gatherings for festivals and funerals — are typical targets. In 1995, for example, the Japanese doomsday cult Aum Shinrikyo attacked the crowded Tokyo subway system. In the summer of 1996, a terrorist's bomb exploded during the Olympic Games in Atlanta, Georgia. Also in 1996, the Irish Republican Army claimed responsibility for a series of bomb attacks in busy areas of London. European, American and Middle Eastern terrorism has also included attacks on automobiles and public transportation, such as the grimly common bus attacks in Israel by suicide bombers. Generally bombs either planted on board the vehicle or detonated in the proximity assault such targets.

Terrorists may also target official buildings or important facilities. These include embassies, international business premises, military installations, and any other place representing values to which the terrorist is opposed or which is crucial to the function of the target society. Recent terrorist planning shows more interest in attacking facilities of infrastructure, such as nuclear power plants, chemical factories, hydroelectric dams and telecommunications hubs. Other places that represent ideological, educational or religious values are also potential targets.

Over the past four decades, terrorists have also targeted commercial aircraft for two distinct kinds of attack: hijacking and bombing. As modern jet travel is an integral part of international commerce, terrorists have many points of entry or access to airplanes. The quality of airport security varies from one location to another, though this is becoming more standardized internationally. Airlines operating to or within North Africa, southwestern Asia or the former Soviet republics are particularly vulnerable.

BASIC COUNTERMEASURES

Terrorism, whether perpetrated for political or military aims, is at its base a tool the success of which depends on public outrage, paranoia and confusion. It is important to bear in mind the terrorist has achieved partial success – before any bombs are detonated or hostages taken – if he convinces the public to curtail its freedoms, disrupt normal commerce or otherwise give in to fear.

Should your job or status, or the places you frequent, mark you as a potential target some precautions may be prudent. Among the first considerations in reducing vulnerability to terrorist attack are maintaining a low public profile and being alert to signs of trouble. Ensure the workplace offers adequate security. Hiring a reputable security firm with diverse clientele, with ex-military (particularly Special Forces soldiers) on staff is an advantage. Such firms have been trained for the full spectrum of threat assessment and response in crisis situations. Carefully review the security firm's accreditation, endorsements and

Car search

A car search involves carefully and methodically checking a vehicle at the indicated points, looking **for signs of tampering, incongruous wiring, suspect packages and mechanical modifications.**

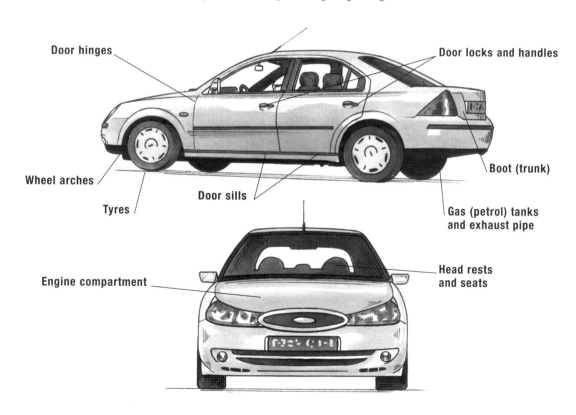

Door hinges

Door locks and handles

Wheel arches

Tyres

Door sills

Boot (trunk)

Gas (petrol) tanks and exhaust pipe

Engine compartment

Head rests and seats

training programme. The latter should be comprehensive and include elements such as bomb-threat awareness, surveillance, location security and perhaps close-protection services.

Travel presents the greatest opportunity for terrorist attack. Terrorist planning relies on predictable timetables, so vary your routes to and from work and alter the times and method of travel. It may be important for family members of potential targets to vary their travel routines as well. All routes contain vulnerabilities, therefore it is important to be conscious of the ideal places for attack, such as at traffic lights, road intersections, tunnels, narrow alleyways and the like. Blind bends, steep gradients or one-way streets also present choke points where an attack is more likely to be successful.

Routes should be selected with as few stops as possible, using open roads and avoiding heavy, slow-moving traffic.

Vehicle hostage rescue

Anti-terrorist forces may use a four-car box to trap a terrorist vehicle which contains a hostage. If you are that hostage, curl up on the seat or on the floor so that you give your rescuers clear lines of fire through the vehicle windows.

TAKING HOSTAGES

Terrorists have resorted to taking hostages for a variety of reasons, including extracting information, using the hostages to bargain for political ends and raising ransom money.

If you are taken hostage, you are most vulnerable in the first few minutes of the situation. The terrorists will be emotional and nervous, and consequently more liable to use violence to control the situation. If you cannot escape unseen, the safest course is to comply with terrorists' orders. Remember this advice:

- Do not confront the hijackers verbally or physically.
- Avoid eye contact with the hijackers.
- Hide or discard any documents that may arouse the interest of the hijackers, such as military, government or corporate identification, government paperwork, and so on.
- Remove expensive jewellery or clothing if you can – terrorists generally dislike signs of wealth.
- Do not debate the politics of the hijackers.
- Do not talk among yourselves – the hijackers might think you are plotting.
- Do not show signs of fear and weakness – these are likely to attract contempt rather than pity from the terrorists.

It is useful to remember that professional hostage-rescue services will be engaged early in a crisis. The best course is to give rescue services time to do their work. During captivity, avoid debate with the terrorists, but reply with short, sensible answers if questioned directly. The terrorists are likely to set rules for hostage conduct, movement,

AIRCRAFT HIJACK TIPS

Terrorists may select an aircraft as the arena for a hostage-taking operation. To be prepared for a hijacking, it is important that passengers pay attention to the preflight safety briefing – you must know exactly where emergency exits and other key features of the plane are located in the event you need to make a rapid escape from the aircraft. Keep your shoes on at all times for this same reason. Terrorist activity will tend to be concentrated around the cockpit, so try to seat yourself in the middle and rear sections of the aircraft to attract less attention.

Gun hijack

As a general rule, comply totally with a terrorist armed with a gun. However, if you believe you are about to be killed, a disarmament technique such as shown here might be attempted.

communication and toilet visits, and these rules should be obeyed without question to avoid unnecessary confrontation.

Avoid doing anything that singles you out from the group, and remember that the longer a hostage situation goes on, the greater the chance of your rescue. Your biggest challenges will probably be physical and mental discomfort. Relieve mental stress by keeping your mind occupied. Do mental puzzles in your head, talk with your fellow hostages (if allowed) about issues other than the hijack and think of positive images. However, stay aware of your immediate surroundings in case a new threat emerges. To relieve physical discomfort, keep stretching and tensing limbs, joints and muscles to maintain good circulation. When allowed, stand and stretch or exercise. Likewise, sleep if possible to avoid becoming fatigued. Go to the toilet at every opportunity, and eat and drink when provisions are available – the next opportunities to do these things may be a long time in coming.

If you are released at any point during the hostage-taking or hijack situation, you will be thoroughly debriefed by security forces. They will ask you numerous questions, so be observant

during the hijack situation, but do not write down any notes to yourself. Typical debriefing questions include:

- How many terrorists are present?
- Where are the terrorists located and do their movements follow a schedule or pattern?
- What do the terrorists look like and what are their ethnic or cultural origins; what language do they speak?
- How are the terrorists armed; do they have automatic weapons and explosives?
- Have the terrorists set traps or made other modifications to the area?
- What are the emotional and mental states of the terrorists and the hostages?

At some point – usually if negotiations have reached an impasse or a hostage has been executed – the security forces may launch a violent rescue action. Stay alert for indications that such an operation is about to take place. For example, a loud noise, large fire or an explosion may be used as a distraction technique to enable hostage-rescue units to deploy. The electricity to the building or aircraft may suddenly be cut. When entering an aircraft or building, hostage-

Hijacker techniques

Hijackers will often attempt to disorientate their victims, blindfolding them so that they cannot identify their location, the route they took to their location and their captors.

rescue units usually throw in stun grenades first. These grenades release loud noise and intense light, but cause little physical injury. The hostage-rescue assault teams follow closely in the wake of such explosions and may use deadly force against the terrorists. During a hostage-rescue assault, lie down or, if on an aircraft, take cover behind the seat. The rescue force will need clear fields of fire to target the terrorists. Following the assault, you may be handcuffed and forced to lie on the floor while the rescue unit confirms everyone's identity.

BOMBING

The use of explosives is the hallmark of modern terrorism. From the dynamite used by early twentieth-century anarchists, to the sophisticated synthetic explosives that today's skilled bomber may apply, bombs have become the weapons of choice of many terrorists.

   As with other forms of terror attack, planning a bombing in public places offers the terrorist advantages in logistics and escape opportunities. In cities, trash cans (litter bins), public toilets and mailboxes all may be used to conceal bombs – be suspicious if you see someone putting a large wrapped package or sealed bag in one of these locations. Other things to look for include unattended parcels, suitcases, boxes or other

Stun grenade

Stun grenades are commonly used in the initial stages of a hostage-rescue action. They emit a huge bang and intense light, but without delivering fragmentation injuries.

SUSPICIOUS VEHICLES

The following signs could alert you to a potential car bomb.
- **A vehicle that is parked illegally, near a significant building or possible target**
- **A vehicle that has apparently been abandoned**
- **A vehicle that has been parked along the route or place of a special event, such as a parade**
- **A vehicle obviously weighted down on its suspension at the rear; this may indicate that the boot (trunk) contains a heavy explosive device.**

The first action when dealing with a genuinely suspicious vehicle is to contact the police. Warn others away and wait until the police arrive.

containers left in public places. The police should be notified of the presence of such items.

Some forms of bombing attack can be directed to specific individuals, such as is the case with letter or package bombs. First consider the physical properties of a suspicious package. Is it irregularly shaped or excessively heavy for its dimensions? Is it strangely rigid? Are there any noises coming from it? Can you feel any wiring? Is the parcel stained or discoloured in a way that might indicate evidence of engineering? Does it have excessive amounts of packaging?

Next evaluate the context of the package. Consider whether the delivery is anticipated. If the parcel is unsolicited or does not correspond with an event such as a birthday, be suspicious of its contents. Also be cautious if the stamps indicate postage from a foreign country with which you have no dealings or political connections. Look at the address. Warning signals include misspellings of name and address; excessive postage; no return address; and restrictive markings such as 'personal' or 'private' (the terrorist might want to ensure that you personally open the package).

If any package is suspicious, leave it where it is, get everybody out of the building and inform the police. Better to be safe than sorry.

Another form of bombing attack is the car bomb. Car bombs vary in sophistication, placement and method of detonation. Crude car bombs may consist of nothing more than the trunk filled with rudimentary explosives,

detonated in the proximity of buildings and large groups of people either by remote control or as part of a suicide attack. Alternatively, car bombs may be planted specifically to kill the car's occupant. This usually involves small devices planted in the vehicle interior or hidden around the bodywork. These types of bombs tend to be detonated remotely or by an automatic electrical or chemical switch.

Some basic safety precautions may be taken to reduce the risk of your car being used or targeted for a car bombing. Fit the vehicle and its garage (if you have one) with an alarm system. Keep the car locked in the garage when not in use. Do not leave it for long periods of time in unguarded areas, and ensure that security is tight at the mechanics if the vehicle goes in for maintenance. In particularly dangerous areas, avoid washing the car as dirty bodywork shows handprints and other evidence of human interference.

Should circumstances arouse suspicion, particularly if your vehicle has moved from its original position, a vehicle search may be in order. Look around you first. Can you see anybody acting suspiciously in the distance, possibly watching you? They may be waiting to detonate the bomb by remote control, so stay away from the vehicle. If during a comprehensive

Booby trap
This booby trap consists of a hand grenade with its pin removed but placed in a can to restrain its fuse lever. A tripwire pulls the grenade from the tin, the lever flies off and the grenade explodes.

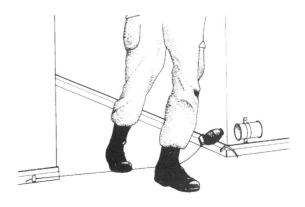

Anti-terrorist sniper

If you are in a hijack situation, be aware that police/military snipers will be deployed. To allow them a clear shot, try not to put yourself between the terrorists and any windows (if you are held inside a building) and, should a rescue attempt take place, never pick up a terrorist weapon, as the sniper may think you are a terrorist and shoot you.

search suspicious devices or tampering is discovered, get away from the vehicle, warn others to clear the area and contact the police.

During the search touch the vehicle as little as possible. Inspect the car from a distance for any obvious signs of tampering. Can you see any wires or brake cables hanging loose? Anything different from the way the car commonly looks

Danger signs

This package has several danger signs, including oily marks, visible wiring, 'Personal' markings and emission of an odour. Never open such a package; leave it alone and call the authorities.

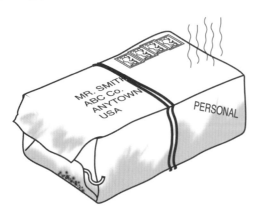

should act as a warning. Move closer, and see if there are any scratches on or around the locks, doors, trunk and bonnet (hood) that might indicate forced entry. Check around the wheels, wings (fenders), doors, fuel tank and exhaust for any visible devices or evidence of modification. Look inside the vehicle. Have seats, floor mats or internal switches been moved from their usual position? Are there any wires visible in the seatbelt reels?

Now slowly open the trunk, checking for suspicious wiring as it inches open. Look around the interior of the trunk for signs of cutting, drilling, or lifting. Release the hood by the same process, and watch out for any nonstandard wiring running from electrical sources or motors, or signs that the radiator or oil filler caps have been tampered with.

To inspect the interior of the car, carefully open a rear passenger door, checking for any wiring around the hinge. Next check every recess of the vehicle, including ashtrays, audio speakers, fittings and cup holders. Avoid leaning or putting pressure on the seats during this process. Finally, enter the car and turn on the engine. Listen for any unusual sounds. When first driving off, be conscious of any unfamiliar sensations in the gears or the driving action. Stop driving immediately if this happens, slowing down using your emergency (hand) brake rather than the main brake.

SUICIDE BOMBINGS

Suicide bombers present a particular challenge: that of dealing with an attacker whose death is part of his or her operational objective. Suicide bombers tend to select public places as targets – such as shopping and entertainment areas, and public transportation.

The suicide bomber's weapon is either a car bomb, personally driven to the target and detonated, or a pack of explosives belted around their torso and concealed beneath clothing. For the latter, there are few outward signs that someone is a suicide bomber. Suicide attackers often appear frightened and agitated, for obvious reasons, and may be sweating profusely with fear. A bomber may be wearing unseasonable clothing – such as jackets or overcoats on a hot summer's day – to conceal bulky packs of explosives. Suicide bombers will often run their hands nervously over their bodies to make sure that the explosives are in place. The bomber may be acting suspiciously, watching a particular place with focused interest.

Stay well away from suspicious individuals and alert the authorities. Some bombers shout out a political or religious statement before exposing and then detonating their explosives. If you have any sort of warning, get down to the ground or floor, and cover your head with your arms, if possible behind or beneath some protective object or surface such as a table or a wall. If you are so close you have no choice but to tackle the bomber, try to grab and pin his or her arms before he or she can put them inside the coat.

CHEMICAL, BIOLOGICAL OR RADIOLOGICAL ATTACK

As horrific as conventional terrorism has shown itself to be, infinitely greater potential tragedy is possible from so-called weapons of mass destruction (WMD). In terms of immediate numbers of casualties, WMD attacks may not rival conventional bombings. However, the use by terrorists of chemical, biological or radiological technologies could result in lingering effects that could raise death tolls from thousands into millions of people.

It is important to keep in mind the risk of an effective WMD attack remains slight. WMD operations require considerable money, scientific and engineering expertise, and supply contacts to

Modern explosives

Modern explosives can be extremely varied in shape, ranging from sticklike lengths to Plasticine-type substances. The detonator cord is usually the giveaway that they are explosives.

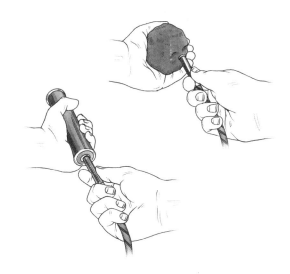

plan, develop and execute. Such resources are beyond the capacity of most terrorist organizations. However, the use of sarin by the Japanese sect Aum Shinrikyo in 1995 and the anthrax attacks in the United States in 2001 demonstrate the seriousness of the threat and warrant some basic security and safety considerations.

Biological weapons are naturally occurring or artificially cultivated diseases, and include anthrax, botulism, bubonic plague, smallpox, tularemia and viral haemorrhagic fevers. Chemical weapons are manufactured agents that attack physiological functions, such as respiration, circulation and the nervous system. Chemical agents include sarin and VX. Effects of all biological and chemical weapons will, if left untreated, result in a high percentage of fatalities. This is particularly the case with chemical nerve agents, which have a fatality rate approaching 100 per cent and can kill within minutes.

Generally speaking, the symptoms of attack by chemical agents emerge within minutes and hours, whereas biological agents may take days to produce noticeable effects. Both will usually overwhelm local emergency treatment facilities near the epicentre of the attack.

EOD vehicle

An Explosive Ordnance Disposal (EOD) vehicle is a remotely operated vehicle fitted with camera devices and kinetic-energy weapons. It is used to inspect and sometimes explode suspect packages.

Many of the early symptoms of chemical and biological attack can be confused with common illnesses, particularly if there are symptoms resembling the flu, headaches, sickness and dizziness. External signs may be nonexistent, but there are certain phenomena that should arouse your suspicion. Be alerted if you suddenly smell something with no obvious source, particularly the scent of almonds, cut grass or hay, or peaches. These may imply cyanide compounds. Visible clouds of dust or coloured vapour mists not related to prevailing climatic conditions should also be treated seriously; observe whether they are low-lying, as many chemical agents are heavier than air. Watch surrounding people and animals for any signs of respiratory troubles, strange convulsive actions and confused mental states, rashes or blistered skin, impaired eyesight or vomiting.

In the event of an actual chemical-biological attack, try to avoid contamination at all costs. Leave a contaminated place immediately and stay upwind of the epicentre. If you are in a building, move to a floor higher than the affected area. Get into a room that has as few openings as possible, and shut and seal all external doors and windows. Switch off air conditioning and heating systems, and cover over ventilation grills and any other openings to the outside. If you are in a car, close up the air vents and shut the windows tightly.

While you are exposed to the agent, cover your mouth with a cloth – if possible soaked in water containing one tablespoon of baking soda – to limit inhalation of the agent. Cover exposed skin with clothing. Make your way as fast as you possibly can to get medical assistance; some chemical-biological agents require treatment with vaccines, which may be effective only if administered within the first few hours after exposure. Until professional medical help arrives, there are a few imperfect personal decontamination procedures. Dispose of contaminated clothing in sealed plastic bags. Scrub the skin with warm, soapy water. Or, cover yourself with a thick layer of talcum powder or flour, leave it on the skin for about 30 seconds, then dust it off with a rag or brush. Do not breathe this dust, and leave the room and close its door after the procedure. Do not allow anyone else to go into the room.

RADIOLOGICAL WEAPONS

While chemical and biological weapons have been used in past acts of terrorism, a release of harmful radiation in an attack has yet to be seen. The potential for weapons-grade uranium or plutonium to fall into the hands of a terrorist organization may be remote, but other methods exist for delivering radioactive particles without requiring knowledge of the complex engineering associated with atomic science.

Perhaps a more realistic near-term threat is posed not by nuclear weapons themselves, but by the possible use of explosive devices to spread radioactive material, such as medical isotopes and waste products from modern atomic energy plants. So-called 'dirty bomb' devices could consist of a conventional high explosive surrounded by pellets of low-level radioactive material. Such a device – while not as lethal as a chemical or biological attack – would have the potential for contaminating urban areas, government buildings or commercial areas, causing illness and chaos.

The first response to a radiological attack is to get as far away as possible from the epicentre of the explosion, leaving any potentially contaminated personal effects behind. Avoid touching anything in and around the scene of the blast. Do not eat food or drink fluids in the affected area, as these may have been contaminated with radioactive dust. Even at a distance from the epicentre, eat only canned food and drink only bottled water until the authorities clarify what is safe. Follow the advice of disaster-response teams and public service broadcasts on reputable, reliable news or radio channels.

To avoid prolonged exposure, get inside a single room in a building, and seal the doors and windows. Remove clothing that may have been exposed to radioactive particles, and wrap the clothes in a sealed plastic bag. Keep these clothes for analysis by the authorities. Take a long shower, washing your skin thoroughly with soap and water to remove as much contamination as possible. If you are outside, look for emergency

Suitcase bomb

A low-yield nuclear device can be small enough to fit into a suitcase, yet could deliver enough explosive force to destroy several square miles of a city centre.

response services, which may have portable showers and decontamination units.

While the terrorist threat from a nuclear weapon is minimal, such an event could occur and certain precautions, largely drawn from the Cold War era, may be in order. The most likely terrorist device would be a so-called 'suitcase bomb'. This would be tiny when compared to military nuclear weapons, but with a one or two kiloton yield (an explosive force equivalent to one or two thousand tons of TNT) the effects in an urban area would be devastating. If you were within a mile of such a blast, your chances of survival would be minimal. At the epicentre, the temperatures would rise to millions of degrees centigrade and blast pressure waves would smash buildings and people at speeds of 6437 km/h (4000 mph).

However, if you were over a mile away, your chances of survival improve when combined with some basic responses. Some seconds may elapse between the flash of detonation and the arrival of the blast wave. Lie flat on the ground, behind a solid physical structure or in a ditch or depression. Remain lying down for at least two minutes to avoid the blast and flying debris. Once the blast has passed, move into shelter as quickly as possible. Look for a stable structure to provide shelter from fire, heat and radioactive fallout.

About 10–15 minutes after the initial blast, particles of highly radioactive dust and debris would begin to fall to Earth and continue to do so over several days. This is 'fallout' and appears as a flaky ash. It represents the long-term lethal threat posed by a nuclear weapon. While the initial blast would be catastrophically destructive to life and to property, the fallout carries and spreads the radioactive effects of the weapon far and wide, decaying over a period of tens, if not hundreds, of years and causing cancers and genetic illnesses. If you are outside when the fallout drops, cover your mouth with a cloth, avoid inhaling the dust and quickly get to a sealed shelter. If possible, wait for instructions from emergency services before venturing outside.

Note: if you are taking shelter in a sealed room, beware the dangers of asphyxiation. When the air seems to be getting very stale, and especially if you are starting to have trouble with breathing and are experiencing feelings of acute sleepiness, vent the room for long enough to refresh the air, then reseal it. Repeat the process as necessary.

INDEX